Around the World in 80 S

The world is currently experiencing a sixth period of mass species extinction, and extinction of flora and fauna is caused by a variety of factors arising from industrial activity and increasing human population, such as global warming, climate change, habitat loss, pollution and use of pesticides. Most causes of extinction are linked to corporate activity, either directly or indirectly.

Around the World in 80 Species: Exploring the Business of Extinction responds to the ongoing mass extinction crisis engulfing our planet by exploring the ways in which accounting, business and finance can be used to prevent species extinctions. From Africa to the Far East and from Europe to the Americas, the authors explore species loss and how businesses can stop mass extinctions through greater transparency, and through closer engagement with their investors and wildlife organisations. The book concludes that global capitalism has led us to this extinction crisis and that therefore the mechanisms of capitalism – namely accounting, finance, investment – can help to pull us out. Businesses must urgently address extinction before it is too late for all species, including ourselves.

As the first book to explore corporate accounting and accountability in relation to species on the brink of extinction, this book will be of great interest to both professionals and a wider audience interested in the causes and prevention of extinction.

Jill Atkins holds a Chair in Financial Management at Sheffield University Management School, UK, and is a visiting professor at the University of the Witwatersrand, South Africa.

Barry Atkins has a background in script-writing and editing for BBC Radio and TV.

Around the World in 80 Species

Exploring the Business of Extinction

Edited by Jill Atkins and Barry Atkins

Routledge
Taylor & Francis Group

LONDON AND NEW YORK

First published 2019
by Routledge
2 Park Square, Milton Park, Abingdon, Oxon OX14 4RN

and by Routledge
711 Third Avenue, New York, NY 10017

Routledge is an imprint of the Taylor & Francis Group, an informa business

British Library Cataloguing-in-Publication Data
A catalogue record for this book is available from the British Library

Library of Congress Cataloging-in-Publication Data
A catalog record has been requested for this book

ISBN: 978-1-78353-822-5 (hbk)
ISBN: 978-1-78353-713-6 (pbk)
ISBN: 978-0-429-43739-7 (ebk)

Typeset in Bembo
by Swales & Willis Ltd, Exeter, Devon, UK

Printed and bound in Great Britain by
TJ International Ltd, Padstow, Cornwall

To our wonderful family
and in loving memory of Brenda Ann Thompson,
Derek Thompson and Walter Atkins

Contents

Illustrations

Figures

Tables

xii *List of illustrations*

14.1 IUCN report criteria   260
15.1 Steps for the validity of findings   277
18.1 Trends in polar bear subpopulations   340
18.2 Content categories screened in annual reports and
      sustainability reports 2012–2015   343
19.1 A panda-centric extinction accounting framework   381

Contributors

Vanessa Amaral-Rogers, RSPB

Barry Atkins, University of South Wales, UK

Jill Atkins, University of Sheffield, UK

Michael Büchling, University of the Witwatersrand, South Africa

Jack Christian, Manchester Metropolitan University, UK

Margaret Clappison, Athabasca University, Canada

Antonio Corvino, University of Foggia, Italy

Federica Doni, Milano-Bicocca University, Italy

Rob Gray, University of St Andrews, UK (emeritus)

Abigail Herron, Aviva Investors

Kristina Jonäll, University of Gothenburg, Sweden

Mervyn E. King, IIRC

Sanjay V. Lanka, University of Sheffield, UK

Lelys Maddock, University of the Witwatersrand, South Africa

Warren Maroun, University of the Witwatersrand, South Africa

Silvio Bianchi Martini, University of Pisa, Italy

Markus J. Milne, University of Canterbury, New Zealand

Martin Mulama, WWF

Sophia Nicolov, University of Leeds, UK

Simon Norton, Cardiff Business School, Cardiff University, UK

Timo Punkari, Aalto University, Finland

Gunnar Rimmel, University of Reading, UK

Svetlana Sabelfeld, University of Gothenburg, Sweden

Mxolisi Sibanda, WWF

Aris Solomon, Athabasca University, Canada

Longxiang Zhao, University of Sheffield, UK

Acknowledgements

In writing this book we have been incredibly fortunate to have support, critical comments, suggestions and encouragement from a large number of friends and colleagues.

First and foremost, we are so grateful to the contributors, without whom the book would have been impossible. So many friends and colleagues from all ends of the world have researched chapters so we can provide an overview of species threatened by extinction, extinction accounting, engagement on extinction prevention, and a wide range of perspectives from different parts of the planet. We are grateful for their patience and hard work in researching complex issues in such a sensitive manner.

We are especially grateful to Professor Mervyn King for his constant, long-term support of our work, and this book in particular. Also, special thanks to Professor Rob Gray for his comments on our chapters and for his suggestions and amendments throughout the writing process. We are very grateful to Mxolisi Sibanda, from the WWF, who has been so supportive of this project and who hosted us at the WWF in Woking so that we could speak to colleagues and discuss our work. We are grateful to Martina Macpherson, who hosted our Species & Extinction Roundtable event at S&P Global in July 2017, where we were able to discuss the frameworks in this book with a large group of investors, practitioners and academics, as well as to the White Rose Extinction Network for their interest in and comments on this project.

We would like to thank Rebecca Marsh from Greenleaf Publishing for her encouragement and support throughout the process of proposing, writing and producing this book as well as to Judith Lorton from Routledge. Thank you to Professor Christopher Napier for his continued support of the ideas encapsulated in this book and the research underpinning it, as well as for his encouragement when the research was in its early stages. We are delighted with the two etchings provided for the book by Izzy Edgley, namely the seahorse and polar bear.

Last but not least, we would like to thank our families for their patience and support during the time we have been researching and writing this book, especially Brenda and Zoe who have listened endlessly (and not always with patience) to our discussions of the work.

Jill and Barry Atkins

Preamble

Tales of innocence and experience

Through the eyes of childhood innocence, the world looks rosy. Growing up usually involves, in most cultures, spending a good deal of time outside, discovering the world. Children probably get closer to nature than adults, apart from those dedicated to an outdoor career such as conservation, biology, botany and horticulture. Certainly, as children growing up in the late 1960s and early 1970s, outdoor play was the norm in Britain. Insects abounded in parks and in the countryside. Walks with the family involved peering into woodland ponds, searching for frogs and newts and frogspawn in the spring. In the summer there were always many different butterflies in the garden: peacocks, red admirals, cabbage whites, even sometimes primrose yellow brimstones. Shield bugs, ladybirds, aphids crept across flowers and shrubs. Earwigs, spiders in different shapes and sizes, centipedes and various species of worm including the earthworm, all appeared as soon as my mum started to dig the flower beds. It was especially thrilling when she came across a chrysalis hidden in the soil which, when we picked it up gently we could see the end wriggling as it prepared for its metamorphosis. Being always fascinated by animals and wildlife, there were many documentaries, especially David Attenborough's many nature programmes, which explored the wildlife in parts of the world we could only start to imagine.

Childhood films and books have always been filled with animal stories and animal characterisations. In past decades, the stories of Rudyard Kipling captivated small minds: 'How the Leopard got his Spots', 'How the Rhinoceros got his Skin', and 'How the Camel Got his Hump' – and of course, the famous *Jungle Book*. Any children's film tends to have animals as key characters with personal favourites being the lady skunk, Flower, in *Bambi*, the black panther, Bagheera, and Shere Khan the evil tiger in the *Jungle Book*. There are so many different species of animal in the animated children's films. One only has to think of Jiminy Cricket in *Pinocchio*. *The Lion King* brings all the beauty of Africa to the big screen, as does *Madagascar*. The more recent animations explore the oceans in *Finding Nemo*, and feature Eastern animals in the adorable *Kungfu Panda*, with his friends being a praying mantis, a tiger and a snake.

These wonderful and exciting creatures become part of a child's psyche and form an important component of their world view. Certainly when we were young, the thoughts of one day travelling to far-distant lands and seeing these species in their natural habitat was always exciting.

Then there are zoos and aquaria. A typical day at a zoo introduces children to a vast array of species from the (often) terrifying spiders and beetles in the insect house, to giants such as rhinoceros, elephant, giraffe and buffalo in the outdoor areas. The world seems idyllic, fascinating, beautiful, bursting with strange creatures, colourful parrots, humming birds, peacocks and immense monsters like alligators and hippopotamus. Then, unfortunately, as teenagers are educated about the world around us and as more adult media begins to infiltrate young minds, the scales fall and we see what is really happening to the world around us. Beautiful coral reefs are becoming deserts, rainforests are continuing to disappear at an alarming rate, amazing species such as the Bornean orang-utan, Asian tigers, the mighty rhinoceros, are, we are told, disappearing. There are flashes of this oncoming sadness in children's stories and films. For example, the heart-breaking shooting of Bambi's mother – which, years later, can still make a grown man cry – was an early introduction to the cruelty of some humans towards other species, and to the harshness and brutality of the 'real' world.

All children learn about dinosaurs and probably have a number of toys, maybe a *Tyrannosaurus rex*, a *Stegosaurus* and a *Pterodactyl* to play with. Their parents will tell them that these immense monsters ruled the earth millions of years ago, but that they are no longer here – they 'went extinct'. What does this really mean for a child? Knowing that they were 'real', but are now relics of a previous era, may be somewhat comforting. Would a four-year-old really want to know that a *T. rex* could suddenly make an appearance at nursery school? Films like *Jurassic Park*, although in one way entirely unbelievable, can also seem uncannily realistic given the incredible computer graphics which effectively make the film look like any regular nature and wildlife documentary. This was particularly the case for the documentary series *Walking with Dinosaurs*, which felt like a typical Sunday night programme exploring an African jungle: quite unsettling in terms of separating fact from fiction, dreams from reality. These are not made up, fictional characters but strange creatures from another era – so a mixture of fact and fiction. Only time divides reality from dinosaur dreams.

Returning to *Jurassic Park*, the concept of being able to use scientific technology to bring a lost species back to life lies clearly within the realms of science fiction but also has an unnerving reality attached to it. We now live in a world where sheep – and people, were ethics to allow – can be cloned; where babies are regularly created in 'test tubes'; where scientists could create a black hole; where we have almost fixed a hole in the ozone (caused by ourselves).

Again returning to the concept of extinction: in a child's eyes, this means the creature has gone forever – or does it? Any child who has watched *Jurassic Park* will probably be confused at a deep psychological level. Maybe also an adult struggles to separate fact from fiction in a similar way. Although we 'know' dinosaurs are extinct, we can see the fossils in natural history museums, we can see them recreated using computer graphics and then we can watch a film showing how science can bring them back from frozen eggs. In today's world, with computer technology and scientific discovery moving at an incredible pace, does the possibility of somehow genetically engineering a *Pterodactyl* from ancient DNA really seem impossible? Who knows in the future?

Despite fantasy and wild imagination, at the present moment this is not possible. Around the world there are large-scale initiatives aimed at preserving species so that their genetic material is not lost forever. In Antarctica there is a frozen laboratory where seeds are kept from hundreds of thousands of species so that, were a species to go extinct, we still have the DNA and seeds to be able to recreate the plant. Similarly, the Kew Gardens Seed Bank holds a huge array of seeds from plants which are threatened with extinction. In a similar way, zoos and aquaria around the world have shifted their function away from being show cases for the public to visit and view unusual species from far distant lands to being active breeding centres for threatened species. Indeed, they cannot gain or maintain a license to operate unless they behave in this way. National parks such as the Kruger in South Africa represent the last bastions of natural habitat for large herbivores and carnivores such as the African 'big five' – the lion, rhinoceros, leopard, elephant and buffalo.

Business activities such as mining, forestry, extractives (oil, gas, coal, precious gems, metals), fracking, agriculture, are continuing to decimate natural habitats. Pristine rainforests are being burnt and hacked down for land use, leaving less and less space for wildlife. Theoretical models show a direct relationship and correlation between space and species populations. As habitat reduces, the number of species in an area falls commensurately. Current estimates suggest species are falling into oblivion every few minutes. Scientists have various estimates for the number of species on the planet but it is acknowledged that these may be nowhere near correct. The Red List of threatened species compiled by the International Union for Conservation of Nature (IUCN) provides numbers of species which are already extinct, extinct in the wild, critically endangered, endangered and vulnerable but these numbers again are by no means exact as they rely on research which is expensive, sporadic and which can at best provide an indication rather than the exact state of nature. However, whether accurate or not, one overriding and extremely alarming fact is unquestionable – species are going extinct on a huge scale and this trend is not reversing but accelerating. The situation for the planet's wildlife is critical. We find ourselves in the sixth period of mass extinction on Planet Earth, with the extinction of the dinosaurs being the fifth and most recent previous mass extinction event.

If this trend is to be stayed and then reversed, urgent action is required. Debates about whether climate change is happening, about the inaccuracies of science and about which species may be more or less 'important' to our 'ecosystem services' are really equivalent to fiddling while Rome burns. Only immediate and drastic action can literally save the planet. Wildlife organisations,

NGOs, local nature groups, governments are enacting policies and initiatives to protect habitats and conserve nature. However, in our view, the business world, accounting and finance are kept apart and separate from the natural world. It is this type of siloing, this reductionist approach to disciplines and activities which is a part of the problem. Only by adopting a truly interdisciplinary approach which brings together economics, finance, accounting with biology, ecology, and wildlife protection, can far-reaching and effective solutions be brought to bear.

This book adopts such an interdisciplinary approach by exploring solutions to species loss problems which can be implemented within businesses and the corporate sector globally. We build a business case for extinction prevention which rests on the interdependence of species within our ecosystems. This business case is grounded in the financial materiality of species loss and the associated financial risk relating to species loss but also seek to incorporate deep ecology into the heart of accounting and finance in a pragmatic manner. The solutions involve developing accounting and reporting frameworks which transform business activities and behaviour as well as frameworks for institutional investor and NGO engagement with companies on extinction prevention. It is our fervent hope that by developing such mechanisms of extinction governance and accountability, we can step back from this extinction precipice and a more natural balance may be attained on our fragile planet.

As the child becomes the adult, innocence is gradually stripped away and replaced by fear, even horror, at the way the world, in fact the human species, behaves towards itself and towards other species. The more we learn and the more we know about the world around us, the easier it is to become disillusioned and despondent. But when we see human crises such as terrorist attacks, or mass starvation, or a refugee crisis, there is an overwhelming response with people offering time, money and putting themselves in personal danger to help those in dire need. Similarly, with wildlife and other species there is the kind, charitable, philanthropic and caring part of human nature which, when awakened, can inspire world-changing action. It is a belief in these aspects of human nature which has driven the desire to produce this book as a call to action and a plea to the business world to alter the way business is done – forever.

> I have enough faith in human nature to believe that when people are both economically secure and aware of the value of biological wealth they will take the necessary measures to protect their environment. Out of that commitment will grow new knowledge and an enrichment of the human spirit beyond our present imagination.
>
> (Wilson, 1989, p. 116)

A note on *Around the World in 80 Species* and Verne's famous story

The inspiration for the title of this book comes, of course, from the famous novel by Jules Verne, *Around the World in 80 Days*. In originally choosing this title, the deciding factor was how neatly it worked; as with Verne's novel, our book was intended to take the reader on a kind of global voyage of discovery, and the device of evaluating the precarious existences of 80 species gave the work a distinct central structure upon which the content could be built.

However, perhaps there was more going on – albeit subconsciously – in our thought processes when naming the book, as there is a much deeper connection between Verne's work and ours (and our contributors') than merely a titular play on words. Verne's central character, Phileas Fogg, is essentially in a race against time; the 80 days in the title is the result of a wager made over a game of cards in London's Reform Club, and were Phileas to fail to complete the journey in that time, he would stand to lose everything. In the event, he succeeds with seconds to spare. And, of course, that is precisely what *our* species is caught up in, whether it likes it or not; a race against time to find solutions to address the sixth mass extinction in our planet's history – like Phileas, too, if we fail, we stand to lose everything, including our *own* existence.

References

Verne, J. (1873) *Around the World in Eighty Days*, London: Sampson Low, Marston, Low & Searle.
Wilson, E. O. (1989) 'Threats to Biodiversity', *Scientific American*, 261(3), 108–116.

Part I

Understanding extinction and introducing extinction accounting

1 Around the world in 80 species

What is mass extinction and can we stop it?

Jill Atkins and Barry Atkins

One aim of this book is to raise awareness of the urgency of addressing the ongoing crisis of mass extinction which faces our planet as well as to seek solutions from the business world. The enormity of this crisis is, as far as we can see, recognised only by ecological organisations and experts, with society in general having a partial and often limited appreciation of its implications and impacts: Not that people are uninterested or uncaring, just that they are not necessarily aware of the fact that we are currently in a sixth mass extinction event on planet earth. However, media coverage is increasing and there is a growing societal awareness of biodiversity[1] loss, habitat loss and species loss.[2] The current state of nature around our beautiful planet is precarious and increasingly fragile. Writing this book has been disturbing, depressing at times, and extremely challenging when reading research about the enormity of destruction which human activities have wreaked, and are continuing to wreak, on the natural world.

Nature documentaries presented by Sir David Attenborough and others from the late 1970s showed viewers the glittering and magical variety of species on our planet, with never-before-seen photographs of birds of paradise, strange insect-eating plants, wonders of the oceans such as the Portugese man o' war jellyfish and other of nature's wonders. Series like *Life on Earth, The Living Planet* and the *Kingdom of the Ice Bear* captivated audiences and demonstrated, through fabulous wildlife photography, how precious, how diverse, how fascinatingly complex, but also how fragile life on planet earth, with every new television documentary, the extent of habitat destruction and degradation, and the increasing numbers of species under threat of extinction, rises significantly. The recent series *Blue Planet II* revealed the terrible problems facing marine life in seas and oceans around the world from plastics pollution. The more we discover about the world around us, the more we realise how it is changing quickly and that without urgent interventions, so many life forms and idiosyncratic species will be lost forever.

Like an ostrich, a natural reaction to growing recognition that mass extinctions of species are taking place, that climate change seems out of control, that the seas are warming and acidifying, killing coral reefs, and that the rainforests are continuing to disappear despite years of lobbying by wildlife groups and activists, makes us want to bury our heads in the sand. Apathy and a sort of exasperated acceptance seem natural reactions to horrifying and deeply depressing global statistics on animal loss, habitat loss, disappearance of birds and increasingly challenging weather patterns.

Another reaction is to grieve at the extent of species loss. It seems natural for people to feel grief and despair at the deterioration of the natural world around us. How could we lose the panda? How could rhinoceroses seriously cease to exist? What if there were no morning chorus? All these feelings, while perfectly natural and understandable, unfortunately lead society sometimes to feel the problems are insurmountable. So many of us feel that it is too difficult for us to do anything to turn the ship around – the planet is heading towards collapse and what can we do about it? How can I, a mere mortal, change the course which we are now on? How can I stop the burning of fossil fuels? How can I stop the extraction of raw materials? How can I stop the cutting down and burning of the rainforests? How can I save the rhino? How can I prevent species extinctions? Indeed, many sociologists have written about the tendency towards apathy among people who are faced with apparently insurmountable risks and problems. Anthony Giddens, in his famous writings on institutions and risk,[3] as well as Ulrich Beck, in his works *Risk Society* and *World Risk Society*,[4] have discussed the way in which societies react to catastrophic risks by effectively shrugging shoulders and burying their heads in the sand. This is an understandable and easy way out for us all. Indeed, many people we come into contact with, when presenting work in the area of extinction accounting or responsible investment, often comment that it is now too late to change things and that we should all 'eat, drink and be merry' – make the most of things as they are. That is fine if you live in a country which is currently relatively unaffected by climate change, by flooding, by droughts, starvation, crop failures, water scarcity and political upheaval. For the many millions of refugees fleeing either because of political problems, military issues or because of extreme changes in climate, it is a very different story. There are already substantial shifts in population and pressure on populations around the world due to climate change and global warming. People affected by these global changes in weather patterns, geopolitics and related disasters are not fortunate enough to be able to enjoy the world around them. It is often difficult enough to find food to eat, or water to drink, let alone make merry! The United Nations and many international bodies recognise the need for urgent action and are developing initiatives such as the Sustainable Development Goals (SDGs) to address problems in developing and emerging economies.[5]

It is critically urgent that the causes of catastrophic change on our planet are addressed now, not later. Raising awareness of the situation is not enough. As well as raising awareness, people can only act if they can see potential solutions to the problems. We want solutions which can be implemented immediately. The United Nations' SDGs should start to elicit change as they are implemented around the world. Global initiatives to stop temperature rise and to clamp down on fossil fuels are under way and should start to have an impact.

The Kyoto, Copenhagen and Paris Summits on climate change are pushing forward global initiatives to slow down and stop human-induced global warming. Most countries in the world have committed themselves to keeping below a two degree limit in global temperature rises.

This book also aims to explore and seeks to provide solutions to just one part – albeit a very important part – of the plethora of issues arising from our changing planetary climate and the impact of human activity on the world around us: the crisis of mass extinction.

Nature is not something separate from us, from society, from business, from the industrial world. Instead, nature is intrinsically linked with us as human beings, with societies in every part of the world. We are a part of nature. We are a species, not so different from any other – dominant over others at the moment but still affected by the laws of nature. Despite industrial development, capitalism, business, economic growth, we cannot escape the basic reality that we are part of the ecological ecosystem[6] and are just as vulnerable to the natural world, climatic conditions, changes in weather patterns and the fate of other species as is any other species on the planet. It is the interdependence of all life on earth which places us in a vulnerable position. If one species of tiny insect, or a mammalian species, or a plant species goes into extinction this may have no impact at all on local or global ecosystems. Or it may be that the species is in fact a keystone species, one whose disappearance has a substantial and possibly devastating impact on the ecological balance and ecosystem in which it lived. This interdependence brings us back to the old adage, 'you don't know what you've got till it's gone' – until a species disappears either locally or universally it is impossible to gauge whether or not its disappearance will have a pervasive impact.

This book seeks to explore the extent to which flora and fauna are going extinct and the ways in which these extinctions are being researched, and known. Further, we explore the causes of the current phase of extinctions, what is known about the causes and why this sixth period of mass extinction is occurring. Primarily, we address the role of business and corporate activity in driving species to extinction. There are strikingly obvious examples such as the Mexican Gulf explosion and Torrey Canyon oil spill, where industrial accidents have devastating consequences on wildlife and habitat, or there are the subtler, slower, and less obvious long-term effects of business activity such as gradual deforestation, use of pesticides and herbicides, habitat degradation and excessive fishing, hunting and farming.

Appreciating the causes of mass extinction, and the role of business activity in driving species towards extinction, allows us to move on to considering how extinctions may be prevented. Our aim is to explore ways in which accounting and finance, in particular, can contribute to reversing extinction trends and stop species extinctions around the world. We are interested in how companies are being called to account for their impact on nature and species and how they are responding to this call. Initially we aim to build a 'business case' for protecting species from extinction. This is challenging, not just because it is hard to demonstrate that species loss represents a material financial loss for businesses and ultimately for shareholders and other stakeholders, but also because there is a widespread opposition in the academic accounting literature and across other disciplines towards any attempt to 'financialise' nature or try to attach some sort of financial value to a species. We therefore seek to show how the loss, or absence, of a species is in fact also a financial loss to business through the absence of the species' contribution to the ecosystem and to 'ecosystem services'. We then go on to explore the ways in which the need for businesses to provide accounts of their activities and impacts can be harnessed to assist in species protection and extinction prevention.

Accounts are (or at least should be) produced because organisations (or individuals) are called to account, are required to discharge an accountability for their actions and the impact of these actions. Accounts do not have to be numerical in nature but can be narrative accounts or even pictorial accounts. Indeed, we include a number of etchings of endangered and threatened species throughout this book which provide a different means of conveying the urgency of extinctions, which perhaps communicate to people more readily the need to protect species and habitats. These pictorial accounts are intended to improve our communication of the richness and beauty of species to the reader as well as the need to preserve the diversity of life on earth.

Some chapters of this book focus on how companies and organisations are accounting (or not) for their impact on specific species. For example, Chapters 18 and 19 respectively explore corporate accounting for preventing the extinction of polar bears and panda. Extinction accounting by organisations such as zoos and aquaria are addressed in Chapters 12 and 16. Other chapters explore the ways in which engagement and dialogue can prevent extinction. For example, Chapter 7 explains how institutional investor engagement with investee companies can prevent extinctions among marine species. Institutional investors, such as pension funds and life insurance companies, engage in dialogue with their investee companies[7] where they meet directly face to face and influence the way companies behave through influencing their decision-making and strategy. Issues such as biodiversity loss and extinction are increasingly becoming an important component of such meetings especially with investors who focus on environmental, social and governance ('ESG') issues. Responsible investors are keen to encourage companies to preserve certain species and protect certain habitats because their potential loss represents a material financial risk to the investment portfolio. Similarly, the process of engagement and dialogue between non-governmental organisations (NGOs), such as the World Wide Fund for Nature (WWF),[8] and companies can also be effective in preventing extinctions. Such engagements feature in many chapters of this book, for example Chapter 10 focuses on the role of the WWF in preventing rhinoceros extinction in East Africa, and Chapter 13 discusses the ways in which the Royal Society for the Protection of Birds (RSPB) is collaborating and partnering with businesses to prevent extinction.

What is extinction and what do we mean by mass extinction?

A historical perspective on extinction reveals that extinction as a concept *per se* has only been in existence for a couple of hundred years. Extinction as a concept, a phenomenon, was not accepted until the end of the eighteenth century. Religious beliefs, grounded in a literal interpretation of the Book of Genesis which describes the creation of all creatures on earth, as well as similar stories in other world religions, made it almost impossible for scientists or others to suggest that a species had evolved (in a Darwinian sense) or that a species had been effectively wiped out. Accepting the notion of species extinction represented a significant paradigm shift just over two hundred years ago. George Cuvier, a lecturer at the Museum of Natural History in Paris, had spent considerable time studying bones in the museum from a variety of fossils brought in by palaeontologists and explorers. One series of fossilised bones from a mastodon, led him to conclude that the bones must come from a species that had been lost to the world. Cuvier presented his findings in a public lecture, 'Mémoires sur les espèces d'éléphants vivants et fossiles',[9] in which he stated:

> What has become of these two enormous animals of which one no longer finds any [living] traces . . . All these facts, consistent among themselves, and not opposed by any report, seem to me to prove the existence of a world previous to ours, destroyed by some kind of catastrophe.[10]

It seems incredible in the modern world that extinction only became an accepted 'fact' a little over two hundred years ago. We are all brought up 'knowing' that dinosaurs disappeared as a result of an asteroid strike. But this theory was only proposed in the 1970s.[11] Not only is the acceptance of extinction as a concept very new to the human race but the concept itself is extremely fluid. We can never be completely certain that a species is extinct. Scientists can only suspect a species to be extinct because they cannot find any survivors. On average, a species is estimated to last between 5 and 10 million years. Extinction is in fact a naturally occurring phenomenon, which manifests as a process rather than an event. One species can achieve dominance for a period of time, such as in the case of the dinosaurs, but will eventually be replaced by other species because of changes in the natural environment or shocking external events such as volcanic eruptions and asteroid strikes. Estimates of the 'background rate of extinction' float around one extinction per million species per year, but can be as low as 0.1 extinction per million species per year.[12]

We, as a species, have been increasingly aware that other species are under threat and are disappearing for a long time. It is not news that the environment and nature have suffered and are suffering from human and industrial activities. A group of scientists including Edward Wilson, in the 1980s, sought to estimate the number of species known to the human race, focusing on those that had been formally described (by assigning a Latin name to them) and came to a figure of 1.4 million although the writer asserted that there were likely to be at least four million or more. Wilson was one of the first scientists to raise awareness of the global decline in biodiversity and to discuss the consequences of extinctions. Another revered scientist, Terry Erwin, around the same time arrived at a rough estimate of ground-dwelling species at a total across the planet of around 30 million.[13] In a later work, Wilson asked, 'how many species of organisms are there on earth? We don't know, not even to the nearest order of magnitude. The number could be close to 10 million or as high as 100 million.'[14]

   The extinction crisis is not limited to one geographic location, or to one group of species, but appears to be a universal phenomenon. The *Living Planet Report* produced by the WWF provides horrifying statistics on the decline in wildlife populations over just a few decades.[15] The latest report indicates a decline on average in wildlife populations by 58 per cent between 1970 and 2012, and predicts these to fall by 67 per cent by 2020. The WWF also produces the Living Planet Index (LPI), which assesses and measures trends of populations of birds, mammals, reptiles, fish and amphibians around the world. The LPI published in 2016 (the most recent index to date) measures the size of populations over time for 1,678 terrestrial species, 881 freshwater species, 1,353 marine species.[16] The LPI indicates that population sizes of vertebrate species have fallen by more than 50 per cent over the last 40 years. The IUCN Red List website provides up to date statistics relating to species threatened with extinction. For example, it records that in 2014, 25 per cent of all mammals were threatened with extinction, as well as 34 per cent of conifer species, 41 per cent of amphibians. In stark contrast, the population of humans was 6.6 billion in 2007, an increase of half a billion from 2001, making us the widest distribution of any terrestrial mammal species on the planet. The current list of extinct mammals and mammals under threat of extinction is sobering. Cheetahs are under threat with only around 3,500 cheetahs recorded in Southern Africa. Giraffes are under threat because their populations are reducing in all regions where they are found. Elephants are threatened by poaching for tusks and rhinoceros for their horns. Creatures which we have grown up reading about and watching on television, or visiting in zoos, and which surely we cannot imagine disappearing within our lifetimes, are disappearing, and in some cases very quickly.

   The IUCN Red List has quite a history as it was first created in the 1960s. The list identifies species which have been assessed by scientific researchers and which have been found to be at risk of extinction. The Red List categorises species according to whether they are extinct, extinct in the wild (as in alive in zoos), critically endangered, endangered, vulnerable, near threatened, or 'of least concern' (which does not imply they are not threatened as they are still on the list). In a way, the Red list provides a type of audit of flora and fauna. The problem is that science actually has a very impartial knowledge of species in existence and those which are actually at risk of extinction. The List relies on data gathered by scientists and as we realise on an almost weekly basis, there are so many new species being discovered all the time. Many newly discovered species may be threatened with extinction as soon as they are found. The Red List has been interpreted as a means of making species 'calculable'.[17] Simply casting an eye through the IUCN Red List of extinct species shows many, many groups of flora and fauna to have lost many members, such as snipes, woodpigeons, quails, robber frogs, pupfish, species of mussels.

The online *Encyclopedia of Life* is a growing resource which is attempting to gather together information from multifarious sources including the IUCN Red List in order to act as a repository for all life. Their stated Vision is to provide global access to knowledge about life on Earth. They also state their vision on their website as, 'To increase awareness and understanding of living nature through an *Encyclopedia of Life* that gathers, generates, and shares knowledge in an open, freely accessible and trusted digital resource'.[18] Wikipedia similarly brings together information from the IUCN Red List and from other sources in order to provide information on species and their status. Indeed, there is a proliferation of online resources which document threats to species' survival, such as *iNaturalist*.[19] *iNaturalist* is an online forum for people around the world to share observations about nature. Currently the website states there are over half a million members and reports that 128,235 species have been observed on the site. There are many such online resources with which people can involve themselves and contribute to, all of which help to raise awareness and gather species information.

We now turn to exploring the world in '80 species'.[20] In terms of our selection method we began by considering a number of species which are already known to be extinct. We then move on to discussing species of flora and fauna which find themselves at various stages of extinction threat, as categorised by the IUCN Red List. We have chosen a sample of those creatures and plants threatened by extinction in order to provide an image, a snapshot in time, of the situation facing the planet. A quite frankly depressing aspect of writing this book was trying to decide which creatures and plants to include in this introductory chapter, in other words to prioritise, when every single one, large or small, is so precious. To choose just one species from the many seemed almost wrong as it does not do justice to all of the creatures. We have sought to represent species of flora as well as fauna, plants and trees as well as mammals and larger more well-known creatures, as well as members of the insect family and sea-dwelling creatures. We have chosen species which dwell on land as well as those which fly and those which are aquatic. We have also sought to select species which represent geographically all the continents and a wide array of countries around the world. We have included high profile species which readers may be more familiar with. To make the reading more approachable we selected species which have an English name as well as a Latin name and we have only provided the English names. This is not a scientific book and bringing in the Latin names in some way detracts from the theme, in our view. We also sought to provide etchings of some species as this, for us, represents an important part of providing a full and rich 'account' of them.

What have we lost already?

The latest version of the IUCN Red List[21] classified 866 species as extinct. Everyone has heard of the poor dodo, which disappeared within only a few years of meeting humans. The passenger pigeon is also famous for the way it was forced into extinction within a few decades by our good selves through being shot and killed for food, feathers and oil.[22] Indeed, the following is a tear-jerking description of the demise of this species:

> The very last passenger-pigeon to inhabit this earth of ours died at five o'clock in the afternoon of 1st September 1914. We know the precise time because somebody saw its head slowly sink to the floor. The bird died in a cage at Cincinnati Zoo in America. It was the only one left out of the countless millions which had flown across the states of Michigan and Ohio about a hundred years earlier.[23]

A creature called Steller's sea-cow was also driven into extinction by Russian hunters who killed and ate them all. Indeed, there are so many colourful creatures with enchanting and fascinating names which are now classified as extinct. One such tantalisingly named snake is the Round Island burrowing boa, another odd-sounding creature is the pig-footed bandicoot. Other birds now classified as extinct include the Tanna ground dove and the Reunion shelduck. There are, of course, shelducks in existence, but species which are specific to certain localities and often isolated ecosystems are not exactly the same as their relatives, as they have evolved in different ways, and therefore when they disappear from a local ecosystem it is the end of the line for that particular creature. Other strange-sounding birds which are now listed as extinct include the St Helena crake and the Labrador duck. The possibly less excitingly named Amsterdam duck is also now classified as extinct as is the (Australian) Norfolk starling and the red rail.

The magical Queen of Sheba's gazelle is listed as an extinct mammal. A native of Saudi Arabia, it was forced into extinction by over hunting. The Gölçük toothcarp again raises eyebrows as the name itself conjures images of some strange type of fish. Similarly, the desert rat kangaroo sounds like some weird hybrid animal and was exactly as it sounds, a jumping rat. The now extinct Navassa rhinoceros iguana also inspires mental images of an almost dinosaur-type individual, a cross between a rhinoceros and a lizard. Insects lost to the world include the chestnut moth. The Pinta giant tortoise became famous as the last of the species was named Lonesome George and passed away in June 2012. Readers may recall the story on the news.[24]

Some extinct creatures are known only by their latinised names, it seems, such as the *Amazona martinicana*, a brightly coloured parrot, and the Chinese fish *Anabarilius macrolepsis*, and, as stated earlier, we are focusing on species with English names as it makes the reading more accessible. A recent and distressing loss is the extinction of the rarest subspecies of black rhinoceros, the West African black rhinoceros. Once found across central Africa, the creature has

Figure 1.1 West African black rhinoceros (extinct)

been forced into extinction primarily through poaching for its horn. It is critical that continuing and increased efforts are made to prevent the whole range
of the rhinoceros species from suffering the same fate. In recent years, rangers
in the South African National Parks such as the Kruger have accelerated efforts
to provide protection to rhinoceros but numbers are still being reduced with
over a thousand rhinoceros a year being poached from the Kruger Park, despite
tracking devices, armed rangers and other anti-poaching initiatives.[25]

Another notorious extinction was the loss of a species of zebra, from
over-hunting, the quagga. Losses among amphibians are on a massive scale,
as we will see in our discussion of endangered species in the following section. One amphibian which has been pushed out of existence in recent years
was Holdridge's toad. This species of toad was a native of the Costa Rican
rainforests and was declared extinct in 2004. This was guessed to be a result
of an amphibian disease, chytridiomycosis, the spread of which is thought to
be linked to climate change and global warming. Flora as well as fauna have
already departed the earth. For example, the chocolate cosmos, originally
native to Mexico, is now extinct in the wild.[26]

What is causing mass extinctions? Seeking to explain extinctions of flora and fauna

What is causing extinctions? We are by no means scientists and are attempting
here to provide an approachable, but hopefully not overly simplistic, discussion

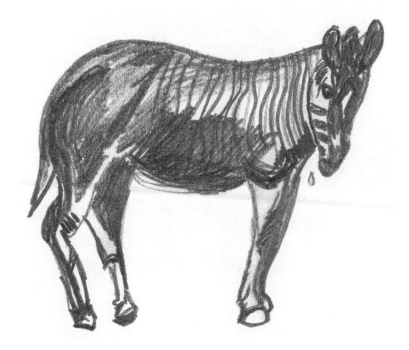

Figure 1.2 Quagga (extinct)

of extinctions and their causes. It is a sad fact that if we examine any species which is currently threatened with extinction or indeed a species which
has passed into extinction then the blame almost entirely points towards us.
However many causes there appear to be for a species dying out, they all seem
to emanate in some way from human activity. The five previous mass extinctions on planet earth occurred firstly at the end of the Ordovician period,
second in the late Devonian period, thirdly at the end of the Permian period,
fourth at the end of the Triassic period and, lastly, at the end of the Cretaceous
period when all of the dinosaurs disappeared. Following a mass extinction
event, it has taken tens of millions of years for a complete recovery in biodiversity.[27] Naturally occurring catastrophic events led to the previous five mass
extinction periods but the current mass extinction trend is very different. It is
the only mass extinction caused by one species:

> we are now living in the middle of another such cataclysm which has a
> new and quite different cause. The absolute, unprecedented dominance of
> one species – us – is putting the existence of a large proportion of all other
> life in jeopardy.[28]

Current mass extinctions have been brought about, according to some writers, by business, capitalism and market forces.[29] There are currently calls from

writers, researchers and practitioners for changes to the nature and form of capitalism around the world. Calls for a more social capitalism, a greener form of capitalism, abound in the press, among politicians, and in the business and social media. We now turn to a historic consideration of the impact of industry and business activity on nature and wildlife.

A historic perspective on industry's impact on the environment and species

The impact of pollution on the natural environment and wildlife has been recognised for many decades, indeed for centuries. Early accounts of the impact of pollution on nature and on human health were described by John Evelyn, who concerned himself with the effects of early industrial smoke and fog in London as early as 1661, in his short book *Fumifugium: Or the Inconvenience of the Aer and Smoake of London Dissipated.*[30] For example, he describes linkages between pollution and nature, specifically impacts on individual species of flora and fauna:

> Avernus to Fowl, and kills our Bees and Flowers abroad, suffering nothing in our gardens to bud, display themselves or ripen; so as our Anemonies and many other choicest Flowers, will by no Industry be made to blow in London . . . imparting a bitter and ungrateful Tast to those few wretched Fruits, which never arriving to their desired maturity, seem, like the Apples of Sodome, to fall even to dust, when they are but touched.[31]

The appalling effects of industrial activity such as the extraction of lead and copper on flora and fauna, were described in early observations at mining sites by early travel writers going on expeditions around Britain and other parts of the world. One eighteenth-century travel writer, Thomas Pennant, described the effects of copper mining in Anglesea, on nature as he toured Wales in 1778:

> The whole aspect of this tract has, by the mineral operations, assumed a most savage appearance. Suffocating fumes of the burning heaps of copper arise in all parts, and extend their baneful influence for miles around. In the adjacent parts vegetation is nearly destroyed; even the mosses and lichens of the rocks have perished; and nothing seems capable of resisting the fumes but the purple Melic grass, which flourishes in abundance.[32]

Gilbert White, an avid eighteenth-century naturalist who kept daily detailed nature diaries documenting his observations of local species in southern England, also concerned himself with the effects of environmental pollution from industrial activity on the air and land. White's account of nature also contains commentary, which raises environmental issues. For example:

> Blue mist. Vulg. Called London smoke . . . Does this meteorous appearance shew itself on the N.E. side of London when the wind is N.E? If that is the case then that mist cannot proceed from the smoke of the metropolis.

This mist has a strong smell, and is supposed to occasion blights. When such mists appear they are usually followed by dry weather. They have somewhat the smell of coal-smoke and therefore are supposed to come from London as they always come to us with a N.E. wind.[33]

The nineteenth century also witnessed a surge in concern about the impact of business activities and industry on the landscape, nature and wildlife. In 1853, a British civil engineer, Frederick Braithwaite (1778–1865), published a report, *On the Rise and Fall of the River Wandle; its Springs, Tributaries, and Pollution.* This report represents to all intent and purposes an 'account' of river pollution and also identifies the polluters:

The firm (Messrs. Dempsey and Hind) used half *a carboy of sulphuric acid weekly*; a carboy, or about 8 gallons, of *muriate of tin per month*; and *5 cwt. of prussiate of potash*, and *5 cwt. of oxalic acid per annum*; also a certain quantity of sulphate of copper, nitrate of iron, chloride of lime, &c, *all of which materials are discharged into the river.*[34]

The Pre-Raphaelite movement created utopian scenes in art and literature which harkened back to a pre-industrial landscape. William Morris's writings abound with concerns for the changing natural environment as he was distressed about the effect of industry on rivers, on the countryside, on forests, for example, he deplored the effects of industry on nature in *How We Live and How We Might Live.*[35]

Interestingly, in *Around the World in Eighty Days*, published in 1873, Jules Verne described Phileas Fogg and Passepartout's journey across India on the Peninsular Railway and highlighted the deleterious effects of the train on nature:

The engine, driven by an Englishman and fuelled with English coal, belched out its smoke over the plantations of cotton, coffee, nutmeg, clove and pepper, while the steam wound its spirals round clumps of palm trees ... Then stretching out of sight, lay a vast expanse of jungle, the home of abounding snakes and tigers, terrified by the snorting screech of the engine; and after this the forests cleft by the line, and still frequented by elephants, that gazed with wistful eye as the train rushed past in its dishevelled fury.[36]

We can see from this smattering of writings spanning a few centuries that humanity has becoming increasingly aware of, and increasingly concerned about, their own impact on nature and on wildlife, whether from mining, industrial activity and pollution, or the growth of transportation. These concerns have become more and more justified as time has moved onwards. It is notable that these early 'accounts' were not provided by the perpetrators of the pollution of air, or land, or water but were instead interested parties, observers of landscape or nature, who took it upon themselves to provide an 'account'. Since the mid-nineteenth century, listed companies have had to produce accounts by law. This process of accounting is a means by which companies may discharge their accountability for their actions and impacts to their stakeholders. As we will see in the following chapter, there has been a move over time from purely financial accounting to accounts which contain environmental and social impacts as well. Before formal accounting began, all we have to document the impacts of business activities on the environment derives from voluntary 'accounts', records, journals produced by interested individuals.

As well as the direct impact of industrial activities on nature, in the 1960s, there were growing societal concerns about pollution and pesticides around the world. *Silent Spring*, the famous work of Rachel Carson, reached across all groups of readers and resulted in the banning of DDT pesticides. Researchers have identified a wide range of pollutants and pesticides and the ways in which they were starting to have deleterious effects on nature and wildlife through air pollution, water pollution, pollution by herbicides and fungicides, dangerous effects from insecticides and pesticides.[37] Climate change is one of the most significant and overriding factors driving the current mass extinction crisis. Until very recently there was continuous debate among the scientific community as to whether climate change was 'definitely happening'. There are still many climate change sceptics and deniers. Putting aside arguments about how we may be entering something similar to the mediaeval warming period, or how this is just a natural planetary phase which we have seen before in previous millennia, let us assume that climate change is happening, that global warming is an indisputable fact and that the world is warming up. The connected assumption to this is that human activity is the root cause of the warming, that human activity is continuing to warm the atmosphere through the burning of fossil fuels and other outcomes of human and in particular, industrial activity. It could also be the case that in addition to human-induced global warming, the planet is experiencing a natural warming period.

In our modern world, with all the conveniences of the West, and increasingly across other parts of the (until now) 'developing' world, it is hard to imagine how things were different only a short time ago. Any historical series on the television, whether it is a cowboy film, or an adaptation of an eighteenth century novel, portrays relatively recent history in a way that makes it feel ancient. Yet television, aeroplanes, trains, toilets, showers, computers, just about any appliance or equipment used in today's society as a basic item, without which people would struggle, were only invented over the last couple of hundred years. This is absolutely inconsequential in the history of our planet and indeed of our species, which has only been around for some 100,000 years. Other species, extinct and existing, are far more ancient, dating back millions of years. The industrial revolution is a relatively recent phenomenon – only in the early 1700s in the UK did the industrial revolution really start to get a grip. Yet it is in that incredibly short period of time, considering the history of the planet, that global warming has taken hold and the climate has started to change so significantly as a direct result of industrialisation, resulting in industrial pollution, the destruction of natural habitat for industrial activity and pillaging of species for food, medicines and for any other purpose, or usefulness, to humans.

Edward Wilson, as we saw above, writing widely on biodiversity and extinction, raised public awareness of extinction trends 30 to 40 years ago. It is sobering to realise that society seems only now to be starting to realise the immensity of the extinction crisis, given the work of scientists like Wilson decades ago. He identifies extinction as the most critical challenge facing our planet: 'In one sense the loss of diversity is the most important process of environmental change. I say this because it is the only process that is wholly irreversible.'[38]

Unless, as discussed earlier, we can create a *Jurassic Park* scenario, extinction of species is the end of millions of years of evolution, the end of the line for idiosyncratic and unique genetic DNA and the last sight of a particular creature, whether immense and charismatic such as the mighty rhinoceros, or small and relatively inconspicuous like a fire ant. Of course, with farming and agriculture, habitat loss and depletion of land and natural resources has a history going back to early human emergence as a dominant species. As soon as cavemen (and maybe cavewomen?) started to hunt and gather, and then practise very early forms of farming, they started to leave their imprint on the land, changing the landscape forever.

Feeding the ever growing human populations around the world is a key cause of extinction, with species of bird, mammal, fish, even insects providing meals of every imaginable kind for people around the world. A truly fascinating book, *The Wordsworth Guide to Edible Plants and Animals*, provides a veritable menu of how we have munched our way through the planet's biodiversity since time immemorial. While on the one hand quaint and interesting, on the other the book shows us the insatiable greed of the human race and their ability to see every single natural item of flora and fauna as a potential delicacy for their personal use.[39] The authors state in the introduction that their book contains around 500 unusual plants and animals that can be eaten in an attempt to preserve knowledge about edible species but also to help cultures understand each other's eating habits and preferences. We were horrified to read the following under the heading 'rhinoceroses':

> the meat is highly prized in some areas and its thick skin is considered to be a delicacy in parts of Asia . . . The rhino is difficult to bring down, partly because of its bulk and partly because of its thick skin. It is, in short, a dangerous animal for the hunter to face, even with modern rifle. It wasn't meat that brought about the rhino's demise, but rather the value of its horns and destruction of its habitat.[40]

And this book was published originally in 1993, only 25 years ago. Attitudes have surely changed, although clearly there are still many around the world who care to hunt rhinos and other game. Although we have spent much time researching the threat to rhinoceros arising from poaching, their being eaten never entered our minds.

Given the fact that orangutans are now on the very brink of extinction due to the destruction of their habitat and increasing swathes of palm oil plantations, we were also mortified to read this under the heading 'orangutans': 'the orang-utan has been eaten for food in times past . . . In Vietnam, the lip of orang-utan was once considered a delicacy'.[41]

Giraffes, also now threatened with extinction, as their populations are shrinking, are also mentioned in this book: 'These long-legged animals also provide one of the greatest delicacies in all Africa: giraffe bone marrow. After the bones are baked in the oven, the marrow is picked out.'[42] Is there any wonder everything is disappearing?

The destruction of the rainforests has had devastating consequences for tropical flora and fauna for decades and no matter how much fuss is made by wildlife activists, NGOs, or other bodies, the clearing of pristine rainforest continues. Sustainable forests and efforts to slow the destruction seem to have minimal impact. The Amazon rainforest is disappearing rapidly, as are the forests in Borneo, Madagascar and in all tropical areas of the world. The last vestiges of real, genuine wilderness are being forced into smaller and smaller spaces, with wildlife parks and areas of protected natural beauty or natural heritage sites being the final outposts for millions of species. As early as the 1980s, it was clear that extinctions were being brought about through tropical deforestation when it was estimated that worldwide the loss of species attributable to clearing rainforest would be between 0.2 and 0.3 of all species in the rainforests each year, around an average of 5,000 species a year, although this was seen as a very conservative estimate. [43]

Urbanisation arising from the continuous growth in human populations around the world presents another threat to species, habitats and ecosystems. As the famous economist Malthus predicted, human populations will reach unsustainable levels and perhaps this is now the case. Chapter 4 discusses the ultimate fate of the human species as a direct result of our own effectively suicidal tendency to destroy the natural world around us:

> We have to recognise that the old vision of a world in which human beings played a relatively minor part is done and finished. The notion that an ever bountiful nature, lying beyond man's habitations and influence, will always (satisfy?) his wants, no matter how much he takes from it or how he maltreats it, is false. We can no longer depend on providence to maintain the delicate interconnected communities of animals and plants on which we depend.[44]

Clearly, there is not one underlying cause of the current extinction trend. Reading and researching species extinction reveals a great number of causes, although all the roots of the current mass extinction trend are bedded in the actions of human beings. While we are not scientists ourselves and do not profess to have a specialist understanding of scientific research, we have read widely and provide an attempt at least to capture the underlying causes. Let us now take a look at groups of species and the factors contributing to their population decline and extinction threat: plants, mammals, invertebrates, fish and water-dwelling creatures, reptiles and amphibians, and birds.

Flora . . .

Plants: trees, flowers, ferns, conifers . . .

Plants are affected by climate change and specifically by increases in CO_2 levels, temperature and moisture changes, changes in rainfall, frost patterns and winds. It is far more difficult for plants to migrate and relocate when habitat conditions change than for mammals or insects, for obvious reasons – they are rooted in the ground. Over time they can migrate through pollination and by spreading to more favourable areas but plant biodiversity is likely to reduce significantly as climate change and global warming continue.[45] The WWF, in the early 1990s, identified habitats where plants were likely to be at highest risk from climate change, including: freshwater and salt wetlands, coastal areas, mountain regions, tundra, and moorland. Alpine plants are considered particularly vulnerable. Also, South Africa is renowned for its rich floral diversity especially in the fynbos region which is seen as a biome of global conservation importance but is at high risk of biodiversity loss due to climate change.[46] Other areas around the world where plants and flowers have been identified as under serious threat from climate change are the Colorado Mountains in the USA, European wetlands, the French Mediterranean dune systems. Forests play a key role in stabilising the earth's environmental system by moderating climate, controlling floods, storing water, holding onto carbon (reducing the effects of global warming) and, most importantly for our purposes here, providing habitat for at least half of the planet's species of flora and fauna.[47] As discussed earlier, tropical rainforests are under constant threat from development and clearing. They also contain some of the greatest biodiversity on the planet. The latest figures included in the LPI indicate that there has been a 41 per cent fall in species endemic to tropical forests between 1970 and 2009.[48] Almost half of the tropical and subtropical dry broadleaf forest had been 'taken' for use by humans by the turn of this century.[49] Around the turn of the century, the US had lost 95 per cent of its natural forest, probably more by now.[50]

The Environmental Conservation Online System (ECOS) lists 950 plants as threatened. Flowering plants included on the list and categorised as endangered and threatened include a great many with captivating names such as Munz's onion, the South Texas ambrosia, large-flowered fiddleneck, dwarf bear-poppy, Sacramento prickly poppy, Dwarf naupaka, and clay-reed mustard. It is sometimes hard to imagine how some of these flowers were named, when we find such strangely named species as the endangered Fosberg's love grass, the Michigan monkey flower, the Minnesota dwarf trout lily, Colorado hookless cactus, Florida skullcap and the Holy Ghost ipomopsis. For others, their naming seems more obvious – for example the endangered 'scrub blazing star', the Ben Lomond wallflower or the threatened 'bush clover'. Under ferns, ECOS includes again many intriguingly named plants such as the American hart's-tongue fern, which is listed as threatened and the slender-horned spineflower. The Blue Ridge golden rod cannot fail to remind some of us of a certain age of the Laurel and Hardy films.

One species of tree listed as critically endangered by the IUCN Red List is the Algerian silver fir.[51] The tree sounds like the silvery leaved foliage from a Shakespeare's *A Midsummer Night's Dream*. This tree is native to Algeria, as its name suggests, and to parts of the Djebel Babor Mountains. Decline in species population is measured by square kilometres of the remaining component of this tree within the forest, which is an interesting indicative measure of extinction risk. According to the IUCN Red List data, there is thought to be less than a square kilometre of the Algerian silver fir remaining. Threats to this tree, stated in the Red List, include forest fires, collection of wood for fuel, and grazing by farmed animals. The whole area of forest is protected as a formalised Nature Reserve with efforts to prevent trees being taken for timber or fuel. It is so sad to see beautiful forests and their increasingly rare trees dwindling and disappearing. Again we can see human activity as the root cause of its demise. A whole range of other plant species appear on the threatened, endangered and critically endangered lists including the bastard quiver tree, the Clanwilliam cedar, the Symonds Yat white beam, Henry's paphiopedilum (an orchid), Attenborough's pitcher plant (named after David Attenborough), the He cabbage tree and Hinckley's oak.

. . . and fauna

Mammals

Mammals are probably the most well-known group of species as they include the cuddliest of all flora and fauna and probably excite the most interest in their appeal as fluffy, cute creatures as well as including huge striking creatures which are imposing and exciting. They are warm-blooded – like us. It is distressing to discover how many mammalian species are at risk of extinction. Big cats, rhinoceros, elephants, giraffes, tigers, panda and smaller mammals such as mice and hedgehogs are all suffering from habitat depletion, pollution, poisoning, chemicals and climate change. As a writer on threatened species commented in the early 1970s, just because an animal may be large does not offer protection from man, 'Size and strength are no match for human vandalism.'[52]

The writer goes on to discuss the threats to large animals from people wanting to hunt and shoot for leisure and to poach for profit. They are also at risk from their lower populations when compared to smaller creatures. The impact of humans on the land is so extensive that habitats are disappearing to the point where land dwelling mammals are running out of places to live. There are, of course, massive nature reserves and protected areas of habitat around the world such as the Kruger Park in South Africa which covers a vast area of land. One would think that species of mammal would at least be safe there but huge creatures such as the mighty rhinoceros are under threat from poachers who kill them in their 'safe' environment in order to take their horns. The fact that some national parks are so huge may be good in one way, as creatures have large areas in which to roam, but they are difficult to protect from poachers and the like. With the clearance of rainforests, the continually growing suffocation of land by agricultural activity, industrial appropriation of land for mining, and human populations encroaching on more and more pristine habitat, species of mammals are at risk of extinction across every continent and country. In addition to threats from habitat loss and destruction, climate change is presenting new and different problems, 'Large and small mammals worldwide are threatened particularly by the potential impact of climate change on remaining wilderness and semi-wild lands.'[53]

A quarter of a century ago, the WWF identified mammals in tundra areas, savannah and tropical rainforests as being most acutely at risk of extinction.[54] Global warming is causing wet areas in Africa to disappear through drought, mangroves to be destroyed, and cold habitats to be lost. As we will see in Chapter 18, polar bears are threatened by the loss of ice through climate change which prevents them from hunting, as well as the loss of their food supply through the effects of global warming on seal populations. Migrating species are affected adversely by habitat loss and degradation. Caribou, for example, which migrate across vast tracts of tundra each year, are a species famous for the distances they travel to align themselves with the most fitting conditions for their survival and breeding.

Habitat fragmentation, resulting in genetic isolation, leads to what is scientifically known as the 'allele problem', which is contributing to extinction risk. Alleles are forms of gene carrying characteristics such as colour or negative traits which can cause mutations among members of a species. In a large population, such mutations are not a problem for a species, or a population, until a population falls below a certain number, then reproduction can lead to an imbalance in characteristics, which can in turn lead to negative alleles dominating, rendering the species vulnerable to extinction: 'Small populations therefore accumulate deleterious mutations. Left unchecked, the effect of these fixed alleles is to reduce the reproductive capacity of a species, eventually to the point of extinction.'[55]

An iconic species, which has become the motif for the WWF, is the adorable panda. Almost unbearably cute and cuddly, this quirky black and white mammal has been the centre of worldwide concerns about extinction threat. The plight of the giant panda is discussed at length in Chapter 19, where we also see examples of panda accounting by Chinese companies which are battling to save panda.

As we see in the following section, species are all interconnected within global and local ecosystems. One species cannot disappear without affecting other species and the interlinkages, although researched by scientists, are not fully known or understood and are mind bogglingly complex. For mammals, where smaller creatures down the food chain disappear, this in itself presents an extinction threat. Many mammals rely on fruits, seeds and insects as their staple diet. What would an anteater eat if not ants? How could a honey badger survive without bees and honey? How could a koala bear live without eucalyptus, or a panda without bamboo?

A further threat is that endangered species are increasingly poached and sold for human food, as human populations continue to expand and societies are threatened themselves by climate change. The pangolin, or scaly anteater, is being hunted and poached as meat. Extreme poaching is driving the species towards extinction. There are eight species of pangolin throughout china and Vietnam and they are on the brink of extinction. TRAFFIC, the international wildlife trade monitoring network has recently stated that the Sunda pangolin as a critically endangered species is being seriously affected by illegal trade and poaching. They state that, as at 21 December 2017, ten thousand pangolins a year are being lost from Indonesia to illegal trade. Further in a recent study TRAFFIC researchers found that pangolin meat is being sold in vast quantities. The IUCN pangolin specialist group and other groups worldwide, including Save Pangolins, are focusing on trying to save the pangolin and preventing wildlife crime.

An intriguingly named creature, the Tasmanian Devil, once abundant in Australia and Tasmania, is also threatened with extinction. The animal has been described as the largest of the marsupial cats and was reported as extinct on the Australian mainland in the early 1980s.[56] Other colourful and magical-sounding creatures which are currently included on the critically endangered species include the black-and-white ruffed lemur, the Bornean orang-utan, the Angel Island mouse, the black-crested gibbon, the pygmy possum, the northern hairy-nosed wombat, the silky sifaka and the Bulmers fruit bat. We provide some sketches of these which in themselves attempt to provide a pictorial 'account' of the species and to communicate their individuality and idiosyncracies. Lemurs, so beautiful and diverse in their species, have been recognised as under threat for decades. Anyone who grew up in the UK during the 1970s will have fond memories of the television presenter Johnny Morris having conversations with the ring-tailed lemur, Dotty, in the wonderful children's programme *Animal Magic*. In relation to the aye-aye, Sir David Attenborough commented in the early eighties that, 'There may be only about 50 of these very extraordinary lemurs left alive'.[57]

The aye-aye, a native to Madagascar, is nocturnal and lives in the canopy of the tropical rainforest. Scientists had believed the animal to be extinct until it was rediscovered in 1961.[58] IUCN assessments have categorised the species as endangered since then apart from once when its status was downgraded to threatened.

One of our favourite creatures, which look like little dinosaurs from a land time has forgotten, is the armadillo. Although they sometimes look reptilian

Figure 1.3 Black-and-white ruffed lemur

due to their bony shells, armadillos are omnivorous mammals.[59] They are the only mammal which wears plates of armour. They live almost exclusively in Latin America. Many armadillo species again have strange and quirky names which conjure up all sorts of images of weird wonderfulness – but these are also under threat. The giant armadillo, probably the most well-known, is classified as vulnerable, as is the Brazilian three-banded armadillo. The amazingly named Chacoan naked-tailed armadillo is classified as near threatened. Fortunately, the screaming hairy armadillo is categorised as of least concern – but this means it is still threatened as it appears on the Red List. The nine-banded armadillo was described as the most widespread of the armadillo species in the early 1980s.[60] It is, however, currently included on the IUCN Red List, albeit 'of least concern'. Another strange and fascinating mammal, which in many ways looks more like a cross between a reptile and a small hog, is the aardvark. For many readers, the word 'aardvark' may conjure up images of Blackadder and his assistant Baldrick frantically trying to rewrite the Dr. Johnson's first dictionary, after they thought they had burned the only version as fuel for their fire, as aardvark has to be the first word in any English language dictionary! Aardvarks are found throughout Africa South of the Sahara desert and their principal food consists of termites. They are currently classified by the IUCN as of 'Least Concern', although their numbers have been decreasing.

Figure 1.4 Aardvark

Big cats are especially close to our hearts, as cat owners and supporters of cat rescue charities. Maybe people take lions for granted? But their survival is not necessarily certain. *The Lion King*, a magical portrayal of lions and the 'Circle of Life', has embedded lions into the hearts and minds of children for many years. How can we dare to imagine a world without the mighty lion, the King of the Jungle? Lions are now categorised as vulnerable by the IUCN. On a recent trip to South Africa we saw a great white lion, stunningly beautiful creature, in a wildlife park near to Johannesburg. He was the star of a film and is carefully guarded and cared for. White lions are albinos of the lion species rather than a separate species. Similarly, the lovingly avuncular Bagheera featured in *The Jungle Book* is a black panther, which again is not a member of a separate species but rather a rare dark pigmentation found in leopards, jaguars and other big cats.[61]

Probably our favourite big cat, if it is possible to identify a favourite among these wonderful creatures, is the elusive and secretive snow leopard. Downlisting a species from one category to another is actually quite controversial. While it may be an indication that the species is at less threat than before of extinction, it could also imply less concern and protection and lead to further falls in population, habitat protection and conservation. This issue is discussed eloquently in Chapter 5 in relation to the downgrading of the grey whale's status. For example, the recent decision by the IUCN to downlist the snow leopard's Red List status from 'endangered' to 'vulnerable' has been opposed by the Snow Leopard Trust.[62] The Snow Leopard Trust asserts that this change of status may lead to less protection for these glorious animals from governments and society. Climate change and global warming are identified as threatening two-thirds of their habitat with other threats including mining, illegal hunting, attempts to allow trophy hunting, and poaching.

It would be wrong not to include a discussion of our 'closest relatives' the primates, which again are suffering from the threats of climate change, habitat loss and degradation and deforestation. One of the saddest stories in the media at the moment is the demise of the Bornean orang-utan, described in 1981 as follows: 'The great red-haired orang-utan of Borneo and Sumatra is the world's heaviest tree-dweller.'[63]

Once prolific in the tropical rainforests of Borneo, they are on the very brink of extinction, mainly as a result of losing their homes. Palm oil plantations are rapidly replacing pristine jungle with orang-utans being left with nowhere to live. Indeed, if you were to take a bus from the north to the south of the Malaysian mainland, it is quite disturbing to find that the drive is flanked almost the whole way on both sides by palm oil plantations. There are only isolated areas of pristine rainforest left such as the Taman Nagara National Park. Gorillas have been a cause for concern among naturalists and scientists for several decades.

It is not just the hot, sticky jungles, tropical forests and warm areas of the world where life is threatened but also in the coldest parts of the planet. The Antarctic is suffering from global warming with scientists reporting the thawing of sea ice and the disappearance of frozen areas at an alarming rate. Everyone

Figure 1.5 Snow leopard

probably associates global warming with photographs of polar bears struggling to feed. With the disappearance of sea ice the immense bears have to swim, sometimes for days, to find 'land'. The threatened polar bear is the subject of Chapter 18.

Birds

There are so many birds, many of which we hear in stories, in documentaries, see around us, or eat, and their variations are immense. Species of petrel, ibis, kite, pheasant, quail, rail, shorebird, auk, pigeon, parrot, owl, hummingbird, woodpecker, bulbul, thrush, tit, wren, warbler, finch all form part of our culture, our knowledge of the natural world around us. But for how long? Even when creatures escape the land and the sea they are just as vulnerable to extinction. Songbirds have been the target of hunting, shooting and captivation as pets for many centuries. The English King Henry VIII, renowned for his love of food and drink, organised immense banquets for hundreds of people during his reign and songbirds in their thousands comprised many of the King's menus. Rachel Carson's *Silent Spring* made society aware of how the world could look without the dawn chorus and the delightful sound of songbirds around us. A rather depressingly titled book, published in 1967, 'Extinct and vanishing birds of the world', takes a virtual tour of the world's bird species to draw attention to the 130 species and subspecies of birds which at that time were known to have become extinct or were under serious threat of extinction.[64] The situation is far worse now than it was 50 years ago. In today's environment, bird species are disappearing at an alarming rate with an estimated 13 per cent of all birds under threat of extinction.[65] In the early 1990s the impacts of climate change and associated shifts in natural cycles were identified as of serious threat to birds. Bird species are especially affected by the disappearance of wetlands as they are wet-land dependent.[66]

> Birds may be affected by direct physical effects of climate change, such as temperature rise, and more widely by disruption of their habitats and food supplies, both through the impact of climate change itself, and through human responses to climate change.[67]

As discussed in the same WWF report, although birds can fly away from trouble, they tend to have very localised habitats and especially those species dwelling in tropical rainforest can be reliant on particular, local habitats which when affected by climatic changes, or destroyed by human activity makes their survival impossible. However, species which are migratory are also at significant risk from climate change as they have to travel across many different habitats in their migratory cycle which, if affected adversely by environmental and climatic changes, make their migratory routes unachievable. In the 1980s it was recognised that half of the bird species of Polynesia had been forced into extinction through human activity including habitat destruction and hunting.[68]

The WWF identified many bird species under threat from climate change-induced reductions in forest habitat, the loss of wetlands due to human pressures on land use and significant global warming, increasingly arid conditions and sea level rises which affect low-lying islands and shallow coastal areas. Similarly changes to fish species arising from climate change affects birds through reducing their food supplies and breeding sites are being lost as habitats are being destroyed by changes in climate but also by industrial activity such as forest clearance, logging and extending agricultural land. Polar regions (and eventually everywhere else) are being affected as ice and snow melt with rising temperatures. Penguins have to be one of the most attractive species of birds, beloved by birdwatchers, children and often the subject of cartoons, pictures and books. One particularly fascinating species is the African penguin, also known as the Jackass Penguin, or the black-footed penguin. Anyone fortunate enough to travel to Cape Town in South Africa can take a short drive along the coast to Boulders Bay and find thousands of these strange and comical birds nesting by the paths and strutting up and down the beach, diving in and out of the sea. However, the IUCN Red List states that the species is classified as 'Endangered' because it is undergoing a very rapid population decline, probably as a result of commercial fisheries and shifts in prey populations.[69] The entry states further that the decreasing trend currently shows no sign of reversing, and immediate conservation action is required to prevent further declines. Scientists have suggested that a primary cause of declining African penguin populations is essentially a lack of food. Penguins eat sardines and anchovies which have been heavily targeted by the fishing industry leaving the penguins with drastically less food available. Another threat affecting this unusual penguin arises from marine oil spills, with conservationists working hard to rescue oiled penguins and rehabilitate them.[70] Another, historic, reason for the decline in African penguin populations is that humans found a use for their 'guano', basically excrement, as fertiliser, removing it in vast quantities which left them without the ability to burrow and nest. There are around 50,000 African penguins left in the wild, only 2 per cent of the original numbers in the 1800s. South African companies are now involved in conservation of the African penguin as well as SANCCOB, the local conservation group. One bank, Old Mutual, is especially involved, sponsoring the penguin programme at the Two Oceans Aquarium. Visitors to the aquarium can see marine life from both sides of South Africa, as the warm Indian Ocean meets the cold Atlantic Ocean at Cape point making the area a place of strange and wonderful combinations of species, including the African penguin which lives in a warm climate unlike its Antarctic relatives. Indeed, one of the most amazing days of our lives was our visit to Cape Point in 2015, where we were able to stand on the Southernmost point of Africa and see both oceans from the top of the mountain as well as looking out to the South in the knowledge that there was nothing between us and the coastline of Antarctica. Cape Point should really be on everyone's bucket list fortunate enough to be able to travel.

Figure 1.6 African penguin

Birds around the entire globe are under serious threat. Puffins are (in our view at least) one of the most charismatic and delightful bird species. Their little dumpy bodies and black and white markings make them look like small gentleman at a black tie do. Atlantic puffins entered the IUCN Red List of endangered species list in Europe in October 2015. Global warming is pushing sand eel populations into deeper, cooler waters and, as they are puffins' favourite food, this is having a severe impact on them. Similarly, sand eels are being overfished in European waters.[71] We can see the painful way in which species interdependence means a kink in one part of the system affects dramatically creatures near the top of the food chain.

Figure 1.7 Puffin

A large island in Polynesia, New Caledonia, was identified as having many rare and threatened species of bird such as parrots and rail with writers in the 1960s stating that the island was home to 68 species of bird, 25 per cent of which were only found on that island.[72] One critically endangered species, as detailed in the Red List is the New Caledonian owlet-nightjar. The Jamaican poorwill is a critically endangered species of bird. The Red List identifies the sapphire-bellied humming bird as critically endangered. A bird known as the spoon-billed sandpiper is critically endangered according to the Red List. Another critically endangered species of bird is the Sumatran ground cuckoo and, similarly, the Chilean woodstar is critically endangered.

The Brazilian merganser, a type of duck, is also listed as critically endangered by the IUCN Red List. This bird was described as being very rare in 1901 by Bertoni and the state of this species in 1967 was described as being only a small and scattered population recorded from southeastern Brazil in the states of São Paulo, Santa Catarina, Goyaz, eastern Paraguay and Misiones in Argentina.[73] Later chapters examine the current fate of sparrows, once such a commonly seen species (Chapter 14) and the state of nature in relation to birds and extinction threats in the UK (Chapter 13).

Invertebrates: spiders, worms, bees and other bugs

Invertebrates, creatures without a spine, include all bugs and insects, both terrestrial and water-dwelling, those that crawl, swim and fly. Ancient creatures such as the silverfish are remnants from a prehistoric period, surviving millennia of change on the planet. Climate change and other factors are also seriously affecting populations of invertebrates. Insects, which we spend so much time trying to eradicate from our homes and workplaces, are now at risk of extinction. Researchers consider that different types of insect will fare better than others in the face of global warming and climate change. For example, butterflies and moths are seen as some of the most sensitive as they are affected by climatic changes and even minor environmental changes whereas beetles and species often perceived as pests and parasites can adapt more easily to changes in temperature, especially temperature increases and can also disperse quickly and migrate.[74] There are increasing concerns about the spread of malaria-carrying mosquitos as a result of global warming and there are heightened worries about dengue fever in cities in the Far East, for which there is no inoculation available. In effect, insects are seen to fall into two groups: those which are easily adaptable to climatic changes and those which are not – usually due to their highly specialised nature.

In a recent book, we explored the financial risks relating to pollinators but specifically bees, both threatened wild and commercial bees. Bees are solitary as well as hive-dwelling, and the book entitled *The Business of Bees: An Integrated Approach to Bee Decline and Corporate Responsibility* demonstrated the material financial risks arising from bee decline for businesses and for shareholders.[75] As pollinators, it is relatively easy to assess the ways in which their loss can affect business: mainly through failures in the food chain. Scientists have shown that bee loss is having a significant financial impact on the global food industry. The cause of this decline in bee species has been attributed largely to the use of agricultural pesticides, especially neonicotinoids. Their ban for agricultural use throughout Europe has resulted in some apparent recovery in populations. The widespread and systematic use of agricultural pesticides is having an impact not only on bee populations but also on all invertebrates affected, it appears from research. Insects are crucial to the continuance of life on earth.

Most of life on this planet (flora and fauna) comprises insects, or invertebrates of one sort or another. Although we often think of large mammals, or even ourselves, as being the dominant and most important species on the planet, it is in actual fact the tiny creatures which support everything else. They are the tip of an upside down pyramid. Tiny as they are, if insects disappeared everything else would also collapse into extinction. Estimates of the number of insect species have been arrived at by scientists, for example one estimate in the 1980s was that there were around 30 million insect species.[76] Bacteria, funghi, algae, lichen and microcosms are all critical to the continuance of life on earth but we do not feel able to do these tiny creatures justice in the current book. Needless to say, as with insects, humanity spends most of its time trying to kill bacteria with antibiotics (which are ceasing to work as bacteria adapt), with antibacterial sprays, bleaches and other forms of scientifically devised organism murdering creations. In fact, the importance of insects to our global ecosystem and to the survival of everything including ourselves cannot be overstated.

When we think about it, humans spend a great deal of their time systematically eliminating insects from the home, from their workplace, from their pets, from their gardens, from farms, from parks and from just about everywhere they inhabit. Insecticides, pesticides, parasiticides, fly sprays, ant killer, slug pellets – you name the insect and we have a dedicated poison or spray to eradicate it. From the critically endangered species on the IUCN Red List we selected a small handful of insects and invertebrates for consideration, to illustrate the tiny things which are heading towards eternal darkness.

Similarly, there is evidence of insect-killing chemicals in streams and rivers in Scotland. Essentially, the chemical cocktail present in parasiticides which are used prolifically on pets and farming livestock contain the same essential ingredient as the bee killing pesticides which have been banned across European countries – imidacloprid contains neonicotonoids. Concerns about cat and dog flea collars, for examples, have also been raised by the academic community in relation to their impact on the animals they are meant to protect, their owners, and the natural environment and biodiversity.

Arachnids, or spiders, are an unusual group of creatures, each having eight legs and eight eyes. They are probably one of the animals which induce the most fear among humans. Basically spiders have a bad press. It is not clear why they have been branded as frightening and even terrifying. Children often love playing with spiders but as soon as they become adults many of the preconceptions and societal expectations kick in and they become frightened of them.

Figure 1.8 Rusty patched bumble bee

Some are admittedly extremely poisonous and they can look scary when they seek to protect themselves by raising their front legs or scuttling away quickly into a safe place.

A selection of some insects with amazing names which are, sadly, classified as critically endangered include the Rumplestiltskin pygmy grasshopper, the red legged fire millipede, the Lion's hill velvet worm, the Cyprian grey bush cricket, the Socorro snail and the rusty patched bumble bee. Spiders, although not insects, are probably seen by most people as the same sort of creature and they, too, are suffering from extinction threat. Two randomly selected from the list of critically endangered creatures include the peacock tarantula and the Zulu ambush katydid.

Butterflies and moths are some of the most scintillatingly beautiful creatures on earth but are also some of the most fragile and vulnerable to climatic change and other factors. In Chapter 17 there is a detailed analysis of the situation for the celebrated Monarch butterfly, known for the clouds of this butterfly hanging from trees across the US. In Britain, one species of butterfly, the large blue, became extinct in the UK in the late 1970s after a long period of decline, mainly as a result of habitat loss. It has now been reintroduced through the efforts of conservationists and naturalists[77] but the species is currently classified as endangered by the IUCN.

Fish and other creatures of the seas, oceans, lakes and rivers

As was demonstrated eloquently in the latest series narrated by Sir David Attenborough, *Blue Planet II*, it is not just terrestrial creatures which are seriously endangered. The seas and oceans of the world are being contaminated by industrial activity, by plastics, pollutants, waste. Also, climate change and global warming are causing warming of the oceans as well as increases in acidity. Fresh water fish species have been identified as being at particular threat from climate change, as they are isolated within lakes or freshwater inland areas, being unable to escape to more tolerable conditions when conditions change, as a result of global warming and associated factors.[78] Fish and other species within river systems are especially affected by human manipulation of rivers and waterways, especially the building of dams.[79] The 'mega-dam' currently being constructed in Ethopia is likely to have untold consequences on habitats and species.

Marine fish are more adaptable to changes in climatic conditions than fresh water fish, as they can migrate to areas where conditions may be more suitable. The WWF[80] highlights some groups of marine species which are, however, at greater threat from climate change, such as: cold water fish which have no colder areas to move to as seas warm; fish found in areas such as mangrove swamps which are disappearing. However, they do state that 'the size, relative stability and interconnectedness of the world's oceans may help reduce the effects in terms of biodiversity loss'.[81]

If climate change were the only threat to the seas and oceans of the world, then perhaps the fact that they are all connected would mean marine life may not be at significant threat of extinction – but there are so many other factors contributing to the loss of marine species. All of these, again, arise from human and business activity. Seas and oceans cover almost three quarters of the surface of our planet.[82] The latest figures produced by the WWF (namely the marine LPI) indicate a 36 per cent fall in marine species, which primarily include fish (although the index does also include marine birds, mammals, reptiles) between 1970 and 2012. Excessive fishing represents the primary threat to marine fish species and over 30 per cent of global fish stocks are estimated to be over-fished.[83] The Northern Pacific bluefin tuna is at risk from over-fishing. Another horrifying statistic is that a third of sharks, rays and skate are considered to be threatened by extinction due to overfishing.[84]

Species biodiversity varies across different types of water system and water-based system. The latest LPI produced by the WWF[85] indicates that on average, populations (abundance of populations monitored, to be specific) of species within freshwater has fallen by 81 per cent between 1970 and 2012. Plastics in the oceans and seas are an immense and growing problem. As Mervyn King asserts in Chapter 6, plastic beads and plastic pollution are killing vast swathes of creatures. Some of the most affected areas are the treasured coral reefs. Coral reefs have always been held up as some of the wonderful examples of creation, evolution and biodiversity, being living masses of diverse and often tiny, life. Coral reefs are being bleached by warmer waters and are dying *en masse*, leaving coral graveyards over huge expanses of seabed. With the death of the coral we are witnessing the death and disappearance of all the massive diversity of life which inhabited the reefs.

> Bleaching occurs when corals are stressed by unusual conditions such as high water temperatures. If the water gets too warm, corals expel the tiny algae living in their tissues, causing the coral to turn completely white. Heat stress can kill corals directly or indirectly via starvation and disease . . . In a severe bleaching event, large swathes of reef-building corals die.[86]

The latest estimates suggest that three quarters of all coral reefs are under threat.[87] In 2007, species of coral were added to the IUCN Red List's annual report of species threatened with extinction for the first time.[88] They identified two species as critically endangered: floreana coral and Wellington's solitary coral. In the same report, the Red List classified 74 seaweeds, or 'micro-algae' from the Galapagos as critically endangered.

Lake Victoria is an exceptionally sad case in point. By the 1980s it was recognised that hundreds of species, found only in Lake Victoria were being threatened with extinction. The root cause appeared to be the introduction of the Nile perch. More recently scientists are suggesting that Lake Victoria is actually dying. There are extensive areas of the massive lake which appear to

Figure 1.9 Seahorse

contain no life at all. Fishing and hunting but also pollution and the use of pesticides in agricultural facilities bordering the lake, have been identified as causal factors in the encroaching 'death' of the Lake.[89] The Lake extends over more than 68,000 square km and provides food from fishing as well as employment for neighbouring peoples in Kenya, Tanzania and Uganda.

From the vast lists of threatened species of fish and other water-dwelling creatures we only have space to mention a few. The elongate bitterling has an intriguing name. It is a Chinese freshwater fish only found in Lake Dianchi in the Yunnan Province of China and the Red List categorises the species as critically endangered but comments it may actually be extinct. The online *Encyclopedia of Life* provides a series of photographs of this small fish. There is very bad news for anyone who enjoys caviar, as the Russian sturgeon, from which caviar is harvested, is also listed as critically endangered by the IUCN. Surprisingly, given its name, the common skate is another species of fish on the critically endangered Red List as is the Ganges shark. Seahorses, probably the most mystical little creatures of the sea, akin to legendary dragons, are also threatened by changes in temperature and from fishing and pollutants.

Chapters 5 and 16 address the threat of extinction faced by whales (which are mammals) and other cretaceans and highlights the problems associated with attempting to keep such huge and incredible creatures in captivity. Further, Chapter 7 looks at ways in which engagement by investors can help to save marine life.

Reptiles and amphibians

Dinosaurs were reptiles and we know what happened to them – they were brought to extinction at the end of the Jurassic period probably as a result of a massive asteroid striking the earth. Reptiles today are just as prone to extinction threat as other forms of fauna and flora. Again we have selected a tiny sample of reptiles which are critically endangered to discuss the causes of their extinction threat. They span many countries and geographic areas of the world. Among some of the weird and wonderful critically endangered reptiles is the geometric tortoise. This amazing looking creature was clearly named because of its strange geometric markings and shell which almost resembles the prehistoric Aztec buildings. Amphibians are also threatened by extinction the world over, as we saw from the gruesome statistics quoted earlier. Species such as the natterjack toad and the great-crested newt have been the focus of conservation and protection efforts in the UK for decades.

The latest research concluded in 2017 provided sober reading for chameleons. The wonderful creatures that can change colour, with googly eyes and amazing technicolour skin are in serious trouble. The IUCN/SSC Chameleon Specialist Group (CSG) completed their assessments of over 98 per cent of the 206 recognised species of chameleon and found that over 100 species are now categorised as near threatened, vulnerable, endangered or critically endangered.

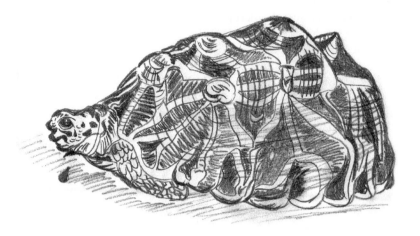

Figure 1.10 Geometric tortoise

Of these, 11 are critically endangered, in other words close to extinction. Over half of Madagascan chameleons are threatened. One of the endangered species is the lesser chameleon, pictured below, as is the West Usambara blade-horned chameleon. Chapman's pygmy chameleon may already be extinct. The wonderful names of these species are only matched by their amazing shapes, colours, characters and diversity. Habitat degradation seems to be one of the primary causes of chameleons' demise.[90]

Figure 1.11 Lesser chameleon

Kemp's Ridley turtles are critically endangered. Other critically endangered reptiles and amphibians with fascinating and intriguing names include the Siamese crocodile, the Luaun ground snake and Sierra Juarez rubber frog. The gentle and ghostly axolotl is also now critically endangered. We now turn to considering an often unrecognised factor contributing to species extinction: the taxonomic impediment.

The taxonomic impediment – another cause of mass extinction?

Another factor which is contributing to the extinction crisis is known as the taxonomic impediment. Wilson highlighted the need for more attention to taxonomy when he stated, 'Both developed and developing (mostly tropical) countries need to expand their taxonomic inventories and reference libraries in order to map the world's species and identify hot spots for priority in conservation.'[91]

So what is taxonomy and what constitutes the taxonomic impediment? In 1972, Jennifer Owen, a university professor with a biology degree, embarked upon a project spanning nearly four decades. This project, which yielded two ground-breaking books,[92] documented what she discovered when she and her zoologist husband, Denis, decided to record every living thing that they found in the garden of their ordinary suburban home in an ordinary suburban street.

During the course of this pioneering study, she recorded 2,673 species including numerous invertebrates such as butterflies, hoverflies and beetles, in addition to plants, birds and mammals. It is estimated that with additional expertise, and had illness not intervened, the final tally may well have approached 8,000 species.

Along with the remarkable tallies of flora and fauna recorded, two things stand out starkly, especially when considered within the frame of a sixth extinction event; firstly, the records chart a sobering trend of a dramatic decline in the numbers of moths, butterflies, bees and ladybirds, among others, observed in her garden during the course of the study; and secondly, over the duration of the research, Owen recorded 20 species never before seen in the British Isles and, in the case of parasitic wasps, for example, she discovered six species that had never been recorded and described *anywhere*. And this, of course, was in just *one* British garden; there are, give or take, 20 million gardens in the UK alone.

The overriding inference to be drawn from this is clear; if, on the one hand, a period of study such as this can chart a dramatic decline in species numbers and yet, on the other, can yield the discovery of species hitherto unrecorded, then it surely follows that – if we extrapolate these findings into a global context – there must be not only a vast number of species worldwide that have yet to be discovered or described,[93] but also that the number of species that become, and have become, extinct before ever being recorded may be equally mind-boggling.

Which brings us to the subject of taxonomy. Or, to be more specific, the *taxonomic impediment*. Taxonomy, which originated with Carl Linnaeus, a

Swedish botanist, in 1758, can be described broadly as the process of discovering, describing, naming and classification of species into groups. The information yielded by this practice can then be used in many ways but, specifically – within the sphere of interest of this book – is an essential tool in the monitoring and conservation of species that are vulnerable, threatened or critically endangered. The UN-sponsored Convention on Biological Diversity posed the question, 'Why is Taxonomy Important?' and gave the answer, 'It provides the foundation of our understanding of biological diversity', and then goes on to define the taxonomic impediment as:

> The knowledge gaps in our taxonomic system . . . the shortage of trained taxonomists and curators, and the impact these deficiencies have on our ability to conserve, use and share the benefits of our biological diversity.[94]

To seek to address these issues, its Global Taxonomy Initiative was introduced in 1998, although, as Drew states, 'Still, the problem persists'.[95] Indeed, taxonomists are in critically short supply, particularly in those regions with the greatest need; most taxonomists work in developed nations which tend to have less biological diversity than economically poorer but biodiversity-rich regions. The irony of this is compelling; if there were an IUCN list of endangered environmental professionals, then taxonomists would probably appear under the heading 'Critically Endangered'.

So why has the taxonomic impediment happened? As always, as with *any* major problem, there is no single reason but, rather, a conflation of several – and, we would argue, these can usefully be whittled down to two overriding factors; professional and academic scorn; and, the short-termism and target-driven orientation of universities and other higher-education institutions.

According to Enghoff, professional and academic 'understanding of taxonomy has been hampered by confusion vis-à-vis systematics'.[96] Indeed, the two terms are often used as a synonym for each other. Enghoff quotes Mayr, who characterised taxonomy as 'the theory and practice of classifying organisms', whereas he described systematics as 'the science of the diversity of organisms'.[97] In other words, says Enghoff, systematics was considered a 'science', with taxonomy mere 'theory and practice', 'like plumbing, haircutting and other respectable but clearly non-scientific activities'. He goes on further to quote an unnamed high-ranking European science administrator who, at a conference on the role of natural history museums a few years previously, had epitomised this dismissive attitude – bordering on contempt – by opining that, 'In the natural history museums, there are scientists as well as taxonomists'.[98]

These examples are symptomatic of a disdain and disregard that runs deep; as Agnarsson and Kuntner note, 'Taxonomy is often considered to have little intellectual content'; however, as they later assert, 'Most of biology relies on taxonomic hypotheses, yet we treat taxonomy as a 'B' discipline'.[99]

On its own, this endemic disrespect would probably be enough to engender the taxonomic impediment, but its effect is bolstered further by what could arguably be described as the short-termism in academic thinking and planning brought about by assessment and ranking systems such as the Research Excellence Framework (REF); its focus on judging the worth – both academic and financial – of research professionals (and the universities that employ them) largely by the amount of papers they publish in high-quality, peer-reviewed journals produces what Lucinda A. McCabe of the Academy of Natural Sciences, quoted by Drew, describes as a 'remarkable mismatch between professional productivity . . . and the prevailing academic assessment system'.[100] Drew defines this productivity as including 'specimen collecting; curation; digital objects such as data, video, and images; software applications; and other work that does not fit into the traditional peer-reviewed-publication formula'.[101] As Agnarsson and Kuntner – damningly – observe, 'Taxonomic expertise is rarely required, or even relevant, when it comes to securing a job, especially in academia'.[102] Finally, as if these downward pressures on forging a successful career in taxonomy weren't already powerful enough, there is one further obstacle to the dissemination of taxonomic findings and hypotheses into the wider academic – and professional – community; as Agnarsson and Kuntner put it, 'One major hurdle for taxonomy is a result of a peculiar convention: it is considered unnecessary to cite original taxonomic descriptions or subsequent taxonomic revisions . . . even when those hypotheses crucially impact a given study and its design', concluding that, 'We see this as the major reason why journals avoid taxonomic publications: they are unlikely to be cited, thus lowering the journal's overall impact factor.'[103]

Who would have thought that a handful of academic KPI's could prove to be so deleterious to the future of bio-conservation? Someone ought to write a paper on it. So, to recap; Taxonomists are not scientists but, rather, more akin to plumbers and hairdressers – nothing wrong with those professions, of course, but their skilled execution will do little to protect our fragile biodiversity. Taxonomy is also regarded by some as 'outdated', with its practitioners depicted as mere 'postage-stamp collectors'.[104] Furthermore, as Tahseen points out, 'there is a tendency among young and modern ecologists to view museums and herbaria as "dusty" places with old-fashioned people working in them'.[105] Taxonomists are also less likely to be employed by universities because they probably wouldn't be able to fulfil their quota of publications, or secure meaningful grant-funding, thus negatively impacting upon an institution's future income. So, professional disdain; an acute image problem; and, diminishing prospects in academia . . . No wonder that providing the foundation of our understanding of biological diversity can seem like a poor career choice for the bright young graduate!

The taxonomic imperative: is there a future in describing the past and the present?

The answer to this question is, perhaps, obvious: there *has* to be, otherwise one of the key resources in our struggle to understand and conserve our planet's rich, but fragile, biodiversity will surely wither on the vine. Certainly, a number of practicing taxonomists do not entirely escape blame. As Evenhuis states,

some taxonomists are simply not as productive as others, and 'these "taxonomic deadbeats" are content to either collect, or sort, or both, but reluctant
to sit down and crank out the written results of their discovery of new taxa
and give them names and publish them'.[106] In addition, there is clearly a need
for taxonomists to move with the times, to incorporate – for example – DNA
barcoding and molecular data into their hypotheses. However, in the final
analysis, only a sea-change in attitudes towards the profession, driven by ever
more lobbying and awareness-raising by environmentalist NGO's, academics
and scientists in the corridors of power, can lead realistically to a fundamental
understanding of the crucial importance of taxonomy, and a root-and-branch
reform of the support structures, training, funding and career pathways that
could yet tempt a new generation of questing, rigorous minds into the field.
So . . . all that's needed, then, is a political system driven by long-term goals,
cross-party collaborations and an unqualified acceptance that our global biodiversity is under imminent threat. Is this possible? We now turn to considering
the crucial fact that species are all interdependent and what that implies for
extinction prevention.

The interdependence of species within ecosystems

> Take biodiversity. The richness and diversity of life on Earth is fundamental
> to the complex life systems that underpin it. Life supports life itself. We are
> part of the same equation. Lose biodiversity and the natural world and the
> life support systems, as we know them today, will collapse.
>
> (Marco Lambertini, director general of
> WWF International)[107]

Every species has its special place within its local, and the more global, ecosystem. If each and every species operated in isolation and its existence had little
or no impact on the existence and survival of other species then the loss of a
species would be largely irrelevant to the survival of the rest. This is not the
case at all. Instead each and every species is inextricably linked to others within
their ecosystem. Ecosystems and biota are fragile: 'Biologists now know that
biotas, like houses of cards, can be brought tumbling down by relatively small
perturbations in the physical environment. They are not robust at all.'[108]

Biodiversity is no accident. The wide variety of species within a particular
ecosystem, for example in the tropical rainforests of Borneo, have evolved as
a result of the natural environment, the temperature. The balance of nature
and species within this environment is not robust but extremely fragile and
can be altered and affected adversely by even small changes in temperature,
humidity or other factors. Rainforests are areas of the highest biodiversity on
the planet. Removing rainforest not only removes the trees themselves but also
immense populations of insects, mammals, plants, more than can be imagined.
An understanding of how important each and every species is to the ecosystem
requires a brief tour of ecology and biology.

A species is commonly defined as 'a population whose members are able to interbreed freely under natural conditions'.[109] Further, a species is a 'closed gene pool' and is the end of millions, if not billions, of years of evolution. Darwin's theory of evolution via natural selection, or survival of the fittest, has been reinterpreted and to a large extent supported, through genetics in recent decades. Biodiversity, however, is seen as a by-product of evolution.[110] Evolution of species can occur in a linear fashion such that the number of species remains the same, in which case there would be no increase in biodiversity. Some hold beliefs in alternative paths to species proliferation such as the Creationist view, taking Genesis (the first book of the Bible) as a literal account of how all life on earth (biodiversity) was created at one point in time. Taking an evolutionary perspective, there are other accepted forces which have led to the vast variety of species on earth. For example, intrinsic isolating mechanisms arise from events as simple as a river cutting through a species population such that over time the two separated groups may develop different mating calls or a preference for different habitats which prevents them from interbreeding and results in ultimately a separate species. This is one of many ways scientists believe biological diversity has evolved. Others include genetic drift, the 'founder effect', mutation and adaptive radiation.[111] Time also appears to be a crucial element: 'Great biological diversity takes long stretches of geological time and the accumulation of large reservoirs of unique genes. The richest ecosystems build slowly over millions of years.'[112]

However species were created, they are now disappearing. The interdependence of species within the ecosystem cannot be overestimated:

> A great many species are critical for the functioning of ecosystem processes such as regulation and purification of water and air, climatic conditions, pollination and seed dispersal, and control of pests and diseases. And by affecting nutrient and water cycling systems and soil fertility, some species indirectly support the supply of food, fibre, fresh water and medicines.[113]

Some species, such as bees, have an obvious 'use' to the human race and their decline and for many bee species their impending extinction, are already presenting serious problems for world food production due to the depletion of pollination 'services'. However, why would species such as earwigs, cockroaches, scary spiders and other creepy crawlies be worth conserving? There is a simple answer. All species are interconnected within the planet's ecosystem and within their own, local habitats and ecosystems, such that we cannot begin to truly understand how the extinction of one species can affect the whole. The following chilling quote drives this message home:

> if invertebrates were to disappear, I doubt that the human species could last more than a few months. Most of the fishes, amphibians, birds and mammals would crash to extinction about the same time. Next would go

the bulk of the flowering plants and with them the physical structure of the majority of the forests and other terrestrial habitats of the world. The earth would rot.[114]

Insects are just one vital group of species upon which all others depend, along food chains and in ecosystems, as 'there are many individual species which have hundreds of other species completely dependent on their existence – because they provide food, shelter, sanctuary or some other crucial resource'.[115]

There are, it appears from research and experience, 'keystone' species, whose disappearance can have devastating effects on their local ecosystem. A tiny handful of such species, which we are aware of, include the sea otter, rhinoceros, elephant, driver ants and pollinators.[116] The infinite complexity of interconnectedness between species which constitute ecosystems cannot be overemphasised and, with current knowledge, is by no means understood:

> [T]he unpredictability of ecosystems is a consequence of the particularity of the species that compose them. Each species is an entity with a unique evolutionary history and set of genes, and so each species responds to the rest of the community in a special way . . . [O]nly with a detailed knowledge of the life cycles and biology of large numbers of constituent species will it be possible to create principles and methods that can precisely chart the future of ecosystems in the face of the human onslaught.[117]

The consequences for humans of species loss, given the interdependencies between species, habitats, ecosystems and business are becoming increasingly evident as species are lost and habitats destroyed. If we simply consider the way in which a forest is intricately linked with species survival and human survival, the system is so complex it is astounding:

> A standing forest is a resource in itself, performing vital functions beyond economic measure. Forests moderate climate, control floods, and store water against drought. They cushion the erosive effects of rainfall, build and hold soil on slopes, and keep rivers and seacoasts, irrigation canals and damn reservoirs, free from silt. They harbour and support many species of life. The tropical forests alone, which cover only 7 percent of the earth's surface, are believed to be the home of at least 50 percent of the earth's species. Many of those species, from rattan vines to mushrooms to sources of medicines and dyes and food, have commercial value, and cannot exist without the sheltering trees that form their habitat.[118]

Other critically precious systems within our overall planetary system are soil systems, water systems – oceans, seas, rivers, lakes. The balance of these systems is crucial and there has been growing concern over recent decades that the human race has surpassed basic planetary boundaries, as an understanding of planetary boundaries, such as loss of biodiversity and species, can help us grasp the complexity of human impacts on the planet:[119] 'Pushing the boundaries of nine Earth system processes may lead to dangerous levels of instability in the Earth system and increasing risk for humans.'[120]

Ecosystem services is the term used to refer to the 'services' provided by all of these, sometimes undiscovered, species to the planet and humanity. These services include: purification of water and air; absorption and storage of water; mitigation of floods and drought; decomposition, detoxification and sequestering of wastes, pollination and dispersal of seeds, regeneration of soil nutrients, natural pest control, climatic stabilisation; natural provision of food products for human use and medicinal products. The survival of every species on the planet including our own depends entirely on the survival of this interdependent, interlocking jigsaw which humanity has called the ecosystem. It is our intention, in Chapter 2, to find a way of representing the business risk attached to species loss in terms of their contribution to this living planetary system and their possibly crucial role in its survival.

All species are interdependent and interlinked. The extent to which flora and fauna are interdependent is not known by science although knowledge is increasing all the time and researchers are gaining an increasingly clear understanding of how species affect each other. Many theorists, writers and thought-leaders have adopted frameworks considered appropriate for understanding ecology and environmental issues, which derive from an understanding of systems and system dynamics. The sociological paradigm which engendered systems thinking and theoretical understandings of systems is known as cybernetics. General systems theory was first introduced by Ludwig von Bertalanffy, who described the theory as a 'general science of wholeness'. General systems theory is about interconnectedness, wholeness, and involves adopting a holistic approach. The theory attempts to move away from 'reductionist reasoning', and towards a theoretical approach which seeks to encompass the complexities of a system as a whole. Following the concepts of systems theory, Gaia theory, developed by James Lovelock, views the Earth as a self-regulating system which has a 'goal' of regulating surface conditions on the planet to render them as favourable to existing life as possible. Lovelock emphasises the interconnectedness of everything in relation to the threats of climate change in his 2009 book, *The Vanishing Face of Gaia*, making the point that humans could not survive for an instant on a dead planet.[121]

In the seminal book *Limits to Growth*, published in 1972, again building on a systems approach, the world was introduced starkly to the terrifying precipice towards which human population expansion, economic growth, capitalism and profit seeking are pushing us.[122] The authors had been commissioned to write the book by the Club of Rome, a group of international scientists, politicians and business leaders in order explore the long-term effects of population expansion (human), industrial activity, consumption of resources and pollution. This project employed system dynamics theory and computer modelling. Although many saw the book as doom-mongering, it raised the alarm for our planet's survival. Using a computer model, the authors explored how the future could look if humanity continued on the course it was following at that time. The book concluded that the physical limits to the use of energy and raw materials by the human race was some decades into the future. As the authors explain, they view the world around us from a systems perspective where they focus on connections rather than single pieces of a system, on interconnections and interactions within one planetary system. When the same authors returned to their initial project 20 years later, their conclusions were rather different. In the sequel, *Beyond the Limits*, their conclusion was that the world had already surpassed its sustainable limits in various ways in terms of resource use and pollution. This led the authors to state: 'The human world is beyond its limits. The present way of doing things is unsustainable. The future, to be viable at all, must be one of drawing back, easing down, healing.'[123]

Which in turns leads us to ask, just over a quarter of a century later, has the human race drawn back, eased down and started to heal the planet? *Beyond the Limits* identified species extinction as one of the ongoing outcomes of excessive growth:

> One thing is certain. As humans take more of the primary productivity of the earth for themselves and the life forms of their choice (such as corn and cows), they leave less for other forms. The result is a loss of economic value: game, fish, chemicals, medicines, foods may be disappearing with species that no one has even identified. There is also a spiritual and esthetic loss, a loss of colourful companions in creation. There may be, for all anyone knows, a loss of critical pieces that hold together ecosystems. There is certainly a loss of genetic information that has taken billions of years to evolve – and that humanity is just beginning to learn how to read and use.[124]

While overtly anthropocentric, this quotation illuminates the linkages between human survival, in terms of what economic processes and business activity provides for us from non-human species around us and the immense threat to humanity from their disappearance. In 2004 a third book was published, *Limits to Growth: The 30-Year Update*, which further assessed the human trajectory and the extent to which efforts at sustainable living were succeeding in improving the situation on planet earth.

New species being discovered – and their impending extinction

One of the craziest ironies in the current extinction crisis is that we are constantly discovering new species. In December 2017, it was reported that over one hundred new species had been discovered in the Greater Mekong region of Southeast Asia, an average of two species a week being discovered. The disheartening and actually depressing aspect of these discoveries is that as each species is discovered their future security and continuity seems questionable. Many of the newly discovered species are under threat of extinction as soon as they are found. As the Stranger Species article on the WWF website informs us:

While it's amazing to see the diversity of species being discovered every year, many of these species are under direct threat from human activity. Fish and forest species are under mounting pressure from infrastructure development such as roads and hydropower dams, while rare, edible or charismatic species such as the crocodile lizard and snail-eating turtle are targeted by poachers for the pet and meat trade.[125]

Unsustainable development of mines, roads and dams threatens the survival of the Greater Mekong area while newly discovered species are at threat of wildlife crime, illegal wildlife trade. So many species will be lost before the scientists can even discover them. The discoveries include a crocodile lizard, a horseshoe bat, a brightly coloured frog, two new species of mole, two fish, 88 plants and three mammals across Vietnam, Thailand, Myanmar, Laos and Cambodia. The total number of new species discovered in this region between 1997 and 2016 is a staggering 2,524. Sadly, the newly discovered Vietnamese crocodile lizard is threatened by habitat destruction, coal mining and the illegal pet trade, with fewer than 200 individuals in the populations, clearly unsustainable. Some good news reported on the WWF website is that the moles are thriving because they can hide from threats.

There are, of course, some species which are positively thriving in human-dominated environments, such as rats, urban fox, house mice, and cockroaches. Unfortunately, because of their proximity to humans and their ability to adapt to city conditions and polluted environments, people tend to label them as 'pests' and 'vermin'. If there was a sudden abundance of panda in cities around the world because they managed to adapt to eating from dustbins, changing their diet from bamboo to food waste, would they too become 'vermin'? Certainly, starving polar bears are seen as a dangerous problem by people living on the edges of their habitat and they are not made welcome. When will polar bears be referred to as vermin?

Solutions to the extinction crisis

The evidence that we are currently in a sixth era of mass extinction on planet earth is unquestionable and scientists are continually discovering more existing species which are heading for extinction as well as finding new species which are similarly under threat from a wide range of causal factors. It is not as if nothing is being done to stop this extinction process and to reverse the mass extinction trend. Immense efforts are being made by wildlife organisations, especially the WWF, as well as by lesser known nature and wildlife organisations and local community groups, and organisations. The IUCN Red List itself is dedicated to cataloguing, categorising and in this way raising the alarm about the extinction crisis. Just looking at the WWF website reveals many, many initiatives and programmes focusing on habitat protection and species conservation. The WWF partners with organisations the world over to find innovative ways of protecting habitats and ecosystems and conserving and preserving species. There is a wide array of initiatives discussed throughout this book, where the WWF has developed strategic partnerships, for example in China for pandas (Chapter 19) and polar bears in Chapter 18.

The concept of an Ark of accountability mechanisms which, working together, are fighting to save species from extinction was published in a recent academic paper on extinction accounting.[126] We have built on this concept here to bring together initiatives by a wide range of interested parties which are working towards saving species and their habitats, including: non-governmental organisations, wildlife lobby groups, international bodies, governments, local governments as well as businesses and organisations in the financial and accounting sector. It is the elements of this 'Ark' arising from accounting, investment and engagement which we explore in Chapter 2 and how accounting and engagement may help to prevent extinctions. There are literally thousands and thousands of initiatives and strategies being developed and operationalised for tackling species and biodiversity loss due to climate change and other factors by wildlife groups, local communities, NGOs, governments – and businesses. Many of these are discussed in the rest of this book in relation to specific species or geographic regions. The work of the United Nations and their Convention for Biological Diversity represents a substantial international commitment to species protection. Areas of focus for policy makers include great and small projects and protection plans, such as the following:

- managing and preserving protected areas and reserves both marine and terrestrial;
- establishing corridors for wildlife; restoration ecology, translocation and assisted migration;
- establishing zoos, aquaria and botanic gardens for breeding programmes;
- the World Commission on Forests and Sustainable Development;
- the Forest Stewardship Council; the Marine Stewardship Council;
- sustainable palm oil;
- increasing and extending legislation protecting endangered species; and
- legislation on pesticides use.

Many of the programmes and initiatives focused on extinction prevention run by organisations such as WWF, also partner closely with businesses. There are reasons to be optimistic – and cheerful – about our abilities to turn things around. As outlined in an assessment just after the turn of the century:

> the world has implemented new technologies, consumers have altered their buying habits, new institutions have been created, and multinational agreements have been crafted . . . Awareness of environmental issues is much higher today than in 1970. There are ministries of environmental affairs in most countries, and environmental education is commonplace. Most pollution has been eliminated from the smoke stacks and outflow pipes of factories in the rich world, and leading firms are pushing successfully for ever higher eco-efficiency.[127]

There are signs, then, that human beings can work together to address problems. This book seeks to develop frameworks of accounting and engagement which can and will save species. Many would argue (and do, vociferously) that nature, wildlife and species have nothing to do with capitalism and business. Many feel passionately that the business world and industry have no place in environmental stewardship, conservation or species protection. We take a different view. As can be seen from the above discussion, business activity, the industrial revolution and the capitalist society are the principal cause of the extinction crisis but, we believe, can also be part of the solution.

Whether we like it or not, global capitalism is going nowhere at the moment, unless it is to the door marked exit for ourselves and for the rest of life on earth. The capitalist societies around the world, whether we love them or hate them, are not heading for extinction any time soon. Much as it would be a utopian dream to transform the business world overnight and replace it with something genuinely sustainable, natural and environmentally friendly, this is a dream and not something which can happen before more species extinctions take place. Species are going extinct as we read this sentence, as we make a cup of tea, as we drive to work. Capitalism and the business world have created this situation – we have created this situation by building and participating in global capitalism – and therefore businesses, accounting, finance, industry have the greatest responsibility for addressing the current extinction crisis. Only by harnessing capitalism in all of its often appalling power and dominance and insisting that businesses act now to improve habitats, protect the environment and prevent extinctions can we find a realistic solution. Of course, it has to be acknowledged that the business world alone cannot save the planet – it has to be a combined and collective effort, as demonstrated by the Ark concept. But substantial changes in the way businesses account for their impacts and the way investors relate to companies can contribute to extinction prevention. The ways in which this can be achieved are the focus of the rest of this book. The following chapter focuses on the development of an extinction accounting and reporting framework which can be used by businesses but also by other organisations in the public, voluntary and charity sectors, as well as by governments and larger, state- and country-level entities.

> Changing mental models, societal attitudes and values underlying the current structures and patterns of our global economy is a more challenging course of action. How can we 'repurpose' businesses so that they are not just focusing on short-term profit but are also expected to be accountable for social and environmental benefits? Or how should we redefine what desirable economic development looks like? And how can we reduce the emphasis on material wealth, confront consumerism and the throw-away culture, and promote the desirability of more sustainable diets? These kinds of changes to societal values are likely to be achievable only over the long term and in ways that we have not yet imagined.[128]

Notes

1 Biodiversity has been defined as 'the variability among living organisms from all sources including [among other things] terrestrial, marine and other aquatic ecosystems and the ecological complexes of which they are a part ... [including] diversity within species, between species and of ecosystems' (quoted in Spicer, 2006, p. 2).

2 Losing a specific species is species extinction but loss of biodiversity is concerned with the reduction in the diversity of life, flora and fauna, within ecosystems and habitats. Biodiversity loss can result in extinction of a species within a habitat but not necessarily the extinction of the entire species.

3 See Giddens (1990).

4 See Beck (1992, 1999).

5 See King with Atkins (2016) for a full discussion of the SDGs and other current initiatives.

6 An ecosystem is defined as 'a dynamic complex of plant, animal, and micro-organism communities and their non-living environment interacting as a functional unit' (Convention on Biological Diversity, quoted in Earthwatch, 2002, p. 11).

7 By 'investee companies', we are referring to those companies in which the institutional investors hold shares.

8 Formerly known as the World Wildlife Fund.

9 This 'memoir on the species of elephants, both living and fossil', was read at the public session of the National Institute on 15 Germinal, Year IV (4 April 1796) by Georges Cuvier.

10 Published in Rudwick (1997, pp. 22–24). See also Kolbert (2014).

11 See Allaby and Lovelock (1985).

12 De Vos et al. (2015).

13 See figures quoted in Wilson (1989).

14 Wilson (1992, p. 124).

15 WWF (2016).

16 Information gathered from the WWF website at http://wwf.panda.org/about_our_earth/all_publications/living_planet_index2.

17 Cuckston (2018).

18 See http://eol.org/about.

19 This resource may be viewed at www.inaturalist.org.

20 '80 species' arises from our allusion to Jules Verne's *Around the World in 80 Days* and does not imply that we have included exactly 80 species in this book – rather 80 is taken to imply a representative sample of threatened and endangered species rather than an exact number.

21 The list was accessed for this information on 9 January 2018.

22 This is discussed in a colourful way in Kolbert (2014).

23 Hillaby (1960, p. 44).

24 Nicholls (2017).

25 For a full discussion of these initiatives and the current state of rhinoceros populations in South Africa, see Atkins et al. (2018).

26 See www.flowers.org.uk/news/rare-and-endangered-flowers.

27 See Wilson (1992).

28 Schoon (1996, p. 20), emphasis added.

29 Browswimmer (2003).

30 *Fumifugium* has been analysed as a very early environmental account of the impacts of industrial pollution on nature and wildlife in Atkins and Thomson (2012).

31 Evelyn (1933, p. 19).
32 This quotation is taken from Thomas Penant's Tour of Wales, Vol. II, 1778, but is presented in Lloyd Owen's *A Wilder Wales: Travellers' Tales 1610–1831* (Lloyd Owen, 2017, p. 333).
33 This is from Gilbert White, quoted in Johnson (1970, p. 24).
34 See Braithwaite (1853, pp. 200–201), emphasis added.
35 Morris (2015).
36 Verne (1994, p. 39).
37 See, for example, Mellanby (1967).
38 Wilson (1989, p. 536).
39 Livingston and Livingston (1996).
40 Ibid., p. 117.
41 Ibid., p. 989.
42 Ibid., p. 61.
43 Wilson (1989).
44 Attenborough (1984, p. 308).
45 See WWF (1993).
46 Ibid.
47 See Meadows et al. (2004).
48 WWF (2016).
49 See WWF (2016).
50 Meadows et al. (2004).
51 The species population was last assessed in 2010 by Yahi, Knees and Gardner (2011).
52 Quoted in Sparks (1973, p. 139).
53 WWF (1993, p. 104).
54 WWF (1993).
55 Whitlock, (2000, p. 1855).
56 Attenborough (1981).
57 Ibid., p. 190.
58 See the WWF website for more information at http://wwf.panda.org/about_our_earth/teacher_resources/best_place_species/harry_potter_top_10/aye_aye.cfm.
59 For information about armadillos, see www.nationalgeographic.com/animals/mammals/group/armadillos.
60 Attenborough (1981).
61 See https://news.mongabay.com/2013/01/in-the-kingdom-of-the-black-panther.
62 See www.snowleopard.org/statement-iucn-red-list-status-change-snow-leopard/
63 Attenborough (1981, p. 199).
64 See Greenway (1967).
65 WWF (2016).
66 Ibid.
67 Quotation from WWF (1993, p. 100).
68 Wilson (1989).
69 BirdLife International (2013).
70 See Parsons and Underhill (2005).
71 Evans Ogden (2015).
72 See Greenway (1967).
73 Ibid.
74 WWF (1993).
75 Atkins and Atkins (2016).
76 See Wilson (1985).

77   Schoon (1996).
78   WWF (1993).
79   WWF (2016).
80   See WWF (1993).
81   Quotation from WWF (1993, p. 99).
82   WWF (2016).
83   Ibid.
84   Ibid.
85   See WWF (2016).
86   Ibid., p. 42.
87   Ibid.
88   Conservation International (2007).
89   See, for example, Ryan (2015).
90   Anderson (2017).
91   Wilson (1989, p. 116).
92   Owen (1991, 2010).
93   There is a significant difference between the two words; it has been suggested that one of the best ways of discovering a new species is to visit the archives of Natural History museums, where samples of species, collected years before but remaining undescribed and therefore unknown to science, have often been found languishing in drawers.
94   Convention on Biological Diversity (1998).
95   Drew (2011).
96   Enghoff (2009).
97   Mayr (1969).
98   Ibid.
99   Agnarsson and Kuntner (2007).
100   Drew (2011).
101   Ibid.
102   Agnarsson and Kuntner (2007).
103   Ibid.
104   Gewin (2002).
105   Tahseen (2014).
106   Evenhuis (2007).
107   WWF (2016, p. 6).
108   Wilson (1989, p. 110).
109   Wilson (1992, p. 36).
110   Wilson (1992).
111   Ibid.
112   Ibid., p. 68.
113   WWF (2016, p. 50).
114   Quotation from Wilson (1987, p. 345).
115   Schoon (1996, p. 17).
116   Wilson (1992).
117   Ibid., pp. 169–170.
118   Meadows et al. (2004, p. 74).
119   See Rockström et al. (2009); Steffen et al. (2015).
120   WWF (2016, p. 12).
121   See Lovelock (1979, 2009).
122   See Meadows et al. (1972).
123   Meadows et al. (1992, p. xv).

124 Ibid., p. 66.
125 WWF (2018).
126 See Atkins and Maroun (2016).
127 Meadows et al. (2004, p. xiii).
128 WWF (2016, p. 122).

References

Agnarsson, I. and Kuntner, M. (2007) 'Taxonomy in a Changing World: Seeking Solutions for a Science in Crisis', *Systematic Biology* 56(3), pp. 531–539.

Allaby, M. and Lovelock, J. (1985) *The Great Extinction: What Killed the Dinosaurs and Devastated the Earth?* Paladin Books, London.

Anderson, C. (2017) 'IUCN Red List Assessment Update for Chameleons', retrieved from www.chameleonforums.com/threads/2017-iucn-red-list-assessment-update-for-chameleons 158153.

Atkins, J. F. and Atkins, B. C. (eds) (2016) *The Business of Bees: An Integrated Approach to Bee Decline*, Greenleaf Publishing, Saltaire.

Atkins, J. F. and Maroun, W. (2016) 'Accounting for Wildlife and Biodiversity through Nature Diaries'. Working paper, originally entitled 'Nature Diaries: Reports of Nature and Biodiversity', presented at the annual British Accounting Association (BAA, now BAFA) conference, Cardiff University, in 2010.

Atkins, J. and Thomson, I. (2012) 'Accounting for Nature in 19th Century Britain: William Morris and the Defence of the Fairness of the Earth', in Michael Jones (ed.), *Accounting for Biodiversity*, Routledge, Abingdon.

Atkins, J. F., Maroun, W., Atkins, B. C., Barone, E. (2018) From the Big Five to the Big Four? Exploring Extinction Accounting for the Rhinoceros? *Accounting, Auditing and Accountability Journal*, 31(2), 1–31.

Attenborough, D. (1981) *Discovering Life on Earth*, William Collins Sons and Co., London. Revised edition of the original *Life on Earth* published in 1979.

Attenborough, D. (1984) *The Living Planet*, Book Club Associates, London.

Beck, U. (1992) *Risk Society: Towards a New Modernity*, Sage Publications, London.

Beck, U. (1999) *World Risk Society*, Polity, Blackwell Publishers, Oxford.

BirdLife International (2013) '*Spheniscus Demersus*', IUCN Red List of Threatened Species, version 2015.2, retrieved from www.iucnredlist.org (accessed 2 August 2015).

Braithwaite, F. (1853) 'On the Rise and Fall of the River Wandle: its Springs, Tributaries, and Pollution; Account from Survey No. 1023', *Institution of Civil Engineers Minutes of Proceedings*, XX, pp. 190–209.

Browswimmer (2003) *Ecocide: A Short History of the Mass-Extinction of Species*, Pluto Press, London.

Conservation International (2007) 'Corals Added To IUCN Red List Of Threatened Species For First Time', 13 September, retrieved from www.sciencedaily.com/releases/2007/09/070912094029.htm.

Convention on Biological Diversity (1998) 'Global Taxonomy Initiative', retrieved from www.cbd.int/gti.

Cuckston, T. (2018) 'Making Extinction Calculable', *Accounting, Auditing and Accountability Journal*, 31(3), March.

De Vos, J. M., Joppa, L. N., Gittleman, J. L., Stephens, P. R. and Pimm, S. L. (2015) 'Estimating the Normal Background Rate of Species Extinction', *Conservation Biology*, 29(2), April, pp. 452–462.

Drew, L. W. (2011) 'Are We Losing the Science of Taxonomy?', *Bioscience*, 61(12), pp. 942–946.

Earthwatch (2002) *Business and Biodiversity: The Handbook of Corporate Action*, Earthwatch Institute (Europe), International Union for Conservation of Nature and Natural Resources, World Business Council for Sustainable Development, Gland, Switzerland.

Enghoff, H. (2009) 'What is Taxonomy? An Overview with Myriapodological Examples', *Soil Organisms*, 81(3), pp. 441–451.

Evans Ogden, L. (2015) 'Atlantic Puffins Listed as Endangered Species in Europe: Climate Change to Blame and Could Soon Affect Puffins in Maine', CBC News online, 19 November, retrieved from www.cbc.ca/news/technology/puffins-atlantic-threatened-species-europe-1.3324848.

Evelyn, J. (1933) *Fumifugium: Or the Inconvenience of the Aer and Smoake of London Dissipated Together with Some Remedies*, The National Smoke Abatement Society, Manchester (first published in 1661).

Evenhuis, N. L. (2007) 'Helping Solve the "Other" Taxonomic Impediment: Completing the Eight Steps to Total Enlightenment and Taxonomic Nirvana'. *Zootaxa*, 1407, pp. 3–12.

Gewin, V. (2002) 'All Living Things', *Nature*, 418, pp. 362–363.

Giddens, A. (1990) *The Consequences of Modernity*, Stanford University Press, Stanford, CA.

Greenway, J. C. Jr. (1967) *Extinct and Vanishing Birds of the World*, Dover Publications, Constable and Company, London.

Hillaby, J. (1960) *Nature and Man*, Phoenix House, London.

Johnson, W. (ed.) (1970) *Gilbert White's Journals*, Routledge & Kegan Paul, London (first published in 1931).

King, M. E. with Atkins, J. F. (2016) *The Chief Value Officer: Accountants Can Save the Planet*, Greenleaf Publishing, Saltaire.

Kolbert, E. (2014) *The Sixth Extinction: An Unnatural History*, Bloomsbury, London.

Livingston, A. D. and Livingston, H. (1996) *The Wordsworth Guide to Edible Plants and Animals*, Wordsworth Editions, Hertforshire.

Lloyd Owen, D. (2017) *A Wilder Wales: Travellers' Tales 1610–1831*, Parthian, Cardigan, Wales.

Lovelock, J. (1979) *Gaia: A New Look at Life on Earth*, Oxford University Press, Oxford.

Lovelock, J. (2009) *The Vanishing Face of Gaia: A Final Warning*, Allen Lane, Penguin Books, London.

Mayr, E. (1969) *Principles of Systemic Zoology*, McGraw-Hill Book Co., New York.

Meadows, D. H., Meadows, D. L. and Randers, J. (1972) *The Limits to Growth*, Universe Books, New York.

Meadows, D. H., Meadows, D. L. and Randers, J. (1992) *Beyond the Limits: Global Collapse or a Sustainable Future*, Earthscan Publications, London.

Meadows, D., Randers, J., Meadows, D. (2004) *Limits to Growth: The 30-Year Update*, Chelsea Green Publishing, VT.

Mellanby, K. (1967) *Pesticides and Pollution*, New Naturalist Series, Collins, London.

Morris, W. (2015) *How We Live and How We Might Live*, Five Leaves, Nottingham (first published in 1887).

Nicholls, H. (2017) 'Welcome Home, Lonesome George: Giant Tortoise Returns to Galapagos', *Guardian*, 17 February, retrieved from www.theguardian.com/science/animal-magic/2017/feb/17/welcome-home-lonesome-george-giant-tortoise-returns-to-galapagos.

Owen, J. (1991) *The Ecology of a Garden: The First Fifteen Years*, Cambridge University Press, Cambridge.

Owen, J. (2010) *Wildlife of a Garden: A Thirty-year Study*, RHS, London.

Parsons, N. J. and Underhill, L. G. (2005) 'Oiled and Injured African Penguins Spheniscus Demersus and Other Seabirds Admitted for Rehabilitation in the Western Cape, South Africa, 2001 and 2002', *African Journal of Marine Science* 27(1).

Rockström, J., Steffen, W., Noone, K., Persson, Å., Chapin, III, F. S., Lambin, E. F., Lenton, T. M., Scheffer, M., Folke, C., Schellnhuber, H. J., et al. (2009) A Safe Operating Space for Humanity. *Nature*, 461(7263): 472–475.

Rudwick, M. J. S. (1997) *Georges Cuvier, Fossil Bone, and Geological Catastrophes. New Translations and Interpretations of the Primary Texts*, University of Chicago Press, Chicago, US.

Ryan, R. (2015) 'Africa's Biggest Lake is on the Verge of Dying', 2 April, retrieved from www.news.com.au/travel/world-travel/africa/africas-biggest-lake-is-on-the-verge-of-dying/news-story/364bdb4e810ab33aa6434f3b71a473dc

Schoon, N. (1996). *Going Going Gone: The Story of Britain's Vanishing Natural History*, Bookman Projects and Nicholas School.

Sparks, J. (1973) *Animals in Danger*, Hamlyn Publishing Group, London.

Spicer, J. I. (2006) *Biodiversity: A Beginner's Guide*, Oneworld Publications, Oxford.

Steffen, W., Richardson, K., Rockström, J., Cornell, S.E., Fetzer, I., Bennet, E.M., Biggs, R., Carpenter, S.R., De Vries, W., De Wit, C.A., et al. (2015) 'Planetary Boundaries: Guiding Human Development on a Changing Planet', *Science*, 347(6223), pp. 1259855-1–259855-10. (doi:10.1126/science.1259855)

Tahseen, Q. (2014) 'Taxonomy – The Crucial yet Misunderstood and Disregarded Tool for Studying Biodiversity', *Journal of Biodiversity and Endangered Species*, 2, p. 128.

Verne, J. (1994) *Around the World in Eighty Day & Five Weeks in A Balloon*, Wordsworth Editions, Hertford. Originally published in 1873.

Whitlock, M. C. (2000) 'Fixation of New Alleles and the Extinction of Small Populations: Drift Load, Beneficial Alleles, and Sexual Selection', *Evolution*, 54(6), pp. 1855–1861.

Wilson, E. O. (1985) 'The Biological Diversity Crisis: A Challenge to Science', *Issues in Science and Technology*, 2(1), pp. 20–29.

Wilson, E. O. (1987) 'The Little Things that Run the World', *Conservation Biology*, 1(4), pp. 344–346.

Wilson, E. O. (1989) 'Threats to Biodiversity', *Scientific American*, 261(3), pp. 108–116.

Wilson, E. O. (1992) *The Diversity of Life*, Penguin Books, London.

WWF (1993) *Some Like it Hot*, WWF International, Gland, Switzerland.

WWF (2016) *Living Planet Report 2016: Risk and Resilience in a New Era*, WWF International, Gland, Switzerland.

WWF (2018) 'Stranger Species', retrieved from http://greatermekong.panda.org/discovering_the_greater_mekong/species/new_species/stranger_species.

Yahi, N., Knees, S. and Gardner, M. (2011) '*Abies Numidica*', IUCN Red List of Threatened Species, retrieved from www.iucnredlist.org.

2 How can accounting, integrated reporting and engagement prevent extinction?

Jill Atkins, Warren Maroun and Barry Atkins

In Chapter 1, we explored the meaning of extinction, an understanding of 'mass extinction', and considered the symptoms and causes of the current (sixth) period of mass extinction on Planet Earth. The interdependencies between species were outlined and the complex systems which characterise our planet were viewed with reference to a systems theory perspective. It is the intention of this chapter to demonstrate inextricable links between species, their interdependence within ecosystems, extinction and the business world. In particular, we focus on how accounting can be harnessed as an agent of transformation and change which, for our current purposes, can be used to prevent extinction of species.[1] This discussion involves an appraisal of the ways in which accounting has evolved over time to incorporate environmental issues and biodiversity. We also suggest that institutional investor engagement and engagement of business by NGOs can similarly prevent species extinction.

Extinction of species: building a business case

> Every species extinction diminishes humanity.
>
> (E. O. Wilson)[2]

It is not easy to convince anyone, let alone those running multinational organisations, that allowing a species to go into extinction, whether a large mammal, a tiny insect, or a bullfrog, represents a financial risk for businesses. Trying to explain to a chief executive officer or a financial director from a global organisation such as a pharmaceutical company or a food producer, that the loss of several insect species could constitute a substantial and imminent financial risk that could materially damage their business, is likely to result in disbelief and probably a request to leave their office rather quickly. But things are changing. It is increasingly evident that the loss of one small creature, such as a bee, can have a devastating effect on businesses worldwide.

A few years ago we were met by vague amusement from fellow academics, when we talked about the need to develop a bee accounting framework. Since publishing *The Business of Bees* in 2016,[3] we have encountered a very different reaction, especially from the institutional investment community. Introducing the book at several investment institutions in the City of London, at the European Union's European Landowners' Organisation and at a conference organised by the Italian Financial Analysts' Association, we detected a shift in attitude. Indeed, there has been a sea change in attitude among the financial community towards financial risks arising from the demise of this small insect, as well as in other areas of wildlife conservation and species protection. It all comes down to basic finance and financial management. A company operating in the food production or food retail industry relies on stable food supplies which are consistent and which do not vary wildly in price and cost of production through their supply chain. The baseline for bee–pollinated products is: no bees, no pollination, no crops, no food supply, no food, no cash flow, no profits, no business.

Using bees as an illustration is a useful way of conveying the impact of species loss on financial return and profitability. There is a direct and obvious link – although it is surprising how the business world has only recently identified and acted on this link. The demise of bee populations worldwide and the problems associated with pollinator decline, represent a relatively easy and accessible way of explaining to businesses why wildlife and species matter.

It is far more difficult to convince the business world and investors that each and every species counts. Indeed, it is hard to find ways of explaining why the loss of any one species could affect businesses adversely through ecosystem collapse. As we saw in the previous chapter, we do not know all the 'keystone' species, those species whose disappearance from a local ecosystem could cause the collapse of that ecosystem. In business speak, such a collapse would lead to loss of 'ecosystem services', which then has a detrimental impact on businesses such as agriculture, pharmaceuticals, and many other industrial processes. If direct effects of species extinction on a business are not always immediately obvious to managers and investors, then indirect effects of species loss are even more difficult to appreciate. We feel the best way of attempting to communicate the importance of species loss and extinction to business from a financial and risk perspective, is to focus on the interdependence of species as discussed in Chapter 1. The next stage is to demonstrate the potentially financial impact of the absence of a species.

The 'value' of nature and wildlife to humanity has been recognised for many decades, if not for centuries. Value can mean economic and financial value but also, from a more ecological perspective, intrinsic value, aesthetic value. For deep ecologists, species have an intrinsic value, and attempts to place any other value on nature is strongly contested.[4]

There is huge controversy over whether financial or economic value should be considered in relation to life on earth, arguments which we understand and agree with in principle but to persuade businesses to act to save species, we feel it is necessary to argue some form of financial, especially financial risk, 'value'. This means incorporating the concept of natural capital, a term for nature that we are not at all enamoured of, but which is part of business vocabulary and as such, provides a means of communicating issues of extinction. In terms of value, as applies to developing a financial risk argument for saving species, economists have talked of 'natural capital' for many decades. This is an example of such writing from the late 1970s:

> Nature is our capital. The interest it yields is all we may use. If we persistently encroach on that capital, we shall eventually go bankrupt. . ... But we are using up our natural capital all over the world instead of leaving it intact, so that not only is nature being wiped out but we are bringing the same fate upon ourselves.[5]

Also in the late 1970s, the British Royal family lectured around the world on the need for conservation and made clear linkages between wildlife protection and business, providing early foundations for a business case for extinction prevention:

> The conservation of the environment . . . must be taken into account at all levels and in all departments of government and in the boardrooms of every industrial enterprise. It is no longer sufficient simply to quantify the elements of existence as in old-fashioned material economics; conservation means taking notice of the quality of existence as well. The problem is of course to give some value to that quality . . . money spent on proper pollution control, urban and rural planning and the control of exploitation of wild stocks of plants and animals on land and in the seas, is the less expensive alternative in the long run.[6]

The concept of 'natural capitalism' grew from the idea of an economic shift from an 'emphasis on human productivity to a radical increase in resource productivity'[7], and proposes that future human prosperity depends upon an understanding and acceptance that ecosystem services are finite − at least in the way that current industrial processes use (and abuse) them; natural resources are transformed into products for profit, with the waste from the process (and, eventually, the products themselves) disposed of elsewhere. To counter this, natural capitalism proposes four interrelated and interdependent strategies for change:

- *radical resource productivity*, which slows depletion and lowers pollution;
- *biomimicry*, or the redesigning of industrial systems along biological lines, enabling the constant reuse of materials;
- *service and flow economy*, in which the relationship between Producer and Consumer would move away from the acquisition of goods, to the provision of services derived from those goods; and
- *investing in natural capital*, the reinvestment in sustaining, restoring and expanding natural capital.

Although such a radical shift of frame and emphasis has not been – and was never going to be – adopted globally, nationally, or even locally, overnight, it has generated widespread interest, such as with a multi-stakeholder body, the Natural Capital Coalition, which seeks to bring together 'leading initiatives and organisations to harmonise approaches to natural capital',[8] and it certainly captures the zeitgeist of a growing public awareness of a species (us) making demands upon an environment that increasingly cannot be met. Most crucially, it has a raft of credible strategies already in place should politicians decide to come calling – the timing of which will likely depend entirely upon the day when polling reveals that saving the world is a vote-winner.

The concept of natural capital can also be considered the birthing pool of economic models such as green or eco capitalism, which attempt to address the competing demands of generating profits in a capitalist society, and protecting an environment affected by the processes that generate those profits. Perhaps the most significant impact yet delivered by eco capitalism has been that of carbon trading, the exchange of credits designed to reduce emissions of carbon dioxide. This system, which was adopted by many countries in order to meet the carbon emissions targets specified in the 1997 Kyoto Protocol, enables nations that exceed their carbon emissions cap to buy the right to release more carbon dioxide into the atmosphere from those countries that have lower emissions. The shift of emphasis here is in the absorption of a cost previously considered to be an *externality* (e.g. health costs and environmental costs associated with the use of fossil fuel) into companies' profit and loss sheets; that is, if you produce a negative externality, you have to pay for it. The pressure, therefore, is on high-emissions corporations and nations to invest in more energy-efficient and environmentally friendly technology and processes as an economical imperative.

There are numerous attempts ongoing to give capitalism a friendlier face. The term 'responsible capitalism' as a term could broadly apply to Western capitalist economies today, at least with regards to the sorts of societies that our leaders insist that they *aspire* to. Broadly, then, although in essence describing a fully fledged free market economy, responsible capitalism also implies a measure of government regulation and intervention to temper the worst excesses of 'turbo capitalism',[9] along with a welfare state safety net, progressive tax rates and a private enterprise/public ownership mix.

As such, it is less rigorously idealistic than turbo-capitalism, and sufficiently bendy enough to be claimed by the right, left and centre ground in politics as 'their own'. Indeed, as recently as 22 May 2013, Ed Miliband – speaking at Google's Big Tent event – defined responsible capitalism as 'an agenda being led by business, where companies pursue profit but we also have an equal society, power is in the hands of the many and where we recognise our responsibilities to each other'. Fine words, or the slightly awkward offspring of an unholy one-night stand between capitalism and socialism? You decide. For many, the whole approach taken in this book towards creating a capitalism which embraces and enshrines deep ecology, may be seen as just another attempt to make capitalism look prettier, with no real underlying change. We hope it is more than that. We hope that it is possible to create an ecological capitalism, founded on the need to preserve species, habitats and ecosystems.

The appalling impact of capitalist activities on ecology and the environment is only too clear to see from large scale events. Sporadically, corporate accidents occur which bring home the stark and often immediate impacts of business activity on wildlife and natural habitats. Environmental disasters arising often from corporate irresponsibility, or just bad luck, can be so significant that their effects pervade for decades following the event, having untold consequences for species. One such devastating accident occurred in March 1967 when a crude oil tanker, the Torrey Canyon, ran aground off Land's End in UK waters. The disaster had terrible impacts on marine life not only from the oil itself but also from detergents used in the clean-up process. So many species were killed and damaged including algae, mussels, limpets, winkles, barnacles, shrimps, urchins, as well of course as thousands of seabirds. A scientific report into the ecological consequences of the spill concluded with the following terse critical reflection: 'We are progressively making a slum of nature and may eventually find that we are enjoying the benefit of science and industry under conditions which no civilized society should tolerate.'[10]

Not only do such events have devastating effects on nature and wildlife but today they also have severe financial implications for the businesses involved due to legal liabilities. Indeed, one aspect of developing a business case for extinction prevention, as well as an extinction accounting framework, which we feel deserves specific attention, is the risk of legal liability from damaging threatened species. There is already a rather undeveloped form of 'extinction accounting' within corporate reports, in the form of disclosures of fines and financial criminal liabilities relating to wildlife. Environmental law and legislation protecting endangered species must, if effective, have financial implications for those who do not comply, providing additional financial incentives for business to prevent extinction and protect species. The Convention on International Trade in Endangered Species of Wild Fauna and Flora (CITES) is a multilateral treaty established in 1975 for the protection of endangered animals and plants. CITES protects around 5,000 animal species and 29,000 plant species against overexploitation through international trade. Despite CITES being effective since 1975 it seems this regulation has not remained uncontested and indeed there have been many efforts to overturn the legal restriction on 'taking' endangered species.[11] Legal scholars have sought to explain the meaning of 'taking', stating that Section 9 of the Endangered Species Act prohibits the 'take' of any endangered species, where 'take' means to harass, harm, pursue, hunt, shoot, wound, kill, trap, capture, or collect a species specified as endangered, or to attempt to engage in any such conduct. The literature suggests that that there has been controversy around the Act and explains the difficulties in identifying the cause of harm – a change in habitat can cause extinction or loss but cannot necessarily or easily be proven to be a direct effect. There are distinct and acknowledged financial and business implications of species loss, associated with species interdependence, ecosystem functioning and an ecosystem services approach:

the ESA has become vulnerable to constitutional challenge because the basis for species protection is not exclusively commercial in nature, but is instead a mixture of philosophy, morality, aesthetics, and utility. Although the statute is widely defended on moral and aesthetic grounds, the utilitarian argument for protecting endangered species is actually quite strong if understood to include more than just the commercial, medicinal, or recreational uses of particular species and to encompass the role of species as indicators of the health of ecosystems necessary for human health and welfare.[12]

Linked to legislation and environmental laws such as CITES, another element of an 'extinction accounting' framework, as developed in this chapter, manifests in the reporting on liabilities, fines and other costs associated with damage or harm to endangered species in breach of environmental law and legislation. Probably the most financially crippling corporate event concerning species endangered by extinction is the 2010 oil spill by BP plc in the Mexican Gulf. Although companies report on fines and also potential liabilities relating to environmental damages linked to impacts on endangered species, such reporting lacks detail. For example, BP reported financial details in the notes to the accounts on damages paid in relation to Deepwater Horizon, but did not provide details of how many species were affected to accompany those figures. An illustration of this endangered species impact relates to BP's legal payments as follows:

> Under the terms of the criminal plea agreement, a total of $2,394 million is required to be paid to the National Fish & Wildlife Foundation (NFWF) over five years. In addition, $350 million is required to be paid to the National Academy of Sciences (NAS) over five years.[13]

The materially financial implications of harming species threatened with extinction are evident in BP's note 2 to their financial statements for 2015, where they state, 'The cumulative pre-tax income statement charge since the incident amounts to $55.5 billion'.[14]

BP provided detailed information concerning the amounts paid but did not disclose information on specific species affected, or the ways in which populations were impacted, to accompany the financial information. We feel that a more hybrid form of disclosure would improve communication and transparency. BP discussed in the notes to the accounts uncertainty attached to future liabilities still arising from the event:

> It is not possible, at this time, to measure reliably other obligations arising from the incident, nor is it practicable to estimate their magnitude or possible timing of payment. Therefore, no amounts have been provided for these obligations as at 31 December 2015.[15]

We therefore recommend that damages to habitat and related species impacts should be included in an extinction accounting framework as an important element of an organisation's disclosures. These details provide context for the reader and bring out transparency in relation to corporate impact on extinction as well as on efforts to clean up and therefore prevent extinction. By reporting more detail in this area, companies would be discharging higher levels of accountability both for mistakes made, as well as for efforts made to reverse damages to sperm whale, gulf sturgeon, manatee, sea turtles and other threatened species. A narrative species discussion attached to the disclosure of any financial fines would represent a form of extinction accounting. This narrative is complemented by providing details on actions to prevent extinction. The impact and importance of legal structures which seek to protect endangered species are explored fully in Chapter 8. We now turn to consider how accounting may be linked to extinction prevention.

How can accounting relate to species extinction?

Accounting is just about numbers. Or is it? Accounting is seen by many as a calculative device for recording an organisation's financial performance and profitability as well as its losses and liabilities. Accounting was developed as a means of discharging an accountability, demonstrating responsibility, for an organisation or business. Anyone holding a financial stake, a share, in a company wants to know that their investment is being looked after properly. Financial accounting attempts to satisfy requirements for companies to provide shareholders with some form of account of their financial transactions each year, their assets and liabilities and a balance sheet. However, in the second half of the twentieth century, shareholders and other stakeholders (those with an interest in the company who do not necessarily hold shares) began to be increasingly interested in other aspects of a company's activities, for example their social and environmental impacts. Since the 1970s especially, companies have started to produce different forms of 'accounting' including social and environmental accounting, where they seek to explain their impact on society and the environment. It is also important to stress that environmental and social accounting are not restricted to listed companies. We view 'accounts' as relevant to all forms of organisation and indeed interested parties across all sectors: private, public, voluntary, charity, including governments and supra-national bodies. Companies have increasingly produced some form of separate, stand alone, social and environmental account for several decades.

The responsibility of accounting in relation to environmental pollution began to be a focus of academic research and accounting practice in the 1970s and early 1980s.[16] There is today a substantial and growing body of academic and other literature on the development, and content of these forms of social and environmental accounting. As this book focuses on extinction accounting, we need to explore its 'ancestors', especially accounting for biodiversity.

One of the academic pioneers of social and environmental accounting, Professor Rob Gray, has provided thoughtful and critical discussions of the emergence and development of social and environment accounting over several decades. His professional article, 'The Accountant's Task as a Friend to the Earth',[17] was probably the first publication demonstrating the potential for accounting to help in preserving nature. Indeed, this short professional article explores a 'possible innovative role' for accountants in developing the (then) emergent concept of 'green' accounting but one which, 'must be approached with some care', given the contradictory nature of bringing together financial business concerns and preservation of the natural environment. The various experiments such as the connected reporting framework, developed by the Prince of Wales Accounting for Sustainability (A4S) project, the triple bottom line approach, and now integrated reporting are all efforts to develop complex frameworks which seek to include 'nature' in the form of natural capital, or in some sense to monetise nature.

The founding and development of the Centre for Social and Environmental Accounting Research (CSEAR)[18] originally at Dundee University and now St Andrews, provides a forum for social and environmental accounting researchers, establishing an annual CSEAR Summer School which has now grown to include CSEAR conferences worldwide. As social and environmental accounting has proliferated in practice internationally, so research into these now highly developed areas of accounting has grown commensurately. Scholars worldwide are focusing more and more on the details of social accounting, drilling down into understanding the motivations for, drivers of, and content within corporate reporting on climate change, water usage, pollutants, emissions, biodiversity indicators and corporate impacts on habitats and ecosystems. Accounting academia has been aware of the environmental and ecological impacts from business activity, and the importance of integrating these into accounting and corporate reporting, for decades. The following shows how extinction was recognised in the accounting literature as an imminent global crisis nearly 30 years ago:

> a break in the ecological chain can happen for many reasons . . . but it takes little imagination to see that once it has started, the process is irreversible and will, potentially, accelerate. The process of extinction is now rapid.[19]

Indeed there were various attempts at making business more environmentally and ecologically aware around this time.[20] Yet, here we are, well into the twenty-first century, and the ecological situation continues to deteriorate, with business activities growing and taking over more and more tropical rainforest, more pristine wildlife areas, more natural resources. Surely more can be done. Suffice to say, the frameworks which currently are in place may be improving the situation and slowing extinction rates but is this happening fast enough given the urgency we described in the previous chapter?

A recent book, *The Chief Value Officer: Accountants Can Save the Planet*,[21] identifies ways that accounting, reporting and other corporate governance and accountability mechanisms can (and must) be orientated towards saving the environment and preventing extinction, or at least reducing deleterious impacts. The book contains the first explicit example of an extinction accounting framework.

One area where environmental accounting has grown recently is in the area of accounting for biodiversity. Indeed, there has been an impressive increase in the amount of information now provided by many companies on their impact on biodiversity through their operations as well as concerning their initiatives and 'biodiversity action plans' which they are putting place to conserve and enhance biodiversity. However, some forms of reporting on social and environmental issues dates further back in time and extends much further into our history than social and environment accounting 'experiments' in the last few decades. As we saw in Chapter 1, a study of river pollution, as described by an engineer, examined the effects of industrial pollution on a London river, providing what can be interpreted as an environmental account of pollution and environmental degradation in the 1800s.[22] Other research similarly identifies examples of environmental and social 'accounting' and reporting from earlier centuries. One paper offers a historical analysis of social disclosure by a large Australian company over a hundred-year period commencing in 1885.[23] The findings are similar to those reported in a study which deals with an exponential increase in a type of corporate reporting to employees in the UK from 1920 to 1970.[24] Environmental reporting appears to have followed later, gaining prominence in the 1980s and 1990s.[25] This was probably because of growing scientific evidence on the deteriorating state of the planet and the ability of large multinational corporations, 'to control and move resources internationally [becoming] a subject of worldwide concern'.[26]

By the beginning of the twenty-first century, empirical and theoretical analysis of social and environmental disclosures shifted from viewing them as separate parts of a corporation's engagement with stakeholders to understanding how social and environmental issues were inter-connected, and affected a company's long-term sustainability.[27] This coincided with the proliferation of what is often (in our view somewhat erroneously) referred to as non-financial reporting[28] and a concerted effort by the academic community to synthesise the growing body of research on different forms of social and environmental disclosures. For example, some researchers shed light on variations in reporting practices by country[29] while others are concerned with how regional cultures impact on the prevalence of non-financial reporting.[30] Researchers have also grappled with providing a framework for analysing and explaining changing reporting trends. This has drawn on different ontological perspectives and principles from, inter alia, economics, business management, institutional theory, political economy and ecology[31] to frame environmental and social reporting as either an 'addendum' to existing accounting discourse or a central feature in 'organisation–society dialogue'.[32]

Early forms of social and environmental disclosures were not guided by a single body of knowledge or unifying theoretical framework.[33] This may explain the significant variation in the types of issues being reported to stakeholders and the plethora of names used to label reports dealing with social and environmental issues such as corporate citizen report, social report, environmental and social report, sustainability practice report or good practice report.[34] This changed during the 1990s when, '. . .reporting research and practice increasingly began to consider the social and environmental dimension simultaneously in a joint report which [was] often published alongside traditional financial reports'.[35] Consolidating social, environmental and financial reporting, soon to be renamed 'sustainability reporting', gained favour in North America and Europe and quickly spread to other regions.[36] Regulation by governments and stock exchanges played a key role in driving an increase in the amount of environmental and social disclosures and the standardisation of the form and content of sustainability reports.[37] The growth of the responsible investment community, lobbying by non-governmental organisations, and emergence of codes of corporate governance further stimulated the sustainability reporting movement.[38] As some of the world's most prominent companies subscribed to sustainability reporting and formalised some type of sustainability report, these were quickly replicated by organisations in different parts of the world. As a result, sustainability reports became more standardised.[39] This was especially true following the release of codified guidance on how to prepare a sustainability report by the Global Reporting Initiative, the GRI. In 1987 and 1992, the United Nations hosted two important conferences on human impact on the planet and the need for companies to become more environmentally responsible. These led to the 1995 World Business Council on Sustainable Development (WBCSD) which laid the foundation for a framework to guide and report on sustainable business practices, namely the GRI, which was founded in 1997. The GRI's 'G2 guidelines' were issued in 2002.[40] The most recent guidelines, the GRI G4, were issued in 2016 and are seen by many to provide the basis for sustainability reporting:

> An ever-increasing number of companies and other organizations want to make their operations sustainable. Moreover, expectations that long-term profitability should go hand-in-hand with social justice and protecting the environment are gaining ground. These expectations are only set to increase and intensify as the need to move to a truly sustainable economy is understood by companies' and organizations' financiers, customers and other stakeholders.[41]

Further, the guidelines state that if sustainability reports are prepared sincerely, then the reporting

> . . . helps organizations to set goals, measure performance, and manage change in order to make their operations more sustainable. A sustainability report conveys disclosures on an organization's impacts – be they positive or negative – on the environment, society and the economy. In doing so, sustainability reporting makes abstract issues tangible and concrete, thereby assisting in understanding and managing the effects of sustainability developments on the organization's activities and strategy.[42]

Recent surveys of sustainability reporting practice, conducted by one of the major four accounting firms, KPMG, confirm that sustainability reporting according to GRI principles has become well established.[43] The surveys indicated that in 2015, over 70% of the world's largest companies were preparing a sustainability report, and that by 2017, this had increased to 90% of the largest 250 companies.

Despite its popularity, sustainability reporting has attracted extensive criticism, especially from the academic accounting community. Scholars have raised concerns that sustainability reports are used as part of an impression management strategy, with no guarantee that corporate action and reporting are consistent.[44] Practitioners and stakeholders have also pointed out that the disclosures recommended by the GRI are not being reported in a way which makes the relevance of social and environmental issues for business management, risk assessment and strategy sufficiently clear.[45] Criticisms of sustainability reporting compare it to financial reporting:

> Sustainability reports have similarly suffered weaknesses, usually appearing disconnected from the organisation's financial reports, generally providing a backward-looking review of performance, and almost always failing to make the link between sustainability issues and the organisation's core strategy. For the most part, these reports have failed to address the lingering distrust among civil society of the intentions and practices of business. Stakeholders today want forward-looking information that will enable them to more effectively assess the total economic value of an organisation.[46]

In response to such concerns, a new form of accounting, 'integrated reporting', was proposed as a way of explaining the interconnection between information being reported in financial statements and sustainability reports. South Africa took a leading position in the development of integrated reporting, issuing a discussion paper on the topic in 2011[47] and taking an active role in the development of an integrated reporting framework released by the International Integrated Reporting Council (IIRC) in 2013.[48] In the same year, the country required listed companies to prepare an integrated report or provide reasons for not doing so, a move regarded as making integrated reporting by South African listed companies mandatory.[49] The primary purpose of an integrated report is

> . . . to explain to providers of financial capital how an organization creates value over time. An integrated report benefits all stakeholders interested in an organization's ability to create value over time, including employees, customers, suppliers, business partners, local communities, legislators, regulators and policy-makers.[50]

Integrated reporting has not become as widespread as sustainability reporting and it has been criticised by some for placing too much emphasis on the providers of financial capital to the detriment of the sustainability movement.[51] However it is impossible that this outcome, if really as negative as suggested by some academics, was at all the intention of Mervyn King and his committee given his total commitment to a stakeholder inclusive approach to governance and accounting.[52] Integrated reporting is still in its developmental stages[53] and there are signs that companies adopting and applying the framework are experiencing positive change. This includes a better understanding of business processes and their financial, economic and social impact and an improved ability to explain how organisations ensure long-term sustainability,[54] something which is valued by investors and other stakeholders.[55] The journey to widespread adoption of integrated reporting and also, integrated thinking, upon which it depends, is taking time and it is our view that extinction is such an urgent issue that it needs individual attention from the accounting community.

Given the urgency of the current ongoing species crisis and daily extinctions, developing a completely new and alternative system of capitalism is not possible unless the incumbent system ceases to function – which it will unless change occurs. We are therefore seeking to develop and implement a framework which can work from within the current capitalist system, which can slot into integrated reports or sustainability reporting. However controversial this may be for some academics, we feel it is the only viable alternative at present if mass extinctions are to be tackled within the business community, the perpetrators of habitat destruction and many other factors discussed in Chapter 1. Even if a capitalist 'within system' approach only leads to a slowing down of extinction rather than prevention, at least that slowing down provides policy makers and environmentalists inter alia the time to seek other solutions. Every single extinction is the end of a genetic line, with no going back, no return. Every species saved is a victory. Saving creatures via the capitalist system may not be consistent with deep green thinking, but it is better than not saving anything at all. The following attempts to square this circle:

> . . . grounding the extinction accounting framework in existing accounting practices and systems ensures that that it resonates with practitioners and has, at least, some chance of being adopted and applied. This is especially true when it comes to using an anthropocentric view of nature to frame the impact of an absence of ecosystem services. On one hand, attempting to assign a monetary value to nature poses a number of technical and moral challenges. On the other, the academic community needs to appreciate that companies and investors are unable to consider the environment from a non-financial or non-economic perspective.[56]

Although the GRI's Principles, in their latest form, do encourage companies to report information relating to species threatened with extinction which are affected by their business activities, the relevant principles have come under substantial criticism from accounting academia. For example, one study criticises the GRI for failing to define 'sustainability' and 'sustainable development' explicitly.[57] We note also that the GRI does not explain exactly how a company should incorporate biodiversity management as part of its risk assessment, strategy and operational practices. The GRI Principles relating to extinction are, it seems, rather broad and do not provide adequate guidance to companies on how they should be applied in the unique contexts of their business model and may be interpreted by companies as a disclosure checklist rather than a framework for reducing biodiversity risks or preventing extinction.[58] Basically, scholars in accounting tend to feel that the GRI Principles are inadequate in terms of leading to protection of species, biodiversity and habitats and that something far stronger and more effective needs to be found if extinctions are to be prevented.[59] We suggest that merely following the current GRI Principles will lead to little more than a *fossil record*, through the historic annual and sustainability reports of companies, and other organisations, of the species which they have failed to protect and save.

As we can see from the above discussion, a considerable amount of the academic literature in the area of social and environmental accounting has, unfortunately, come to the conclusion that existing forms of biodiversity accounting do not tend to be very effective either in communicating to an audience about the company's impacts on species, on habitats, or in explaining year on year how effective they are being in protecting and enhancing populations affected by their operations. Furthermore, the consensus in the existing research, which explores these forms of accounting, is that the reporting is totally focused on species which are useful to us as, in other words the accounts centre around protecting species which are useful to society in some way either because they provide an essential ecosystem service or because they are especially attractive to people. Cuddly species such as bears and monkeys, or bees because of their pollination services, tend to be the focus of such accounting and corporate initiatives. There is very little mention in corporate accounts of creepy crawlies, worms, spiders, cockroaches and the like. Even the very term 'accounting for biodiversity' has been held up as a hindrance in raising awareness of species extinction and the need to protect wildlife and nature, as it 'is not immediately understandable, sounds scientific and does not perhaps convey either the notion of accountability for species and wildlife, nor does it communicate the urgency of species extinction'.[60]

If accounting is to become a force for transformation and change, and attain its emancipatory potential, then it needs to embrace the urgency of species extinction. Biodiversity accounting has effectively failed to 'do the job' of raising public awareness and prevent species extinctions. A form of accounting which will genuinely lead to changes in business behaviour and to extinction prevention needs to be far more than a recording of species affected by business activity, far more than a mere biodiversity audit. In other words, extinction accounting has to be different from, and an evolution from, existing forms of biodiversity accounting. It has to go further in the language used, the way in which species under threat are communicated to the reader, and the extent of effort made to prevent extinction by the business and in partnership with other interested parties. The transformational potential for accounting to 'save the planet' has been raised in the academic accounting literature before yet there seems to have been little progression given the dire situation we currently find ourselves in. We now consider how accounting can be emancipatory.

What do we mean by emancipatory accounting?

The concept of emancipatory accounting has grown gradually and evolved within the academic accounting literature. The earliest explicit usage of the term 'emancipatory accounting' appears in the works of a leading critical accounting academic, Tony Tinker.[61] Indeed, these works, published over thirty years ago, recognised the contemporaneous failure of accounting to deal with the negative effects of commercial activity on the environment and society. They highlighted the failure of accounting, as a mechanism of the capitalist system, to encompass negative social and environmental impacts into their remit and address them for the good and betterment of society and the planet. For example, this quotation introduces the concept of an 'emancipatory accounting' as a potential cure and solution to this failure of the accounting function, given the ability of accounting to incorporate different forms of communication and broader types of information:

> Emancipatory accounting includes information systems capable of recognizing the alienating effects of capitalism and therefore is more effective in detecting capitalist alienation than any of the other accountability systems discussed previously. The need for the critical potential of emancipatory accounting is illustrated by those occasions on which private and public interests are at variance. For instance, the market imperative makes it irrational for Hooker Chemical,[62] or any other producer of toxic waste, to do anything other than minimize costs of disposal (including any litigation costs).[63]

Using Tinker's analysis, it is the alienation of business from the natural environment, ecological systems, wildlife and species, which has led us to the terrible extinction situation in which we now find ourselves. We, however, consider that accounting can assist in healing this alienation and lead to improvements for people and planet. Accounting as a mechanism of communication and a system of information can, and must, address problems created by businesses and the capitalist system. What our capitalist system has created, it can also mend. Surely accounting can be the cure as well as the cause? As Tinker explained:

> We have reconceptualised accounting by enriching it with work from economics, anthropology, sociology, philosophy, and other disciplines. This reconceptualization . . . has enabled to see accounting not as a mere bookkeeping and record keeping, but as capitalism's prime adjudicator in social conflict.[64]

We are similarly attempting to reconceptualise accounting by enriching it with ecology, science, deep ecology and other related disciplines. Some may think by this that we mean giving simply a financial or numerical value to species. This is not the case at all. Instead, we want to encourage narrative reporting and indeed, hybrid reporting on species, habitats and ecosystems which leads organisations to change practices. Where there are attempts to estimate financial value it is only for the purpose of highlighting a material risk to a business of species loss, species disappearance and absence, in order to strengthen a business case which has to exist for businesses and capitalism to take species loss seriously. Would it were different – but the harsh reality is that unless there is a financial benefit to preserving species, businesses will not embrace biodiversity and species protection, for purely ethical and moral arguments, given the pressures for growth and profit seeking. Since Tinker's work, there has been significant development of the 'emancipatory concept', which could help to 'expose, enhance and develop social relationships through a re-examination and expansion of established rights to information'.[65]

Some of the most significant contributions to developing and understanding the concept of emancipatory accounting are found in the writings of critical accounting theorists Sonja Gallhofer and Jim Haslam, who suggest:

> Accounting has the potential to be mobilized for the critical and emancipatory project. It can challenge current norms, traditions, ways of 'doing things' and expose inequalities, injustices, oppression and exploitation. Through this, accounting can help engender change, contributing to the building of a more liberated, democratic and happier society.[66]

The authors have written extensively on how accounting can become more emancipatory leading to transformation, or at least progression, towards a better world.[67] For example, they explain how a more emancipatory form of accounting is a vision of a means of changing the world for the better: accounting can bring about the enhancement of social welfare:

> A vision of accounting as an emancipatory force is consistent with seeing accounting as a communicative social practice that functions as a system of informing that renders transparent and enlightens with the effect of social betterment. It is a vision in which a progressive community comes to control accounting rather than be controlled by it, a reflection of a proper accountability.[68]

Their most recent papers show how the concept of emancipatory accounting has evolved since the early explorations by Tony Tinker, as discussed above, to a form of accounting which is not necessary radical in its approach but more pragmatic. In other words, the notion of emancipatory accounting is now more about progressing towards change within the capitalist system, as it is currently functioning, than about trying to shake everything up and start again:

More generally, there is a move away . . . from the position that emancipatory accounting – if still a radically progressive notion – necessarily
reduces to an accounting that is an instrument of revolutionary or grand
radical transformation consistent with the position suggested in the Marx-
inspired line of thought pursued by Tinker.[69]

Applying this approach to address the current extinction crisis could, if successful, lead to an emancipatory outcome: namely, extinction prevention and
ecological betterment. As we saw in the earlier discussion, current attempts
to enhance biodiversity through accounting and corporate reporting are not
necessarily achieving transformation and change but are instead embedding the
power of organisations over nature and furthering the dominance of the human
species over others.[70] We therefore seek to provide a framework which may be
at least progressive, moving towards a significant change in business practices, if
not entirely emancipatory. However, we also stress the need for the framework
to achieve maximum transformative change if species are to be saved.

From accounting for biodiversity towards an emancipatory extinction accounting framework

As we saw above, social and environmental accounting has a long history but
accounting for biodiversity is a relatively new form. Accounting academics in
the 1990s began to provide examples of accounting for biodiversity, which
sought to effectively audit species. One of the first examples of an alternate
chart of accounts which can be used to track changes in biodiversity developed
a type of natural inventory schematic which is categorised according to the
number of species found in a particular location, population sizes and level
of extinction risk.[71] Rather than attempting to monetise any natural capital,
information is reported to stakeholders according to an ecological grading,
based on biodiversity richness and vulnerability. The application of this type of
biodiversity reporting was illustrated in a small nature park in Wales.

Since these initial explorations in accounting for biodiversity research,
the area has blossomed. In 2013, a leading international accounting journal,
Accounting, Auditing and Accountability Journal, published a special issue on
'Accounting for Biodiversity', which effectively paved the way for further
research in this burgeoning area. Within the special issue are a number of
papers which explore different aspects of accounting for biodiversity. The edi-
torial paper outlined a variety of perspectives on biodiversity and sought to
build a case for why companies 'should' be accounting for biodiversity.[72] For
example, one paper employed a biodiversity disclosure matrix to show the
extent of reporting on specific biodiversity themes. Examples include social
engagements, partnerships formed to manage biodiversity impact and specifics on biodiversity risk assessment.[73] More recently, the international research
effort aimed at understanding current practice and providing recommendations
for improvements has been significant.

The prior research gives readers a respectable overview of how annual, sustainability or integrated reports can be modified to address biodiversity-related concerns directly. They also complement existing guidelines – such as those issued by the GRI – which make some reference to biodiversity but lack detail on the nature and form of a biodiversity account.[74] This is not to say that biodiversity reporting has not earned negative feedback. Reporting on biodiversity can become part of discursive, narrative or aesthetic accounts which are useful for generating awareness and advancing a normative position on environmental accountability.[75] This type of reporting is, however, very descriptive and its emotive tone can be dismissed in a corporate context. Biodiversity reporting can also become compliance-focused, especially as different measures of biodiversity risk and impact are codified in reporting guidelines. This significantly undermines the change potential of reporting on biodiversity.[76] We now, as a result, depart from the biodiversity reporting models described in the prior literature and present an emancipatory accounting framework outlined in a recently published special issue of *Accounting, Auditing and Accountability Journal*.[77]

Defining 'extinction accounting': hybrid disclosure on the absence of nature and species

'Extinction accounting' may be described as 'an attempt by companies to report on and evaluate the *absence* of *specific* species'.[78] This chapter adopts a 'within-system', approach, provides a framework for extinction accounting which works within our current system of accounting and is especially compatible with integrated reporting.

In seeking to 'account for' extinction prevention we avoid financialising species – in other words we do not seek to place a defined financial value on a species. Such an approach would not only contradict deep green ecological beliefs that nature has intrinsic value but would also be at odds with our intention to bring all aspects of the value of flora and fauna into accounting. Although for many the very attempt to use accounting to address species extinction may be deeply offensive, our approach seeks in some way to find a middle ground, a compromise, between widely differing views. In attempting to define extinction accounting we are at all times mindful of the warnings from the environmental accounting literature which views the capitalist system as totally separate from, and incompatible with, nature, 'The march of a financial market-driven, financial reporting-enabled international capitalism leaves in its wake a planet barely able to continue supporting life.'[79]

This quotation *per se* demonstrates the difficulties involved in trying to develop extinction accounting which could be acceptable to people with disparate views of nature and the environment. Our definition of extinction accounting and the hybrid disclosure framework we propose, seeks to encourage 'accounting for species' while at the same time not diminishing their intrinsic value and ignoring their contribution to the ecosystem – which is indeed *in*valuable. The inability to tag any actual financial value on any species due to its interrelationship with others and its contribution to the survival of an ecosystem renders any attempt to place an *exact* financial value on a species as meaningless. However, using broad financial estimates can help to provide a business case to underlie hybrid disclosures.

As argued earlier, it is highly unlikely that businesses and investors will accept a need to provide extinction accounting unless a business case grounded in financial risk and materiality appears to exist, although there are many individuals working in industry and investment who are passionate about wildlife and nature. Such people however are tied by their legal liabilities to prioritise shareholder value and cannot pursue personal passions instead. Deep ecological arguments of morality and ethics are, unfortunately, inadequate in our capitalist-driven system. While taking heed of warnings in the existing literature,[80] our framework is based on the 'deprival value' arising from the extinction of a species. This type of 'reverse reasoning' leads us to seek an accounting which attempts to 'value' the *absence* of species – tries to place a value on how much extinction could cost business in financial terms, to bolster a business case for extinction prevention. To assist us in this argument, we have turned to science to find any existing estimates of how much is at stake were a species or an ecosystem to disappear. The anthropocentric approach to nature, which seeks to value 'ecosystem services' (that is – the 'services' rendered to humans by nature and the natural world for our use – a concept which is deeply controversial) has been the focus of policy makers at an international level.[81] The total value of the world's 'ecosystem services' has been estimated as equivalent to an eye-watering $33 trillion, which almost doubles global GNP (effectively global economic production), which is estimated at $18 trillion. It has also been estimated that changes in land use globally between 1997 and 2011 led to a loss of ecosystem services somewhere between $4.3 and $20.2 trillion per year. Further, total global ecosystem services were estimated at $125 trillion per year or $145 trillion per year for 2011. The authors highlight that their estimates are conservative and emphasise the importance of viewing these estimates as representations of the enormity of 'value' attached to the ecosystem and the diverse ways in which nature supports the human species. Their paper stresses how massively 'we' as the human race depend on nature and the survival of the ecosystem. Such an approach is heavily criticised as leading to the commodification of nature. Further, such figures are actually meaningless if we reflect on Chapter 1 and the fact that we are in a period of mass extinction – unless extinctions are prevented there will be no ecosystem. In turn, there will be no 'ecosystem services' and ultimately no people to miss them.

So, the prospect of extinctions leading to ecosystem collapse and the loss of ecosystem services presents a serious challenge for businesses worldwide and one which needs to be recognised as engendering huge financial risk. As seen from the discussion in Chapter 1 on species interdependence, no one knows for sure which species could, if lost, destroy a local ecosystem which could in turn destroy business and human life. Based on a precautionary approach is it not safer to protect every species from extinction? We argue that an exact 'number' should not and cannot be placed on a species but that there is a financial business case based on the way in which each and every species *contributes* to the whole, whether that 'whole' equates to $30 trillion or $100 trillion. The amounts are irrelevant, it is the complexity of the natural system and its fragility and vulnerability to species loss which counts.

Having, hopefully, established a convincing business case for providing extinction accounting, we now consider how a form of extinction accounting can actually prevent extinctions (i.e. can be emancipatory, transformational and progressive).

An emancipatory framework for extinction accounting

This book argues that extinction accounting should promote change in an effort to reverse existing extinction trends. This means that extinction accounting cannot be limited to disclosures on species or generic details on how the loss of species is being managed. It should be embedded in an organisation's strategy, risk management, internal control and operating practices.[82] Financial impact may be used to make a business case for protecting species and preventing extinction in line with an anthropocentric view on nature but there are also elements of deep ecology. This is because extinction accounting complements the economic impact of extinction with a genuine moral, social and ecological perspective on extinction.[83] The result is that extinction accounting acts as a possible enabler of change. This draws on an emerging body of research which argues that the act of providing an account of a defined subject matter can reveal, enhance and develop interrelationships between organisations, society and the environment and, at the very least, make people aware of the need for change.[84] This was discussed above in relation to the meaning and development of emancipatory accounting.

Extinction accounting, as an illustration of emancipatory accounting, can take different forms. For example, one study considers how geometrical mathematics can be used to offer an alternative basis for measuring biodiversity and generating ecological accounts which are not limited by a single monetary value. This allows corporate reports to provide a perspective on the beauty and importance of nature and, by inference, the consequences of a loss of biodiversity.[85] Another recent paper suggests that visual counter-accounts can be used by environmental and animal rights activists to illustrate unsustainable and unethical business practice and to champion the need for change.[86] As a final illustration, a recent paper explains how accounts should be provided at the level of the relevant ecosystem.[87] This form of ecologically centred reporting can be used to specify and describe conservation efforts, measure impacts and 'produced a visible and comprehensible standard for biodiversity conservation'.[88]

An extinction account needs to provide sufficient information on species at risk of extinction, why extinction is something which the public and the reporting organisation should be concerned about and the specific strategies put in place and actions taken to prevent extinction.[89] This is summarised in the framework shown in Table 2.1.[90]

Element 1 of Table 2.1 is informed by disclosures recommended by the GRI Principles[91] and should take economic, social and ecological factors into account. Elements 2 and 3 are concerned with proactive reporting. The emphasis is on demonstrating how the reporting entity is managing the risk of extinction, rather than on managing impressions. Codes of best practice can inform the nature and extent of the disclosures but these should also be tailored according to the specific facts and circumstances and the context in which the reporting entity operates.

To ensure that the extinction account is comprehensive, it is necessary to include a detailed review of whether or not conservation targets have been met, challenges encountered and any changes to plans or strategies (Elements 4 and 5). This not only ensures transparent reporting but also gives stakeholders an understanding of how extinction prevention is a dynamic process.[92] Finally, the reporting entity ensures that each element in the extinction accounting model has been explained accurately and completely. The objective is to ensure that there is a clear interconnection between all parts of the model and that the reporting does not become an exercise in checking disclosures against a list. Illustrations of emergent 'extinction accounting', which is to some extent emancipatory, by a number of South African listed companies are presented in a recent study.[93] For example, toad accounting is featured in the integrated report of BHP Billiton:

> Wetlands around the Jansen Potash Project, in Saskatchewan, Canada, are home to a range of sensitive amphibian species including the Canadian toad. To mitigate potential effects the Jansen Project may have on these toads, the Canadian Toad Relocation and Monitoring Program was initiated in 2012. To date, 45 adult toads have been collected, 44 of which had their feet tagged with a fluorescent elastomer. These adults and subsequently 204 metamorphs and 21 toad tadpoles were released into wetlands that will not be disturbed by Project activities and have habitat to which they are accustomed.[94]

The way this company explains the details of their programme to relocate toads, despite the small numbers involved and the way they demonstrate an improvement in the toad population, represents genuine emancipatory extinction accounting – a form of accounting which not only records what species are in danger but also what they are doing to prevent their extinction as well as how effective their programme is. If this emergent form of extinction accounting can be rolled out across far more species, more habitats, far more programmes and far more organisations then we may be progressing towards extinction preventions.

There is already some evidence of the emergence of an early form of extinction accounting in these corporate reports as a paper exploring accounting

Table 2.1 Elements in an extinction accounting framework

	Element	Purpose	Elements
1	Extinction accounting context	Describe the extinction risk in the context of the organisation's business and the diverse reasons for wanting to address this risk	Record a list of plant and animal species, identified as endangered by the IUCN Red List, whose habitats are affected by the company's activities
			Report where, geographically, the company's activities pose a threat to endangered plant and animal species, as identified by the IUCN Red List
			Report potential risks/impacts on these specific species arising from the company's operations (equivalent to the existing GRI principles to this point)
			Incorporate images (such as photographs, etchings, botanical drawings example) of vulnerable, threatened, endangered, critically endangered species which are affected by the company's operations and which the company has a duty of care to protect
			Report full details (narrative as well as financial figures) relating to any fines or ongoing claims relating to endangered species legislation arising from the company's activities (e.g. CITES)
			Report corporate expressions of moral, ethical, emotional, financial and reputational motivations for preserving species and preventing extinction (to respond to diverse needs and requirements of different stakeholders/readers)
2	Action-focused reporting	Explain the actions the company takes and plans to take to reduce extinction risk	Report actions/initiatives taken by the company to avoid harm to, and to prevent extinction of, endangered plant and animal species including efforts to protect habitats and local ecosystems
3	Partnership reporting	Complement action-focused reporting by explaining broader partnerships/initiatives formed to combat/reverse extinction trends	Report partnerships/engagement between wildlife/nature/conservation organisations and the company which aim to address corporate impacts on endangered species and report the outcome/impact of engagement/partnerships on endangered species, habitats and ecosystems

#		
4	Analysis and reflection	Evaluation of extinction prevention initiatives against aims/targets to inform changes to actions and partnerships	Report assessment and reflection on outcome/impact of engagement/partnerships and decisions taken about necessary changes to policy/initiatives going forward
5	Assessment	Audit of affected species/ populations/biomes	Report regular assessments (audit) of species populations in areas affected by corporate operations as well as assessments of habitat degradation or improvement Report assessment of whether or not corporate initiatives/actions are assisting in prevention of species extinction and habitat protection
6	Reporting	Provide an account of the progress made to date on preventing or mitigating extinction, planned future actions and risk exposure	Report strategy for the future development and improvement of actions/initiatives: an iterative process Ensure that the whole process of 'extinction accounting' is integrated into corporate strategy and is incorporated into the company's integrated report, the company's business plan, corporate strategy and risk management/internal control system not resigned to separate sustainability reports or websites Potential liabilities relating to future possible legal fines/claims relating to endangered species impacts Discussion of ways in which the company is working to prevent future liabilities related to harming endangered species Provide pictorial representation of success in conservation – and of failure (i.e. species loss)

for the rhinoceros discusses the extinction threat facing the species, especially within the African context, and analyses corporate disclosures by South African listed companies on their initiatives aimed at preventing rhinoceros extinction.[95] Also, a recent book focuses on the accounting and finance issues relating to bee decline, as discussed earlier.[96] In both instances, the researchers find that companies rely on different types of reporting and disclosures (including a mix of qualitative and quantitative information) to construct their accounts of extinction and extinction prevention. However, attempts to consider accounting for specific species are still limited in the literature.

Extinction accounting needs to be mindful of the limitations of earlier forms of environmental accounts which over-emphasise the input–output model derived from economics and 'information throughput' rather than corporate action.[97] 'Accounting' needs to be conceptualised more broadly to accommodate different methods for providing an account[98] at both the organisational and ecological level[99] and mindful of the fact that continuity of the planet does not require humanity.[100] Two recently published special issues on extinction accounting (2018) and ecological accounts (2017) in *Accounting, Auditing and Accountability Journal* provide important insights in this regard.

It is unlikely that anthropocentrism – and its close association with the dominant financial discourse of contemporary accounting – can be replaced by an alternate philosophy in the short term.[101] As a result, rather than ignore principles from finance and economics, these can be mobilised to support the emancipatory objectives of extinction accounting. For example, two studies report that schemes for off-setting adverse biodiversity effects are marred by a number of challenges but the financial concept of off-setting and synthetic instrument trading are resilient ones which can be modified to contribute positively to environmental governance.[102] The same may be the case with full cost accounting and financial valuation which, while running the risk of obscuring biodiversity loss,[103] could be adapted as part of a broader assessment of extinction risk and how to prevent it.[104]

This does not, however, mean that extinction accounting ignores deep ecological views on nature and the danger of monetising flora and fauna under the broad heading of 'natural capital'.[105] For example, 'inventories' of different species can be organised by scientific classification, role in the ecosystem and level of extinction risk to provide context for extinction accounting without having to assign a financial value.[106] To avoid creating the impression that nature can be ranked, ordered and valued, it may also be possible to draw on ideas from fractal geometry to provide a multi-dimensional view of biodiversity. This would entail giving a detailed description of plant and animal species and accounts of natural capital which signal changes in biomass rather than creating the impression that complex ecosystems can bounded by accounting's binary asset-liability model.[107] As part of this, quantitative information on the population sizes, levels of extinction risk and changes in animals' ranges can still be provided. These are complemented by the impact of a company's operations on biomass and qualitative assessments of nature at *both* the deep ecological and anthropocentric level.[108]

Extinction accounting will also need to move beyond individual entities.[109] There are several examples of this. For example, a recent paper explains how 'counter-accounts' can have a transformative potential by challenging the status quo.[110] The meat and dairy industry in Finland is used as a case study to illustrate how animal rights activists can use a type of accounting to call for change. From a different perspective, another study highlights the importance of government involvement in policy development designed to reduce biodiversity impacts and change people's attitudes and behaviours toward sustainability.[111] Also dealing with the public sector, a recent paper reminds us of the role which local government has to play in protecting biodiversity.[112] The authors find that biodiversity is conceptualised mainly as an issue of human welfare and resource availability. There is, however, evidence of an awareness of accountability and stewardship as well as a sense of commitment to conservation which may point to the emancipatory potential of this type of reporting by local governments. This is especially true when public sector reporting deals with how local governments are monitoring and managing the loss of species and their efforts are supported by active public involvement.[113] From a different perspective, another study uses principles from geography to provide an illustration of what may be a type of extinction accounting at the ecological level.[114] The author shows how it may be possible to provide an account of a peatland habitat using scientific classifications for species which gives a sense of the level of extinction risk and can be used to drive conservation projects aimed at restoring biodiversity.

Lastly, for extinction accounting to live up to its emancipatory potential, it is important for it to develop in an interdisciplinary environment. Accountants are not well placed to gather, analyse and interpret data on ecosystems and biodiversity. As a result, active engagement with the scientific community is essential to ensure that key environmental issues are identified and understood before an extinction accounting framework is applied.[115] Accountants will also need to rely on the expertise of computer programmers, engineers, management experts and natural scientists to ensure that the necessary systems and processes are in place to collect and analyse data needed for providing an accounting of extinction, reform business practices and manage conservation initiatives.[116] An interdisciplinary and multidisciplinary approach is crucial and is inkeeping with a systems theory approach as discussed earlier. This is essential if extinction accounting is to overcome the fact that most integrated and sustainability reports usually neglect humanity's central role in driving species extinct and stop short of offering a clear indication of *how* extinction trends will be reversed.[117]

Emancipatory extinction engagement

In this book, we are also keen to explore the potential – and ongoing efforts – for finance and financial management to contribute to extinction prevention. If accounting can be emancipatory and be tuned toward preventing species extinction, then so can finance and financial management. The engagement role of institutional investors and financial institutions has an enormous potential to change business behaviour and to, in this case, prevent extinctions. Earlier work has explored the ways in which responsible investors can influence corporate strategy on social and environmental issues through engagement and dialogue. This form of engagement constitutes an important aspect of what is known as 'responsible investment'. Responsible investment is investment which takes into consideration environmental, social and governance (ESG) issues. Responsible investor engagement is the process by which institutional investors meet with their investee companies face to face to discuss how the company is dealing with ESG risks and how these are being incorporated into corporate strategy and internal control mechanisms. Such private ESG engagement represents a critically important mechanism of holistic corporate governance and stakeholder accountability.[118] A specific illustration of such engagement is the ways in which responsible institutional investors are engaging with companies on bee and pollinator decline. They are asking questions of investee companies about how bee loss is being addressed within the companies' supply chains, for example.[119] The following list presents a schema for responsible investor engagement on species extinction, which builds on a recently published tentative framework for responsible investor extinction engagement:[120]

- How do you inform yourselves about species decline and extinction threats in relation to your business activities?
- How do you track your impact on habitats and ecosystems?
- In what ways is your supply chain, both upstream and downstream, likely to be affected by species loss?
- Have you commissioned any studies to determine which species threatened with extinction on the IUCN Red List are directly or indirectly affected by your operations, or those of organisations within your supply chain?
- If you have commissioned studies, what were the outcomes? Have you identified which species are most at risk and what the financial (and other: reputational, social responsibility, ethical, moral) consequences of decline and extinction of these species are for your organisation?
- Are you engaging, or partnering, with any wildlife organisation regarding species threatened with extinction, for example the WWF? If so what are the outcomes of these engagements/partnerships?
- What contingency measures, risk scenarios and mitigation strategies have you considered regarding species decline and extinction?
- What measures are you taking to reduce and limit the impact of your operations on threatened species, habitats and the ecosystem more generally?
- What initiatives, policies and strategies have you implemented in order to prevent species extinction and to preserve and enhance habitats and ecosystems?
- Have you assessed the impact of these initiatives, policies and strategies on species populations, habitats and ecosystems?
- Have your assessments led to alterations and improvements in your initiatives, policies and strategies?

- If they have, in what ways has your extinction prevention strategy altered?
- Can you explain the extent to which your strategies, partnerships and initiatives have succeeded or failed in preventing species population decline and species extinction?
- How do you intend to improve on your performance in this area?

The above engagement framework transfers the reporting elements of the extinction accounting framework into a series of questions which institutional investors can apply in their meetings with companies. We hope fervently that this framework (as well as the extinction accounting framework) can be used in practice and can assist in extinction prevention. We also hope that this approach to reporting and questioning can be of use to wildlife NGOs, such as the WWF, in developing their partnerships and engagement relationships with companies and other organisations.

The structure of this book

We now take a brief tour of the remaining chapters of this book, which explore various aspects of extinction and extinction accounting.

Part II addresses extinction from various philosophical, moral, literary, business and legal perspectives. In Chapter 3, Jack Christian provides a fascinating imaginary conversation between a group of people including a naturalist (played by himself), two farmers (good farmer and bad farmer), a conservationist and an accountant. They focus on the impacts of agriculture on biodiversity within a UK perspective and discuss many of the initiatives and strategies currently in place to enhance and protect biodiversity from negative agricultural impacts. The chapter adopts a deep ecology approach and provides rich and colourful descriptions of nature and wildlife.

Chapter 4 focuses on the potential and probably imminent extinction of one specific species: ourselves. From a deep ecology perspective, the writers clearly demonstrate how capitalism and human activity have led us to the 'absurd' situation we are now in whereby all of nature is threatened. Our own extinction could be the solution to the problem for non-human species and the planet. In our view, Rob Gray and Markus Milne actually provide a rationale beyond argument for extinction accounting despite this being the last thing they intended. Yes, it would be wonderful to change everything and move into a utopian bliss of ecological and Gaian balance. But it is not going to happen – until and unless we are all gone, as in all of the human species. To some extent, the argument that when 'we' go everything else will start to improve is appealing except for the fact that some of us tend to have a survival instinct. So, this is a last ditch attempt to alter things from within the current system. If it fails, then balance will be restored by our own demise! The contrast between Chapter 4 and this chapter should fuel some intense and serious debate around the role of capitalism and capitalist structures and mechanisms in preventing extinction and other aspects of environmental degradation.

In Chapter 5, Sophia Nicolov considers the history, present and future for the grey whale, drawing on a wide range of literary texts and narratives. Especially important to this book is her discussion of the problems arising from categorisation of threatened species and especially the repercussions from downgrading a species' status.

Chapter 6 presents a succinct view on the need for natural capital to be included in integrated reports, as well as a discussion of some of the most pertinent threats to the natural world from Mervyn King, who has contributed so massively to the development of integrated reporting and the GRI as well as to the evolution of corporate governance in South Africa and elsewhere.

Chapter 7, written by Abigail Herron, provides an institutional investor perspective on how responsible investor engagement can assist in preventing the extinction of marine species. By listing questions used by investors in engagement and dialogue with companies, we can see how substantial the potential is for the institutional investment community to elicit change among businesses – a genuine example of emancipatory extinction engagement and dialogue.

Chapter 8 gives us a detailed analysis of the existing legislation surrounding endangered species protection and identifies strengths, weaknesses and the effectiveness of this legislation. The legal foundations of species protection seem, according to Simon Norton, to be working to some extent but there are clear areas for improvement.

Part III travels around the world exploring species threatened by extinction, extinction accounting and other extinction prevention efforts and initiatives. Indeed, these chapters demonstrate the enormity of the human effort, across the globe, to save habitats and species. The writers consider extinction from Africa to Europe and Scandinavia, across the Atlantic to the USA, Mexico and Canada, and finally to the Far East and the polar regions.

Several of the chapters apply our extinction accounting framework as a basis for their analysis of different species, different countries and different sectors. For example, in Chapter 9, Warren Maroun uses the framework to explore extinction accounting practice by South African listed companies, and in Chapter 11, Maroun and Michael Büchling use the framework to illustrate the construction of an extinction account by SANParks, the national parks in South Africa.

Chapter 10, written by Mxolisi Sibanda and Martin Mulama, addresses the plight of the black rhinoceros in East Africa and outlines the efforts of private business to address the extinction risk for rhinoceros. Chapter 12, by Gunnar Rimmel, explores extinction accounting practice by zoos across Europe, and in Chapter 13, Vanessa Amaral Rogers discusses extinction and extinction prevention for birds in the UK, from the perspective of the RSPB's strategies and initiatives. In Chapter 14, Timo Punkari also considers birds at risk of extinction with a focus on the surprising fact that red kite, once threatened, are thriving, whereas the simple house sparrow, so prevalent in the past, is now at risk of extinction.

Chapter 15 turns attention to flora rather than fauna, by investigating plants threatened by extinction as a result of the activities of the Italian paper tissue industry. Chapter 16 provides an analysis by Aris Solomon and Margaret Clappison of the role of aquaria and marine centres in Canada in 'saving' species but also the demise of many individuals. Sanjay Lanka, in Chapter 17, takes a butterfly-centric approach to assessing the situation for Monarch butterflies in the USA and Mexico.

A focus on specific species is also found in Chapter 18, where Kristina Jonäll and Svetlana Sabelfeld consider whether oil companies are genuinely addressing the risk that polar bears are threatened with extinction, by analysing their extinction accounting practice. Similarly, in Chapter 19, Longxiang Zhao and Jill Atkins analyse the accounts and websites of Chinese companies to evaluate their extinction accounting for panda as well as providing an extinction accounting framework for saving panda.

The book concludes in Chapter 20 with some reflections on extinction accounting, engagement and species.

Notes

1 This chapter draws heavily on the content of three published academic papers: Atkins et al. (2018) on accounting for the rhinoceros, which introduces the extinction accounting concept for the first time; Atkins and Maroun (2018), which presents a framework for extinction accounting and engagement as well as an Ark of extinction accounting and accountability; and Maroun and Atkins (2018), which provides some tentative KPIs for extinction prevention as well as illustrations of emergent extinction accounting from South African listed companies' integrated reports.
2 Wilson (1989, p. 114).
3 Atkins and Atkins (2016).
4 The deep ecology perspective is enshrined in the work of Arne Næss; see Glasser (2005).
5 This book, entitled, *Nature's Price: The Economics of Mother Earth*, arose from a report into the value of nature, commissioned by the WWF. See van Dieren and Hummelinck (1979, p. 3) for this quotation.
6 This lecture is included in HRH Prince Philip (1978, p. 12).
7 Hawken et al. (1999).
8 See naturalcapitalcoalition.org.
9 *Turbo capitalism*, which could also be referred to as *unrestrained capitalism* or *free market capitalism* (Pettinger 2017), was coined by Edward Lattwak (1998) and denotes a completely unregulated capitalist system replete with financial deregulation, privatisation, lower taxation rates for high-earners and an unregulated labour market. The advent of the term can be seen as a reflection upon the unfettered capitalism of some Western economies during the 1980s and, as Pettinger (2017) points out, 'Arguably, this led to rising income inequality and also the financial deregulation played a key role in the unsustainable credit bubble of 2001–2007.'
10 Smith (1970, p. 184).
11 See Blumm and Kimbrell (2004).
12 Blumm and Kimbrell (2004, p. 313).

13 BP (2015, p. 241).
14 Ibid.
15 Ibid.
16 See the introduction to Tony Tinker's seminal work, *Paper Prophets: A Social Critique of Accounting* (Tinker 1985).
17 See Gray (1990), which explores early experiments in environmental accounting as well as contemporaneous policy and political attempts to 'green' business.
18 Founded by Professor Rob Gray.
19 See Gray (1992, p. 406).
20 See also CERES (1990).
21 See King with Atkins (2016).
22 See Solomon and Thomson (2009).
23 Guthrie and Parker (1989).
24 Lewis et al. (1984).
25 See Guthrie and Parker (1989) and Gray et al. (1995b) for discussions of its development.
26 Gray et al. (1990, p. 598).
27 Fifka (2013).
28 Hughen et al. (2014).
29 Fifka (2013) and Orlitzky et al. (2003).
30 Khlif et al. (2015).
31 Gray et al. (1995a), Parker (2005), De Villiers and Maroun (2017) and Russell et al. (2017).
32 Parker (2005, p. 845).
33 Gray et al. (1995a) and Parker (2005).
34 Fifka (2013), Hahn and Kühnen (2013) and Junior et al. (2014).
35 Hahn and Kühnen (2013, p. 5).
36 KPMG (2012) and Fifka (2013).
37 Mock et al. (2013).
38 Solomon (2013), Mock et al. (2013) and KPMG (2017).
39 De Villiers and Alexander (2014).
40 Mock et al. (2013) and GRI (2015).
41 GRI (2016, p. 3).
42 Ibid.
43 KPMG (2015, 2016, 2017).
44 See, for example, Milne et al. (2009), Gray (2010) and Tregidga et al. (2014).
45 Solomon and Maroun (2012) and Atkins and Maroun (2014, 2015).
46 Foreword by Mervyn King in IRCSA (2011, p. 1).
47 Ibid.
48 King with Atkins (2016).
49 See discussions in Solomon and Maroun (2012), Solomon (2013), De Villiers et al. (2014) and Atkins and Maroun (2015).
50 Quotation from IIRC (2013, p. 4).
51 Flower (2015) and Thomson (2015).
52 King with Atkins (2016).
53 De Villiers et al. (2017) and McNally et al. (2017).
54 Eccles and Saltzman (2011), Adams et al. (2016), De Villiers et al. (2017) and Guthrie et al. (2017).
55 Atkins and Maroun (2015) and Zhou et al. (2017).
56 Atkins and Maroun (2018, p. 31).
57 Milne et al. (2009).

58 See Farneti and Guthrie (2009), Milne et al. (2009) and Jones and Solomon (2013).
59 See Maroun and Atkins (2018) for a fuller discussion of this.
60 See Jones and Solomon (2013, p. 683).
61 Tinker (1984, 1985).
62 This reference is to Hooker Chemical's pollution of Love Canal in Niagara in the 1940s which resulted in deaths and illnesses among local residents becoming apparent in the 1970s when deadly toxins such as tetradioxin (used to make Agent Orange) were found to have been dumped by the company. Tinker (1985) outlines the details of this notorious case and also explains how accounting was at the root of the problem. The company failed to report potential legal liabilities associated with dumping the deadly chemicals, with their impacts only becoming apparent some 40 years later.
63 See Tinker (1985, p. 202).
64 This quotation is from ibid., p. 205.
65 Gray (1992, p. 413).
66 Gallhofer and Haslam (1996, p. 25).
67 See the following works, which develop this theoretical framework: Gallhofer and Haslam (1996, 1997, 2003, 2011, 2017) and Gallhofer, Haslam and Yonekura (2013, 2015).
68 Gallhofer and Haslam (2003, p. 7).
69 Gallhofer and Haslam (2017, p. 6).
70 See, for example, Tregidga (2013).
71 See Jones (1996).
72 Jones and Solomon (2013).
73 See van Liempd and Busch (2013).
74 See Jones and Solomon (2013).
75 See Dillard and Reynolds (2008), Atkins et al. (2015a, 2015b) and Russell et al. (2017).
76 Atkins and Maroun (2018).
77 Ibid.
78 Ibid., p. 11.
79 Gray (2006, p. 797).
80 Specifically Gray (1990, 1992, 2006).
81 For example, initiatives by the United Nations' Millennium Ecosystem Assessment (MEA), the UN Environment Programme initiative, and the Economics of Ecosystems and Biodiversity (TEEB).
82 See Atkins and Maroun (2018).
83 See Gaia and Jones (2017), Russell et al. (2017) and Atkins and Maroun (2018).
84 Gray (1992) and Dillard and Reynolds (2008).
85 See also Dillard and Reynolds (2008) and Atkins et al. (2015, 2015b).
86 Laine and Vinnari (2017).
87 Cuckston (2017).
88 Ibid., p. 159.
89 See the full discussion of the derivation of this accounting framework in Atkins and Maroun (2018).
90 This framework has been adapted from the framework published in Atkins and Maroun (2018).
91 GRI (2016).
92 Atkins and Maroun (2018).
93 Maroun and Atkins (2018).
94 BHP Billiton (2015), emphasis added.

95   Atkins et al. (2018).
96   Atkins and Atkins (2016).
97   Gray et al. (1995a) and Russell et al. (2017, p. 1426).
98   Dillard and Reynolds (2008) and Atkins et al. (2015a, 2015b).
99   Cuckston (2017).
100 Gray and Milne (2018).
101 Atkins and Maroun (2018).
102 Ferreira (2017) and Cuckston (2013).
103 Tregidga (2013).
104 Freeman and Groom (2013), Atkins et al. (2015a, 2015b) and Atkins and Maroun (2018).
105 Jones and Solomon (2013), Tregidga (2013), Sullivan and Hannis (2017) and Gray and Milne (2018).
106 Jones (1996, 2003) and Siddiqui (2013).
107 Sullivan and Hannis (2017).
108 Atkins et al. (2015a, 2015b), Cuckston (2018) and Maroun and Atkins (2018).
109 Milne and Gray (2013).
110 Laine and Vinnari (2017).
111 Lanka et al. (2017).
112 Gaia and Jones (2017).
113 Weir (2018).
114 Cuckston (2017).
115 Maroun (2016).
116 See, for example, Melnyk et al. (2003), Alrazi et al. (2015) and Feger and Mermet (2017).
117 See Russell et al. (2017), Adler et al. (2018) and Gray and Milne (2018).
118 See Jones and Solomon (2013).
119 Atkins and Atkins (2016).
120 See Atkins and Maroun (2018).

References

Adams, C. A., Potter, B., Singh, P. J. and York, J. 2016. Exploring the Implications of Integrated Reporting for Social Investment (Disclosures). *The British Accounting Review*, 48(3), 283–296.

Adler, R., Mansi, M. and Pandey, R. 2018. Biodiversity and Threatened Species Reporting by the Top Fortune Global Companies. *Accounting, Auditing and Accountability Journal*, 31(3), 787–825.

Alrazi, B., De Villiers, C. and van Staden, C. J. 2015. A Comprehensive Literature Review on, and the Construction of a Framework for, Environmental Legitimacy, Accountability and Proactivity. *Journal of Cleaner Production*, 102, 44–57.

Atkins, J. F. and Atkins, B. C. (eds). 2016. *The Business of Bees: An Integrated Approach to Bee Decline*. Sheffield: Greenleaf Publishers.

Atkins, J. and Maroun, W. 2014. *South African Institutional Investors' Perceptions of Integrated Reporting*. London: Association of Chartered Certified Accountants.

Atkins, J. and Maroun, W. 2015. Integrated Reporting in South Africa in 2012: Perspectives from South African Institutional Investors. *Meditari Accountancy Research*, 23(2), 197–221.

Atkins, J. and Maroun, W. 2018. Integrated Extinction Accounting and Accountability: Building an Ark. *Accounting, Auditing and Accountability Journal*, 31(3), 750–786.

Atkins, J. F., Solomon, A., Norton, S. and Joseph, N. L. 2015a. The Emergence of Integrated Private Reporting. *Meditari Accountancy Research*, 23(1), 28–61.

Atkins, J., Atkins, B., Thomson, I. and Maroun, W. 2015b. 'Good' News from Nowhere: Imagining Utopian Sustainable Accounting. *Accounting, Auditing and Accountability Journal*, 28(5), 651–670.

Atkins, J. F., Maroun, W., Atkins, B. C. and Barone, E. 2018. From the Big Five to the Big Four? Exploring Extinction Accounting for the Rhinoceros? *Accounting, Auditing and Accountability Journal*, 31(2), 1–31.

BHP Billiton. 2015. *Sustainability Report*. Melbourne: BHP Billiton.

Blumm, M. C., and Kimbrell, G. 2004. Flies, Spiders, Toads, Wolves and the Constitutionality of the Endangered Species Act's Take Provision. *Environmental Law*, 34, 309–361.

BP. 2015. *Annual Report*. London: BP.

CERES. 1990. *The 1990 Ceres Guide to the Valdez Principles*. Boston, MA: Social Investment Forum.

Cuckston, T. 2013. Bringing Tropical Forest Biodiversity Conservation into Financial Accounting Calculation. *Accounting, Auditing and Accountability Journal*, 26(5), 688–714.

Cuckston, T. 2017. Ecology-Centred Accounting for Biodiversity in the Production of a Blanket Bog. *Accounting, Auditing and Accountability Journal*, 30(7), 1537–1567.

Cuckston, T. 2018. Making Extinction Calculable. *Accounting, Auditing and Accountability Journal*, 31(3), 849–874.

De Villiers, C. and Alexander, D. 2014. The Institutionalisation of Corporate Social Responsibility Reporting. *The British Accounting Review*, 46(2), 198–212.

De Villiers, C. and Maroun, W. 2017. *Sustainability Accounting and Integrated Reporting*. Abingdon: Taylor & Francis.

De Villiers, C., Pei-Chi, K. H. and Maroun, W. 2017. Developing a Conceptual Model of Influences around Integrated Reporting, New Insights and Directions for Future Research. *Meditari Accountancy Research*, 25(4), 450–460.

De Villiers, C., Rinaldi, L. and Unerman, J. 2014. Integrated Reporting: Insights, Gaps and an Agenda for Future Research. *Accounting, Auditing and Accountability Journal*, 27(7), 1042–1067.

Dillard, J. and Reynolds, M. 2008. Green Owl and the Corn Maiden. *Accounting, Auditing and Accountability Journal*, 21(4), 556–579.

Eccles, R. and Saltzman, D. 2011. Achieving Sustainability Through Integrated Reporting. *Stanford Social Innovation Review*, Summer. Retrieved from http://202.154.59.182/mfile/files/Jurnal/MIT%202012–2013%20(PDF)/Achieving%20Sustainability%20Through%20Integrated%20Reporting.pdf.

Farneti, F. and Guthrie, J. 2009. Sustainability Reporting by Australian Public Sector Organisations: Why They Report? *Accounting Forum*, 33(1), 89–98.

Feger, C. and Mermet, L. 2017. A Blueprint towards Accounting for the Management of Ecosystems. *Accounting, Auditing and Accountability Journal*, 30(7), 1511–1536.

Ferreira, C. 2017. The Contested Instruments of a New Governance Regime: Accounting for Nature and Building Markets for Biodiversity Offsets. *Accounting, Auditing and Accountability Journal*, 30(7), 1568–1590.

Fifka, M. S. 2013. Corporate Responsibility Reporting and its Determinants in Comparative Perspective – a Review of the Empirical Literature and a Meta-analysis. *Business Strategy and the Environment*, 22(1), 1–35.

Flower, J. 2015. The International Integrated Reporting Council: A Story of Failure. *Critical Perspectives on Accounting*, 27, 1–17.

Freeman, M. C. and Groom, B. 2013. Biodiversity Valuation and the Discount Rate Problem. *Accounting, Auditing and Accountability Journal*, 26(5), 715–745.

Gaia, S. and Jones, M. J. 2017. UK Local Councils Reporting of Biodiversity Values: A Stakeholder Perspective. *Accounting, Auditing and Accountability Journal*, 30(7), 1614–1638.

Gallhofer, S. and Haslam, J. 1996. Accounting/Art and the Emancipatory Project: Some Reflections. *Accounting, Auditing and Accountability Journal*, 9(5), 23–44.

Gallhofer, S. and Haslam, J. 1997. Beyond Accounting: The Possibilities of Accounting and 'Critical' Accounting Research. *Critical Perspectives on Accounting*, 8(1/2), 71–95.

Gallhofer, S. and Haslam, J. 2003. *Accounting and Emancipation: Some Critical Interventions.* New York: Routledge.

Gallhofer, S. and Haslam, J. 2011. Emancipation, the Spiritual and Accounting. *Critical Perspectives on Accounting*, 22(5), 500–9.

Gallhofer, S. and Haslam, J. 2017. Some Reflections on the Construct of Emancipatory Accounting: Shifting Meaning and the Possibilities of a New Pragmatism. *Critical Perspectives on Accounting*, in press.

Gallhofer, S., Haslam, J. and Yonekura, A. 2013. Further Critical Reflections on a Contribution to the Methodological Issues Debate in Accounting. *Critical Perspectives on Accounting*, 24(3), 191–206.

Gallhofer, S., Haslam, J. and Yonekura, A. 2015. Accounting as Differentiated Universal for Emancipatory Praxis: Accounting Delineation and Mobilization for Emancipation(s) Recognising Democracy and Difference. *Accounting, Auditing and Accountability Journal*, 28(5), 846–874.

Glasser, H. (ed). 2005. *The Selected Works of Arne Naess*, Volumes 1–10. Berlin: Springer.

Gray, R. H. 1990. The Accountant's Task as a Friend to the Earth: How Can the Profession Contribute to the Way in Which Business Will Operate in the Green 1990s. *Accountancy*, June, 65–69.

Gray, R. 1992. Accounting and Environmentalism: A Exploration of the Challenge of Gently Accounting for Accountability, Transparency and Sustainability. *Accounting, Organizations and Society*, 17(5), 399–425.

Gray, R. 2006. Social, Environmental and Sustainability Reporting and Organisational Value Creation? Whose Value? Whose Creation? *Accounting, Auditing and Accountability Journal*, 19(6), 793–819.

Gray, R. 2010. Is Accounting for Sustainability Actually Accounting for Sustainability . . . and How Would We Know? An Exploration of Narratives of Organisations and the Planet. *Accounting, Organizations and Society*, 35(1), 47–62.

Gray, R. and Milne, M. J. 2018. Perhaps the Dodo Should Have Accounted for Human Beings? Accounts of Humanity and (its) Extinction. *Accounting, Auditing and Accountability Journal*, 31(3), 826–848.

Gray, S. J., Radebaugh, L. H. and Roberts, C. B. 1990. International Perceptions of Cost Constraints on Voluntary Information Disclosure: A Comparative Study of U.K. and U.S. Multinationals. *Journal of International Business Studies*, 21(4), 597–622.

Gray, R., Kouhy, R. and Lavers, S. 1995a. Corporate Social and Environmental Reporting: A Review of the Literature and a Longitudinal Study of UK Disclosure. *Accounting, Auditing and Accountability Journal*, 8(2), 47–77.

Gray, R., Walters, D., Bebbington, J. and Thompson, I. 1995b. The Greening of Enterprise: An Exploration of the (Non)Role of Environmental Accounting and Environmental Accountants in Organizational Change. *Critical Perspectives on Accounting*, 6(3), 211–239.

GRI. 2015. The GRI's History. Retrieved from www.globalreporting.org/informa tion/about-gri/gri-history/Pages/GRI's%20history.aspx (accessed 1 August 2015).

GRI. 2016. Consolidated Set of GRI Sustainability Reporting Standards (2016). Retrieved from www.globalreporting.org/standards/gri-standards-download-center /?g=ae2e23b8–4958–455c-a9df-ac372d6ed9a8.

Guthrie, J. and Parker, L. D. 1989. Corporate Social Reporting: A Rebuttal of Legitimacy Theory. *Accounting and Business Research*, 19(76), 343–352.

Guthrie, J., Manes-Rossi, F. and Orelli Rebecca, L. 2017. Integrated Reporting and Integrated Thinking in Italian Public Sector Organisations. *Meditari Accountancy Research*, 25(4), 553–573.

Hahn, R. and Kühnen, M. 2013. Determinants of Sustainability Reporting: A Review of Results, Trends, Theory, and Opportunities in an Expanding Field of Research. *Journal of Cleaner Production*, 59(Supplement C), 5–21.

Hawken, P., Lovins, A. and Lovins, L. H. 1999. *Natural Capitalism: Creating the Next Industrial Revolution*. Boston, MA: Little, Brown and Company.

HRH Prince Philip. 1978. *The Environmental Revolution: Speeches on Conservation, 1962–1977*, Beekman Books, London.

Hughen, L., Lulseged, A. and Upton, D. 2014. Improving Stakeholder Value through Sustainability and Integrated Reporting. *CPA Journal*, 84(3), 57–61.

IIRC. 2013. *The International Framework: Integrated Reporting*. Retrieved from www. theiirc.org/wp-content/uploads/2013/12/13–12–08-THE-INTERNATIONAL-IR-FRAMEWORK–2–1.pdf (accessed 1 October 2013).

IRCSA. 2011. Framework for Integrated Reporting and the Integrated Report. Integrated Reporting Committee of South Africa. Retrieved from www.sustaina bilitysa.org (accessed 5 June 2012).

Jones, M. J. 1996. Accounting for Biodiversity: A Pilot Study. *The British Accounting Review*, 28(4), 281–303.

Jones, M. J. 2003. Accounting for Biodiversity: Operationalising Environmental Accounting. *Accounting, Auditing and Accountability Journal*, 16(5), 762–789.

Jones, M. J. and Solomon, J. F. 2013. Problematising Accounting for Biodiversity. *Accounting, Auditing and Accountability Journal*, 26(5), 668–687.

Junior, R. M., Best, P. J. and Cotter, J. 2014. Sustainability Reporting and Assurance: A Historical Analysis on a World-Wide Phenomenon. *Journal of Business Ethics*, 120(1), 1–11.

Khlif, H., Hussainey, K. and Achek, I. 2015. The Effect of National Culture on the Association between Profitability and Corporate Social and Environmental Disclosure: A Meta-analysis. *Meditari Accountancy Research*, 23(3), 296–321.

King, M. with Atkins, J. 2016. *The Chief Value Officer: Accountants Can Save the Planet*. Abingdon: Routledge.

KPMG. 2012. *Carrots and Sticks: Promoting Transparency and Sustainability: An Update on Trends in Voluntary and Mandatory Approaches to Sustainability Reporting*. Retrieved from www.globalreporting.org/resourcelibrary/Carrots-And-Sticks-Promoting-Transparency-And-Sustainability.pdf (accessed 30 June 2013).

KPMG. 2015. *Currents of Change: The KPMG Survey of Corporate Responsibility Reporting 2015*. Retrieved from https://assets.kpmg.com/content/dam/kpmg/pdf/2016/02/kpmg-international-survey-of-corporate-responsibility-reporting–2015.pdf (accessed 11 December 2016).

KPMG. 2016. *Carrots and Sticks: Global Trends in Sustainability Reporting Regulation and Policy*. Retrieved from https://assets.kpmg.com/content/dam/kpmg/pdf/2016/05/carrots-and-sticks-may–2016.pdf (accessed 30 June 2017).

KPMG. 2017. *The Road Ahead: The KPMG Survey of Corporate Responsibility Reporting 2017*. Retrieved from https://assets.kpmg.com/content/dam/kpmg/xx/pdf/2017/10/kpmg-survey-of-corporate-responsibility-reporting–2017.pdf (accessed 20 November 2017).

Laine, M. and Vinnari, E. 2017. The Transformative Potential of Counter Accounts: A Case Study of Animal Rights Activism. *Accounting, Auditing and Accountability Journal*, 30(7), 1481–1510.

Lanka, S. V., Khadaroo, I. and Böhm, S. 2017. Agroecology Accounting: Biodiversity and Sustainable Livelihoods from the Margins. *Accounting, Auditing and Accountability Journal*, 30(7), 1592–1613.

Lattwak, E. 1998. *Turbo-Capitalism: Winners and Losers in the Global Economy*. London: Weidenfeld & Nicholson.

Lewis, N. R., Parker, L. D. and Sutcliffe, P. 1984. Financial Reporting to Employees: the Pattern of Development 1919 to 1979. *Accounting, Organizations and Society*, 9(3–4), 275–289.

Maroun, W. 2016. No Bees in Their Bonnet: On the Absence of Bee Reporting by South African Listed Companies. In K. Atkins and B. Atkins (eds), *The Business of Bees: An Integrated Approach to Bee Decline and Corporate Responsibility*. Sheffield: Greenleaf Publishers.

Maroun, W. and Atkins, J. 2018. The Emancipatory Potential of Extinction Accounting: Exploring Current Practice in Integrated Reports. *Accounting Forum*, in press.

McNally, M.-A., Cerbone, D. and Maroun, W. 2017. Exploring the Challenges of Preparing an Integrated Report. *Meditari Accountancy Research*, 25(4), 481–504.

Melnyk, S. A., Sroufe, R. P. and Calantone, R. 2003. Assessing the Impact of Environmental Management Systems on Corporate and Environmental Performance. *Journal of Operations Management*, 21(3), 329–351.

Milne, M. and Gray, R. 2013. W(h)ither Ecology? The Triple Bottom Line, the Global Reporting Initiative, and Corporate Sustainability Reporting. *Journal of Business Ethics*, 118(1), 13–29.

Milne, M., Tregidga, H. and Walton, S. 2009. Words Not Actions! The Ideological Role of Sustainable Development Reporting. *Accounting, Auditing and Accountability Journal*, 22(8), 1211–1257.

Mock, T. J., Rao, S. S. and Srivastava, R. P. 2013. The Development of Worldwide Sustainability Reporting Assurance. *Australian Accounting Review*, 23(4), 280–294.

Orlitzky, M., Schmidt, F. L. and Rynes, S. L. 2003. Corporate Social and Financial Performance: A Meta-Analysis. *Organization Studies*, 24(3), 403–441.

Parker, L. D. 2005. Social and Environmental Accountability Research: A View from the Commentary Box. *Accounting, Auditing and Accountability Journal*, 18(6), 842–860.

Pettinger, T. 2017. Types of Capitalism. Retrieved from www.economicshelp.org/blog/4896/economics/types-of-capitalism.

Russell, S., Milne, M. J. and Dey, C. 2017. Accounts of Nature and the Nature of Accounts: Critical Reflections on Environmental Accounting and Propositions for Ecologically Informed Accounting. *Accounting, Auditing and Accountability Journal*, 30(7), 1426–1458.

Siddiqui, J. 2013. Mainstreaming Biodiversity Accounting: Potential Implications for a Developing Economy. *Accounting, Auditing and Accountability Journal*, 26(5), 779–805.

Smith, J. E. 1970. *'Torrey Canyon' Pollution and Marine Life: A Report by the Plymouth Laboratory of the Marine Biological Association of the United Kingdom*. Cambridge: Cambridge University Press.

Solomon, J. and Maroun, W. 2012. *Integrated Reporting: The New Face of Social, Ethical and Environmental Reporting in South Africa?* London: Association of Chartered Certified Accountants.

Solomon, J. F. and Thomson, I. 2009. 'Satanic Mills? An Illustration of Victorian External Environmental Accounting?' *Accounting Forum*, 33, 74–87.

Sullivan, S. and Hannis, M. 2017. 'Mathematics Maybe, But Not Money': On Balance Sheets, Numbers and Nature in Ecological Accounting. *Accounting, Auditing and Accountability Journal*, 30(7), 1459–1480.

Thomson, I. 2015. 'But Does Sustainability Need Capitalism or an Integrated Report' A Commentary on 'The International Integrated Reporting Council: A Story of Failure' by Flower, J. *Critical Perspectives on Accounting*, 27, 18–22.

Tinker, T. (ed.). 1984. *Social Accounting for Corporations: Private Enterprise Versus the Public Interest*. New York: Markus Wiener.

Tinker, T. 1985. *Paper Prophets: A Social Critique of Accounting*. London: Holt, Rinehart & Winston.

Tregidga, H. 2013. Biodiversity Offsetting: Problematisation of an Emerging governance regime. *Accounting, Auditing and Accountability Journal*, 26(5), 806–832.

Tregidga, H., Milne, M. and Kearins, K. 2014. (Re)presenting 'Sustainable Organizations'. *Accounting, Organizations and Society*, 39(6), 477–494.

Van Dieren, W. and Hummelinck, M. G. W. 1979. *Nature's Price: The Economics of Mother Earth*. London: Marion Boyars.

Van Liempd, D. and Busch, J. 2013. Biodiversity Reporting In Denmark. *Accounting Auditing and Accountability Journal*, 26(5), 833–872.

Weir, K. 2018. The Purposes, Promises and Compromises of Extinction Accounting in the UK Public Sector. *Accounting, Auditing and Accountability Journal*, 31(3), 875–899.

Wilson, E. O. 1989. *The Diversity of Life*. London: Penguin.

Zhou, S., Simnett, R. and Green, W. 2017. Does Integrated Reporting Matter to the Capital Market? *Abacus*, 53(1), 94–132.

Part II

Philosophical, moral, literary, business and legal perspectives on extinction

3 A deep ecology perspective on extinction

Jack Christian

It is said that the world is in the throes of a sixth mass extinction. Uncountable numbers of species are being lost at a rate of almost one a day.[1] Certainly animal populations are in decline, the WWF report a 52% decrease in over 10,000 animal populations they have monitored for 40 years.[2] Iconic individual species such as the white rhinoceros[3] are very likely to vanish from existence in the near future unless action is taken to protect or conserve them.

Of course many species have already vanished, such as the great auk[4] and the passenger pigeon,[5] and the evidence points to one cause – humankind. As the human population has expanded and spread across the globe we have taken plants and animals with us, often to the detriment of those species already living in the areas we colonise. Further, we have exploited the indigenous species, often for food, hunting them to extinction. Finally, and perhaps most significantly, we reduce the land and resources available to the other life forms we share the planet with, to the point where these life forms can no longer exist.

The WWF attributes the following causes to the decline in the animal populations it surveys:[6]

1 Exploitation: 37%.
2 Habitat degradation/change: 31.4%.
3 Habitat loss: 13.4%.
4 Climate change: 7.1%.
5 Invasive species/genes: 5.1%.
6 Pollution: 4%.
7 Disease: 2%.

In this chapter I will focus primarily on humankind's impact on habitat as the major threat to other life forms, in particular I will focus on agriculture. Humanity has to feed itself, and with a population that has more than doubled in the last 60 years and is expected to grow by at least another 25% to 9 billion people by the middle of the this century,[7] it is inevitable that more terrestrial and oceanic resources will be required to provide food. Can this be done without reducing further the life forms we share our planet with?

In trying to answer this question I have explored agricultural activity in the UK. How does one of the largest economies in the world farm? What thought does it pay to those other life forms we share the planet with? Surely in a land of plenty we have room to spare for these Others? My explorations have led me to Government policy documents, to the conservation activities of the Royal Society for the Protection of Birds (RSPB), the UK Wildlife Trusts and others, and to conservation incentives and schemes aimed at farmers such as the Linking Environment and Farming (LEAF) accreditation scheme. I have discussed these policies, activities and schemes with three individuals; a farmer working for the RSPB, a planning officer from one of the larger Wildlife Trusts, and a manager at an agricultural accreditation scheme.

What follows is an imaginary conversation between various actors representing the conservation, farming, and policy-making communities. This dialogue both summarises the different views and highlights the tensions between them. It also includes the views of a hiker who represents the deep ecology movement. The origins, philosophy and relevance of this movement will become apparent during the dialogue. Summaries of the movement can of course be found in many business textbooks;[8] however; these do not explain what it feels like to be a deep green. This chapter attempts to fill that gap.

When the conversation ends the hiker reflects on what he has heard and asks himself what the future might hold and what he should do. To this end he draws on three Kantian questions posed by Horkheimer[9] and Mouffe's conception of agonistic democracy.[10]

The dialogue begins with a description of how the hiker feels as he makes his way across the countryside.

> He breasted the hill and looked across the plain to the sea. At moments like this his being expanded and he felt eternal. He was part of all this and more. There was no Cartesian dualism, he was of the land and would return to the land. Mind and body are one and while neither are eternal in themselves, in Nature they are. He could reach the sea if he chose, or he could reach the fallen tree and rest. The only difference was time and time is eternity, joining the future to the past. Only humans slice it up and try to rush through it; failing to feel the now, and the interconnectedness of all things.
>
> He heard, felt, smelt, touched and tasted the wind. A low whoosh as the branches on the trees swayed and the cold rippled across the skin on his face, the farmers had been feeding the fields and he tasted a deep, rich fruitiness as he breathed in. Jackdaws argued and seagulls scolded in the fields, a flock of finches spiralled through the air. Brothers and sisters every one. He felt pleased they were feasting.
>
> The skull of a dead, half-eaten fox grinned at him by the roadside. Death arrives in many ways but it is inevitable, the old must eventually give way to the new. Every spring life begins anew on our planet and with it comes as yet unseen wonders each of which adds to the rich diversity

that is the hallmark of life. He rejoiced in that thought even as he felt sadness at the blind destruction currently striking at that same diversity.

"Penny for 'em."

"Eh, what?" The hiker broke out of his reverie.

"Penny for your thoughts," laughed an elderly figure wearing a green gilet over a chequered shirt and grey slacks tucked into wellington boots.

"I was just celebrating all this beauty we are part of," replied the hiker "and ruing the way in which we are treating it."

"Well I'm a farmer," responded the elderly chap, "and I remember when these fields were devoted to pasture. Broke my father's heart to plough 'em up but, well, the government wanted food self-sufficiency and the money was in crops."

"The problem with crops is they become monocultures and destroy biodiversity. It's a tragedy. The way we use land, and animals for that matter, leaves less and less space for the other life forms we share the planet with and is driving, has driven, many of them to extinction," replied the hiker.

"And that matters to you does it?" asked the farmer.

"It certainly does," answered the hiker. "I'm a real believer in a philosophy, ecosophy even, developed by Arne Naess.[11] He termed it deep ecology and it calls for the recognition of the inter-connectedness and equality of all life forms. He referred to the relational total field image and biospherical egalitarianism. He also suggested we need to protect biodiversity."

"Vegetarian was he?" asked the farmer with a hint of a grin.

"No," responded the hiker, noting the grin and smiling back. "He recognised the complexity involved in living by his ecosophy, the difficulties involved in interpreting it,[12] but in truth that has not stopped it being criticised. Further he himself was party to some significant adjustments to his original principles – in 1984 he spent some time with a guy called George Sessions and the two principles I highlighted above were somewhat watered down.[13] Personally I think he was responding to a different culture, a different understanding of nature, that had developed in the USA over the previous century or so. I am talking about the work of Thoreau, Muir, Leopold, Snyder and others."[14]

"You know some of us farmers care about this biodiversity thing you refer to," said the farmer, "we call it nature and we know how important she is. The way I see it my crops wouldn't grow without the worms, fungi and other stuff in the soil; they wouldn't pollinate without the bees and other insects and they would succumb to disease if I didn't let the ground rest and recuperate from time to time with a covering of clover or some such."

The hiker raised his eyebrows.

"Oh yes," continued the farmer, "many of us know that the land isn't a machine. It's a gift and we need to look after it, sustain it. My missus says that if we do that there will be plenty for everyone, and that includes the birds, the rabbits and the deer."

"I can't tell you how much that brightens my world," replied the hiker. "I have read of such possibilities. How with careful stewardship land can be set aside for nature and yields not suffer[15] and even how the whole country could be fed from our own fields."[16]

"I'm not so sure about that," responded the farmer, "it sounds a bit ambitious. I think we would need some major shifts in public attitude towards food and the price of it to achieve that. Anyway I am turning off here, I am surveying the footpaths on my land – gives me an excuse for a walk – just making sure they are passable."

"I didn't know farmers did that sort of thing either," said the hiker.

"It's all part of the LEAF[17] accreditation scheme," the farmer informed him. "It's nice to have accreditation, it helps with marketing, but more importantly it offers guidance on how to look after your land to the benefit of all stakeholders, humans and other creatures too."

"A ploughman's lunch and a pint of bitter shandy," requested the hiker, who had reached a public house and decided to stop for a bit of lunch.

While waiting for his meal he took out his mobile phone and googled LEAF. He discovered the Linking Environment and Farming (LEAF) organisation was founded in 1991. It described itself as 'the go-to organisation for the delivery of more sustainable food and farming' whose priorities include increasing the adoption of more sustainable farming practices; leading a collaborative approach within the industry for better public engagement among consumers; and positively influencing consumer attitudes towards, and knowledge of food, farming and the environment. Further it sought to achieve this through developing and promoting integrated farm management. This had three core pillars:

1   facilitating knowledge generation and exchange among farmers and researchers;
2   developing market opportunities; and
3   engaging the public in sustainable food and farming.

Its vision, it said, is "a world that is farming, eating and living sustainably".[18]

Not far away a conversation was under way. Two smartly dressed men were discussing economics; one apparently a large-scale farmer, the other some sort of governmental policy maker.

"We need to get two things sorted ASAP," said the farmer, "the BPS[19] and this overemphasis on the precautionary principle."[20]

"Let's look at the economics first," said the policy maker. "Whilst it seems the minister is prepared to keep up current subsidies post-Brexit[21] and that, he wants a move away from them in the longer term. This fellow Helm[22] is putting together some good arguments and outfits like the National Trust and the RSPB are also talking about market initiatives and the like."[23]

"The RSPB have got a nerve," replied the farmer, "even under the BPS we look after the various threatened environments leaving fallow land, buffer strips, field margins, green cover and all sorts. We even weed by hand in some areas. We rotate crops, work to reduce soil erosion and most painful of all we have to record all this."

"Some would say that is just good farming," suggested the policy maker a little pointedly.

Ignoring him the farmer went on, "Then there is the Countryside Stewardship[24] scheme. We prioritise all sorts of stuff from woodland management and protecting biodiversity, through looking after water quality and flood management, to protecting the historic environment and facilitating educational access. I'm a farmer for goodness sake but I employ an environmental team these days."

"I know, you have done some great things, in both your lowland meadows and on the sand dunes where you handed over that land to complete the reserve," responded the policy maker. "I am sure the lapwings and the natterjack toads appreciate it."

The farmer smiled, unoffended. "It just makes me cross when we are not appreciated."

"Well I think the RSPB are on your side as far as the grants are concerned, they suggest we 'support farmers and fishermen to look after the natural resources'[25]," noted the policy maker. "It's Helm who isn't. He prefers to call grants subsidies and wants them done away with. He also seems to prefer regulation and internalising external costs. The current system is the wrong way round, 'farmers are paid to do less environmental damage, subsidised not taxed'[26] he says."

"Cheeky so-and-so," exploded the farmer. "We are the stewards of the land."

"He rejects that too," added the policy maker. "He describes agriculture as 'the history of fighting back nature'[27] reducing and eliminating competitors to crops and herds."

"In essence," he continued, "he argues that farmers should be made to clean up their damage to the land through the like of fertilisers, pesticides and herbicides and pay taxes or penalties if they don't. Further it should not be up to them to decide on how our countryside should be managed. He sees the countryside as a public good and hence the public should prioritise its use. He appears to think that any public money should be channelled through public institutions such as the National Trust for example."

"I am mightily unimpressed by that," grunted the farmer.

"It almost echoes some of the thoughts coming out of the UN," continued the policy maker. "A recent report from UNEP[28] talks about identifying land potential along the lines of productivity, risks and biodiversity; and making land use plans backed up by taxes and incentives. They note how inappropriate use is leading to soil losses far in excess of soil creation. A rather sad but interesting figure[29] shows soil loss in the UK to be particularly bad."

"Still unimpressed," muttered the farmer rather more defensively.

"The RSPB of course want the grant systems to continue," went on the policy maker, "which puts them on your side in one sense. However they certainly want relevant regulations and legislation more strictly enforced.[30] They are pushing for more power for the Environment Agency, something we are struggling with as we are trying to reduce costs. They are also calling on the government to somehow increase consumer awareness around the cost of food production. They want waste reduced which is good but they somehow envisage a supposedly fairer pricing system that will pay farmers to manage the land more sustainably."[31]

"Oh yes, I am back on their side with that one," concluded the farmer.

In another corner of the public house another conversation was taking place. An accountant had applied for a job with an environmental conservation society and was being interviewed by a wildlife conservation expert.

"Accounting for Biodiversity? That's a new one on me," said the Conservationist.

"It is pretty new," responded the accountant, "The first major book I am aware of was edited by Mike Jones,[32] with sections on theory, practical applications and alternative views. That said it was predated by a special edition of the *Accounting, Auditing and Accountability Journal* edited by Jones and Jill Solomon,[33] and there were occasional earlier papers such as Accounting for the Environment again by Jones.[34] As a subject it lies within Environmental Accounting which some commentators date back to the 1980s."[35]

"What sort of subject matter is it concerned with?" asked the conservationist.

"Jones and Solomon explore what the term biodiversity actually means and ponder whether it somehow hides, for example, "the urgency of species extinction" as an issue.[36] They offer terms such as 'wildlife' or 'life on earth' as more meaningful alternatives," replied the accountant. "Three of the articles in the paper offer economic perspectives which tend to see nature in all her forms as a resource.[37] One of the authors talks about offsetting, fearing the 'quantification' of nature as a means rationalising the destruction of biodiversity,[38] another paper describes the lack of interest in biodiversity shown by business,[39] and the last follows up the work of Jones, taking an inventory approach to accounting for nature."[40]

"And the book?" asked the conservationist.

"Well the book itself is a collection of views. Jones himself talks of stewardship as the basis for accounting for biodiversity and offers two approaches," continued the accountant almost seamlessly. "There are perhaps three ecocentric approaches[41] including a specifically deep ecology approach. By way of a contrast two of the authors[42] take an anthropocentric, resource based view of biodiversity and this is reflected in their suggested accountings. In the penultimate chapter Atkins and Thomson[43] look at art forms as a means of accounting for nature. Two other chapters[44] look at accreditation schemes as accounting mechanisms."

"This is interesting," commented the conservationist. "Has anything been said more recently?"

"Not very much really," said the accountant somewhat despondently. "There are special editions of *Critical Perspectives on Accounting* and *Accounting, Auditing and Accountability Journal* due out in the next year or so, I believe. Otherwise the work has been focused on what is now referred to as natural capital,[45] which I feel will work to the detriment of nature. Crompton and Kasser[46] explained the psychology behind why this might be some time ago. There is also a good critical piece by Sullivan,[47] more about offsetting but which also critiques anthropocentric views in general."

Back nearer the bar the farmer had just begun, "As I said, we have got to tackle this over emphasis on the precautionary principle . . ."

The conservationist must have heard him and she immediately turned round to see who was talking. There was only the hiker, farmer and the policy maker in the place (apart from herself and the accountant) and she directed her comment towards the well-dressed pair at the table. "Whoa, wait a minute, sorry to interrupt, but the precautionary principle is very important to me[48] and I couldn't help but overhear your reference to it. Are you referring to our impact on the environment?"

The farmer was visibly taken aback but the policy maker looked at the conservationist and asked, "Yes, but why is it so important to you?"

"I work in wildlife conservation," replied the conservationist, "and I suppose I take a somewhat contrary view to that your colleague just intimated. Sorry to jump into your conversation, I probably have no right, but it was pure reaction, I do feel deeply."

The farmer, having recovered his poise, said, "As I do, but why is it so with you?"

"I am a conservationist," was the response, "and I do this job because I love nature. Over the years I have watched the decline in many of our bird and insect species, and indeed in our plant species. These are well documented in the 2016 State of Nature report[49] with declines in the population of 56% of UK species and 15% of recorded species threatened with or already extinct. The most likely causes are known and include, among others, overuse of pesticides, herbicides and fertilisers. I firmly believe in withholding the use of various brands and chemicals unless it can be shown they are not causing harm."

"Surely it is up to you conservationists to show that they are causing harm in the first place," responded the farmer.

"I think it is more a case of showing they might be causing harm rather than actually causing harm. That's why it is precautionary," said the conservationist, "and we do that."

"I'm not so sure," came back the farmer once more. "You criticise everything from glyphosate to neonicotinoids with precious little direct, that is scientific, evidence to back up your claims."

"If by scientific evidence you want proof of some form of cause and effect then I would have to say that isn't possible, there are too many variables ranging from individual plant or creature resistance to climatic variation," explained the conservationist, "but we have long term correlations between changes in agricultural practice and declining biodiversity. Rachel Carson[50] brought that to our attention nearly 60 years ago."

"Correlation simply isn't good enough," argued the farmer, "the relationship might just as easily be due to some other factor."

"I think we all know that outside the purely physical sciences we have to rely on probability and statistics; and that is why we have to take a precautionary approach," retorted the conservationist.

"Give me some examples," interrupted the policy maker in an emollient tone.

"Well obviously herbicides and pesticides are designed to eliminate certain plants and creatures, primarily insects, and will therefore reduce the abundance of, if not wipe out, these particular life forms. Beyond that though there are the unintended consequences. The loss of these plants and creatures means there is less food and other resources for other, non-targeted species. As farming has intensified, particularly we since 1970, we have seen a 54% decline in farmland bird populations generally with species such as the turtle dove almost wiped out – numbers declining by 91% since 1995. 12 out 26 species of farmland breeding birds are now red listed. Also since 1970 we have seen a 41% decline in farmland butterfly populations,"[51] replied the conservationist.

"The main causes are generally held out as (1) production driven farm practices, (2) intensification of grazing, (3) loss of habitat, (4) increased fertiliser usage and, of relevance here (5) increased use of pesticides and herbicides,"[52] she continued.

"So there are other causes besides pesticides and herbicides?" interjected the policy maker.

"Absolutely," responded the conservationist. "The use of phosphate and nitrogen fertilisers enriches soils but it is often inadvertently spread onto other fields and/or leaks into water courses. The result is that plants that can survive in poorer soils lose out to those that prefer the enriched soils and basically die out. Worse effected water can get covered with algae blooms that take the oxygen out of the water suffocating other creatures that might have lived there."

"In fact in global terms we are now producing more nitrogen based fertilisers than the whole of nature's natural processes and this is threatening life all over the planet,"[53] she continued.

"I have a feeling you have more to say," said the policy maker smiling wryly.

"Oh yes," replied the conservationist. "I could talk about the indiscriminate use of anti-biotics on farm animals, purportedly to protect them against disease, which has led to faeces that will not rot and carcasses that cannot be consumed leading to the spread of diseases and the evolution of super-bugs. I could point to the black grass that has evolved and now infests many of the cereal fields in our country. Nature is clever, she evolves and finds ways to defeat our herbicides and pesticides. These are not the answer to our food supply problems."

"So what is?" asked the farmer pointedly.

"Well first I would start to look at the way we have bred our food plants," said the conservationist. "We have taken wild stock and bred it so as to maximise yield, but in order to achieve this yield we have removed its natural protections strengths and protections so now it needs our fertilisers and herbicides to protect it. And do you know that in 146 countries in the world a meagre 100 species of crops provide 90% of the food. Globally we are putting nearly all our eggs in one relatively small basket.

"If we work with nature rather than against her we might abrogate the need for chemicals and poisons – and they get everywhere, 175 agrichemicals have been found in beeswax for example."[54]

"These are very noble sentiments," said the farmer, "but they will not enable the feeding of an increasing global population. Demand for food is set to increase by 70% by 2050."[55]

"I am not so sure," replied the conservationist, "a recent report suggests that with suitable wildlife friendly farming techniques including wider field margins to create pollen and nectar habitats and in-field grass banks to increase beneficial predatory insects could well increase yields and profits.[56] An older paper also shows how even a country as populated as the United Kingdom could be self-sufficient in food."[57]

"I can understand the value of wider field margins for insect pollinated crops," said the farmer, "but they wouldn't do much for my wind pollinated cereals. I am also sceptical that self-sufficiency is possible without fertilisers."

"Well I guess that is fair comment," replied the conservationist, "upgrading trials nationwide is something we would all have to work on."

"And only the other day I was talking to someone about that," said the policy maker. I was at a conference discussing soil protection primarily but I met somebody from an outfit called LEAF who talked about soil management, then crop health and protection, pollution control[58] and – particularly relevant at this juncture – facilitating knowledge generation and exchange."[59]

The hiker was suddenly all ears; LEAF again, twice within the hour.

"Heard of them," said the farmer, "they are fairly well known in the horticultural sector. What took you to the soil conference?"

"As we discussed earlier soil degradation is becoming a big issue. I believe there is a spot in Cambridgeshire somewhere where we have lost 4 metres of soil in the last 150 years,"[60] replied the policy maker. "Anyway this lady from LEAF was explaining their Integrated Farm Management accreditation scheme. It has nine sections covering things like soil management, crop protection, pollution control, nature conservation and even community engagement. Indeed all the things we have been talking about."

"I'm not too sure about community engagement," said the farmer, "but we have been looking at it from a marketing point of view. We are wondering if the LEAF Marque will open up any new markets."

"I think you need to take a more strategic view on community engagement," interjected the conservationist. "If you engage people and give them a better understanding of the countryside and the role of farming you might get them to understand the need for fairer prices and local sourcing for example."[61]

"An interesting thought," mused the policy maker. "But back to the idea of upgrading trials. The lady from LEAF also talked about knowledge generation and exchange. About farmers trialling ideas to find out what is best for their particular farm and then sharing the results with other farmers. A sort of Kaizen[62] approach. LEAF is part of the Sustainable Intensification Platform (SIP), which sounded a particularly good idea."

"SIP is a good idea," suggested the conservationist, "DEFRA[63] and the Welsh Government are looking at how farming and conservation can work together on landscape scales which is vitally important."

"Mmm, not really up on that one," said the farmer, "Wales is a long way from my cereal fields. But no one could criticise the idea of sharing knowledge that's for sure."

"There is an international standard on sustainable agriculture," pointed out the accountant.

The others turned to face her, a little surprised by her contribution.

"There is an outfit based in Mexico I think, called the Sustainable Agricultural Network and they issue a standard, voluntary obviously. I am interested in something called Integrated Reporting and whilst investigating it I came across this standard. I was particularly interested in Stakeholder Engagement and their network includes producers, workers organisations, traders, NGOs and civil society organisations, governments, retailers, academia and scientific research institutions."[64]

"Stakeholder engagement, knowledge sharing, better informed customers, there's something in all this," said the policy maker.

"But don't forget the precautionary principle," added the conservationist, "and we still need to make space for nature."

"Ah yes, the Lawton Report,"[65] responded the policy maker.

"Too much fluff," added the farmer, "and not enough substance. That analogy with the cathedral for example; he is appealing to emotions rather than acknowledging the facts, we need the countryside for food."

"I think it is a fair analogy," responded the conservationist. "In the last 100 years we have lost 11% of our prime conservation sites and all but destroyed another 32%. Imagine, as Lawton suggests, the outrage, the sense of loss, had we destroyed 12 of our 27 ancient cathedrals in that time."[66]

"I suspect there is limited interest in either," returned the farmer. "I still say the countryside is for farming, nature is fine as long as it doesn't get in the way."

"Farming is set in nature, it can't push nature out of the way, it has to exist within the ecosystems around it. Fighting them is simply vexatious and ultimately self-defeating," replied the conservationist.

"Vexatious maybe, but I think we are winning," the farmer retorted.

"What do you mean by ecosystems?" asked the policy maker.

"Lawton explains the importance of the natural environment in non-emotive, instrumental terms by listing numerous benefits that nature provides," explained the conservationist. "These include soil formation, water and nutrient cycling and primary production by harnessing the energy of the sun. He also mentions carbon retention, water filtration and flood control."[67]

"Properly martialled they sound like they could be sensible arguments," noted the policy maker.

"And there are the psychological benefits," added the accountant.

The farmer raised his eyebrows.

"I suspect our colleague here is referring to the more emotional and aesthetic arguments that Lawton puts forward," suggested the policy maker. "He talks of public access, the enjoyment of landscapes and cultural heritage, and the existence of other creatures that enrich our lives."[68]

"Like I said minority pursuits, and for the well off at that," added the farmer.

The hiker could not resist, "Visiting the countryside is far from a minority pursuit, and it is not just for the rich. It was the working class boys of Manchester and Sheffield who opened the thought processes that led to the National Parks. They found their freedom on the moors and crags of the Dark Peak and they still do today. And now they take their families too."

The conservationist glanced up at him before adding, "And they bring money and jobs to the countryside too. Today they can afford farmhouse teas, and bed and breakfast sometimes too."

"True, by and large it's a wealthier world we live in today," acknowledged the hiker.

"The hikers bring nothing to my cereal fields except litter and sometimes worse," replied the farmer. "Oh and extra work and costs as I tidy hedgerows and clear footpaths."

"It makes me sad you see it that way," responded the hiker. "I met a farmer earlier who took pleasure in maintaining his footpaths and sharing his space. With people and his fellow creatures he said."

"That last statement makes me happy," said the conservationist. "We need to care for our wildlife, for its own sake and because it is an integral part of the ecosystems that service our food production and other needs."

"And what does that involve?" asked the policy maker.

"Habitat protection and habitat improvement," answered the conservationist unequivocally.

"More space then?" asked the policy maker.

"Absolutely," responded the conservationist, "the government's own reports say that 40% of priority habitats and ecosystem services are declining, and as a result 30% of priority species are also declining."[69]

"So we are losing species?" queried the policy maker.

"Yes," responded the conservationist urgently. "At a recent RSPB conference[70] there were papers on capercaillies, black grouse, stone curlews, turtle doves, black tailed godwits, roseate terns, hawfinches and twite; and even one on the pine marten. We need to look after these species."

"And habitats?" asked the policy maker.

"Well habitat is an issue in all those cases but there were a couple of more general papers on livestock treatments and neonicotinoid seed treatments and their impact," replied the conservationist.

"Here we go, blame the farmer," said the farmer.

"Well farming does have impacts that could be avoided," insisted the conservationist. "As I said before it is a case of working with nature rather than against it."

"What other sorts of impact are you talking about?" continued the policy maker.

"Well, as I said earlier, 54% of farmland species have declined since 1970; 12% of the 1118 species monitored are under threat of extinction, including 12 out of 26 farmland birds," replied the conservationist.

"That's outcomes, I meant causes," returned the policy maker sounding a little impatient.

"And don't forget several species have increased in abundance," interjected the farmer.

"That's true," said the conservationist, "but it doesn't make up for the loss of the other species."

"Now, the causes . . ." she continued, "again, as we said earlier, in farmland we can look at production-driven farming systems, intensive grazing regimes, loss of things like hedges and ponds, and increased use of fertilisers, pesticides and herbicides."

"All the things we have been discussing then?" responded the policy maker.

"Yes," replied the conservationist. "There are other impacts in the uplands and woodlands. Sheep and deer farming for example, and burning for grouse management. But I guess those of us in this part of the world are probably mostly concerned with agriculture."

"I'm a bit of a polymath," smiled the policy maker. "What's happening in woodlands?"

"Pretty much the same as elsewhere," answered the conservationist, "53% of species have declined, 11% of species under threat of extinction with 16 out of 49 species of bird under threat."

"The main problem in the UK," she continued, "is the lack of wood-land. With only 13% of our land area covered by trees we are one of Europe's least wooded nations.[71] As other environmental factors take effect, such as global warming, many of our woodland species will find it difficult to translocate elsewhere."

"Looks like we might want farmers to give over some of their land to forestry," said the policy maker.

"As you did with the coastal strip you gave over to the dune reserve," he added looking at the farmer.

"That was you, was it?" asked the conservationist, following the policy maker's glance.

"Thank you," she added sincerely.

"Well I am finding this conversation more and more interesting," said the policy maker. "Where do we go from here?"

"One word," said the conservationist, "partnership."

"Partnership?" echoed the policy maker.

"Yes," replied the conservationist. "Despite our differences we have to work together if we are to provide the needs of what is likely to be a growing population with protection for the environment and ecological systems that are necessary to underpin that provisioning."

"Fine," said the policy maker, "but a bit more detail please."

"Well it goes back to the Lawton Report again," said the conservation-ist. "We need to build ecological networks. To quote Lawton, we need to 'secure a suite of high quality sites which collectively contain the range and area of habitats that species require and ensure that ecological connections exist to allow species, or at least their genes, to move between them'."

"'It is this network of core sites connected by buffer zones, wildlife corridors and smaller but still wildlife-rich sites that are important in their own right and can also act as stepping stones that we call an 'ecological network',"[72] she continued.

"You had that at the front of your mind," smiled the policy maker.

"It's my life's work," returned the conservationist.

"But I thought we had a network of high quality sites?" queried the policy maker.

"We have had a host of environmental protection legislation since 1941,"[73] said the conservationist, "but there was no systematic notifica-tion of these sites still less adequate protection. Further the government demand for increased agricultural production over the last 70 years has side-lined the importance of these sites and many have been neglected."

"Let's blame the farmers again," grumbled the farmer.

"Now look," he continued, "I know I always sound defensive but I do think farmers have done sterling work over the years. We have done what was asked of us! If you are now changing the rules let's make these new rules clear."

"Lawton suggests ecological networks need core areas already of high nature conservation value plus new restoration area to create further high value areas. Between them we need corridors and stepping stones enabling species to migrate. Further we need buffer zones around these areas and beyond that a wider landscape focussed on sustaining natural resources," explained the conservationist.

"That sounds like a lot of land," responded the farmer. "Land that might currently be producing crops."

"That's why we need to work together," returned the conservationist. "Conservationists cannot do it alone. We now have Local Nature Partnerships[74] and Nature Improvement Areas[75] such as those in Humberside and the Nene Valley working at strategic, landscape levels."

"We have an LNP," said the farmer, "but it's a bit of a talking shop really. The real incentive, which they acknowledge implicitly, is cash and the stewardship schemes offered by government."

"Back to cash," sighed the policy maker.

"Tell me," he looked at the conservationist, "is there any evidence that schemes such as that you have described work?"

"They have to be made to work, there is no choice," responded the conservationist. "There are many challenges – population growth, increasing consumption, climate change – but we have the possibility of new technologies that might increase yield, the opportunity to increase societal awareness and preferences and, post-Brexit, new policies and regulations."

"All possibilities but no firm evidence," bemoaned the policy maker.

"Well, as Lawton reminds us, we know that when we make the effort we can make a difference. He points to the return of the stone curlew for example," returned the conservationist, for the first time a little defensively.

"All achieved with the help of farmers," she added looking at the farmer.

"I am not sure how many farmers, or consumers for that matter, will respond to the well-being of stone curlews," noted the policy maker, a little pointedly.

"All I can say is that there are many international agreements on this dating back to at least Rio 1992,"[76] returned the conservationist, "and as long ago as 2002 the Convention on Biological Diversity in Johannesburg noted there needed to be a significant reduction in the rate of biodiversity loss to alleviate poverty . . ."

"And to the benefit of all life on earth," interjected the hiker.

All turned to look at him.

"I guess I am one of those people Lawton described as feeling a strong emotional connection to nature, who gives wildlife – indeed all life – intrinsic value and hence on who has a moral conviction that all plants and animals a right to their existence," explained the hiker.

"Fine sentiments," smiled the policy maker, "but they won't pay the farmers."

"It's about education," responded the hiker, "and determination."

"Determination?" queried the policy maker.

"Yes," said the hiker. "It's an investment you see, and you have to make it work."

"Now you have lost me," said the policy maker.

"I suspect he is talking about societal benefits," suggested the accountant. "It is said that healthy natural environments can reduce the crime rate in some areas. They seem to encourage greater social activity and neighbourliness.[77] In fact, a survey carried out by a collaboration of 26 conservation organisations appeared to find 90% of the population felt that our well-being and quality of life is based on nature and biodiversity.[78] Of course these types of benefit are very difficult to quantify in monetary terms."

"Yes that and the fact that access to green spaces seems to encourage people to take exercise which would make them healthier and save the NHS[79] cash," responded the hiker. "Not to mention all those environmental benefits I heard you talking about earlier."

"So it is down to the politicians is it?" asked the policy maker, "Or, more precisely, the likes of me. We have to put together radical new policies telling the public that they will have to pay more for food in order to protect Nature. I don't see that as an easy sell!"

"And what is to stop the supermarkets buying their fruit and vegetables, and their meat and fish from abroad anyway?" asked the farmer.

"I guess it would have to start with an educational programme," mused the policy maker. "The sort of thing where we route National Lottery[80] money to organisations from the Ramblers Association to the RSPB, from the National Trust to the Wildlife Trusts and they get people into the countryside or at least outside walking whilst explaining to them how the countryside works."

"But these campaigns take years," he added.

"Payback will be the withdrawal of the various stewardship grants," the accountant reminded him.

"And there will be resistance along the lines that we are espousing inflation, imposing real costs in a time of austerity," continued the policy maker.

"Not to mention those who would say 'leave it to the scientists, they will find a way'," added the farmer, still cynical but somehow more conciliatory than before.

"Aye especially if you introduce regulation to level the playing field against imported foodstuffs," commented the conservationist.

"It's about leading the world, setting out best practice," claimed the hiker.

The policy maker looked at him. "Where does all this come from?" he asked. "you have an almost religious fervour."

"It's a philosophy," replied the hiker, "or rather an ecosophy. A philosophy informed by the science of ecology – that's how Arne Naess described it."[81]

"Deep ecology," exclaimed the accountant, "I heard about that when I was researching accounting for the environment and biodiversity."[82]

"I thought it was a religion," said the farmer. "I have heard people who describe themselves as deep green talking about the earth as if it was alive. Gaia I think they call her."

"Well certainly there are those who have described Deep Ecology as a religion[83] but there again they define religion quite widely," replied the hiker. "Personally I can't deny a spiritual connection to Nature and my fellow creatures but I realise the wider world requires more down to earth arguments; if you will pardon the double entendre."

"But I guess this spiritual connection guides your arguments?" noted the policy maker.

"Inevitably," replied the hiker, "but I would say that all of us have worldviews that shape our knowledge and underline how we interact with the world. As a hiker though I probably do spend more time reflecting on mine than most."[84]

"And?" asked the policy maker.

"I find myself fully aligned with Naess's version of deep ecology. And in particular the principle of protecting biodiversity," admitted the hiker, "which obviously underlines, some might say biases, my view in this particular conversation."

"Nothing wrong with that," came a voice from the doorway. It was the farmer the hiker had seen earlier. "We all have beliefs, it is important to acknowledge them, that's all."

All eyes looked over to him, "I met that young chap earlier," he explained. "Seems to me he feels nature like a good farmer does. It's not all a matter of science and analysis and returns, or at least it shouldn't be. It's about judgement, reflection and thinking of others. It's just as much about 'what kind of world do you want to live in?' as it is about making money."

"That's right," added a woman entering the room behind him. "You go and get the drinks, Elam, while I explain a bit more."

She sat down.

"Hi, I'm Leslie," she began. "Elam and I run a farm not far from here and we are both from farming families. We have seen the changes in society over the years, the growing population and increased wealth, and how that has changed the demands made of farmers. We have talked over and over again about how to respond to the changes and that response has been underwritten by our beliefs. It has to be. How can you live in a community if you have no sense of right or wrong, and how can you live with yourself if you don't do what is right?"

"So we are with that young fellow all the way," she finished, looking at the hiker.

"Well that's a fair comment," answered the policy maker, "but maybe not everyone sees the world like you?

"True," replied Leslie, "so you have to look for the middle ground. The area where you can agree. And you have to look how you can set an example, show how things can be done. In the first instance Elam and I looked to the folk around us and talked to them about the countryside and farming, and what they are for and who they are for. In the second instance we looked for ideas about 'good practice', about how things should be done. Astonishingly, both journeys took us to the same place. The Linking Environment and Farming scheme."

"Well," said the policy maker, "we're back to LEAF."

"So you know of the marque?" asked Leslie.

"We referred to it earlier," answered the policy maker, "but we don't really know that much about it. Perhaps you can tell us why you set so much store by it."

"And don't forget the bad bits," added the farmer.

"Sorry," he continued with a hint of a self-deprecating smile, "I can't help myself sometimes. I am interested though."

"Well," began Leslie, "there is too much to tell in a short lunchtime so I will focus on what I think you have all been talking about; landscape and nature conservation. This is one of nine sections that make up what LEAF call Integrated Farm Management."

"LEAF are very much aware that enhancing the public's experience of the countryside is vital for the future of farming.[85] To this end they produce several pamphlets including Simply Sustainable Biodiversity that offers six simple steps for managing biodiversity. These are identify habitats, identify key species, manage farmland sympathetically, be pro-active in managing habitats, enhance existing habitats and populations and lastly work with others."

"Partnership is so important," interjected the conservationist.

"Precisely," said Leslie, "and the book offers guidance on all these steps; defining habitats, referring to soil, water and crop management sympathetic to biodiversity – and all these have booklets and LEAF standards of their own, and how to enhance existing habitats and populations. There is also a section on working with others including staff, local farmers, local communities and interest groups and local schools."

"There is of course," she continued, "a series of standards to be met before you can gain accreditation in respect of this particular standard."

"First you need to map key environmental features and note any potential risks to these features. Then you have to draw up a five year enhancement plan, linked to local biodiversity action plans and identifying four specific species as a focus. These are ongoing commitments to be reviewed annually by the farmer and every five years by a specialist advisor."

"Time and money," interjected the farmer.

"Vital if we are really farmers," responded Leslie.

"And not an agribusiness lobby group," added the accountant.

"As the Ethical Consumer organisation described National Farmers Union recently,"[86] she continued as the others turned to look at her.

The farmer grimaced as she spoke.

Leslie continued, "We have to keep special records of events such as bringing uncultivated land into use, hedge cutting, and other boundary management, water course management and especially any tree felling. We have to maintain two-metre wide field margins with minimum use of fertilisers and pest margins. Large fields have to include native habitat banks. We keep records of flowers and fauna, in particular bees and nesting birds ensuring adequate food supplies are available."

"Everything that make Making Space for Nature a reality," sighed the conservationist.

"And last but not least," Leslie finished, "we must keep our staff appraised of how and why we do it."

"When I saw Elam earlier he said he was checking the footpaths?" noted the hiker.

"That's for another section of the LEAF marque," replied Leslie. "Community engagement.

"We have to evidence regular communication with local communities and participation in local initiatives. Further we have to, as Elam was doing keep public and traditional paths clear of obstructions and make sure they are clearly marked."

"So," said the policy maker looking at the farmer, "there are different perspectives within the farming community?"

"Yes, and much of it depends on how much you want to pay for your food," responded the farmer. "All that land committed to nature is lost production, and record keeping and auditing costs money."

"Well as an accountant I have to declare an interest," said the accountant, "but frankly I think accounting for the real world rather than symbolic monetary representations is where accounting should be."

"Oh," exclaimed the policy maker, "please expand."

"Well it has been said that accounting is all about laws and economics and calculation,"[87] began the accountant, "but in the 1980s, about the time of the Brundtland Report,[88] accountants began to wonder how they could contribute to this then new idea of sustainable development. The first seminal text in the UK, Accounting for the Environment by Rob Gray, Jan Bebbington and Diane Walters appeared in 1993 and covered topics such as environmental policy, management accounting, reporting and auditing. A second edition of the book was published in 2001.[89]

"In 2007," she continued, "Bebbington, Jeffrey Unerman and Brendan O'Dwyer produced a book entitled *Sustainability Accounting and Accountability*, which further broadened the topic area to include stakeholder engagement, education and standardisation.[90] And perhaps the most recent book on the subject is *Accountability, Social Responsibility and Sustainability* by Rob Gray, Carol Adams and David Owen, published in

2014.[91] This is a more critical book that does not really add to the subject matter but which argues strongly for more stakeholder engagement and some form of mandatory reporting on environmental matters by business in particular."

"Ah, mandatory reporting, that will be good for the accountants," interspersed the farmer.

Ignoring him, the accountant continued, "Over the years there has been a massive amount of literature in academic journals. Reporting has been a particularly hot topic with carbon accounting and some elements of management accounting rising to the fore from time to time. To be honest though there seems to have been little progress in changing the profession. Gray himself notes that SEA has failed to change practice in depth, showing itself 'largely impervious to evidence, argument and practical solutions unless, that is, the evidence, argument and solutions can either go with the grain of current orthodoxy or can be seen as a useful addendum to that orthodoxy'.[92] In particular Gray suggests that the efforts to make corporate reporting meaningful have failed."

"I am probably not surprised by that last statement," said the policy maker. "But that is all very general. What contribution has accounting to make on nature specifically?"

"Well I was explaining to my colleague here earlier," replied the accountant, "that Mike Jones had produced a book called *Accounting for Biodiversity* in 2014 and there have been a number of academic papers on the subject."

"Why are the accountants who write these books and articles concerned about the environment and biodiversity?" interrupted the hiker.

"That seems to vary," replied the accountant. "Some seem to see nature as a resource but others appear to believe nature has intrinsic as well as instrumental value. However so far at least it appears that the arguments for environmental accounting have been based on instrumental values in an attempt to win over the profession at large. A strategy that appears to be failing as I noted above and environmental accounting has been criticised and labelled quietist by more critical scholars."[93]

"What about this idea of natural capital I have heard some of my colleagues talking about?"[94] asked the policy maker.

"There have been attempts by economists[95] and accountants[96] —it is an extension of what they call full cost accounting[97] – to monetarise environmental impacts and currently there is huge project on in the UK trying to establish a methodology for valuing so–called natural capital. It is not without its critics,[98] though as a concept it does seem to appeal to the business and accounting fraternities," replied the accountant.

"Critics?" asked the policy maker.

"Yes," replied the accountant. "Perhaps summed up best by Ruth Hines: 'It is in the name of Net Profit, Budget Surplus and Gross National Product that the natural environment in which we all co-exist is being destroyed. Those who speak this language have more social power to influence thinking and actions than they perhaps realise, or utilise.'"[99]

At that point Elam brought two glasses of beer to the table.

"The food is on its way," he said.

"Well, that is probably a good point to end this conversation," said the policy maker. "I have to get back to the city for a meeting this evening."

"And that means it is time for me to go too," added the farmer.

"Not something I said?" asked Elam.

"No but it probably would be if I stayed," responded the farmer. "We are in the same job, producing food, but I can't help but think we are light years apart in how we want to do it."

Elam simply smiled.

"I think we can go too," said the conservationist, "That has been a truly interesting conversation."

She and the accountant said their goodbyes and left with the policy maker and the farmer.

"Are you off too?" Leslie asked the Hiker.

"I'm afraid so," he replied. "I have another four hours or so of walking to my next stop and I want to be there well before dark. I am hoping to find some natterjack toads down on the coast."

"There used to be some on the Point," said Elam.

"You will hear them if they are there," added Leslie. "Just listen out as it starts to go dark."

As he walked the hiker reflected on what he had heard. He smiled at the thought of Elam and Leslie and pondered over the tension between them and the other farmer. Perhaps the latter was not a farmer at all but simply a business man as suggested by the accountant. He remembered Horkheimer raging against rationalisation, "Yet even here the small farmer (the only farmer in the proper sense of the word) no less than the artisan is learning from personal experience that he has been born out of time."[100] Truly Elam was of the land and recognised a duty of care for it. Not so the other man for whom the precautionary principle was but a nuisance.

He was saddened by the way an anthropocentric perspective had prevailed throughout the discussion. Yet he recognised, underlying this was another view, a view that allowed nature some value in herself; an intrinsic value. The accountant had opened his eyes; in that most instrumental and reductive of professions there were some who cared for nature for her own sake. Perhaps though they needed to state this more openly. Their so-called objective and instrumental arguments were all well and good but they were not working. They needed to bring all their thoughts into what Mouffe called "the political", that "dimension of antagonism that is inherent in human relations", an "antagonism that can take many forms and emerge in different types of social relations".[101] Only with their beliefs, intuitions, ontologies even, standing openly and proud, could they hope to join that fray and influence the politics – that "ensemble of practices, discourses and institutions which seek to establish a certain order and organise human co-existence in conditions that are always potentially conflictual".[102]

At this point he remembered how the conservationist had talked of partnership, and how Elam and Leslie had spoken enthusiastically of the LEAF marque and the sharing of ideas and community involvement. This sharing of ideas was surely the way to influence the organisation of human existence and in doing so make "a space for nature".[103] Humanity will always need food and shelter he thought but only now are some of us realising that the Earth is a finite resource. We must work to make this known to all and work out how to share her resources; not just among humans but with the rest of nature as well. He smiled at the limitation that put on the idea of pricing as a solution to the problems of distribution; there was no money in a kangaroo's pocket and what did the as yet unborn have to offer. No we have to keep working on identifying what is valuable and that task does not take place in the arena of cost/benefit analysis or so-called natural capital; it takes place in "the political".

He finished his thoughts with the three Kantian questions posed by Horkheimer: "What do I know?", "What ought I to do?" and "What may I hope?"[104]

What I know he decided is that nature in her immensely diverse form is both the fruit and the beautiful uniqueness of our planet. Further we, *Homo sapiens*, are part of nature and destroying nature as we are doing will ultimately destroy us. Whatever we leave behind in such circumstances, if anything, will not be *Homo sapiens*. What I ought to do he thought, is to argue for a space for nature in such a way as to allow her to express herself, evolve even; to this end I should also argue for a world of sharing, a world where we share ideas and resources. Finally, accepting Mouffe's concept of an "ineradicable pluralism of value",[105] what I may hope for is a world where people can at least appreciate the value of nature and make space for her diversity and beauty to continue to evolve. In such a world surely humanity too could prosper.

At that point he stopped thinking and looked around. For hundreds of yards in every direction all he could see was rape.[106] There was no movement anywhere. The footpath wound through the silent field of yellow flowers. "Rape," he thought, "an appropriate name to describe this violation of the landscape."

Then his mind moved to another scene. A landscape full of small holdings where the air was filled with the cackling of geese and hens, pigs lay lazing in the sun and the sound of sheep bells drifted musically from the fields. Sparrows chirped endlessly and the air was alive with a myriad swifts feasting on a million midges. Above them an osprey circled high in the sky, moving all the while across the plain with no apparent effort.

The roadside verges were a tangle of flowers, red poppies, purple thistle, pink vetches, every colour in creation. Hedgerows followed ditches while grasses and yet more flowers invaded fields of barley and flowering fruit trees. As he walked through this crazy confusion of colour butterflies flew around his knees. Fiery coppers, golden yellows, chequered whites and purple blues. Dragonflies too; blue skimmers and blood red darters. And flying beetles as big as almonds it seemed.

Was he looking at the future or the past, he wondered? Would this scene too 'follow the money' and vanish forever? Or was it the future suggested by Douglas Tompkins where the myth of progress has been deposed, "the notion of ever-developing megatechnologies . . . has fallen from grace" and "the Earth has recuperated from its dark times of biodepletion"?[107]

Here in the twenty-first century it seemed to him a new politics was in its infancy, a politics with a place for nature. There was much to do and would there be time to prevent a sixth mass extinction? There would be problems and issues along the way, but, yes, there was hope.

Notes

1 See Wilson (1992) and Ceballos, Ehrlich and Dirzo (2017).
2 See WWF (2014, p. 16).
3 See Atkins et al. (2018).
4 See Kolbert (2015).
5 See Hinchliffe, Blower and Freeland (2003, pp. 90–102).
6 See WWF (2014, p. 20).
7 See Juniper (2013, p. 38).
8 See for example Pepper (1996) and Belshaw (2001).
9 "What can I know? What ought I to do? What may I hope?" (Horkheimer 2012/1957, p. 2).
10 Mouffe (2005/2000) argues that 'the multiplicity of ideas of the good is irreducible' (p. 139) and there will be a 'never ending interrogation of the political by the ethical' (p. 140).
11 Naess outlined the original principles of Deep Ecology in *The Shallow and the Deep* (1973), though these were further developed in ensuing years.
12 See Naess (1984).
13 See Devall and Sessions (2007).
14 For an introduction to these writers see Keller's (2010) anthology.
15 See Pywell et al. (2015).
16 See Fairlie (2007–2008).
17 Linking Environment and Farming – an organisation whose mission is to inspire and enable sustainable farming.
18 LEAF (undated).
19 The Basic Payment Scheme, the European Union's grant and payment scheme to farmers. See Raymond (2016, p. 3).
20 Ibid.
21 This conversation is set in 2017 and Brexit refers to the United Kingdom's imminent exit from the European Union. See Harper (2016a).
22 See Helm (2016).
23 See Green Alliance (2016) and RSPB Scotland (2015).
24 Countryside Stewardship is a government scheme providing incentives for land managers to look after their environment.

25 See Harper (2016b).
26 See Helm (2016, p. 5).
27 Ibid.
28 The United Nations Environmental Programme.
29 See UNEP (2016, p. 23).
30 See the RSPB (2013).
31 RSPB Scotland (2015).
32 See Jones (2014).
33 See Jones and Solomon (2013).
34 See Jones (2010).
35 See Van der Veen (2000).
36 Jones and Solomon (2013, p. 683).
37 See Cuckston (2013), Freeman and Groom (2013), and van Liempd and Busch (2013).
38 See Tregidga (2013).
39 See Rimmel and Jonall (2013).
40 See Siddiqui (2013).
41 See Raar (2014), Christian (2014), and Thomson (2014).
42 See Houdet and Germaneau (2014) and Davis (2014).
43 See Atkins and Thomson (2014).
44 See Borsato et al. (2014) and Elad (2014).
45 Natural Capital refers to nature as a finite capital resource which we can draw on but must replace in much the same way we would monetary capital if we are to remain solvent.
46 See Crompton and Kasser (2009).
47 See Sullivan (2014).
48 See Hinchliffe, Blower and Freeland (2003, p. 147) for list of international treaties incorporating the precautionary principle.
49 See Hayhow et al. (2016, p. 6).
50 See Carson (1962).
51 See Hayhow et al. (2016, p. 17).
52 Ibid., p. 18.
53 See Juniper (2013, p. 64).
54 Ibid., p. 116.
55 Ibid., p. 38.
56 See Pywell et al. (2015).
57 See Fairlie (2007–2008).
58 LEAF (2016, pp. 24–28).
59 Ibid., p. 14.
60 See Juniper (2013, p. 28).
61 See RSPB Scotland (2015).
62 Kaizen is an industrial term from Japan referring to a process of continuous improvement.
63 The (UK) Department for Environment, Food and Rural Affairs.
64 See http://san.ag for further information on the Sustainable Agricultural Nertwork.
65 See Lawton (2010).
66 See Lawton et al. (2010, p. 1).
67 Ibid., pp. 5–6.
68 Ibid., p. 5.
69 See Department of Environment, Food and Rural Affairs (2011, p. 9).
70 The RSPB Annual Science Meeting 2016.
71 See Hayhow et al. (2016, p. 29).

72 See Lawton et al. (2010, p. 14).

73 Ibid., pp. 12–13.

74 Local Nature Partnerships are partnerships of a broad range of local organisations, businesses and people who aim to help bring about improvements to their local natural environment.

75 Natural Improvement Areas were established to create joined up and resilient ecological networks at a landscape scale. They are run by partnerships of local authorities, local communities and landowners, the private sector and conservation organisations.

76 The United Nations Conference on Environment and Development.

77 See Department of Environment, Food and Rural Affairs (2011, p. 4).

78 See Response for Nature partnership (2015).

79 The (UK) National Health Service.

80 The UK National Lottery donates 28% of its takings to charities.

81 See Naess (1973).

82 See Gray, Bebbington and Walters (1993) and Gray, Adams and Owen (2014) for references to deep green ecology.

83 See Taylor (2010).

84 See Gros (2015) and Thoreau (1993/1862).

85 LEAF (2016, p. 38).

86 See Ethical Consumer (2017).

87 Dillard (1991).

88 WCED (1987).

89 See Gray and Bebbington (2001).

90 Unerman, Bebbington and O'Dwyer (2007).

91 See Gray, Adams and Owen (2014).

92 See Gray (2014, p. 101).

93 See for example Spence, Hysillos and Correa-Ruiz (2010) and Correa and Laine (2013).

94 In fact Natural Capital became an integral part of UK Government policy in 2018. See Department of Environment, Food and Rural Affairs (2018).

95 See for example Markandya and Richardson (1992) and Hodge (1995).

96 See Chua, Hime and Herbertson (2015).

97 See for example Bebbington et al. (2001).

98 See Sullivan (2014) and Herbohn (2005).

99 See Hines (1991, p. 29).

100 See Horkheimer (2012/1957).

101 See Mouffe (2005/2000, p. 101).

102 Ibid.

103 See Lawton et al. (2010).

104 See Horkheimer (2012/1957, p. 2).

105 See Mouffe (2005/2000, p. 102).

106 A plant of the mustard family grown primarily for its seed which is used to produce rapeseed oil.

107 See Tompkins (2016).

References

Atkins, J. F., Maroun, W., Atkins, B. C. and Barone, E., 2018, From the Big Five to the Big Four? Exploring Extinction Accounting for the Rhinoceros, *Accounting, Auditing & Accountability Journal*, 31(2), pp. 674–702.

Atkins, J. and Thomson, I., 2014, Accounting for Nature in 19th Century Britain: William Morris and the defence of the fairness of the Earth, in M. Jones, ed., *Accounting for Biodiversity*, Abingdon: Routledge.

Bebbington, J., Gray, R., Hibbit, C and Kirk, E., 2001, *Full Cost Accounting: An Agenda for Action*, London: Certified Accountants Educational Trust.

Belshaw, C., 2001, Environmental Philosophy: Reason, Nature and Human Concern, Chesham: Acumen Publishing.

Borsato, R., Filho, J. T. M., Milano, M. S., Salzmann, A. M., Brasil, B., Alexandre, M. A., Nunes, M de L. S., Borges, C and Posonski, M., 2014, Biodiversity Accountability in Brazil: The Role of LIFE* Certification, in M. Jones, ed., *Accounting for Biodiversity*, Abingdon: Routledge.

Carson, R., 1962, *Silent Spring*, New York: Houghton Miflin.

Ceballos, G., Ehrlich, P. R. and Dirzo, R., 2017, Biological Annihilation via the Ongoing Sixth Mass Extinction Signalled by Vertebrate Population Losses and Declines, retrieved from www.pnas.org/cgi/doi/10.1073/pnas.1704949114.

Christian, J., 2014, Accounting for Biodiversity – A Deep Ecology perspective, In JONES, M. ed., *Accounting for Biodiversity*, Abingdon: Routledge

Chua, F., Hime, S. and Herbertson, P., 2015, Natural Capital and the Accountancy Profession: Applying Traditional Skills to New Thinking and Practice, London: ACCA, Fauna & Flora International and KPMG.

Correa, C. and Laine, M., 2013, Struggling Against Like-Minded Conformity in Order to Enliven SEAR: A Call for Passion, *Social and Environmental Accountability Journal*, 33(3), pp. 134–144.

Crompton, T. and Kasser, T., 2009, Meeting Environmental Challenges: The Role of Human Identity. Godalming: WWF UK.

Cuckston, T., 2013, Bringing Tropical Forest Biodiversity Conservation into Financial Accounting Calculation, *Accounting, Auditing and Accountability Journal*, 26(5), pp. 688–714.

Davies, J., 2014, Full Cost Accounting – Integrating Biodiversity, in M. Jones, ed., *Accounting for Biodiversity*, Abingdon: Routledge.

Department of Environment, Food and Rural Affairs, 2011, *The Natural Choice: securing the value of nature*, Norwich: The Stationery Office.

Department of Environment, Food and Rural Affairs, 2018, *25 Year Environment Plan*, Norwich: The Stationery Office.

Devall, B. and Sessions, G., 2007, *Deep Ecology: Living as if Nature Mattered*. Layton: Gibbs Smith.

Dillard, J. F., 1991, Accounting as a Critical Social Science. *Accounting, Auditing and Accountability Journal*, 4(1), pp. 8–28.

Elad, C., 2014, Forest Certification and Biodiversity Accounting in the Congo Basin Countries, in M. Jones, ed., *Accounting for Biodiversity*, Abingdon: Routledge.

Ethical Consumer, 2017, The NFU – An English Agribusiness Lobby Group, retrieved from www.ethicalconsumer.org/commentanalysis/corporatewatch/thenfureport.aspx.

Fairlie, S., 2007–2008, Can Britain Feed Itself, *The Land*, Winter 2007–2008.

Freeman, C. and Groom, B., 2013, Biodiversity Valuation and the Discount Rate Problem, *Accounting, Auditing and Accountability Journal*, 26(5), pp. 715–745.

Gray, R., 2014, Ambidexterity, Puzzlement, Confusion and a Community of Faith? A Response to My Friends, *Social and Environmental Accountability Journal*, 34(2), pp. 97–105.

Gray, R. and Bebbington, J., 2001. *Accounting for the Environment*. London: Sage Publications.

Gray, R., Adams, C. A and Owen, D., 2014, Accountability, Social Responsibility and Sustainability: Accounting for Society and the Environment, Harlow: Pearson Education.

Gray, R., Bebbington, J and Waters, D., 1993, *Accounting for the Environment*. London: Paul Chapman Publishing.

Green Alliance, 2016, New Markets for Land and Nature: How Natural Infrastructure Schemes Could Pay for a Better Environment, London: Green Alliance.

Gros, F., 2015, *A Philosophy of Walking*, trans. J. Howe, London: Verso.

Harper, M., 2016a, Good News for a Friday (1): Future Funding for Wildlife Friendly Farming, www.rspb.org.uk/community.

Harper, M., 2016b, What Does Brexit Mean for Nature and the RSPB? *Nature's Home*, Winter 2016, p. 37.

Hayhow, D. B., et al., 2016, The State of Nature Partnership, retrieved from www. rspb.org.uk/stateofnature.

Helm, D., 2016, British Agricultural Policy after BREXIT: Natural Capital Network – Paper 5, retrieved from www.dieterhelm.co.uk/natural–capital.environment.

Herbohn, K., 2005, A full cost environmental accounting experiment. *Accounting, Organizations and Society*, 30, pp. 519–536.

Hinchliffe, S., Blowers, A and Freeland, J., 2003, *Understanding Environmental Issues*. Milton Keynes: Open University.

Hines, R., 1991. On Valuing Nature. *Accounting, Auditing and Accountability*, 4(3), pp. 27–29.

Hodge, I., 1995, *Environmental Economics: Individual Incentives and Public Choice*, Basingstoke: Macmillan.

Horkheimer, M., 2012/1957, *Critique of Instrumental Reason*, London: Verso.

Houdet, J. and Germaneau, C., 2014, Accounting for Biodiversity and Ecosystem Services from an EMA Perspective: Towards a Standardised Biodiversity Footprint Methodology, in M. Jones, ed., *Accounting for Biodiversity*, Abingdon: Routledge.

Jones, M., 2010, Accounting for the Environment: Towards a Theoretical Perspective for Environmental Accounting and Reporting, *Accounting Forum*, 34, pp. 123–138.

Jones, M., 2014, *Accounting for Biodiversity*, Abingdon: Routledge.

Jones, M. J., and Solomon, J. F., 2013, Problematising Accounting for Biodiversity, *Accounting, Auditing and Accountability Journal*, 26(5), pp. 668–687.

Juniper, T., 2013, *What Has Nature Ever Done For Us? How Money Really Does Grow On Trees*, London: Profile Books.

Keller, D. R., 2010, *Environmental Ethics: The Big Questions*, Chichester: Wiley-Blackwell.

Kolbert, E., 2015, *The Sixth Extinction: An Unnatural History*, London: Bloomsbury Publishing.

Lawton, J. H., et al., 2010, *Making Space for Nature: A Review of England's wildlife Sites and Ecological Network*, London: Department of Environment, Food and Rural Affairs.

LEAF, 2016, *Global Impacts Report 2016*, Stoneleigh Park, Warwickshire: LEAF.

LEAF, undated, *Five Year Strategic Direction: 2016–2021*, Stoneleigh Park, Warwickshire: LEAF, retrieved from https://archive.leafuk.org/eblock/services/resources.ashx/001/240/521/LEAF_5_Year_Strategy_A4_FINAL_without_print_marks.pdf.

Markandya, A. and Richardson, J., 1992, *The Earthscan Reader in Environmental Economics*, London: Earthscan Publications.

Mouffe, C., 2005/2000, *The Democratic Paradox*, London: Verso.

Naess, A., 1973, The Shallow and the Deep, Long-Range Ecology Movements: A Summary, *Inquiry*, 16, pp. 95–100.

Naess, A., 1984, Intuition, Intrinsic Value, and Deep Ecology, *The Ecologist*, 14, pp. 201–203.

Pepper, D., 1996, *Modern Environmentalism: An Introduction*. London: Routledge.

Pywell, R. F., Heard, M. S., Woodcock, B. A., Hinsley, S., Ridding, L., Nowakowski, M and Bullock, J. M., 2015, *Wildlife-Friendly Farming Increases Crop Yield: Evidence for Ecological Intensification*, Edinburgh: RSPB.

Raar, J., 2014, Biodiversity and Regional Authorities: A Common-Pool Resources and Accounting Perspective, in M. Jones, ed., *Accounting for Biodiversity*, Abingdon: Routledge.

Raymond, M., 2016, View from the President, *British Farmer and Grower Magazine*, September, p. 3.

Response for Nature Partnership, 2015, Response for Nature: England, retrieved from www.rspb.org.uk/responsefornature.

Rimmel, G. and Jonäll, K., 2013, Biodiversity Reporting in Sweden: Corporate Disclosure and Preparers' Views, *Accounting, Auditing and Accountability Journal*, 26(5), pp. 746–778.

RSPB, 2013, *The RSPB's Response to the Triennial Review of Natural England and the Environment Agency February 2013*, RSPB, Sandy, retrieved from ww2.rspb.org.uk/Images/triennial-review_tcm9-358640.pdf

RSPB Scotland, 2015, *The Future of Scottish Agriculture: A Discussion Document: A Response by RSPB Scotland*, retrieved from http://rackspace-web2.rspb.org.uk/Images/a_vision_for_scottish_agriculture_tcm9-414322.pdf

Siddiqui, J., 2013, Mainstreaming Biodiversity Accounting: Potential Implications for a Developing Economy, *Accounting, Auditing and Accountability Journal*, 26(5), pp. 779–805.

Spence, C., Hysillos, J. and Correa-Ruiz, C., 2010, Cargo Cult Science and the Death of Politics: A Critical Review of Social and Environmental Accounting Research, *Critical Perspectives on Accounting*, 21, pp. 76–89.

Sullivan, S., 2014, *The Natural Capital Myth; or Will Accounting Save the World? Preliminary Thoughts on Nature, Finance and Values*, The Leverhulme Centre for the Study of Value Working Paper Series No. 3, University of Manchester, Manchester.

Taylor, B., 2010, *Dark Green Religion: Nature Spirituality and the Planetary Future*, Berkeley, CA: University of California Press.

Thomson, I., 2014, Biodiversity, International Conventions, Government Strategy and Indicators: the Case of the UK, in M. Jones, ed., *Accounting for Biodiversity*, Abingdon, Routledge.

Thoreau, H. D., 1993/1862, *Civil Disobedience and Other Essays*, New York: Dover Publications.

Tompkins, D. R., 2016, Turning Around from the Wrong Road Taken, *The Trumpeter*, 32(1), pp. 10–15.

Tregidga, H., 2013, Biodiversity Offsetting: Problematisation of an Emerging Governance Regime, *Accounting, Auditing and Accountability Journal*, 26(5), pp. 806–832.

UNEP, 2016, *Unlocking the Sustainable Potential of Land Resources: Evaluation Systems, Strategies and Tools. A Report of the Working Group on Land and Soils of the International Resource Panel*, Nairobi: UNEP.

Unerman, J., Bebbington, J and O'Dwyer, B., 2007, *Sustainability Accounting and Accountability*, Abingdon: Routledge,

Van der Veen, M., 2000, Environmental Management Accounting, in A. Kolk, ed., *Economics of Environmental Management*, Harlow: Pearson Education,

Van Liempd, D. and Busch, J., 2013, Biodiversity reporting in Denmark, *Accounting, Auditing and Accountability Journal*, 26(5), pp. 833–872.

WCED, 1987, *Our Common Future* ['the Brundtland Report'], World Commission on Environment and Development (WCED), Oxford, Oxford University Press.

Wilson, E. O., 1992, *The Diversity of Life*, New York: Norton.

WWF, 2014, *Living Planet Report 2014: Species and Spaces, People and Places*, eds R. McLellan, Ivengar, L., Jeffries, B. and Oerlemans, N., Gland, Switzerland: WWF.

4 Species extinction and closing the loop of argument

Imagining accounting and finance as the potential cause of human extinction

Rob Gray and Markus J. Milne

Introduction

When Umberto Eco speaks of *hyperreality* he seeks to challenge the (often) lazy and (frequently) easy acceptance of a socially constructed reality that is (to appropriate a phrase) "better than life".[1] Such hyperreality is constructed for us by an array of stories, narratives, ideologies, representations – accounts if you will – that may often exploit the worst of the moral feebleness of post-modernity and charm us into a lotus-eater's self-delusion about what it is to be human and the state of our tenure of the planet. As hyperreality takes hold, humankind's narratives about progress, striving, success and worth increasingly lead, it seems, to a state where we start to treat the totally absurd as the undeniably "real": we enter what Curtis (2016) calls hypernormalisation.[2] This hypernormal state is essentially a condition where, *despite overwhelming evidence to the contrary*, whole groups, professions, even societies continue to maintain a myth that all is well . . . that our world is indeed Panglossian. This seems to arise in large part because society seems incapable of imagining any other possibility ("reality") than that which continues the momentum of the present; incapable of thinking of any possibility that is not, essentially, just "more of the same". Over time, the myth becomes "real" and then, in fact, it becomes the only acceptable reality. At this point, it becomes almost impossible for anybody to raise the question of alternatives or even to debate the danger of the myths and self-delusions.[3] The society acts autopoietically and refuses to even acknowledge evidence or argument that will not code to the myth, that will not code to the hyper-normal, (Vinnari and Dillard, 2016; Khan and Gray, 2016). Humanity, arguably, is currently in just such a thrall where the undoubted successes of modernity, science and capitalism are challenged (or should be challenged) by the undoubted crises of species endangerment and extinction, climate change, pollution, resource use, inequality and so on . . . in essence by unsustainability. You don't have to be Albert Camus to find the whole thing somewhat absurd.[4] In the face of our own despoiling of the planet – and of our fellow humans – we continue to strive for meaning. It is difficult not to be persuaded that we have embraced Nietzsche's approach and given meaning to human life through illusion – illusions of progress, worth and achievement perhaps. Camus, not much given to laughter may well find our head long pursuit of the death of our species while bolstered by tales of our excellence, genuinely risible.

However, it is essential that we should stress here that it is *not* that the details of unsustainability and its causes are absolutely settled: although the arguments in its support are substantive and, to our mind entirely persuasive, they are *not* completely resolved. Rather, it is the true absurdity that such substantive and potentially devastating arguments about unsustainability and its causes *cannot* be admitted to mainstream debate and consciousness. The arguments cannot, it seems, be followed through and carefully considered. Such an absurdity is clearly a cause for concern but is at its most devastating, and least defensible, we would argue, when it is present in education and academe.

It is our intention in this short chapter to explore some of this absurdity: particularly as it relates to species extinction and endangerment. In doing so, we will try to sketch in a number of wider matters such as the almost complete absence from mainstream conversation of *any* apparent recognition that it is humanity's institutionalised structures and behaviours that are, in all probability, the primary cause of the symptoms of unsustainability such as species extinction.[5] In doing so, we will seek to expose accounting and finance as key components of any species extinction and that the extinction of humanity is both consequently likely and arguably desirable. The chapter is organised as follows. First we review, very briefly, the broad argument linking unsustainability to humanity's modernity and institutionalised systems of organising. We then argue that consideration of individual extinctions is a study of effects when the cause we should be studying is humanity's failure to manage itself. The following section briefly offers up human extinction as a natural consequence of non-human extinction and explores the absurd irony of this situation, while the final section suggests a few positive ideas to leaven the (some might think) unremitting gloom[6] of the rest of the chapter.

The source of the issue

The essence of the argument relating the institutions of modernity so directly to unsustainability, goes approximately as follows. Although as Steven Pinker (2018) so rigorously and energetically argues, so many people on the planet have "never had it so good" in terms of life expectancy, material well-being, health, travel, freedom and so on, the price of that well-being has been a profound disruption of environmental, ecological and social systems. What seems incontrovertible is that humankind's tenure of the planet is currently unsustainable as judged by all but the most abstract of science fiction possibilities[7]. Climate change, habitat destruction, waste, pollution, species endangerment and extinction, inequality, desertification, alienation, and so on. . . are all getting worse and the ecosystems upon which we all – human and non-human species alike – depend is critically threatened in so many ways.

Paul Ehrlich (Ehrlich and Holden, 1971, 1972; Ehrlich and Ehrlich, 1978) produced his famous heuristic that posited that environmental impact (I) was a direct function of human population (P), affluence (A) and technology (T). The heuristic is as good an indicator of the source of environmental endangerment as anything else of which we are aware. Thus, we may reason, the impact on the planet, including species endangerment, is almost certainly a function of the number of human beings who collectively (stress "collectively") consume too much and who are in thrall to a technology and innovation process that generates as least as many *bads* as *goods*. That is – and this point cannot be stated often enough – species extinction, as with other examples of environmental degradation, is a *systematic* consequence of humanity and its current ways of organising.[8]

But why (and perhaps how) did humanity become so manifestly destructive? It seems too much to suggest than humanity is and always will be a destructive creature – there is too much evidence to offer counter narratives to this. While the reasons for the size of population (P) might be diverse (Billari, 2015; Coleman and Basten, 2015; Lutz and Striessnig, 2015) the sources of affluence (A) and technology (T) are not: they arise and have continued growing primarily through industry and, especially, through capitalism. Again, this seems relatively incontrovertible. But the argument does not stop there. The principal engine of capitalism is undoubtedly the 60,000 or so multinational enterprises which dominate the world economy (Korten, 1995, 2015). These organisations are, for the most part, publicly quoted on the world's financial markets. The companies are geared to grow and, while there is no absolute inherent necessity that a business needs to grow, it is a *sine qua non* that quoted companies must grow: otherwise they cannot pay the rapacious rentiers who own them, the dividends and returns they expect. And the hyperreality of finance (McGoun, 1997) has come to dictate that not only is continual growth desirable and normal but a failure to grow is considered to be the worst kind of failure – so, regardless of what the organisation might do, its products, its impacts, its employment etc., the market will "discipline it". Thus, while the managers of multinational enterprises might be perfectly content with a growth imperative; they fundamentally have no choice: grow or get out. Growth is an institutional requirement of financial capitalism – not an ultimate truth about humanity![9]

You are probably aware that one cannot have multinational organisations without accounting of some sort (otherwise central managers could not exercise control at a distance on behalf of growth and the shareholders; see for example Robson, 1992) and the separation of ownership (shareholders) and control (directors) that is essential for international financial multinationals would not be possible). International financial markets make possible the enormous size and conglomeration of the world's staggeringly large corporations. Accounting makes it possible for multinational corporations to function; finance makes their growth and size both possible and inevitable.

Multinational corporations are crucial – not least because it is through them that A and T are delivered in increasing levels by increasingly sophisticated methods and technology. And as we can see, A and T are essential components of the intolerable pressures, I, on the planet.

Furthermore, if we factor in that as the purpose of the capitalistic company is to maximise returns for shareholders (as it is normally expressed: Bakan, 2004; Collison et al., 2011) then, to put it crudely, the purpose of a company is to make the richest people (the shareholders) richer still. Companies can be seen, essentially, as a legitimatised mechanism for creating inequality.[10]

Thus, we can see, there is a demonstrably substantive argument that accounting, finance, companies, international capitalism – and population – are the primary causes of all elements of unsustainability. The intrinsic structure, motivation and nature of these institutions makes such unsustainability inevitable. Only a fundamental, root and branch dismantling of our current human and economic institutions can address this substantially.[11]

How often is that recognised in the classroom? In corporate dialogue? In politics? In the media? In fact, as we can speak from considerable experience, it is ignored at best and suppressed at worst.

Accounts of extinction

There are few, if any extinctions that we know about in the last 100 years that would have taken place without human activity.

(Kolbert, 2014, quoted in Drake, 2015)

The growth in concern over species extinction (see, for example, WWF, 2016; IUCN, 2017) is surely a manifestation of a civilised society concerned to identify endangered species and seek to manage them in order to bring them back from crisis. There are many success stories to be told here. But there are at least three weaknesses in this traditional response. First, as Spash (2015: 1) notes, our research into – and cataloguing of – species endangerment is a measure of "how humanity watches, observes and statistically enumerates the ongoing destruction [it is] not a measure of life but rather the death toll relating to human appropriation". Second, many of the narratives of species extinction and successful challenges overcome are about the management of the species and their habitat, when, in all probability, it is the management of the causes of the endangerment that should be addressed. Dealing with symptoms cannot be ultimately successful. Third, and most importantly, species extinction is, in most cases, not a single event. Pressure on one species or habitat consequently engenders pressure on other species such that, more accurately, we need to consider simultaneous or co-endangerments/extinctions. Species extinction is, almost exclusively, a systematic symptom of humanity's failure to manage its own actions. The root problem is humanity's continual growth, its ever-expanding footprint, its movement of invasive species, its manufacture of waste, its destruction of forests, its attachment to mono-culture, over-fishing etc., etc., (see especially, Kolbert, 2014; WWF, 2016).

Scott (2008) makes this argument very clearly and graphically and Figure 4.1, while not proof of causation is profoundly suggestive.

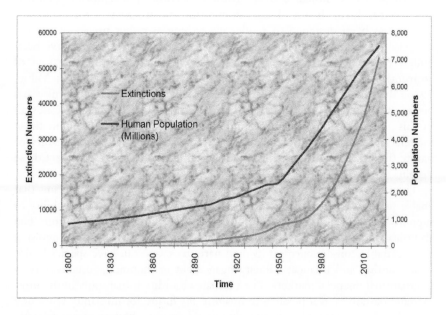

Figure 4.1 Species extinction and human population
Source: Scott (2008), used with permission

We have no need to belabour this point, others have done it far better than we can (see, for example, Haberl et al., 2004; Quinn, 2010; M. Jones, 2014; WWF, 2016; Wilson, 2010). In essence, given current levels of A and T then the world is (to use the notion of Toth and Szigeti, 2015) *over-full*: P, A and T are just too high and humanity is simply appropriating too much of the Earth's ecosystem that all other species need for survival (Vitousek et al., 1986; Daly, 1998). E. O. Wilson's (2016) most recent plea for biodiversity is that we leave half-Earth for all other species survival, such is the scale of our (human) continuing appropriation.

This awareness leads, we would suggest, to the notion that a study of individual species endangerment and extinction, while worthy enough in itself, is actually slightly absurd when to do so effectively ignores the principal causes of that extinction. We need to study humanity more carefully and honestly (Rolston III, 2010).

The extinction of humanity

Essentially, a key component of modernity has been the creation of narratives through which humanity has come to conceive of itself as different from "nature" and, from there erect the edifice of artificiality through which calculation and dominance over "nature" become (hyper)normal (Vinnari and Dillard, 2016). It is no longer contentious to suggest that the economic project has been designed to render everything as either priced or worthless, visible or invisible (Thielemann, 2000). And such sentiments have been widely recognised in accounting in works which expose the omissions of conventional accounts (see, for example, Hines, 1991; Gray, 1992; Milne, 1996; Broadbent, 1998; Shearer, 2002; Hopwood, 2009). Modernity has been a triumph of mankind over nature. And Daly (1998) synthesises all of this as he remarks upon mankind's obsession with investment in those matters which destroy humanity/nature; rather than directly in humanity or nature (ibid.: 276). But, somehow, our narratives of self, fail to connect these insights (Hamilton, 2010; Latour, 2017).

The irony of modernity (Dresner, 2002) is that the very mechanisms that enable us to catalogue and examine the demise of our planet and its ability to support life are the very mechanisms that are wreaking that devastation. The absurdity of modernity is that humanity seems entirely incapable of recognising the inevitable consequences of its own narratives: one can have species health *or* accounting and finance; habitat engagement *or* shopping; sustainability *or* international financial markets. The ultimate absurdity is that, only in the most extreme narratives, is it possible to imagine *any* future for humanity without a flourishing ecosystem. Humanity is set upon destroying its very means of existence but seems incapable of confronting this. While humanity needs "nature" to continue; it seems exceptionally unlikely that any of "nature" needs humanity for anything at all. The simplest way in which we might aid planetary sustainability would be hasten humanity's extinction; while modernity, too, seems intent upon achieving this very aim through a destruction of ecology in the name of self-congratulatory accounts of human progress.

Humanity has only existed for a very short period – as species go. And yet we seem incapable of imagining a world without humanity (Foreman, 2010). Human extinction should not be unthinkable.[12] All species, as far as we are aware, eventually face extinction (Ceballos et al., 2015) and although humanity is a relatively young species (Leslie, 1996) its vulnerability to potential extinction level events seems considerable. In addition to the "natural" events such as volcanoes, meteors and disease, humankind has added what Bostrom (2006) calls *existential risks* such as anthropogenic climate change, chemical and biological warfare, environmental collapse, technological blowback including nuclear meltdown, financial and economic implosion etc. (McPherson, 2011b; Leslie, 1996; Auerbach, 2015). Indeed, the possibility/probability of our own (near) extinction is a matter that one might have thought was somewhat compelling to the modern scholar. However, despite important insights on the issues (see, for example, Livi-Bacci, 2015; Morgan, 2009; Carpenter and Bishop, 2009), these ideas, as Bostrom (2006) observes, rarely enter mainstream debate and reflection.

Speculation on humanity's extinction is a matter of some serious study (see especially Tonn and MacGregor, 2009; Tonn and Stiefel, 2014; Bostrom, 2009) and there are those who thoughtfully express anxiety that such extinction is possible, even likely, within decades rather than millennia (Leslie, 1996; Auerbach, 2015; McPherson, 2011b).[13] It is clearly a matter which deserves to be taken very seriously.

For those of fainter heart, some consolation might be found in the argument that the complete extinction of humanity is probably unlikely: it seems more likely that our concern here is with near-extinction or, perhaps, extinction in part (Bryner, 1999; Diamond, 2005; Kolbert, 2014).

Such anticipation of partial extinction seems broadly justified on a number of grounds. *First*, although humanity's survival/extinction depends, instrumentally, upon the planetary ecology and biodiversity and reductions in biodiversity offer one of the major existential threats to humanity's well-being and continuance (Rockstrom et al., 2009), Kolbert (2014) argues that humanity has managed to survive to the 21st century with the loss of many species; it could probably continue to do so with the loss of yet more species. While humankind's ingenuity seems unable to find ways to prevent our destruction of other species, it does continue to find ways to manufacture substitutes (proteins, plasma etc) which fill some of the gaps left by humanity's "stewardship" of the planet. Whether this could ever be sustainable is a matter of some doubt but there is little question that such acts also increase the existential risks we face as a species (Bostrom, 2009). Rifkin (1980), for example, in contemplating the future of humanity sees two major paths forward, one in which we increasingly seek to exist in a world divorced from our place in the cosmos and become entirely reliant on synthetic substitutes – such a world, he suggests, is being promoted by powerful corporate elites. And another in which we accept planetary limits, fundamentally recognise the implications of the second law of thermodynamics, and adopt a moral imperative to preserve all forms of life for as long as possible.[14]

The *second* argument in support of something other than humanity's complete extinction is that as it appears to be that as "technical advances will in themselves render society more vulnerable to disruption" (Rees, 2003: 21), those less technological societies may exhibit more resilience and/or be less vulnerable to the existential crises through which modernity has rendered humanity vulnerable to extinction. There is little question that modernity and economics have created the parameters of this crisis and the effects are felt well beyond the locus of their cause, nevertheless, societies are clearly not homogeneous, and many non-western societies may be less vulnerable to the threats of extinction – assuming of course that western international financial capitalism has not completely destroyed *their* basis of life (Elliott, 1999).

Third, we might argue at a reflective level and wonder if humanity has already lost its *species-being* and is no longer the "humanity" about which we concern ourselves. Modernity has: encouraged large swathes of the species to embrace a reduction of all values to the economic; encouraged the species to become distanced from the natural world of which it is a part; thereby led to an ignoring of the signs of limits in the natural world. This, in turn, might lead us speculate that any notion of an aspirational, spiritual, human kind – in western contexts at least – is already near extinct? Such dystopian memes are clearly visible in so much of the commentary we have reviewed here. Commentators such as McPherson (2011a), Leslie (1996), McKibben (2012), Kolbert (2014) and Ceballos et al. (2015), all seem to be able to confront the notion that, as a species, humanity no longer has any claims to legitimacy. As we read these exegeses, they are so much more than fantasies of Christian original sin and a yearning for redemption. Rather they speak to us of an inchoate reaching for some means of articulating and understanding the accounts of humanity on which our histories and selves are built: but they do so while gripped by a sense that those aspirational, inspirational accounts may indeed be accounts of either another species than humanity or of a species of humanity which no longer exists (see, for example, Katovich, 2010).

As Rolston III (2010: 71) puts it, will Earth's managers produce a sustainable development or a sustainable biosphere? It is only in the latter that we and a great many other species will survive. Humankind's apparent inability and/or apparent reluctance to consciously address such issues – and, indeed, in doing so to render such consideration illegitimate – leaves us unable to break out of a potentially fatal immanence (Levitas, 2013: 10; see also Latour, 2017).[15] It seems to us that accounts of human extinction are essential if accounts of other species endangerment are to be addressed seriously: species extinction is fundamentally inseparable from humanity's existence and humanity's putative extinction. Humanity, it seems to us, has relatively few such accounts (beyond, for example, Biblical accounts of the Flood).

Reflections and conclusions

> Having abandoned reciprocity with the natural world in pursuit of command over it, modern civilization has broken an ancient covenant with nature . . . but until the present era, humanity and the living Earth itself were not threatened.
>
> (Caldwell, 1999: 3)

Our purpose in this brief chapter has been to make just three simple, if disturbing, points. These are (i) that accounts of species extinction make no sense unless grounded in the context of causes – these being humanity's manifest failures; (ii) that the systematic extinction of species leads to the very real possibility of humanity's extinction (and, as an ethical aside, the potential desirability of such extinction); and (iii) the bewildering inability, it seems, of mainstream argument – whether in politics or academe, business or the media – to follow through the arguments of causes and effects and thus address the potential need for deep, fundamental, root and branch change in our organs of modernity (most notably, such shibboleths as accounting, financial markets, multinational corporations and growth). *We have maintained that it is the failure to confront the arguments that is the true absurdity.* We know that no forecast is ever entirely correct, no argument is ever immutable, no interpretation unquestionable, but to ignore such a wealth of substantive argument when the consequences are so enormous is bewildering and, arguably, absurd.

It is as though western, modern humanity does not (currently) possess either the necessary imagination to conceive of a possible future in which the species is steadily taken to a state of near-extinction or the imagination to conceive of a world where humanity renews, what Caldwell (1999) called, our reciprocity with the natural world. We seem unable to imagine what a path towards a state of grace might look like. That gap in imagination can be filled by a variety of endeavours: new accounts (as we accountants might choose to understand them) is one; stories, music, film, poetry and other cultural communications are others which satisfy the need that a society has for new narratives when faced with substantial upheaval (Norminton, 2013: vii). Other commentators reinforce this notion: so, for example, Benking (1999: 203) calls for more attention to the "pictures and icons we use to paint and communicate possible futures", while the novelist Ursula LeGuin says "Resistance and change often begin in art. Very often in our art, the art of words" (Le Guin, 2014).

Accounts of endangerment and extinction very properly engage us in the process of exploring how such threats might be explained, overcome, mitigated or even reversed. However, our primary challenge here is to suggest that we must balance all such accounts (i.e. accounts about symptoms) with meta-accounts about causes. In that sense, this essay might be seen as a (counter) account for counter-accounters. Such an account, hopefully, might: offer an alternative account to those concerned with specific species' endangerment; encourage wider consideration of context in the act of species accounting; and suggest that a very proper lens of species accounts might embrace an analysis of threats to human continuance.

The problem of species extinction is, in all probability, a problem with humankind and its modern ways of organising – most obviously through international financial capitalism. It is a problem of spirituality, growth, profit, consumption, individualism and the pursuit of more. It is a problem rooted in the very essence of our craft (Hines, 1991) and the very core of our being, (Hamilton, 2010). What we need are honest and penetrating accounts of humanity that sit alongside imaginative new accounts of a selfhood that is part of – and that renews its covenant with – nature (see also Vinnari and Dillard, 2016). For this we need accounts that challenge our sense of modernity and which, as Bostrom (2009) so eloquently argues, and Korten (2015) pursues, change the stories we tell ourselves about ourselves and about new and more admirable possibilities. And an increasingly well-developed sense of our absurdity might not go amiss either.

Acknowledgements

This chapter draws heavily from Gray and Milne (2018). In this chapter we have consciously sought to simplify the essential themes and arguments.

Notes

1 "Better than life" is a game created by the TV series *Red Dwarf*, in which the immersive experiences are, indeed, better than life.
2 The idea probably derives originally from Yurchak (2005).
3 This is a lot like Owen Jones's (2014) argument about the Overton window.
4 See, for example, Maguire (2015) and Jeffries (2010).
5 Although we do acknowledge that the more recent conversations in both the social sciences and natural sciences such as geology and climate science with regard to the Anthropocene do, in fact, begin to expose the collective impact of humanity on nonhuman species and inanimate Earth science processes. See, for example, Crutzen (2006), Steffen et al. (2007), Haraway (2015) and Latour (2014).
6 There is a case to be made that the possibility of human extinction should be treated as a cause of optimism ... no more brutality and nonsense waste of potential and a planet that gets to go on its merry way without interference. What's not to like?
7 Humanity has already survived the extinction of many species and may survive further extinctions through technologies such as the synthesis of proteins, etc. See for example Kolbert (2014).
8 The role(s) of accounting in these ways of organising, as in the ways of organisations, needs no further development here (Miller and O'Leary, 1987; Gray, 2013).
9 Similar arguments also prevail in regard to many nations and their governments concerning the management of economies for economic growth. Ever increasing levels of GDP, which notoriously captures both economic goods and expenditure and efforts on cleaning up social and environmental harms, are the primary objective of many if not all governing parties. For a critique of GDP, see for example, Stiglitz et al. (2010).
10 For a while the trickle-down effect was presumed to overcome this problem but there never was much evidence for it and it is now largely considered to be yet another of our hypernormal myths, (see, for example, Galbraith, 1973; Piketty, 2014).
11 A point we acknowledge is hardly new. Concern with many facets of the "scale" of the human enterprise can be found in the works of Kohr (1957), Schumacher (1973) and Sale (1980) for example.
12 If for no other reason than common (if not always accurate) human narratives of prior apparent (local) extinctions like that associated with Rapa Nui (Easter Island). See, for example, Diamond (2005).
13 Frank Fenner, a world renowned virologist who helped eradicate smallpox states: "Homo sapiens will become extinct, perhaps within 100 years ...A lot of other animals will, too. It's an irreversible situation. I think it's too late. I try not to express that because people are trying to do something, but they keep putting it off. Mitigation would slow things down a bit, but there are too many people here already" (Jones, 2010; see also Sweet, 2010).
14 This latter position recognises that in Earth's future the Sun's energy is ultimately finite, albeit in the very far distant future, and ultimately all life will cease to exist. Furthermore, when energy is used by one life form, because of the second law of thermodynamics (entropy) it is degraded and less available for another. To preserve the process of life for as long as possible, Rifkin believes we have a moral obligation to pursue our existence drawing down the least necessary amount of energy.
15 The point being made here is that the *possibility* (to our mind, actually, *probability*) that the achievement of any substantive notion of sustainability can only be conceived of by stepping outside the normal assumptions of capitalism, growth, population etc. is too frequently excluded from discussion. Accounting's significant implication in this conservative take on the challenges of sustainability is relatively self-evident (Bebbington and Larrinaga, 2014; Byrch et al., 2015; Milne et al., 2009).

References

Auerbach, D. (2015) "A child born today may live to see humanity's end, unless . . .". 18 June. Retrieved from http://blogs.reuters.com/great-debate/2015/06/18/a-child-born-today-may-live-to-see-humanitys-end-unless (accessed 14 February 2018).

Bakan, J. (2004). *The corporation: the pathological pursuit of power and profit*. New York: Free Press.

Bebbington, J. and C. Larrinaga (2014) "Accounting and sustainable development: An exploration". *Accounting, Organizations and Society*, 39(6): 395–413.

Benking, H. (1999) "Show or Schau?". *Politics and the Life Sciences*, 18(2): 203–205.

Billari, F. C. (2015) "Integrating macro- and micro-level approaches in the explanation of population change". *Population Studies*, 69(sup1): S11–S20.

Bostrom, N. (2006) "Dinosaurs, dodos, humans?". *Global Agenda* January: 230–231.

Bostrom, N. (2009) "The future of humanity". In Jan-Kyrre Berg Olsen, Evan Selinger and Soren Riis (eds), *New Waves in Philosophy of Technology*, pp. 186–216. New York: Palgrave Macmillan.

Broadbent, J. (1998). "The gendered nature of 'accounting logic': pointers to an accounting that encompasses multiple values". *Critical Perspectives on Accounting*, 9(3): 267–297.

Bryner, G. (1999) "Protecting humanity's future: threat, response, and debate". *Politics and the Life Sciences*, 18(2): 201–203.

Byrch, C., M. Milne, R. Morgan and K. Kearins (2015) "Seeds of hope? exploring business actors' diverse understandings of sustainable development". *Accounting, Auditing and Accountability Journal*, 28(5): 671–705.

Caldwell L. K. (1999) "Is humanity destined to self-destruct?". *Politics and the Life Sciences*, 18(1): 3–14.

Carpenter P. A. and P.C. Bishop (2009) "The seventh mass extinction: Human-caused events contribute to a fatal consequence". *Futures*, 41(10): 715–722.

Ceballos Gerado, Paul R. Ehrlich, Anthony D. Barnosky, Andrés García, Robert M. Pringle and Todd M. Palmer (2015) "Accelerated modern human-induced species losses: Entering the sixth mass extinction". *Science Advances*, 1(5): e1400253.

Coleman D. and S. Basten (2015) "The Death of the West: An alternative view". *Population Studies*, 69(sup1): S107–S118.

Collison D., S. Cross, J. Ferguson, D. Power and L. Stevenson (2011) *Shareholder primacy in UK corporate law: an exploration of the rationale and evidence*. Research Report 125. London: Certified Accountants Educational Trust.

Crutzen, P. J. (2006). "The 'anthropocene'". In Eckart Ehlers and Thomas Krafft (eds), *Earth system science in the anthropocene*, pp. 13–18. Berlin: Springer.

Curtis, Adam (2016) "HyperNormalisation". Retrieved from www.bbc.co.uk/programmes/p04b183c

Daly H. (1998) "From empty-world economics to full-world economics". In P. Demeny and G. McNicoll (eds), *Population and Development*, pp. 270–278. London: Earthscan.

Diamond, J. (2005) *Collapse: How societies choose to fail or succeed*. London: Penguin.

Drake, N. (2015) "Will humans survive the sixth great extinction?". *National Geographic*, 23 June. Retrieved from http://news.nationalgeographic.com/2015/06/150623-sixth-extinction-kolbert-animals-conservation-science-world (accessed 14 February 2018).

Dresner (2002) *The principles of sustainability*. London: Earthscan.

Ehrlich P. R. and A. H. Ehrlich (1978) "Humanity at the crossroads". *Stanford Magazine*, Spring/Summer. Reprinted in H. E. Daly (ed.) (1980) *Economy, ecology, ethics: Essays toward a steady state economy*, pp. 38–43. San Francisco: W. H. Freeman.

Ehrlich, P. and J. Holden (1971) "Impact of population growth". *Science*, 171: 1212–1217.

Ehrlich, P. and J. Holden (1972) "One-dimensional economy". *Bulletin of Atomic Sciences*, 28(5): 16–27.

Elliott L. (1999) "Social choices for sustainability: a question of equity and justice". *Politics and the Life Sciences*, 18(2): 210–212.

Foreman, D. (2010) "Wild things for their own sakes". In K. D. Moore and M. P. Nelson (eds), *Moral ground: Ethical action for a planet in peril*, pp. 100–102. San Antonio, TX: Trinity University Press.

Galbraith J. K. (1973) *Economics and the public purpose*. Harmondsworth: Penguin.

Gray, R. (1992). Accounting and environmentalism: an exploration of the challenge of gently accounting for accountability, transparency and sustainability. *Accounting, Organizations and Society*, 17(5): 399–425.

Gray R. (2013) "Back to basics: What do we mean by environmental (and social) accounting and what is it for?—a reaction to Thornton". *Critical Perspectives on Accounting*, 24(6): 459–468.

Gray R. and M. Milne (2018) "Perhaps the dodo should have accounted for human beings? Accounts of humanity and (its) extinction". *Accounting, Auditing and Accountability Journal*, 31(3): 826–848.

Haberl, H., M. Wackernagel, F. Krausmann, K. H. Erb and C. Monfreda (2004). "Ecological footprints and human appropriation of net primary production: a comparison". *Land Use Policy*, 21(3): 279–288.

Hamilton C. (2010) *Requiem for a species: Why we resist the truth about climate change*. Abingdon: Earthscan.

Haraway, D. (2015) "Anthropocene, capitalocene, plantationocene, chthulucene: Making kin". *Environmental Humanities*, 6(1), 159–165.

Hines, R. (1991) "On valuing nature". *Accounting, Auditing and Accountability Journal*, 4(3): 27–29.

Hopwood, A. G. (2009) "Accounting and the environment". *Accounting, Organizations and Society*, 34(3): 433–439.

IUCN (2017) "The IUCN Red List of Threatened Species". Retrieved from www.iucnredlist.org.

Jeffries, S. (2010) "Review: 'The age of absurdity: Why modern life makes it hard to be happy' by Michael Foley". *Guardian*, Books Review, April. Retrieved from www.theguardian.com/books/2010/apr/10/age-absurdity-modern-life-foley (accessed 20 February 2018).

Jones, Cheryl (2010) "Frank Fenner sees no hope for humans". *The Australian: Higher Education*, 16 June. Retrieved from www.theaustralian.com.au/higher-education/frank-fenner-sees-no-hope-for-humans/story-e6frgcjx-1225880091722.

Jones, M. (2014) "Accounting for biodiversity: Rationale and overview". In M. Jones (ed.), *Accounting for Biodiversity*, pp. 3–20. Abingdon: Routledge.

Jones, O. (2014) *The establishment and how they get away with it*. London: Allen Lane.

Katovich, M. A. (2010) "The futureless past". *Studies in Symbolic Interaction*, 35: 345–356.

Khan, T. and R. Gray (2016) "Accounting, identity, autopoiesis + sustainability: A comment, development and expansion on Lawrence, Botes, Collins and Roper (2013)". *Meditari Accountancy Research*, 24(1): 36–55.

Kohr, L. (1957) *The breakdown of nations*. London: Routledge & Kegan Paul.

Kolbert E. (2014) *The sixth extinction*. New York: Henry Holt & Company.

Korten D. C. (1995) *When corporations rule the world*. San Francisco, CA: Kumarian/Berrett-Koehler.

Korten, D. C. (2015) *Change the story, change the future: A living economy for a living earth.* Oakland CA: Berrett-Koehler Publishers.

Latour, B. (2014) Agency at the time of the Anthropocene. *New Literary History*, 45(1): 1–18.

Latour, B. (2017) *Facing Gaia: Eight lectures on the new climatic regime.* John Wiley & Sons.

Le Guin, Ursula (2014) "Books aren't aren't just commodities". Speech at National Book Awards. Retrieved from www.theguardian.com/books/2014/nov/20/ursula-k-le-guin-national-book-awards-speech (accessed 14 February 2018).

Leslie, J. (1996) *The end of the world: The science and ethics of human extinction.* Routledge: London.

Levitas, R. (2013) *Utopia as method: The imaginary reconstruction of society.* Basingstoke: Palgrave Macmillan.

Livi-Bacci, M. (2015) "What we can and cannot learn from the history of world population". *Population Studies*, 69(sup1): S21–S28.

Lutz, W. and E. Striessnig (2015) "Demographic aspects of climate change mitigation and adaptation". *Population Studies*, 69(sup1): S69–S76.

Maguire, Laura (2015) "Camus and absurdity". 27 February. Retrieved from www.philosophytalk.org/blog/camus-and-absurdity (accessed 20 February 2018).

McGoun, E. G. (1997) "Hyperreal finance". *Critical Perspectives on Accounting*, 8(1/2): 97–122.

McKibben, B. (2012) "Global warming's terrifying new math: Three simple numbers that add up to global catastrophe – and that make clear who the real enemy is". *Rolling Stone*, 19 July. Retrieved from www.rollingstone.com/politics/news/global-warmings-terrifying-new-math-20120719 (accessed 14 February 2018).

McPherson, G. R. (2011a) *Walking away from empire: A personal journey.* Baltimore, MD: PublishAmerica.

McPherson, G. R. (2011b) "Three paths to near-term human extinction". 20 August. Retrieved from http://guymcpherson.com/2011/08/three-paths-to-near-term-human-extinction (accessed 14 February 2018).

Miller, P. and T. O'Leary (1987) "Accounting and the construction of the governable person". *Accounting, Organizations and Society*, 12(3): 235–266.

Milne, M. J. (1996). "On sustainability; the environment and management accounting". *Management Accounting Research*, 7(1): 135–161.

Milne, M. J., H. M. Tregidga and S. Walton (2009) "Words not actions! The ideological role of sustainable development reporting". *Accounting Auditing and Accountability Journal*, 22(8): 1211–1257.

Morgan, D. R. (2009) "World on fire: two scenarios of the destruction of human civilization and possible extinction of the human race". *Futures*, 41(10): 683–693.

Norminton, G. (2013) *Beacons: Stories for our not so distant future.* London: OneWorld.

Piketty, T. (2014). *Capital in the 21st century.* Cambridge, MA: Harvard University Press:

Pinker, S. (2018) *Enlightenment now.* New York: Allen Lane.

Quinn, D. (2010) "The danger of human exceptionalism". In K. D. Moore and M. P. Nelson (eds), *Moral ground: Ethical action for a planet in peril*, pp. 9–14. San Antonio, TX: Trinity University Press.

Rees, M. (2003). *Our final hour: a scientist's warning: How terror, error, and environmental disaster threaten humankind's future in the century--on Earth and beyond.* New York: Basic Books.

Rifkin, J. (1980) *Entropy: A new world view.* New York: Viking.

Robson, K. (1992) "Accounting numbers as 'inscription': Action at a distance and the development of accounting". *Accounting, Organizations and Society*, 17(7): 685–708.

Rockström, J., et al. (2009) "A safe operating space for humanity". *Nature*, 461(7263): 472–475.

Rolston III, H. (2010) "A hinge point of history", In K. D. Moore and M. P. Nelson (eds), *Moral ground: Ethical action for a planet in peril*, pp. 70–74. San Antonio, TX: Trinity University Press.

Sale, K. (1980/2010). *Human scale*. New York: New Society Publishers.

Schumacher, E. F. (1973). *Small is beautiful: a study of ecomonics as if people mattered*. London: Vintage.

Scott, J. M. (2008) "Threats to biological diversity: Global, continental, local". Shifting Baselines and New Meridians: Water, Resources, Landscapes, and the Transformation of the American West, Summer Conference, 4–6 June. Retrieved from http://scholar.law.colorado.edu/water-resources-and-transformation-of-American-West/15

Shearer, T. (2002) "Ethics and accountability: from the for-itself to the for-the-other". *Accounting, Organizations and Society*, 27(6): 541–573.

Spash, C. (2015) "The dying planet index: Life, death and man's domination of nature", *Environmental Values*, 24(1): 1–7.

Steffen, W., P. J. Crutzen and J. R. McNeill (2007) "The Anthropocene: are humans now overwhelming the great forces of nature". *AMBIO: A Journal of the Human Environment*, 36(8): 614–621.

Stiglitz, J. E., A. Sen and J. P. Fitoussi (2010). *Mismeasuring our lives: Why GDP doesn't add up*. New York: New Press.

Sweet, Melissa (2010) "Obituaries: Frank Fenner". *British Medical Journal*, 341: c6850.

Thielemann U. (2000) "A brief theory of the market – ethically focused". *International Journal of Social Economics*, 27(1): 6–31.

Tonn, B. and D. MacGregor (2009) "Are we doomed?". *Futures*, 41(10): 673–675.

Tonn, B. and D. Stiefel (2014) "Human extinction risk and uncertainty: Assessing conditions for action". *Futures*, 63: 134–144.

Toth, G. and C. Szigeti (2015) "The historical ecological footprint: From over-population to over-consumption". *Ecological Indicators*, 60: 283–291.

Vinnari, E. and J. Dillard (2016) "(ANT)agonistics: Pluralistic politicization of, and by, accounting and its technologies". *Critical Perspectives on Accounting*, 39: 25–44.

Vitousek, P. M., P. R. Ehrlich, A. H. Ehrlich and P. A. Matson (1986). "Human appropriation of the products of photosynthesis". *BioScience*, 36(6): 368–373.

Wilson, E. O. (2010) "The fate of creation is the fate of humanity". In K. D. Moore and M. P. Nelson (eds), *Moral ground: Ethical action for a planet in peril*, pp. 25–29. San Antonio, TX: Trinity University Press.

Wilson, E. O. (2016) *Half-earth: our planet's fight for life*. New York: W. W. Norton & Company.

WWF (2016) *Living planet report 2016*. Gland, Switzerland: World Wide Fund for Nature.

Yurchak, Alexei (2005) *Everything was forever, until it was no more: The last Soviet generation*. Princeton, NJ: Princeton University Press.

5   Recovered species?

The eastern North Pacific grey whale
unusual mortality event, 1999–2000

Sophia Nicolov

Between 1999 and 2000, the Pacific shorelines of North America and Mexico witnessed an unprecedented series of events. 651 eastern North Pacific (ENP) grey whales (*Eschrichtius robustus*) were found stranded in what was considered an exceptional 'unusual mortality event' (UME) for this species. With the longest migration of any mammal, grey whales make a 10,000 to 12,000 mile round trip from the birthing lagoons in Mexico's Baja California; past California, Oregon and Washington; then along Vancouver Island, British Columbia, Canada; past Alaska and eventually into their Arctic feeding grounds of the Bering and Chukchi Seas. Shockingly, stranded whales were found along the length of this coastline.[1] A UME is defined under the 1972 US Marine Mammal Protection Act as 'a stranding that is unexpected; involves a significant die-off of any marine mammal population; and demands immediate response'.[2] While whales and other cetaceans have stranded for millennia and it is indeed a natural phenomenon, in 1999 strandings of grey whales shot up drastically. 283 animals were discovered in comparison to the average of 41 during the three previous years. It was after this alarming increase that the National Marine Fisheries Service (NMFS) of the US government body National Oceanic Atmospheric Administration (NOAA), consulted the official Working Group on Marine Mammal Unusual Mortality Events. The group formally declared this wave of deaths as an UME, reinforcing the extraordinary nature of this incident and the importance of scientific investigation. But the die off did not end there. In 2000, strandings increased further, with 368 animals reported along the coastline – raising concern among the scientific community and the general public in these regions.[3]

Perhaps most concerning of all is that these strandings were believed to be part of a wider population decline. The ENP grey whale was twice hunted to the brink of extinction, once in the mid-1800s and the second time in the early 1900s.[4] Long before whaling became a taboo associated with brutality and human rapacity of the natural world – as it did in the second half of the twentieth century – the species was afforded relatively early protection in the 1930s. All hunting of grey whales was banned by the League of Nations in what was the first international agreement protecting whales. Since the establishment of the International Whaling Commission in 1946, the ban on commercial hunting of grey whales has been upheld.[5] Protected by the US Endangered Species Act (ESA) since 1973, the population steadily rose to an estimated 21,000 and, as the population was believed to have returned close to its pre-whaling numbers, it was removed from the ESA list of endangered species in 1994 as recommended by the NMFS.[6] For this reason, the grey whale has been heralded as one of the greatest conservation success stories, an icon of Western society's environmental movement and our changing relationship with wild animals. However, having reached a peak population of 26,000 in 1998, by 2002 the population had dropped to an estimated 17,500 – a decline of around a third.[7] The strandings were merely the tip of the iceberg.

One major reason why this UME provoked a powerful response in the people who inhabit the Pacific coastlines of Mexico and North America, is that this species carries out its life cycle in physical proximity to humans. As they migrate up and down the west coast of North America and Mexico, they swim relatively close to shore and can be seen from the land. They are intrinsic to the view and have become emblematic of the Pacific shoreline.[8] Moreover, this closeness has resulted in a series of key viewing points along the migration being established, and it is from here that migration is tracked and the number of whales counted by NOAA as well as volunteers from non-profit groups such as Gray Whales Count.[9] This proximity meant that there was a heightened awareness of changes in the migration between 1999 and 2000, including fewer whales, skinny animals, a reduced calf count, the migration starting later and, of course, stranded bodies on the coastline.[10]

But what had caused this die off and, crucially, what had caused so many whales to strand? Whale strandings are visually disruptive, emotive and disturbing, and questions about possible causes are asked by scientists and lay people alike.[11] Since the end of widespread commercial whaling, whales – and cetaceans more broadly – face new threats caused by anthropogenic activity in and degradation to the marine environment. Our imagining of whales is transforming as our perceptions of the natural world give way to a new understanding of its decline at the hands of humans. As might be expected, mass mortality on this scale triggers alarm. In a die off such as this, where the calls for answers get louder, determining whether human activity may have played a role is crucially important. To this day, however, the cause of this particular mortality event remains 'undetermined'.[12] Unsurprisingly, this is a common conclusion in the case of beached cetaceans. Strandings take on an ambiguous nature, with speculation coming from both scientific spheres and popular society and, inevitably, there are conflicting explanations and hypotheses. Stranded whale bodies become scientific objects, analysed and tested in order to discover clues.[13] With the whale body as the main source of evidence, it is often impossible to pinpoint exactly why the animal beached and/or died. This becomes even harder if a post-mortem cannot be carried out. In the case of the grey whales, only three whales were necropsied – just 0.5% of the animals that actually stranded.[14] Thus limited knowledge was gathered in this way. Instead, the collection of body parts and tissue samples for analysis becomes essential for insight. Each stranded whale discovered is recorded and preserved in its individuality in the data it becomes. The animal has individual scientific value while also representing the generality. Thus, stranded whales are critically important for gaining knowledge about what is happening both to the species and the marine environment.[15]

A paper published by NOAA's Technical Memorandum in 2005 stated that a number of factors could have been possible causes of the UME, including 'chemical contaminants, biotoxins, infectious diseases, parasites, fisheries interactions and ship strikes'. These were identified as some of the possible causes during the three post-mortems and are also some of the more common factors believed to cause strandings globally.[16] It was not suggested, however, that this definitely caused the mortality event, reinforcing the lack of clarity about cause of death. Furthermore, in a significant proportion of animals examined, blubber lipid content was considered low and many were emaciated, suggesting that starvation may have played a role. Many living whales, in particular females, were also reported as skinny and malnourished and there were fewer reported calves during this period. In 2005, however, 'the underlying cause of starvation during this event is [still] unknown'.[17]

In the early 2000s, there were two explanations for the mortality event and the reduction of the population that appear to have had significant traction. The first was that it was caused by a particularly strong El Niño/La Niña weather event between 1997 and 2000.[18] El Niño and La Niña are the terms given to climatic events concentrated in the central and east Pacific and are the two phases of the El Niño-Southern Oscillation (ENSO) cycle. They recur as part of a natural cycle every few years. El Niño is used specifically for warming of sea surface temperature, usually for around twelve to eighteen months. La Niña is the term for the phase of cooler sea surface temperatures.[19] Scientists speculated that the changes in water temperature may have had a negative impact on the productivity of the main food source of grey whales, amphipods, tiny shrimp-like creatures that lives in the sediment. This, combined with more Arctic sea ice extending into the Bering and Chukchi seas between mid-1998 and 2001 due to the La Niña weather event, meant that the animals were unable to feed as much or for as long.[20] The second explanation was that NOAA researchers speculated that the grey whale feeding grounds in the north might have reached long-term carrying capacity – the maximum population of a species that an ecosystem can support indefinitely – because the population had rebounded to pre-whaling abundance. They based this on the population having reached a peak of approximately 26,000 in 1998 and the particularly low population estimates during 2001 and 2002. Perceived as a great conservation 'success', this wave of deaths was considered by some to perhaps be a natural course of events.[21]

Less than a decade later, however, ground-breaking research by American Stephen Palumbi, Eric Rynes and S. Elizabeth Alter, suggested that the pre-whaling population of grey whales in the Pacific was more likely to have been between 78,500 and 117,700. They used advancing technology to analyse the

DNA of the current population, including samples from stranded grey whales, to determine the species' genetic diversity. The genetic diversity identified in grey whales was too high for a pre-whaling population of just 22,000 to 26,000, which has been the average population size since the 1990s.[22] Genetic diversity can be relatively unaffected by short-term reductions in population size, such as that caused by whaling.[23] Researchers have suggested that the Bering and Chukchi seas can no longer support a larger population because global warming is causing the temperature of the water to increase which, in turn, has negatively impacted the Bering's benthic marine community, resulting in a decline in the abundance of grey whales' main food source.[24] In 2012, Palumbi and Alter published further research with Seth D. Newsome from their investigations into grey whale diversity by testing DNA from ancient whale remains, which revealed high genetic diversity again. They stated that this may support the possibility of a larger pre-whaling population.[25] DNA analysis of other species of whales – including the humpback whale and fin whale – has also suggested that pre-whaling populations were higher than previous estimates, providing new awareness of the reduction in these animals' ranges. Global strandings have been central to many of these discoveries.[26] These researchers' investigations reveal the ways in which scientific knowledge shifts over time and how alternative hypotheses can be both conflicting and contradictory. In light of this changing knowledge, the UME and wider population decline could no longer be attributed to a positive rebound in the population with certainty.

While the species was removed from the endangered species list in 1994, can a population three to five times smaller than its original abundance truly be considered a conservation success? Even before these advancements in technology, historical accounts of the ENP grey whale describe numbers far greater than those witnessed today, calling into question NOAA's contention that numbers had rebounded to their pre-whaling levels. For example, in one eighteenth century explorer's account of grey whales around Monterey Bay, California, he declared that 'It is impossible to describe either the number of whales with which we were surrounded, or their familiarity', while another described them as 'numberless'.[27] One of the most infamous whalers, Captain Charles Scammon, whose discovery of the birthing lagoons of Baja California, Mexico, in the mid-nineteenth century led to the cruel over-exploitation and near-extinction of this species, described how whales in the lagoons, mainly female and calves, 'huddled together so thickly that it was difficult for a boat to cross the waters without coming into contact with them'.[28] As leading marine biologist Callum Roberts has discussed in his work *The Unnatural History of the Sea*, in the 1850s around 1000 greys were counted daily passing along the shore during the southbound migration. Following their relentless hunting in Baja and along the coast of California, within twenty years the migrating whales counted from shore had dropped to just forty a day.[29] In 2016, volunteers of the Gray Whales Count, based at the Santa Barbara channel, reported an average of 16 grays a day migrating northbound, with a maximum of 54 on one day.[30]

This could be seen as an example of where shifting baseline syndrome has occurred. In 1995, renowned fisheries expert Daniel Pauly coined the term in relation to fisheries, calling for more inclusion of anecdotal accounts as valuable sources. Here, he states that:

> essentially, this syndrome has arisen because each generation of fisheries scientists accepts as a baseline the stock size and species composition that occurred at the beginning of their careers, and uses this to evaluate changes. When the next generation starts its career, the stocks have further decline, but it is the stocks at that time that serve as a new baseline. The result obviously is a gradual shift of the baseline, a gradual accommodation of the creeping disappearance.[31]

Marine ecologist Jeremy Jackson and environmental studies scholar Jennifer Jacquet have noted that 'no rational person would deny' that the bison on the plains of North America ranged in the millions pre-settler expansion, simply because there is 'no ecological survey data'. The evidence is there in the many historical descriptions. However, this is 'in effect . . . what most marine ecologists have done until very recently for the former extraordinary abundance of large animals in coastal seas around the world'.[32] The term has now been extended to a range of conservation issues and is useful when considering the ENP grey whale. Through a combination of archaeological and historical data – much of which is qualitative – as well as more recent DNA testing techniques, the long-term detrimental impact of humans on this species becomes clearer. The discoveries made have serious ramifications for the limitations of ecosystem restoration.[33]

ENP grey whales play a major 'ecological role' in the Arctic feeding grounds. Palumbi, Newsome and Alter suggest that the reduction in numbers may have had 'profound ecosystem impacts'.[34] They propose that, at previous population levels, grey whales – which are bottom feeders, and therefore suck up and filter out mouthfuls of nutritionally rich sediment through their baleen plates – seasonally may have 're-suspended 700 million cubic metres of sediment' which amounts to as much as 12 Yukon Rivers. The Yukon River runs through Alaska and British Columbia and is the largest river emptying into the Bering Sea, which suggests grey whales were responsible for massive levels of productivity in this ecosystem.[35] This species, therefore, is a 'key ecological structuring agent' in these waters. Reduction in its population may have had a drastic impact on the recycling of nutrients which, together with other ecological changes such as warming waters, is having adverse impacts on the benthic marine communities in these seas, including the seabirds and other terrestrial animals that feed on these. Therefore, the carrying capacity of the Arctic feeding grounds may have declined and is no longer able to support former numbers.[36] The reason this has such significance is that because there has been a presumed recovery, there has been 'a steep decline in extinction risk' and there is a reduced management concern for the ENP grey whale, which may affect the rate at which this species and, ultimately the ecosystem, is able recover. For this reason, knowledge about abundances of animal populations in the past is crucial for the present and future management and restoration of species.[37]

Scientists have suggested that reduced productivity in the benthic community along with greater ice cover in the years 1998–2001 meant that grey whales simply could not access enough food to sustain their migration. The combination of long-term 'shifting climatic conditions' and short-term El Niño and La Niña events was particularly disastrous for females who were pregnant or suckling calves, because they were unable to endure the huge migration burdened with these additional pressures.[38] It has been suggested that the carrying capacity of the Arctic feeding grounds of the Bering and Chukchi seas has declined over time for some of the reasons I have briefly touched on in this chapter. The rise of calving rates to pre-1999 levels, combined with knowledge about genetic variation of the long-term population, suggests that this population of grey whales has not reached its historic abundance, and could continue to increase if present conditions permitted. However, with a reduced carrying capacity and the population confined below 26,000 since the 1990s, scientists argue that this population may be considered 'depleted relative to historical numbers'.[39]

This calls into question the meanings we attach to the word 'endangered', both in the context of official classification and its popular usage. We might also want to think about what this has to say about our perception of 'recovered species'. Perhaps we need a rethink of the discourse surrounding 'successful' conservation stories that more closely reflects the truth. The reality is that the possibility of grey whales returning to their previous numbers is unlikely, and perhaps even impossible, because of 'large-scale' and perhaps irreversible ecological changes in their Arctic feeding grounds.[40] With future predictions of Arctic ecosystem collapse due to climate change and marine defaunation, perhaps it is time to speak more frankly about the future of what supposedly recovered and stable populations of animals might actually be.[41] By acknowledging this, humans may be able to manage marine mammal populations in more responsible ways, while ultimately recognising the limits of human conservation efforts in the face of climate change. This is not to undermine the significance of these whale population recoveries. Instead, it reinforces the need for greater action to be taken to tackle the drivers of these climatic shifts and ecological changes to ensure that species like the grey whale do not disappear from the oceans.

Notes

1 F. M. D. Gulland, et al., 'Eastern North Pacific Gray Whale (*Eschrichtius Robustus*) Unusual Mortality Event, 1999–2000', US Department of Commerce, *NOAA Technical Memorandum*, NMFS-AFSC–150, (2015), pp. 1, 2.
2 Marine Mammal Commission, 'Definitions', in *The Marine Mammal Protection Act of 1972 as Amended*, updated with 2015 Amendments by NOAA's National Marine Fisheries Service, Section 410 (2015), p. 103.

3 Gulland et al., 'Eastern North Pacific Gray Whale', p. 2; Linda Hogan and Brenda Peterson, *Sightings: The Gray Whales' Mysterious Journey* (Washington, DC: National Geographic Society, 2003), pp. 89, 90–91, 256.

4 Richard Ellis, *Men and Whales* (New York: Knopf: 1991), pp. 242–244; Serge Dedina, *Saving the Gray Whale: People, Politics, and Conservation in Baja California* (Tuscon, AZ: University of Arizona Press, 2000), pp. 19–24, 26.

5 Dedina, *Saving the Gray Whale*, pp. 48–49.

6 Doug P. DeMaster et al., 'Status Review of the Eastern North Pacific Stock of Gray Whales', US Department of Commerce, *NOAA Technical Memorandum*, NMFS-AFSC–103 (1999), p. 1; Stephen R. Palumbi and Joe Roman, 'The History of Whales Read from DNA', in *Whales, Whaling and Ocean Ecosystems*, ed. by Robert L. Brownell et al. (Berkeley, CA: University of California Press, 2006), p. 102.

7 Sheela McLean, 'Pacific Gray Whale Population Estimate Released', NOAA Fisheries: Alaska Regional Office (10 May 2002), https://alaskafisheries.noaa.gov/node/10779 [accessed 13 December 2017].

8 See, for example, Hogan and Peterson, *Sightings*, pp. 57, 83, 208.

9 Wayne L. Perryman, Stephen B. Reilly and Richard A. Rowlett, 'Results of Surveys of Northbound Gray Whale Calves 2001–2010 and Examination of the Full Seventeen Year Series of Estimates from the Piedras Blancas Light Station', *Whaling Commission, Scientific Committee*, SC/62/BRG1 (2010), p. 1; McLean, 'Pacific Gray Whale Population Estimate Released'; Gray Whales Count is a Santa Barbara based non-profit and project collaborators include NOAA Southwest Fisheries Science Center, www.graywhalescount.org [accessed 16 February 2018].

10 Dick Russell, *Eye of the Whale: Epic Passage from Baja to Siberia* (New York: Simon & Schuster, 2001), p.250; Hogan and Peterson, *Sightings*, p. 57.

11 Sophia Nicolov, 'On the Beach and Beyond: Responses to and Understandings of Sperm Whale Strandings on the British North Sea Coast since 1980' (unpublished Master of Philosophy thesis, University of Bristol, 2017), p. 65.

12 NOAA Fisheries, 'Marine Mammal Unusual Mortality Events', www.nmfs.noaa.gov/pr/health/mmume/events.html [accessed 12 January 2018].

13 Nicolov, 'On the Beach and Beyond', p. 68; Adrian Franklin, *Animals and Modern Cultures: A Sociology of Human-Animal Relations in Modernity* (London: Sage, 1999), pp. 62–83.

14 Gulland et al., 'Eastern North Pacific Gray Whale', pp. iii, 5, 9–11, 12, 18.

15 Nicolov, 'On the Beach and Beyond', pp. 70–71, 150.

16 Gulland et al., 'Eastern North Pacific Gray Whale', pp. iii, 9–11; See 'Report of an IWC Workshop Developing Practical Guidance for the Handling of Cetacean Stranding Events', *International Whaling Commission*, IWC/66/WKM&WI Rep02 (2016).

17 Gulland et al., 'Eastern North Pacific Gray Whale', pp. iii, 8–9.

18 Gulland et al., 'Eastern North Pacific Gray Whale', p. 15; See, for example, Alejandro Gómez-Gallardo U. et al., 'Abundance and Mortality of Gray Whales at Laguna San Ignacio, Mexico, during the 1997–98 El Niño and the 1998–99 La Niña', *Geofísica Internacional*, 42 (2003), pp. 439–446; B. J. Le Boeuf et al., 'High Gray Whale Mortality and Low Recruitment in 1999: Potential Causes and Implications', *Journal of Cetacean Research and Management*, 2 (2000), pp. 85–9. See also, Russell, *Eye of the Whale*, pp. 518–519.

19 Michael H. Glantz, 'El Niño', in *Currents of Change: Impacts of El Niño and La Niña on Climate and Society*, 2nd edn (Cambridge: Cambridge University Press, 2001), pp. 15–28.

20 Gulland et al., 'Eastern North Pacific Gray Whale', p. 15; Le Boeuf et al., 'High Gray Whale Mortality', pp. 85–99; S. Elizabeth Alter, E. Rynes and Stephen R. Palumbi,

'DNA Evidence for Historic Population Size and Past Ecological Impacts of Gray Whales', *Proceedings of the National Academy of Sciences*, 104 (2007), p. 15166. See also Russell, *Eye of the Whale,* pp. 518–519.

21 Gulland et al., 'Eastern North Pacific Gray Whale', p. 17; McLean, 'Pacific Gray Whale Population Estimate Released'; P. R. Wade, 'A Bayesian Stock Assement of the Eastern Pacific Gray Whale Using Abundance and Harvest Data from 1967–1996', *Journal of Cetacean Research and Management,* 4 (2002), 85–98. Doug DeDemaster of NMFS, 'Arctic Science Journeys', Radio Transcript: Gray Whale Comeback (2000), produced by the Alaska Sea Grant and the University of Alaska Fairbanks, https://seagrant.uaf.edu/news/00ASJ/05.01.00_GrayWhales.html [accessed 12 December 2017]; Alter, Rynes and Palumbi, 'DNA Evidence for Historic Population Size', p. 15162.

22 Palumbi, 'DNA Evidence for Historic Population Size', p. 15165.

23 Palumbi, 'DNA Evidence for Historic Population Size', p. 15162; Callum Roberts, *The Unnatural History of the Sea: The Past and Future of Humanity and Fishing* (Washington, DC: Island Press, 2007), p. 102.

24 Alter, Rynes and Palumbi, 'DNA Evidence for Historic Population Size', p. 15166. Eddy C. Carmack et al., 'A Major Ecosystem Shift in the Northern Bering Sea', *Science*, 311 (2006), pp. 1461–1463; Kenneth O. Coyle et al., 'Amphipod Prey of Gray Whales in the Northern Bering Sea: Comparison of Biomass and Distribution between the 1980s and 2002–2003', *Deep Sea Research II*, 54 (2007), pp. 2906–2918.

25 S. Elizabeth Alter, Seth D. Newsome and Stephen R. Palumbi. 2012. 'Pre-Whaling Genetic Diversity and Population Ecology in Eastern Pacific Gray Whales: Insights from Ancient DNA and Stable Isotopes', *PLOS*, 7 (2012), http://journals.plos.org/plosone/article?id=10.1371/journal.pone.0035039 [accessed 19 February 2018].

26 See Palumbi and Roman, 'History of Whales Read from DNA', pp. 103, 107–113; Roberts, *Unnatural History of the Sea,* pp. 100–102. In 2016 I met with Richard Sabin, Principal Curator of the Natural History Museum, London, and cetacean specialist. During a visit to the Museum's storeroom he explained the scientific value of strandings for determining previous genetic diversity and historic ranges: conversation with Richard Sabin 31 May 2016. See Nicolov, 'On the Beach and Beyond', pp. 74–76.

27 Malcolm Margolin, Jean François de la Pérouse, *Monterey in 1786: The Journals of Jean François de la Pérouse* (Berkeley, CA: Heyday Books, 1989), p. 54; George Vancouver, *A Voyage of Discovery to the North Pacific Ocean and Round the World 1791–1795,* 3 vols (London: Printed for G. G. and J Robinson, and J. Edwards, 1798), i, p. 337.

28 Charles Melville Scammon, *The Marine Mammals of the North-western Coast of North America* (San Francisco, CA: John H. Carmany and Company, 1874), p.25; Ellis, *Men and Whales*, pp. 242–244.

29 Scammon, '*Marine Mammals of the North-western*', p. 23; Roberts, *Unnatural History of the Sea*, p. 98.

30 Gray Whales Count, '2016 Daily Totals of Cetaceans, On-Effort', part of 2016 Gray Whales Count Survey Report 2016, prepared by Michael H Smith, www.graywhalescount.org/GWC/GWC_REPORTS_files/2016Daily%20Totals%20Cetaceans.pdf [accessed 18 February 2018].

31 Daniel Pauly, 'Anecdotes and the Shifting Baseline Syndrome of Fisheries', *Trends in Ecology & Evolution*, 10 (1995), p. 430.

32 Jeremy Jackson and Jennifer Jacquet, 'The Shifting Baselines Syndrome: Perception, Deception, and the Future of Our Oceans', in *Ecosystem Approaches to Fisheries: A Global Perspective*, ed. by V. Christensen and J. Maclean (Cambridge: Cambridge

University Press, 2011), p. 129; A. C. Isenberg, *The Destruction of the Bison* (Cambridge: Cambridge University Press, 2000).

33 Alter, Rynes and Palumbi, 'DNA Evidence for Historic Population Size', pp. 15162–67; Alter, Newsome, and Palumbi, 'Pre-Whaling Genetic Diversity'; Palumbi and Roman, 'History of Whales Read from DNA', pp. 102, 103.

34 Alter, Rynes and Palumbi, 'DNA Evidence for Historic Population Size', p. 15162; Donald A. Croll, Raphael Kudela and Bernie R. Tershy, 'Ecosystem Impact of the Decline of Large Whales in the North Pacific', in *Whales, Whaling and Ocean Ecosystems*, ed. by Robert L. Brownell et al. (Berkeley, CA: University of California Press, 2006), pp. 202, 210–12.

35 Alter, Rynes and Palumbi, 'DNA Evidence for Historic Population Size', pp. 15162, 15166.

36 Alter, Rynes and Palumbi, 'DNA Evidence for Historic Population Size', p. 15166; J. S. Oliver and P. N. Slattery, 'Destruction and Opportunity on the Sea Floor: Effects of Gray Whale Feeding', *Ecology*, 66 (1985), pp. 1965–1975; Carmack, 'Major Ecosystem Shift in the Northern Bering Sea', pp. 1461–1463; Coyle, 'Amphipod Prey of Gray Whales in the Northern Bering Sea', pp. 2906–2918; Sue E. Moore, Jacqueline M. Grebmeier and Jeremy R. Davies, 'Gray Whale Distribution Relative to Forage Habitat in the Northern Bering Sea: Current Conditions and Retrospective Summary', *Canadian Journal of Zoology*, 81 (2003), pp. 735, 739–740.

37 Alter, Rynes and Palumbi, 'DNA Evidence for Historic Population Size', pp. 15162, 15166; Jackson and Jacquet, 'Shifting Baselines Syndrome', p. 136; Palumbi and Roman, 'History of Whales Read from DNA', p. 102.

38 Gómez-Gallardo et al., 'Abundance and Mortality of Gray Whales at Laguna San Ignacio', p. 444; Gulland et al., 'Eastern North Pacific Gray Whale', pp. 7, 15, 16.

39 Alter, Rynes and Palumbi, 'DNA Evidence for Historic Population Size', pp. 15162, 15166.

40 Alter, Rynes and Palumbi, 'DNA Evidence for Historic Population Size', p. 15166.

41 James A. Estes et al., 'Marine Defaunation: Animal Loss in the Global Ocean', *Science*, 347 (2015), 1255641.

6 The Natural Capital Protocol and the honey bee

Mervyn E. King

Life below the water is encapsulated in one of the Sustainable Development Goals (SDGs) agreed to by 193 countries together with some great multinational enterprises at the United Nations in April 2015. The importance of life below the water is that part of humankind's food security is in fact found below the water. One of the challenges of the 21st century is that plastic became part of mass market production in the 20th century. As more and more plastic is used, about a third of the 80 million tons of plastics produced per annum finds its way into the environment, polluting our lands and life below the water.

There is, in effect, a plastic smog in our seas and this smog consists of granules of plastic which life below the water does not distinguish from that which is edible. These micro plastics which are eaten by creatures below the water contaminate the fish and crustaceans that human beings eat.

On land the pollution of plastic is more apparent. Plastic packets driven by wind litter countrysides, finding themselves attached to wire fencing but the plastic smog in our seas and oceans is devastating even though less visible.

In the Six Capitals approach of integrated thinking and "doing" an integrated report of the International Integrated Reporting Council (IIRC) one of the sources of value creation recognised is natural capital. Without natural capital the company, both public and private as we know it today cannot exist. Individuals who are the heart, mind and soul of companies as directors cannot exist unless the world is able to sustain its production of food for an increasing population. Our food comes from the land and from below the water.

Below the water we have the smog of micro plastics. Above the water we have well known pollutants such as carbon emissions, but we also have pesticides to "kill" the bugs that people believe are destroying certain plant life.

This pollution below the water and on our lands led to the establishment of the Natural Capital Protocol (NCP), based on the premise that the natural capital that an organisation owns or for which it is responsible has a value both to the organisation and to society. As stated by Prof Colin Meyer in his introduction to the Natural Capital Committee's Corporate Natural Capital Accounting Project:

> A failure to maintain that natural capital diminishes both the future commercial potential of the organisation and the benefits that society will be able to derive from it. Failure to maintain natural capital therefore reduces

its value and in the same way that organisations account for depreciation of the value of their material assets, so too they should account for the depreciation of their natural assets. The way this is done is to estimate the cost of maintaining or replacing the assets.

Michael Izza, the CEO of ICAEW, who was present when the Natural Capital Protocol was launched at the Chartered Accountants Hall at Moorgate in London, has pointed out that:

> At the heart of what we as a profession do is the measuring and provision of timely, trusted, decision useful information, shaped by insight and judgment." He points out that the SDGs are a vision of a world which by 2030 will be one of fairness, with just societies and one where we are living within our natural means.

The recognition by the accountancy profession of the NCP reinforces my belief that it is accountants who can save the planet during this century. It is to the accountant that the business person first turns to for advice and if the accountant, in the discharge of his or her public interest duties, advises a company to develop strategy, having regard to the natural capitals, the SDGs and the NCP, then we should have a sustainable world by the end of the 21st century.

At the end of 2009 at the UN in Geneva, IFAC acknowledged that financial reporting although critical was not sufficient. I as chairman of the Global Reporting Initiative on Sustainability Reporting acknowledged that sustainability reporting was critical but on its own without the numbers was clearly not sufficient. This resulted in the logical conclusion that a new form of corporate reporting was required. Companies were reporting the financials in a silo and the sustainability issues in a silo. This was not reflective of what was actually happening on the ground in companies. Companies use the six sources of value creation, financial, human, intellectual, manufactured, natural and social capital, the latter including the relationships between a company and its stakeholders. There is a daily integration of the use of sources of value creation and the relationships with stakeholders. This reality led to the concepts of integrated thinking and doing an integrated report and the formation of the IIRC which issued its Framework as a guideline to reporting on an integrated basis.

The IIRC and the Natural Capital Coalition have set out how their approaches are complementary. The Natural Capital Coalition (The Coalition) and the International Integrated Reporting Council (IIRC) both recognise the importance of organisations taking more than financial information into consideration and applying integrated thinking in their decision making. They have developed the Natural Capital Protocol and the International IR Framework respectively for organisations to use to achieve this.

The two approaches are complementary and users of one should consider how the other might support their work. The Natural Capital Protocol provides a systematic, harmonized approach on how to identify, measure and value natural capital, and inform business decisions. Whilst the International

IR Framework, which identifies natural capital, is used by organisations to communicate how their strategy, governance, performance and prospects, in the context of their external environment, lead to the creation of value over time in a sustainable manner.

By adopting both the Natural Capital Protocol and the IR Framework, organisations are able to make changes to the way they work and create value for both themselves and society, while conserving and enhancing the natural world. They are also able to communicate with their providers of financial capital and wider stakeholders on their strategy, opportunities and risks in a concise and integrated way. This will enable capital markets to access more meaningful information to achieve more efficient and productive capital allocation decisions and greater financial stability.

The importance of the above can be seen in just looking at one species, and that is the humble bee, on which we are all dependent for continued food security. The world is experiencing its sixth period of mass species extinction. If the bee becomes extinct, food security will cost an estimated 100 billion to produce because pollination would have to take place by hand or by some robotic intervention. All this has led to extinction accounting and being accountable for the possible extinction of a species linked to one's business.

The International Union for Conservation of Nature has listed the threats of extinction as habitat destruction and degradation; over-exploitation for example extraction; hunting; fishing; pollution; disease; invasions of alien species (for example cats and rats on islands); and global climate change for migratory species and coral bleaching.

Scientists have been reporting about the alarming rate at which species are becoming extinct due to pollution. In this context the biggest challenge for humankind is the possible extinction of the bee population. There has already been a significant reduction in that population. The issue of the continued existence of the honey bee has become so critical that they are being migrated in trucks from one area to another. Beehives are also being established on the tops of buildings in cities.

Albert Einstein said: "Mankind will not survive the honey bee's disappearance for more than five years." He said this with such certainty because the bee is a critical player in mankind's food chain. Without the pollination by bees our food security would be severely adversely impacted.

Newsweek has run an article outlining the US Department of Agriculture's announcement that it is to provide a subsidy to ensure the continued existence of the one creature on planet earth that will either make or break our food security, namely the bee. Bees are dying not only from pollution and pesticides but because of climate change from extreme winters and extremely hot summers.

The factual position is that in the last five years some 30% of the national bee population on planet earth has disappeared. Hence the accountant must come to the rescue. Extinction accounting is something which the accountant has to focus on and develop.[1]

Sheffield University Management School at the University of Sheffield has done much work on a bee centric framework for the accounting of bees. They believe there should be a report by a company of how the bee decline has affected or not its supply chain. Has there been a financial impact of bee decline on the business of the company? Report on why bees are important to the business of the company and its stakeholders. Report on the potential risks or impacts on the bee decline on the company's operations in the longer term. A company should report on what initiatives it is taking to halt the decline of bee populations in its operations. Is the company holding supplies in its supply chain accountable for growing food in conditions which is adding to the decline in the bee population?

The concept is to build an emancipatory framework which encourages companies to protect bees and ensure that extinction is prevented. Some serious application of professional minds is needed to see how natural capital reporting can be combined with reporting on the extinction of species, particularly the honey bee, which is so critical to the continued existence of mankind.

Note

1 This term was first published in M. E. King with J. F. Atkins (2016), *The Chief Value Officer: Accountants Can Save the Planet*, Greenleaf Publishing, Saltaire.

7 Extraction and extinction

The role of investors in ensuring the marine health of the planet

Abigail Herron

This chapter discusses the ways in which responsible investors are engaging with companies on fisheries in order to prevent extinction of marine species. The chapter also touches on the influence of civil society on corporate reputation and the growing reputational risk faced by companies in relation to their contribution to species extinction. I write in a personal capacity.

Introduction

For over three decades, the world's marine fish stocks have come under increasing pressure from fishing, loss of habitats and pollution. Rising sea temperatures and the increasing acidity of the oceans are placing further stress on already stressed ecosystems. Illegal fishing and unreported catches undermine fisheries management, while subsidies continue to support unsustainable fishing practices.

Around 85 per cent of global fish stocks are overexploited, depleted, fully exploited or in recovery from exploitation. Globally, 1,851 species of fish or 21% of all fish species evaluated were deemed at risk of extinction by the IUCN in 2010, including more than a third of sharks and rays.

Using natural resources wisely is the key to maintaining a sustainable economy. The current environmental, social, and governance practices within the seafood industry create significant challenges for commercial fish stocks that are driving many species to collapse and ultimately extinction. Current rates of extraction threaten both the future stability of a multi-billion dollar industry itself and, more importantly, the long-term food security of millions of people and the continued existence of iconic fisheries species.

Fishing effort has often exceeded the ability of fish stocks to maintain themselves and the impact on non-target species (including potentially vulnerable species such as sharks, turtles, and marine mammals) can be severe. The results have often been stark; many fish stocks have declined just when our need for increased food production is greatest and the marine ecosystem has been significantly degraded.

Sustainability is central to the business success of companies that produce, process, or retail seafood because of the significant risks inherent in the supply chain. Companies engaged in the seafood sector have to manage risk factors, such as:

- **Risk of supply chain disruption**

   Wild fisheries can be overexploited, causing a dramatic fall in annual harvests, while fish farms can be ravaged by disease. Seafood companies that process and sell marine products face significant risks in securing a reliable source of raw material – in terms of both availability and price.
- **Risk to reputation**

   Companies with public-facing brands face a risk to their reputations if they do not act to source from responsibly managed fisheries. Many high-profile campaign groups specifically work on issues of corporate responsibility around seafood and will publicly identify companies that fail to act responsibly.
- **Risks associated with using illegal product**

   Illegal fishing, sometimes called pirate fishing or "IUU" (illegal, unreported, unregulated) fishing, is a major problem in seafood supply chains and intertwined with the threat of extinction in our oceans. It is also closely associated with environmental damage and labour abuse. Companies that are found to be using illegal product can face legal action and damage to reputation.

Out of tuna

China Tuna Industry Group shelved a planned $100 million initial public offering in December 2014 after Greenpeace delivered a letter of complaint to the Hong Kong Stock Exchange accusing the company of underestimating its exposure to environmental and sustainability risks. The concerns that tuna quotas had been breached were shared by the regulator, but not by the company or its advisors who failed to mention the endangered status of their primary catch when drafting their listing prospectus.

The widespread depletion of fish at the top of the food chain, such as tuna, shark and swordfish, and indeed any disruption in biodiversity, seldom has a positive systemic effect. The resultant population booms of prey species, such as rays and squid, and negative impact on fish further down the food chain can have wide-ranging implications.

Jaw dropping statistics

A quarter of sharks and related species are threatened with extinction, according to the IUCN Shark Specialist Group. Sharks are the ocean's top predators and are vitally important to maintain the balance of marine ecosystems. Overfishing, especially by the use of indiscriminate long line fishing gear, is the key threat sharks face and the demand for shark fin as a soup ingredient is the driving forces behind this overfishing.

The adoption of mandatory ESG disclosure by the Hong Kong Exchanges and Clearing Limited (HKEx) provides an opportunity for companies to formulate wide-ranging environmental policies and key performance indicators. One example investors can press for is a commitment to implementing WWF-Hong Kong's No Shark Fin pledge.

What is the role of investors?

Positive engagement with management can steer investee companies towards more sustainable strategies that both improve business performance and aid the environment and society. However, shareholders need to be able to ask the right questions of companies and press them for substantial answers.

The most important first step that a company can take towards responsible behaviour is to formulate and adopt a responsible seafood policy. Such a policy does not entail avoiding poorly managed fisheries and confining procurement to "sustainable fisheries", but involves a commitment to continuous improvement and transparency with ambitious targets in the future.

The essential elements of an effective, responsible seafood policy for wild fish are commitments to:

1   Assess all source fisheries for environmental and social risk and report on this process.
2   Achieve sufficient traceability within the supply chain that illegally caught fish cannot be sold and the adoption of sanctions against suppliers convicted of dealing in illegal fish.
3   Reward fisheries that are performing well (for instance, certified to a credible standard like the Marine Stewardship Council) through purchasing decisions and reporting on the proportion of certified seafood used in the business.
4   Reward fisheries that are actively improving through purchasing decisions and support for fishery improvement projects (FIPs) and reporting on the proportion of seafood that comes from fisheries that are engaged in improvement projects.
5   Transparency and the reporting of source fisheries used in the business (for example, through supporting the Ocean Disclosure Project).

Questions that investors should ask companies

The ability of investors to ask penetrating questions of companies represents a major source of leverage in pressing for more sustainable behaviours. Asking for substantial answers to simple questions will have a major impact on companies that deal in seafood. Aviva Investors works closely with Sustainable Fisheries Partnership (SFP) and considers them an invaluable resource to advise and support investors in conducting these conversations. Pertinent questions include:

1   Does the company have a policy regarding the sustainable management of the seafood resources it uses in its business?
2   Has the company assessed the current management status of all the stocks of wild fish that are part of their business?
3   Does the company have traceability systems in place that ensure the avoidance of illegally caught fish? What sanctions have been adopted when illegal raw material has been detected?
4   What is the company policy towards producing/purchasing wild seafood that is certified sustainable?
5   What is the company policy towards producing/purchasing seafood from fisheries engaged in fishery improvement projects?
6   What is the company policy regarding the disclosure of source fisheries that produce raw material for the business?

Conclusion

Positive engagement by responsible investors can steer companies towards more sustainable strategies that improve business performance, deliver environmental and social benefits and impress upon companies the risks of having illegal fisheries in their supply chains.

However, investors need to be able to ask the right questions of companies and press them for substantial answers. Investors and companies should also factor the following contemporary environmental concerns that are fuelling extinction into their thinking on this topic:

Deadzones

In the Gulf of Mexico in 2017 the world's largest ever recorded deadzone was identified by the National Oceanic and Atmospheric Administration (NOAA). A deadzone is an area in the sea where pollutants from predominantly industrial factory farms create algal blooms that kill off or displace marine life.

Plastics

While plastic has many beneficial uses, its production has grown exponentially for many years without sufficient regard to its environmental fate or ability to be recycled. At a time of intense interest in transition to a circular economy, only 14% of plastic packaging is recycled.

There are special concerns about the impact of plastic on oceans, which contain an estimated 150 million tons of degraded plastic, with 8 million tons added annually—equivalent to a garbage truck load every minute. In the marine environment, plastics break down into indigestible particles posing a threat to marine life. Plastic production is projected to triple by 2050. The estimated environmental cost of plastic production for the consumer goods industry is $75 billion annually. Scientists predict oceans will contain more plastic than fish by 2050 if no actions are taken.

The recent publicity given to the issue of marine plastic pollution should help propagate a more receptive consumer and business environment for promoting responsible production and use of plastics. Specific actions investors can ask investee companies to take could include:

- Making all packaging recyclable, reusable, or compostable to the fullest extent possible. Considering alternatives to plastic.
- Engaging with appropriate third parties in markets where company products are sold to ensure that end user brands play a role in programs and funding so that packaging actually gets recycled.
- Supporting the Ellen MacArthur Foundation New Plastic Economy project which seeks to dramatically improve effectiveness of recycling and develop a Global Plastics Protocol to remove disruptive plastics, and redesign materials.
- Development of plastic use reduction goals; this should focus on more than simply light weighting, but actually reducing the number of units generated.
- Determine whether reusable containers can replace single use applications.
- Anticipate and respond to the prospect of regulatory risk posed by potential plastic packaging bans by local, federal or regional government.
- Research the potential for technology and innovation to provide workable solutions.

Ghost fishing

Fishing gear, including nets, long lines, fish traps and any contraptions designed to catch sea life, are still capable of catching fishing when abandoned or lost at sea, this is known as ghost fishing. Its impact in terms of the apex, charismatic and often endangered marine species is significant and headline-grabbing. However, in many ways the impact on commercial species is greater. Ghost-fishing gear accounts for 10% of all marine plastic pollution. It moves, so it can be a major threat far from where it was lost, even in Marine Protected Areas. It is a significant cost to the fishing sector in terms of lost catch and it's responsible for 10% of global fish stock decline (up to 30% in some fisheries).

Climate change

If we limit global warming to one and a half or two degrees, this will dramatically reduce the number of species currently at risk of extinction because of climate change. All investors should be quizzing their investee companies about their strategic response to climate change. Companies should be strongly encouraged to disclosure against the Financial Stability Board's Taskforce on Climate Related Financial Disclosure guidelines. Investors should commit to voting against companies who do not at their Annual General Meetings.

8   The Convention on International Trade in Endangered Species of Wild Fauna and Flora (CITES)

An appraisal

Simon Norton

CITES: a convention of its time

The Convention on International Trade in Endangered Species of Wild Fauna and Flora (CITES) was signed in Washington DC, USA, on 3 March 1973, by representatives of 80 countries, the 'Parties', and was drafted as a result of a resolution adopted in 1963 at a meeting of members of the International Union for Conservation of Nature (IUCN). Its roots were firmly in the 1960s with the nascent ecological movements of that time. Then, there was a growing awareness of the impact of human activity upon both the natural environment and the species within it. Ecologists were becoming increasingly aware that the environment itself was a living, breathing organism comprising complex webs in which fauna and flora interact with each other in dynamic, constantly changing environments which are subject to both anthropogenic and non-anthropogenic causes and effects. Minteer et al. (2004) describe the distinction between the two thus: the former comprise the effects of human intervention in the natural environment, while the latter are confined to biologically or ecologically rooted events such as forest fires, floods, and evolution of species as a consequence of naturally occurring phenomena such as the shortening or lengthening of seasonal weather patterns (Magistro and Roncoli, 2001; Davis et al., 1984).

CITES is an agreement to which States and economic organisations such as the European Union adhere voluntarily; it is not binding, but it is expected that Parties will implement its provisions through their own national legislation. If a State chooses to exceed the Convention's criteria, then this is permissible, but a reduction would be unacceptable. The principal aim of CITES is to ensure that international trade in specimens of wild animals and plants does not threaten their survival through two mechanisms; first, that exports or imports of certain species should require permits or licences, and second, that trade is only permitted if a species is not listed in one of three Appendices. In other words, the CITES regime is essentially negative in approach: it informs what cannot be done, rather than providing positive guidance in the form of lists of species which can be traded. After a species has been listed in Appendix I – the endangered species list – it cannot be traded. The Convention does not concern itself with the economic aspects of trade in species: that drivers of trade in natural resources are invariably the forces of demand and supply, and that an imbalance in one tends to lead to consequences for the other (Igo, 2010; Norton, 2007). For example, if the supply of rhino horn is reduced, possibly because of greater enforcement measures in so-called Range States (states whose territory is within the natural range of distribution of a species), then if price remains stable, perhaps because of its use in traditional medicines in the Far East, then the price of illegally obtained product will rise. As the price rises, so the incentive to break the law through poaching becomes greater relative to the possible range of penalties which may be incurred if 'caught' (Linkie et al., 2003; Yamagiwa, 2008). The economics of conservation was omitted from CITES, and is an issue which will be returned to later in this chapter where analysis of the Endangered Species Act of 1973 by Brown and Shogren (1998) which implemented CITES into US law will be commented upon.

For a country to become a Party to the Convention it must meet four criteria. First, there must be a designation of Management and Scientific Authorities. These police the Convention, and decide on issues of sustainability before making a 'non-detrimental finding'. This in turn forms the basis of the licensing and permit system. Second, there must be domestic laws which prohibit the trade in violation of CITES. Third, there must be penalties in respect of breaches (Jachmann and Billiouw, 1997). This is sometimes a weak point in the CITES regime: penalties are not severe enough relative to the rewards which can be gained through violation of the rules, for example by exporting rhino horn. Fourth, there must be laws for the confiscation of specimens, and their return to their country of origin or to a rescue centre.

Structure and funding

CITES is headed up by the Conference of the Parties which meets at three-yearly intervals. The last CoP, CoP 17, was held in Johannesburg, South Africa, from 24 September to 5 October 2016, and the next, CoP18, will be held in Colombo, Sri Lanka, in May 2019. Beneath the Conference are the Plants Committee, the Animals Committee, and a Standing Committee. These report to the CoP. The structure also comprises a CITES Secretariat, supported by the UN Environment Programme which provides administrative services. Members of the Animals and Plants Committees are individuals from the six geographical regions of Africa, Asia, Europe, North America, Central and South America and the Caribbean, and Oceania. They are elected at the meetings of the Conference of the Parties, with the number of regional representatives weighted according to the number of Parties within each region and according to the regional distribution of biodiversity. The core administrative costs of the Secretariat, the CoP and its subsidiary bodies, the Standing Committee and other permanent committees, are financed from the CITES Trust Fund (www.cites.org/eng/disc/fund.php). This is funded from contributions from the Parties to the Convention based on the United Nations scale of assessment, adjusted to take account of the fact that not all members of the United Nations are Parties to the Convention. The European Commission also provides funding, including for a project, 'strengthening the CITES implementation capacity of developing countries' for EUR 1 million with follow-up funding of EUR 1.5 million. It also provides funds of EUR 500,000 for the implementation of CoP15 Decisions, along with the United States which provides USD 320,000. Other major donors include Denmark, France, Germany, Hong Kong SAR (China), Japan, Norway, Qatar, Sweden, and the United Kingdom. These countries continue to provide funding for capacity building, science-related activities, national legislation, enforcement, the sponsored delegates project, and the Monitoring of Illegal Killing of Elephants Programme (MIKE).

Statement of principles

The introduction to the Convention sets out its basic philosophy as follows:

> The Contracting States,
> Recognizing that wild fauna and flora in their many beautiful and varied forms are an irreplaceable part of the natural systems of the earth which must be protected for this and the generations to come;
> Conscious of the ever-growing value of wild fauna and flora for aesthetic, scientific, cultural, recreational and economic points of view;
> Recognizing that peoples and States are and should be the best protectors of their own wild fauna and flora;
> Recognizing, in addition, that international co-operation is essential for the protection of certain species of wild fauna and flora against over-exploitation through international trade;
> Convinced of their urgency of taking appropriate measures to this end;
> Have agreed as follows:
> The penalties for breaches of the Convention are set out in Article VIII. This states that the Parties shall take appropriate measures to enforce the provisions of the present Convention and to prohibit trade in specimens in violation thereof. These shall include the following measures:
>
> (a) to penalize trade in, or possession of, such specimens, or both; and
> (b) to provide for the confiscation or return to the State of export of such specimens.

These statements are significant because they raise three fundamental assumptions underpinning CITES. First, that flora and fauna are irreplaceable, and as such form part of the 'natural systems of the earth'. Ecosystems tend to be self-repairing (O'Neill, 1998), self-perpetuating, and species within them are integral and essential parts of the processes by which these are achieved. Human intervention can damage such systems; anthropogenic change can result from deforestation to make way for increased soya production, deliberate introduction of new species into an environment to enhance food production, or the cultivation of genetically modified crops which are resistant to so-called pests such as aphids, locusts or weevils, which can lead to a reduction in output and concomitantly a decline in profits as less is available for sale into the marketplace or more significantly, a reduction of food output to a local hungry population. Second, over-exploitation is the problem, and not exploitation per se (Rammel et al., 2007). CITES recognises the need to make use of natural resources, but this should be done in a sustainable and 'non-detrimental' way. The emphasis in the Convention is placed upon 'trade', comprising the importing and exporting of species. Third, there is a need for 'urgency'. This part of the statement raises the question of whether the natural environment has, or should have, stakeholder status. The jury is out on this final question, with eco-theorists divided but largely against such an attribute.

CITES and its Appendices

CITES requires Parties to enforce its provisions through national legislation, and through penalties and/or confiscation of species. At the heart of the system is a licensing regime; all import, export, re-export or introduction of species, including parts such as blood, skins, fur, teeth, shell, feathers, or parts of plants, particularly seeds, or other such derivatives has to be authorised through a licensing system and its approval evidenced by a permit which must be shown upon demand. CITES allows for controlled breeding in zoos as a way of preserving genetic diversity, and research is permitted (Neel and Ellstrand, 2003). However, this sometimes raises problems when it comes to reintroducing a zoo-bred animal to its natural habitat, and the protection, if any, which is afforded to it. The Convention works by listing species in one of three possible Appendices. Allocation of a species is the outcome of significant scientific investigation, at the request of an interested party such as an ecological organisation, or a State or States. Species under threat from extinction are protected under Appendix I. Commercial trade in wild-caught species is illegal. Trade in specimens of these species must be subject to particularly strict regulation in order not to further endanger their survival and must only be authorised in exceptional circumstances. Species listed in Appendix II are not endangered, but CITES aims to ensure that trade remains sustainable and does not have a detrimental impact upon wild populations, and in this way protect such species for the future and ensure that they do not migrate to an Appendix I listing. With regard to sustainability, there must first be obtained a 'non-detrimental finding'. Before an export of the species can take place, a finding, backed up by scientific evidence, must first be obtained to show that the trade will not be detrimental to the sustainability of the species concerned. Appendix III contains species that are protected in at least one country but which are not endangered. These include all species which any Party identifies as being subject to regulation within its jurisdiction for the purpose of preventing or restricting exploitation, and as needing the co-operation of other Parties in the control of trade.

Of approximately 33,600 species protected by CITES, about 800 are listed under Appendix I because they are threatened with extinction. About 32,500 species are listed under Appendix II because they risk becoming threatened with extinction unless trade is regulated through permits and licences. The remaining 300 species listed in Appendix III are not endangered by the country which has requested their listing and which has done so to control trade in a way which is sustainable. The numbers of species listed in the Appendices are shown in Table 8.1, taken from the CITES website.

The meaning of 'Threatened with extinction'

The principal focus of CITES is upon the protection of species which are threatened with imminent extinction, or which, if exploitation continues at a current rate, will place that species in such danger. The difficulty is defining at which point the risk of extinction arises; essentially it is when a decline in a population becomes irreversible (Terborgh, 1974; Mace et al., 2008). If a species is exploited in a sustainable way, then either the population remains stable, with withdrawals being replenished by compensatory natural increases in the stock, or a decline is temporary and will revert to the norm after careful

Table 8.1 Numbers of species listed in the Appendices to CITES

	Appendix I	*Appendix II*	*Appendix III*
Fauna			
Mammals	318 spp. (incl. 13 popns) + 20 sspp. (incl. 4 popns)	513 spp. (incl. 17 popns) + 7 sspp. (incl. 2 popns)	52 spp. + 11 sspp
Birds	155 spp. (incl. 2 popns) + 8 sspp.	1278 spp. (incl. 1 popn) + 4 sspp.	27 spp.
Reptiles	87 spp. (incl. 7 popns) + 5 sspp	749 spp. (incl. 6 popns)	61 spp.
Amphibians	24 spp.	134 spp.	4 spp.
Fish	16 spp.	107 spp.	24 spp. (incl. 15 popns)
Invertebrates	69 spp. + 5 sspp.	2171 spp. + 1 sspp.	22 spp. + 3 sspp.
Fauna total	**669 spp. + 38 sspp.**	**4952 spp. + 12 sspp.**	**190 spp. + 14 sspp.**
Flora	**334 spp. + 4 sspp.**	**29644 spp. (incl. 93 popns)**	**12 spp. (incl. 1 popns) + 1 var.**
Grand total	**1003 spp. + 42 sspp.**	**34596 spp. + 12 sspp.**	**202 spp. + 14 sspp. + 1 var.**

Source: www.cites.org/eng/disc/species.php

Ssp. denotes species; sspp. denotes subspecies; var. denotes varieties; popns denotes populations.

management (Lele, 1991). Different interpretations of this definition have resulted in heated debates at Conferences of the Parties, where one country or group of countries may wish to exploit a natural resource, while others insist that existing numbers are already dangerously low and cannot cope with further depletion. Tensions are further exacerbated by secret ballots which underpin voting at CoP meetings. It has been frequently alleged that some CITES delegations hide behind the secret ballot process so that they can deny responsibility later when a vote to permit controversial exploitation of a species is passed, with some delegates putting their own commercial interests and export earnings ahead of the conservation principle explicitly provided in the Convention. The threat of extinction has been defined in CITES as follows:

Characteristics of a species that meets, or is likely to meet, at least one of the following criteria:

A   The wild population is small, and is characterized by at least one of the following:

An observed, inferred or projected decline in the number of individuals or the area and quality of habitat; or
Each subpopulation being very small; or
A majority of individuals being concentrated geographically during one or more life-history phases; or
Large short-term fluctuations in population size; or
A high vulnerability to either intrinsic or extrinsic factors.

B   The wild population has a restricted area of distribution and is characterized by at least one of the following:

i   Fragmentation or occurrence at very few locations; or
ii   Large fluctuations in the area of distribution or the number of sub-populations; or
iii A high vulnerability to either intrinsic or extrinsic factors; or
iv   An observed, inferred or projected decrease in any of the following:

- the area of distribution; or
- the area of habitat; or
- the number of subpopulations; or
- the number of individuals; or
- the quality of habitat; or
- the recruitment.

C   A marked decline in the population size in the world, which has been either:

v   Observed as ongoing or as having occurred in the past (but with a potential to resume); or
vi   Inferred or projected on the basis of any one of the following:

- a decrease in area of habitat; or
- a decrease in quality of habitat; or

- levels or patterns of exploitation; or
- a high vulnerability to either intrinsic or extrinsic factors; or
- a decrease in recruitment.

Enforcement mechanisms

Article VIII of CITES provides the measures which can be taken by the Parties to the Convention. These include the penalising of trade in, or possession of, such species, or both, and the confiscation or return to the State of export of such specimens. According to Article VIII, 4, where a living specimen is confiscated as a result of these measures, the specimen shall be entrusted to a Management Authority of the State of confiscation. Under Article X, 'Trade with States not Party to the Convention', where export or re-export is to, or import is from, a State not a Party to the Convention, comparable documentation issued by the competent authorities in that State which substantially conforms with the requirements of the Convention for permits and certificates may be accepted in lieu thereof by any Party. If Parties to a dispute cannot reconcile their positions, Article XV111 provides that any dispute with respect to the interpretation or application of the provisions of the Convention shall be first subject to negotiation between those Parties. If the dispute cannot be resolved they may, by mutual consent, submit the dispute to arbitration, in particular that of the Permanent Court of Arbitration at The Hague, and the Parties submitting the dispute shall be bound by the arbitral award. The penalties for breaches of the Convention are set out in Article VIII. This states that the Parties shall take appropriate measures to enforce the provisions of the Convention and to prohibit trade in specimens which is in violation. These include the following measures:

a) to penalise trade in, or possession of, such specimens, or both; and
b) to provide for the confiscation or return to the State of export of such specimens

Where a living specimen is confiscated as a result of measures referred to in paragraph 1 of Article VIII:

a) the specimen shall be entrusted to a Management Authority of the State of confiscation;
b) the management Authority shall, after consultation with the State of export, return the specimen to that State at the expense of that State, or to a rescue centre or such other place as the Management Authority deems appropriate and consistent with the purposes of the present Convention; and
c) the Management Authority may obtain the advice of a Scientific Authority, or may, whenever it considers it desirable, consult the Secretariat in order to facilitate the decision under sub-paragraph (b) of this paragraph, including the choice of a rescue centre or other place.

In the event of a breach of the Rules, the Secretariat will notify the offending Party and give it time to respond. Although the Convention does not provide for arbitration, or for punitive measures against an offending Party, subsequent CoP Resolutions have provided for formal warnings to Parties, and recommendations to all other Parties to suspend CITES related trade with that Party. A recommendation to suspend provides a period of time during which the offending country can move from non-compliance to compliance by introducing suitable national legislation, reducing illegal trade in the species concerned, possibly through increased fines as a sanction, or by submitting missing annual reports regarding compliance or responding to concerns and specific recommendations made by the Standing Committee of CITES.

CITES: successes to date

In an interview on the 40th Anniversary of CITES, the Secretary-General, John E. Scanlon, gave a series of reflections on the Convention's achievements (Neme, 2013). When asked about the main successes of the Convention, he emphasised that one of its main strengths was that it was well-drafted, with clear objectives and guidance on how they could be achieved. He indicated that CITES Parties have done an excellent job in 'filling in the blanks' over the years by creating a body of resolutions and decisions that explain and guide implementation of the Convention's text. Scanlon observed that it is a 'living, breathing convention', which is constantly evolving. However, one of the main weaknesses for him was that CITES lacks its own financial mechanism for implementation, with member states, developed and developing, having to contribute their own resources. Another weakness, according to Scanlon, is that the Convention, while good from technical and operational perspectives, lost sight of the importance of engaging politically. A further success is that the Convention does not operate in a typical way for the United Nations. Conferences of Parties do not have voting blocs; issues are voted on like a 'conscience vote in a parliament, or a congress, or a diet, where states vote freely on issues, depending on how they choose to go'. In this way the Convention is more pragmatic in its implementation, not operating on the traditional-type UN negotiating lines. However, it is with regard to the protection of specific, 'easily identifiable', publicly appealing species that CITES has achieved its most noticeable successes; the African and Asian elephants are perhaps the most well-known examples.

Elephants

The present President and Chief Executive Officer of the International Fund for Animal Welfare, Azzedine Downes, commented in an interview with Al Jazeera News Network on 7 March 2013 on the success of CITES in putting an end to the international ivory trade. He noted that in 1900 there were an estimated 10 million African elephants roaming across sub-Saharan Africa, but by 1989 there were fewer than 500,000 largely due to poaching to meet an increasing international demand for ivory. He noted that while loss of habitat had contributed to this decline, the main driver was demand for their tusks. In October 1989 the African elephant was included in Appendix I of CITES, banning the commercial international trade of all African elephant products, including ivory. Downes regarded this prohibition as being the greatest achievement of CITES to date. The Monitoring of Illegal Killing of Elephants Programme (MIKE) and Elephant Trade Information System (ETIS) are monitoring tools used by CITES to assess trade in elephant products. Both MIKE and ETIS are under the supervision of the CITES Standing Committee, and were established after the 10th meeting of the Conference of the Parties as systems for tracking illegal activities involving elephants in elephant range states. To some extent both were established to reconcile the diversity of opinion regarding exploitation of elephant in terms of long term management of populations, which was undermining the achievement of a broad-based consensus. Both programmes are aimed at ensuring that CITES policy is based upon fact and scientific information, and in this way aim to 'take the heat' out of the issue.

The main purpose of MIKE is to monitor levels of the illegal killing of elephants at a sample of sites across the range of African and Asian elephants. The CITES website provides statistics for the levels in the Proportion of Illegally Killed Elephants (PIKE) relative to those dying from natural causes. The figures for the PIKE trend in Africa show a mixed picture. 2005 showed an estimate of about 31% of dead elephants found being illegally killed. By 2008 this had risen to nearly 58%; for CITES, PIKE levels above 50% are a cause for serious concern since they may result in elephant population declines. By 2009 the figure had fallen back to just under 43%, but this rose to 64% in 2010, and 75% in 2011. However, recent years have shown a downward trajectory. 2012 saw a fall to 68%, 2013 to 64%, 2014 to 63%, 2015 to 60%, and 2016 to 56%. The PIKE trend in Asia has been less, but has recently evidenced a rising trajectory. 2005 saw a proportion of 36%, 2008 to just under 31%, 2010 to 33%, 2011 to 25%, 2012 to 32%, 2013 to just under 30%, 2015 to 42%. Although starting from a lower base line, illegal killing of elephants in Asia indicates a rising trend. CITES has also established national ivory action plans (NIAPs) to strengthen controls of the trade in ivory and ivory markets, and to help combat the illegal trade in ivory. Member States are identified as Parties of 'primary concern', 'secondary concern', and Parties of 'importance to watch'. Parties of primary concern include China and Hong Kong SAR, Kenya, Uganda, Malawi, United Republic of Tanzania, and Vietnam. This identification is made by reference to a country's role as source, transit or destination country of illegally traded ivory. Parties of secondary concern include Cambodia, Ethiopia, Nigeria, South Africa, Sri Lanka and Thailand. Parties of importance to watch include Angola, Japan, Egypt, Mozambique, the Philippines, Qatar, and the United Arab Emirates. Classification within each category is determined by the NIAP which each Party is required to submit.

Weaknesses of CITES

Weaknesses of the Convention include that it is voluntary in nature, and accession countries can enter 'reservations' with regard to specific species when they join. Also, penalties which are imposed may be so low as not to act as a deterrent when illegal traders are able to make significantly higher rewards (Knapp, 2012; Holmern et al., 2007). In other words, the penalty does not match the crime and accordingly offenders make a calculated risk–reward calculation. CITES also lacks its own financial mechanism for implementation; this can present a considerable burden for developing countries in particular. For Sas-Rolfes (2000), habitat conversion, fragmentation and destruction account for most species losses, while excessive commercial exploitation accounts for a much smaller, even if significant, proportion of losses. CITES protects species that are threatened by excessive commercial exploitation, focusing on a very narrow aspect of commercial exploitation, namely transactions that take place across international borders, or international trade. CITES is not designed to address issues such as supply and consumer demand, domestic trading regimes, or the trade in wildlife products. For Sas-Rolfes; 'CITES is therefore, very limited in its potential effectiveness as a conservation tool. Not only does it fail to address issues of habitat loss, but it also fails to create mechanisms to control the supply of wildlife products and it has no direct means to influence consumer demand. As currently structured, CITES operates as a largely restrictive mechanism rather than as an enabling one'. CITES implicitly assumes that all trade is bad for conservation, with the burden of disproof being placed upon those who wish to export. As a consequence, the Convention tends to emphasise limitations on trade instead of taking a more pragmatic approach of considering whether trade will in practice enhance the status of wild species. As an example, Sas-Rolfes cites the case of rhinos. After the white rhino and three Asian species were listed in Appendix I at the founding conference in Washington DC in 1973, and the black rhino moved there in 1977, the price of rhino horn rose sharply in all consumer markets, particularly South Korea, Yemen, Japan and Taiwan, where body parts are used in traditional Chinese medicines, or carved into dagger handles (Yemen). He noted that despite the ban, trade continued with speculative stockpiling. The Appendix I listings had no effect on rhino numbers, and in reality drove up the black market price of rhino horn. Subsequent resolutions which aimed to stop the trade in rhino horn also had no effect. Dissatisfied with results, South Africa and Zimbabwe submitted a proposal to downlist their white and black rhino populations to allow a controlled trade in rhino horn, overseen by wildlife departments in both countries. These proposals were rejected at the Eighth Conference of the Parties in 1992. In 1994 at the Ninth CoP, South Africa again applied to have its white rhino population downlisted to Appendix II, subject to an annotation that only live animals and trophies would be traded commercially. All other trade would remain prohibited. The proposal was passed, but at the 1995 Natal Parks Board auction, the average price of a live white rhino again increased as the market expanded to allow international bidders to participate. A problem also seems to be that during transition periods of a species into Appendix I, demand escalates, as do stockpiles. As stocks become depleted, and demand rises, the risk–reward for illegal poachers becomes more attractive, particularly since penalties under CITES remain relatively weak.

CITES is effectively a negative list process; all trade in species is permitted unless and until it appears on one of the lists, which itself can lead to delay, and is dependent upon the financial and scientific resources of the Party conducting the process. Given that resources are limited and the Convention lacks a financial mechanism, this inevitably results in some endangered species not being considered. Further, if derivatives such as body parts have commercial use in multinational corporations such as pharmaceuticals, there may be well-funded opposition to the listing. If an alternative approach had been taken from the outset in which species could only be traded after listing in a permitted to trade list, this would in itself reduce the financial burden of investigation placed upon signatories, particularly developing countries, and could also result in companies which want to trade in a species, for example pharma, expending their own financial resources proving that in fact a species is not endangered and that the trade would be sustainable in the sense of not putting the level of the species at risk. In other words, the financial burden would be switched from the conservers to the exploiters.

Failure to take account of the economics of conservation

Brown and Shogren (1998) have researched the economics of the US Endangered Species Act of 1973, which implemented CITES into US law. They noted that species extinction is not a new phenomenon. On a geological timescale, five or more mass extinction events have been responsible for the loss of up to 84% of the genera or families that have ever existed (Jablonski, 1991). Prehistoric colonization of Pacific islands destroyed about 2000 species of birds, while at least 15 genera of large animals were lost due to aboriginal colonisation of Australia. At the time of writing, they noted that the current rate of human-induced extinction is new because of its scale. Conservative estimates of global extinction rates for various groups of species vary from 10 to 1000 times the natural rates that would currently prevail (National Research Council, 1995; Nott et al., 1995). The aim of the ESA 1973 was to save *all* species; there was no explicit recognition of relative costs and benefits, and a species with high economic cost of recovery and possibly low economic benefits was given the same standing as a species with large economic benefits and small costs. Mann and Plummer (1995: 156–163) note that the word 'practicable' was omitted from the legislation, attributing this in part to a 'feel good' factor on Capitol Hill which enabled legislators to support bald eagles without any perceived downside economic or cost risk. The inclusion of this word would have allowed for an economic balancing of factors where needed.

Brown and Shogren (1998) describe how use or development of land which is hospitable to an endangered species can become essentially unusable by its owner following a formal listing of the species as endangered. This has provided an incentive for landowners to destroy the habitat before listing occurs, and in so doing, render it inhospitable to the particular species concerned which will then either die or migrate. They term this landowner response as the 'shoot, shovel, and shut-up' strategy. They provide an example. Ten days before the golden-cheeked warbler was rated by the Fish and Wildlife Service, a firm hired workers with chain saws to destroy hundreds of acres of oak and juniper warbler habitat, rendering the land inhospitable before the listing had taken place. Further, with no specific priorities for listing species as endangered, employees in the Office of Endangered Species listed species 'that they liked best', despite the prescription in the Act against ranking. Mammals and birds were favoured above fish, amphibians and reptiles (Brown, 1990). Attitudes towards invertebrates were hostile due to their perceived association with diseases and agricultural damage. In 1982 Congress prohibited listing among types of species. Regarding the economics of conservation, Brown and Shogren comment:

> Essentially, the approach of the Act that prohibits any activity that harms a listed species puts a very large or infinite value on avoiding extinction. This view places endangered species beyond the reach of economic trade-offs, and the economist is relegated to helping find the least cost solution to achieve a biological-based standard. Others take an opposing approach. They want hard evidence that the benefits of preservation exceed the alternative uses of these resources (Epstein, 1995, p. 278). From this view, comparing the costs and benefits of endangered species protection is only logical: resources are scarce, and some attempt should be made to balance the costs and benefits so that policymakers are allocating funds to their highest value use, given plausible adjustments for uncertainty in ecosystem functions and irreversibility.
>
> (Brown and Shogren, 1998, p. 10)

Although economic considerations are implicit in many of the decisions about whether species should be listed as endangered and what sort of recovery plan should be established, the legal role only enters the picture explicitly when the designation of critical habitat for the recovery plan is made. Critical habitat is land essential for the survival of a species. The Secretary of State may 'take into consideration the economic impact, and any other relevant impact, of specifying any particular area as critical habitat' for a threatened or endangered species, and can exclude an area from critical habitat designation if the benefits of exclusion outweigh the benefits to specifying the critical habitat, 'unless failure to designate leads to extinction'. Most of the services provided by endangered species, including their corresponding levels of biological diversity, are not priced by the market. However, natural scientists invariably believe that the rightful objects to save are habitats or ecosystems because of their intrinsic value and because they enhance species survival. To place an economic value on a species is difficult although not impossible in terms of raw market price. For example, an ounce of rhino horn may cost X on a certain day, but may increase to 2X if supply is reduced through government intervention, imposition of penalties at such a rate as to deter illegal poachers, or if demand increases relative to a limited or perhaps seasonally affected supply. Similarly, the pink periwinkle may produce substances which can be processed by Big Pharma to produce a drug which generates revenue. If a substitute is found, for example an artificially created alternative, then demand may fall and stocks rejuvenate, notwithstanding an absence of government intervention. Big Pharma and other corporate processors of raw materials will always seek out or manufacture substitutes which reduce costs and boost profits even if market price stays exactly the same. To some extent the Convention on Biodiversity implicitly recognises that market mechanisms are a driving factor in sustainable exploitation; by establishing the Clearing House it facilitates the finding of 'new ways of doing things'. Interactions within ecosystems maintain balances, and yet if one part of the system is damaged, for example when a species is over-exploited, there is loss not just of that species, but also a potential collapse of the ecosystem of which it is such an integral part. The economic cost of ecosystem collapse is usually higher than the economic value of loss of the individual species contributing to it. In other words, the sum of the system has greater economic value than its individual parts.

Agreements post-CITES

CITES has been supplemented in part, at least in terms of its philosophical tenets, by the Convention on Biological Diversity (CBD), adopted in Nairobi, Kenya, in May 1992 (www.cbd.int). Emphasis in this Convention is placed upon sustainable development and 'the fair and equitable sharing of benefits arising from the use of genetic resources'. The Convention was the result of work commenced by an Ad Hoc Working Group of Experts on Biological Diversity convened under the United Nations Environment Programme in November 1988. The experts in the Group were tasked with taking into account 'the need to share costs and benefits between developed and developing countries', as well as 'ways and means to support innovation by local people'. The Convention was opened for signature on 5 June 1992 at the United Nations Conference on Environment and Development (the 'Rio Earth Summit'). It remained open for signature until 4 June 1993, by which time it had received 168 signatures. The Convention establishes three goals: the conservation of biological diversity, the sustainable use of its components, and the fair and equitable sharing of the benefits from the use of genetic resources. It was followed by the Cartagena Protocol on Biosafety which was adopted on 29 January 2000 and entered in to force on 11 September 2003. The Protocol is an international treaty governing the movements of living modified organisms resulting from modern biotechnology from one country to another which may have an adverse effect on the conservation and sustainable use of biological diversity. In contrast to CITES, the Convention has a financial mechanism. The Protocol established a Biosafety Clearing-House to facilitate the exchange of information on living modified organisms ands to assist countries with the implementation of the Protocol. The Conference of the Parties to the Convention designated the Global Environment Facility to serve as the institutional structure to operate the financial mechanism on an interim basis. It also has a compliance mechanism in the form of a Compliance Committee to address cases of non-compliance and to provide advice and assistance to a Party about ways in which the breach can be rectified.

The Nagoya Protocol

The later Nagoya Protocol on Access to Genetic Resources and the Fair and Equitable Sharing of Benefits Arising from their Utilization followed, entering into force on 12 October 2014. It acts as a supplementary agreement to the Cartagena Protocol. The Access and Benefit-Sharing Clearing-House (ABS Clearing-House) is a platform for exchanging information on access and benefit-sharing established by Article 14 of the Protocol. The Convention's website states:

> The ABS Clearing House is a key tool for facilitating the implementation of the Nagoya Protocol, by enhancing legal certainty and transparency on procedures for access and benefit-sharing, and for monitoring the utilization of genetic resources along the value chain, including through the internationally recognized certificate of compliance. By hosting relevant information regarding ABS, the ABS Clearing-House will offer opportunities for connected users and providers of genetic resources and associated traditional knowledge.
>
> (ABSCH, n.d.)

The Nagoya Protocol will create greater legal certainty and transparency for both providers and users of genetic resources by:

> establishing more predictable conditions for access to genetic resources.
>
> helping to ensure benefit-sharing when genetic resources leave the country providing the genetic resources (CBD, n.d.).

By helping to ensure benefit-sharing, the Nagoya Protocol creates incentives to conserve and sustainably use genetic resources, and 'therefore enhances the contribution of biodiversity to development and human well-being'. The Protocol covers genetic resources covered by the CBD, but also traditional knowledge associated with genetic resources and the benefits arising from its utilization. Domestic-level sharing measures are to provide for the fair and equitable sharing of the benefits arising from the utilisation of genetic resources with the contracting party providing genetic resources (Schroeder and Lasen-Diaz, 2006). Utilisation includes research and development on the genetic or biochemical composition of genetic resources as well as subsequent applications and commercialisation. Sharing is subject to mutually agreed terms, and benefits may be monetary or non-monetary such as royalties and the sharing of research results.

The Convention on Biological Diversity, and its subsequent Protocols, address an issue which was absent in CITES: market demand. Instead of focusing upon prohibitions and being essentially negative in its approach, informing parties what they cannot do as opposed to what they can do, these Protocols recognise that countries will exploit their natural resources and biodiversity as part of economic growth (Dietz and Adger, 2003). The Protocols address market realities: if there is a demand for a resource, perhaps a particular flora or animal derivative needed as the base element in a drug, then supply will be created to satisfy this demand. Then, the issue becomes one of sharing the benefits and preventing a withdrawal of supply which could in turn lead to illegal and unsustainable exploitation to meet unsatisfied demand. The Living Rainforest charity (www.livingrainforest.org) provides an example of a plant from Madagascar, the Rosy Periwinkle. Extracts from the plant provide the foundation for two cancer-fighting drugs, vinblastine and vincristine. The former has helped increase the chance of surviving childhood leukaemia from 10% to 95%, while the latter is used to treat Hodgkins' Disease. Worldwide sales of these drugs are worth about £75 million a year to global drug companies, but almost none of this money is returned to Madagascar which The Living Rainforest notes is one of the poorest countries in the world. Some pharma companies are looking to work with ethno-botanists to share profits more equitably, but this is on a voluntary basis; they retain the right not to share global proceeds of sales of the drugs. The Convention on Biological Diversity seeks to overcome this imbalance and to make sharing mandatory rather than at the discretion of drugs companies which, if faced with declining profits elsewhere, may be tempted to divert money to shareholders in the form of dividends rather than to continue sharing with the country from which the genetic materials are sourced.

CITES: which way forward?

CITES recognised with its formal adoption in 1973 and earlier, in the 1960s when its philosophical roots took hold, the importance of conservation, economic development within a sustainable framework, and the need for urgency to protect the natural environment and its infinitely diverse flora and fauna. Since that time, notwithstanding the Convention's good intent and the direct and indirect actions of an array of environmental lobbying and activist groups, species extinction has continued apace. A report from the World Wildlife Fund in 2014, the Living Planet Report, revealed that 52% of the world's animals have become extinct since 1970. Freshwater creatures have witnessed population collapses of more than 75%, principally due to human activity through habitat loss, deforestation, climate change and over-exploitation of the seas with scant regard for sustainable management. Wildlife declines in low-income countries has been even more dramatic; species have declined by 58% between

1970 and 2010, with Latin America seeing declines of 83% of animals over the same period. Marco Lambertini, Director-General of WWF International, made the following observation in the foreword to the report:

> We are using nature's gifts as if we had more than just one Earth at our disposal. By taking more from our ecosystems and natural processes than can be replenished, we are jeopardizing our very future. Nature conservation and sustainable development go hand-in-hand. They are not only about preserving biodiversity and wild places, but just as much about safeguarding the future of humanity- our well-being, economy, food security and social stability- indeed, our very survival.
>
> (WWF, 2014)

CITES has achieved much in a relatively short period of time. Species have been protected, and Parties have worked together in circumstances where political rivalries would have suggested otherwise. For example, at the Bangkok CoP in March 2013, the US and China co-sponsored proposals to restrict trade in Asian turtles and tortoises, and such collaboration has continued. However, there remain dichotomies and paradoxes at the heart of the Convention. First, it has been demonstrated that just as it prohibits trade, so demand for a protected species rises, pushing up supply as poachers become more willing to risk minor penalties in return for even greater rewards. The paradox here is that prior to a listing in an Appendix, demand and stockpiling both spike, leading to even greater short-term depletion of the very species which are to be protected. Further, by placing secret ballots at the heart of the voting procedure, ostensibly to protect weaker Parties from excessive pressure from stronger, wealthier groups, this has enabled such weaker Parties to 'tow the line' and vote against a species listing without the opprobrium which would have resulted if the process had been transparent. This is the dichotomy of secrecy versus transparency. While there is evidence that government wildlife protection agencies are often drawn to protecting 'chocolate box lid', highly visible species such as elephants and rhinos, the resources expended upon their protection, particularly by developing countries, is often at the expense of less attractive but equally endangered species such as invertebrates and disease-carrying insects which play equally important roles in ecosystems. Resources cannot be spent twice, or thrice, and over-attention to one species inevitably is at the expense of others, a problem and reality exacerbated by the fact that the Convention has no financial mechanism and poorer Parties are largely left to fund their own conservation strategies.

CITES also failed to address the economics of conservation, although at the time of its implementation this was perhaps not the issue that it has become today. Norton has described the dichotomy between the natural environment in a non-marketised context, and the neo-classical approach in economics which needs to monetise assets:

The difficulty for neo-classical economics is that, unless it is possible to monetise an asset, according to Gowdy (1997) it necessarily must be valued at zero. Gowdy (1997 at p 30) has characterised the neo-classical position; because there is no market in biological diversity, its price must be zero and accordingly people will use as much as they please of it in the service of other ends, such as making profit. As a consequence, it will be used up more rapidly than is socially desirable.

(Norton 2007: 391)

Fromm (2000) observed that the main difficulty in placing biodiversity or bio-diversity services (such as ocean currents, soil formation) in an economic context is that these services are not valued on markets; there is a gap between market valuation and the economic value of diversity. The Convention on Biodiversity and subsequent Protocols acknowledged that economic development will take place at the expense of the flora and fauna and ecosystems, and that to simply say 'you must not do this' is not enough. Innovations such as the Access and Benefit-Sharing Clearing-House represent a way forward, and a way of ensuring that Parties which supply their natural resources, including derivatives such as animal skins, fur, and body parts for use by for example global pharma companies, will share in the economic benefits. Sourcing and transactions are more likely to be transparent and auditable in such collaborative ventures, reducing the 'blind eye' phenomenon when resources are supplied but no questions asked as to how they have been obtained. Perhaps the most significant weakness in the Convention is that the economic cost of proof of the need for species protection and listing, and the price of implementing it, is placed upon parties who often do not have the financial resources to mount extended campaigns against well-resourced global interests. This is the consequence of the negative process in the Convention; if a species is not listed, then it can be exploited until such time as it is. If instead the burden of proving that species survival is not put at risk by exploitation, and that conservation strategies will be put in place to minimise any adverse effects, then the cost of the process of positive listing would fall to those who, possibly, have the deepest pockets and are best able to finance and prove the case. In this way if a species is listed then it can be exploited, but if it is not, it cannot. This more pragmatic approach could, potentially, be more in tune with the market realities of supply and demand of today's resource-hungry world.

References

ABSCH. (n.d.). Access and Benefit-sharing Clearing-house. Retrieved from https://absch.cbd.int.

Brown, Jr., G. (1990). Valuation of genetic resources. In Orians, G., Brown, G., Kunin, W. and J. Swierzbinski (eds), *The preservation and valuation of biological resources*, 203–229. Seattle, WA: University of Washington Press.

Brown, G.M., and Shogren, J.F. (1998). Economics of the Endangered Species Act. *Journal of Economic Perspectives*, 12 (3), 3–20.

CBD. (n.d.) The Nagoya Protocol on Access and Benefit-sharing. Retrieved from www.cbd.int/abs.

Davis, M., Hut, P. and Muller, R.A. (1984). Extinction of species by periodic comet showers. *Nature*, 308, 715–717.

Dietz, S. and Adger, W.N. (2003). Economic growth, biodiversity loss and conservation effort. *Journal of Environmental Management*, 68 (1), 23–35.

Downes, A. (2013). How CITES can better protect endangered species. *Al Jazeera News Network*. Retrieved from www.aljazeera.com/indepth/opinion/2013/03/20133782830166135.html.

Epstein, R. (1995). *Simple rules for a complex world*. Cambridge, MA: Harvard University Press.

Fromm, O. (2000). Ecological structure and functions of biodiversity as elements of its total economic value. *Environmental and Resource Economics*, 16 (3), 303– 328.

Gowdy, J.M. (1997). The value of biodiversity: markets, society, and ecosystems. *Land Economics*, 73 (1), 25–41.

Holmern, T., Muya, J. and Roskraft, E. (2007). Local law enforcement and illegal bushmeat hunting outside the Serengeti National Park, Tanzania. *Environmental Conservation*, 34 (1), 55–63.

Igoe, J. (2010). The spectacle of nature in the global economy of appearances: anthropological engagements with the spectacular mediations of transnational conservation. *Critique of Anthropology*, 30 (4), 375–397.

Jablonski, D. (1991). Extinctions: a paleontological perspective. *Science*, 253, 754–757.

Jachmann, H. and Billiouw, M. (1997). Elephant poaching and law enforcement in the Central Luangwa Valley, Zambia. *Journal of Applied Ecology*, 34 (1), 233–244.

Knapp, E.J. (2012). Why poaching pays: a summary of risks and benefits illegal hunters face in Western Serengeti, Tanzania. *Tropical Conservation Science*, 5 (4), 434–445.

Lele, S.M. (1991). Sustainable development: a critical review. *World Development*, 19 (6), 607–621.

Linkie, M., Martyr, D.J., Holden, J. and Yanuar, A. (2003). Habitat destruction and poaching threaten the Sumatran tiger in Kerinci Seblat National Park, Sumatra. *Oryx*, 37 (1), 41–48.

Mace, G.M., Collar, N.J., Gaston, K.J., Hilton-Taylor, C., Resit Akcakaya, H., Leader-Williams, N., Milner-Gulland, E.J., and Stuart, S.N. (2008). Quantification of extinction risk: IUCN's system for classifying threatened species. *Conservation Biology*, 22 (6), 1424–1442.

Magistro, J. and Roncoli, C. (2001). Anthropological perspectives and policy implications of climate change research. *Climate Change*, 19 (2), 91–96.

Mann, C., and Plummer, M. (1995). *Noah's choice*. New York: A. Knopf.

Minteer, B. A., Corley, E.A., and Manning, R.E. (2004). Environmental ethics beyond principle? The case for a pragmatic contextualism. *Journal of Agricultural and Environmental Ethics*, 17 (2), 131–156.

National Research Council (1995). *Science and the Endangered Species Act*. Washington, DC: National Academy Press.

Neel, M.C. and Ellstrand, N.C. (2003). Conservation of genetic diversity in the endangered plant *Eriogonum ovalifolium* var. *vineum* (*Polygonaceae*). *Conservation Genetics*, 4 (3), 337–352.

Neme, L. (2013). CITES 40th anniversary: reflections of CITES Secretary-General John Scanlon. *Mongabay*, March. Retrieved from https://news.mongabay.com/2013/03/cites-40th-anniversary-reflections-of-cites-secretary-general-john-scanlon.

Norton, S. D. (2007). The natural environment as a salient stakeholder: non-anthropocentrism, ecosystem stability and the financial markets. *Business Ethics: A European Review*, 16 (4), 387–402.

Nott, M., Rogers, E., and Pimm, S. (1995). Modern extinctions in the kilo-death range. *Current Biology*, 5, 14–17.

O'Neill, R.V. (1998). Recovery in complex ecosystems. *Journal of Aquatic Ecosystem Stress and Recovery*, 6 (3), 181–187.

Rammel, C., Stagl, S. and Wilfing, H. (2007). Managing complex adaptive systems- a co-evolutionary perspective on natural resource management. *Ecological Economics*, 63 (1), 9–21.

Sas-Rolfes, M't. (2000). Assessing CITES: four case studies. In J. Hutton and B. Dickson, *Endangered species threatened convention: the past, present and future of Cites, the Convention on International Trade in Endangered Species of Wild Fauna and Flora*, 69–75. London: Earthscan.

Schroeder, D. and Lasen-Diaz, C. (2006). Sharing the benefits of genetic resources: from biodiversity to human genetics. *Developing World Bioethics*, 6 (3), 135–143.

Terborgh, J. (1974). Preservation of natural diversity: the problem of extinction prone species. *Bioscience*, 24 (12), 715–722.

WWF. (2014). *Living planet report 2014: species and spaces, people and places*. Retrieved from http://d2ouvy59p0dg6k.cloudfront.net/downloads/wwf_lpr2014_low_res_for_web.pdf.

Yamagiwa, J. (2008). Bushmeat poaching and the conservation crisis in Kahuzi-Biega National Park, Democratic Republic of the Congo. *Journal of Sustainable Forestry*, 16 (3–4), 111–130.

Part III

Extinction accounting and accountability around the world

III.1

Extinction accounting in Africa

9 Extinction accounting by South African listed companies

Warren Maroun

This book deals with the extinction of species from an accounting perspective. This chapter focuses on what South African companies are reporting on risks associated with extinction and what they are doing to avoid the loss of species. Using South Africa as a type of case study for examining the development of what this book refers to as 'extinction accounting' is appropriate because this jurisdiction has one of the most developed corporate governance systems internationally (Solomon, 2010; Maroun et al., 2014). The country's long-standing history with stakeholder-centric governance (Rossouw et al., 2002) and its leading role in the development of sustainability and integrated reporting (Atkins and Maroun, 2015) provides a mature corporate reporting environment which should be able to support an emerging extinction accounting framework. Perhaps more important than this is the enormous wealth of biodiversity in South Africa and the clear need to ensure its protection.

A brief account of South African biodiversity

South Africa is one of the most biologically diverse regions on earth. It includes nine terrestrial biomes which are home to millions of species (Wynberg, 2002). Figure 9.1 shows a map of South Africa's main biomes.

South Africa boasts a number of pristine wildness areas where large numbers of birds, reptiles and mammals (including the iconic 'Big 5'[1]) live with little or no human intervention. Examples include the world-famous Kruger National Park (in the north-east), Addo Elephant Park (in the south west) and Kgalagadi Transfrontier Park (in the north-west). Nevertheless, South Africa's flora and fauna are under threat due to expanding human populations, incorrect management of natural resources and the effects of climate change (EWT, 2016c; SANBI, 2017b). A recently published report by Daly and Friedmann (2016) evaluates 295 species of South African mammals with 57 (19.3%) assigned as being under threat. This includes just under 30 endangered and critically endangered species.

Many of the species in Table 9.1 are not well known outside of the scientific community. Some are, however, part of the country's cultural fabric. The rhinoceros is, perhaps, the best example. The species is under significant threat from the effects of climate change and loss of habitat due largely to human

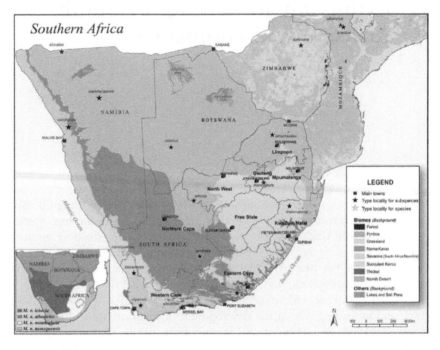

Figure 9.1 Biomes of South Africa
Source: Russo et al. (2010, p. 3)

behaviour. More recently, South Africa has seen an unprecedented level of poaching with over 5000 animals killed for their horn from 2013 to 2017 (Department of Environmental Affairs, 2017). The African Wild Dog is also under threat. The species operates in large territories which are under increased pressure from expanding human populations. This carnivore is often misunderstood and seen as posing an undue threat to livestock and this has resulted in direct conflict with humans (Daly and Friedmann, 2016; EWT, 2016d). Other iconic species including, for example, the elephant, vulture and different species of antelope are also at risk either directly or as a result of human behaviour causing damage to ecosystems (Daly and Friedmann, 2016).

In addition to its mammals, an estimated 12% of South Africa's flora is classified as a 'conservation concern' and approximately 14% is threatened (SANBI, 2017b). This is the result of unsustainable agricultural practices, irresponsible harvesting and clearing of natural habitats for human settlement and industrial use (SANBI, 2015a, 2017b; EWT, 2016a).

Working to fight extinction

Anthropocentrism frames the value of the environment in terms of the benefits its provides to people (Jones and Solomon, 2013). At the anthropocentric level,

Table 9.1 List of engendered and critically endangered species in South Africa

Species	Status
African wild dog	Endangered
Antarctic 'true' blue whale	Endangered
Cape mole-rat	Endangered
Damara woolly bat	Endangered
Four-toed elephant-shrew	Endangered
Gunning's golden mole	Endangered
Hartmann's mountain zebra	Endangered
Indian Ocean bottlenose dolphin	Endangered
Marley's golden mole	Endangered
Oribi	Endangered
Robust golden mole	Endangered
Samango monkey ssp. *Labiatus*	Endangered
Sclater's forest shrew	Endangered
Southern elephant seal	Endangered
Swinny's horseshoe bat	Endangered
Tonga red bush squirrel ssp.	Endangered
Tsessebe	Endangered
White-tailed rat	Endangered
Black rhinoceros	Critically endangered
De Winton's golden mole	Critically endangered
Visagie's golden mole	Critically endangered
Juliana's golden mole	Critically endangered
Rendall's serotine bat	Critically endangered
Riverine rabbit	Critically endangered
Rough-haired golden mole	Critically endangered
Short-eared trident bat	Critically endangered
Van Zyl's golden mole	Critically endangered
Ongoye red squirrel	Critically endangered

the need to conserve South Africa's biodiversity is clear. It is estimated that up to 7% of the country's GDP (or approximately ZAR73[2] billion per annum) is contributed by ecosystem services (Wynberg, 2002). Thousands of South Africans depend on the environment for their livelihood, harvesting flora and fauna for use or sale, in the eco-tourism industry or by indirectly benefiting from ecosystem services such as insect pollination and nutrient recycling essential for the agricultural sector (Melin et al., 2014; SANBI, 2015b; Atkins et al., 2016a; EWT, 2016c).

It is also important to understand the deep ecological value of South Africa's natural systems. Deep ecology is a complex topic and a detailed discussion of its principles is beyond the scope of this chapter. Put simply, deep ecology recognises the intrinsic value of the environment in its own right, rather than in terms of its consumptive value to people. In doing so, deep ecologists stress the moral, cultural and ethical importance of protecting natural systems to ensure continuity of all life on earth (Khisty, 2006; Jones and Solomon, 2013; Christian, 2016; Cuckston, 2018).

A deep ecologist's view of biodiversity is especially relevant when it comes to South Africa. The country has some of the last remaining truly wild areas where animals can still live without material human interference. Many of these species are entirely dependent on these conservancies and are unique to South Africa (Wynberg, 2002; EWT, 2016b). As a result, the preservation of these species and ecosystems is a moral imperative. It should also be remembered that complexity of natural systems is still not fully understood. There is no clear indication of the biological implications of the extinction of one or more species. The cultural cost of extinction adds to the biological and ethical implications of losing these natural systems. Many of the species threatened by human behaviour (such as the rhinoceros, elephant and wild dog) are, ironically, a key part of Africa's heritage, traditions and identity. Their demise would be a huge blow, socially and biologically.

For these reasons, a number of environmental agencies and NGOs are working to mitigate the threat of extinction. SANBI, for example, is tasked with assisting in the management of South Africa's biodiversity. The institute coordinates and participates in different environmental research projects and is responsible for monitoring and reporting on the state of South Africa's biodiversity. It carries out ecosystem rehabilitation, develops and assists with the implementation of biodiversity policy and provides scientific data on biodiversity mass (SANBI, 2015c, 2017a). One of SANBI's partners is the EWT.

Formed in 1973 as a not-for-profit conservation organisation, the EWT operates in Eastern and Southern Africa. Its objective is to 'conserve threatened species and ecosystems by initiating research and conservation action programmes; implementing projects which mitigate threats facing species diversity; and supporting sustainable natural resource management' (EWT, 2016b, p. 7). Its activities include, *inter alia*, urban wildlife, carnivorous species and marine conservation initiatives (ibid.).

SANBI and the EWT work alongside the World Wildlife Fund South Africa (WWF-SA). The WWF-SA use scientific research to inform the development of best practice for wildlife and ecosystem conservation. Its three focus areas include: 'securing the integrity South Africa's ecological assets', 'ensuring that ecosystem services underpin social and economic well-being' and 'building climate resilience' (WWF-SA, 2017). The first involves the protection and restoration of important ecosystems and their responsible integration in agricultural and industrial activity. The second includes partnerships with businesses to develop, implement and drive responsible and sustainable use of natural resources. The last focal point involves the drive for a low carbon society and mitigation of the effects of global warming (ibid.).

An extinction accounting framework

Companies have a role to play in preserving species and ecosystems by providing financial support for environmental agencies and NGOs and by working in partnerships with these bodies to develop more responsible business models and operating practices (Atkins and Maroun, 2018; Maroun and Atkins, 2018). In addition, this book argues that effective reporting on biodiversity loss and the steps taken to mitigate associated risks can be used as a driver of positive change. This is based on an emerging body of academic research which points to the emancipatory potential of accounting.

A detailed review of this literature is provided in Chapter 2. The essential feature of an emancipatory framework is that it sees accounting as more than just a means of collecting and reporting on, typically, financial data (Hopwood, 1987; Dillard and Reynolds, 2008; Atkins et al., 2015a; Gallhofer et al., 2015). Instead, the act of recording environmental metrics such as the number of species affected by an organisation's operations, changes in populations and the extinction risk profile can create an organisational awareness of extinction, establish responsibility for preventing extinction and lead to action (Atkins and Maroun, 2018; Cuckston, 2018).

There is already some evidence of accounting's change potential, albeit in settings unrelated to extinction of species (Guthrie, Manes-Rossi and 2017). For example, a large body of work examines how tracking and recording financial performance is used to communicate expected outcomes, monitor progress towards achieving these gaols and inform changes in operating practices (Hopper and Macintosh, 1993; Cowton and Dopson, 2002). Sustainability reporting provides another example of how accounting processes can drive change. Critics have argued that sustainability reporting has not lived up to its full potential (Larrinaga-Gonzalez and Bebbington, 2001; Milne et al., 2009; Stubbs and Higgins, 2014). Nevertheless, there is some research showing how sustainability reporting encourages companies to incorporate social and environmental considerations in their decision-making processes. As a result, they have become more aware of their impact on different stakeholders and the need to ensure long-term sustainability (Adams and Frost, 2008; Atkins and Maroun, 2015; Massa et al., 2015). A recent research project on the accounting for decline in pollinators supports this assessment. Reporting on the possible demise of the bee (and other insects) gives only a tentative indication of the associated implications and how companies are dealing with the relevant risks. Nevertheless, by disclosing details on pollination services, companies are highlighting a problem which would otherwise have gone unnoticed by some stakeholders, demonstrating a genuine concern for the environment and taking the first steps in addressing a looming environmental disaster (Atkins et al., 2016a; Christian, 2016; Jonäll and Rimmel, 2016). The same may apply to reporting on the risks posed by extinction in general. This is considered in more detail by evaluating what a sample of South African companies are including in their integrated and sustainability reports.

Current reporting trends

The study focused on the largest 40 companies (by market capitalisation) as at 30 November 2016 because these companies are more likely to have the resources and expertise necessary to understand the importance of biodiversity for their business models and prepare detailed sustainability or integrated reports (see Romi and Longing, 2016). Interpretive text was analysis was used to code integrated and sustainability reports issued from 2011 to 2015. The reports were read several times to identify phrases, themes, diagrams or pictures which dealt directly or indirectly with endangered species and conservation projects (including environmental partnerships). This included, for example, references to the IUCN Red List, well-known environmental agencies operating in South Africa and biological terms such as extinction, flora and fauna (GRI, 2010; Rimmel and Jonäll, 2013; Mansoor and Maroun, 2016). Disclosures were recorded in a frequency table and aggregated under broad theme headings (Table 9.2).

Changes in disclosure over time

The initial results are surprising, given the importance of biodiversity to South Africa in both anthropocentric and deep ecological terms. Figure 9.2 shows low levels of reporting over the five years under review.

In 2009, South Africa's third code on corporate governance was issued. King-III reiterated the importance of a balanced approach to reporting which is mindful of a company's social and environmental impact as established by King-I (issued in 1994) and King-II (issued in 2002).

Table 9.2 Disclosure themes

Disclosure theme heading	Explanation
Biodiversity risk statement	A clear statement on the risks posed by biodiversity loss (whether framed in anthropocentric or deep ecological terms) and a broad outline of the policy on protecting and preserving biodiversity in order to prevent extinction
Partnerships	Collaboration with government (for example, SANBI and South African National Parks), NGOs (such as WWF or EWT) and research groups (for example, universities) as part of a conservation initiative
Action plans	Reporting on species policies, plans and actions for combating extinction
Species reporting	Disclosures on specific species or biological areas which the respective company is involved in conserving
Reporting codes	References to well-known environmental codes or reports including, the relevant sections of the GRI, Code for Responsible Investment in South Africa (CRISA) and IUCN Red List

Sources: adapted from Jones and Solomon (2013); van Liempd and Busch (2013); GRI (2016); Mansoor and Maroun (2016)

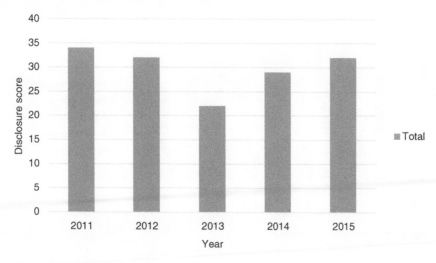

Figure 9.2 Total disclosures over time

King-III also called for a more integrated approach to understanding how companies rely on economic, social and environmental resources to generate returns and for this to be communicated clearly in an integrated report (King, 2012). This message was reaffirmed by the Integrated Reporting Committee of South Africa's (IRCSA) draft paper on integrated reporting in 2011 (IRCSA, 2011). In contrast the disclosure scores remain relatively flat from 2011 to 2012 with an average disclosure of only 0.85 and 0.8 per company per year respectively. The adoption of the International Integrated Reporting Council's (IIRC) framework on integrated reporting shortly after its release in 2013 does not appear to have had an impact on extinction accounting trends. On the contrary, there is a slight decrease in total disclosures from 2012 to 2013 and reporting in 2014 (average = 0.73) and 2015 (average = 0.8) does not exceed the 2011 levels.

Companies should ensure that they do not include repetitive and generic information in their corporate reports (Atkins and Maroun, 2015). Very low disclosure scores cannot, however, be attributed to an attempt to provide more focused reporting. On the contrary, it appears that many South African companies do not see extinction as sufficiently material to warrant inclusion in their integrated or sustainability reports (see also Mansoor and Maroun, 2016; Maroun, 2016; Adler et al., 2018). There are, however, exceptions.

What companies report

Low total reporting scores should not be interpreted as implying that *all* South African companies are marginalising extinction. Figure 9.3 shows that, while limited, some organisations are providing information on different extinction accounting elements.

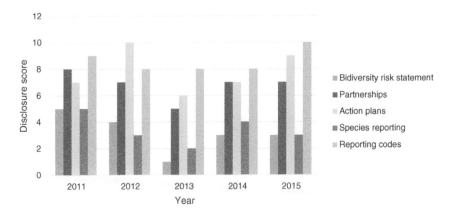

Figure 9.3 Disclosure per theme

Extinction-related reporting usually includes a reference to environmental codes or standards. The following is an example of a commonly-found commitment to environmental responsibility dealing with the IUCN Red List:

> Our operations work to avoid the loss of any International Union for Conservation of Nature (IUCN) Red List threatened species. We respect land with a high biodiversity value and that which is legally designated as protected; we closely monitor our activities in or near these areas.
>
> (Company 3, Sustainability Report, 2011)

Similarly, a second company deals with codes of best practice which require financial services firms to take environmental issues into account when formulating their investment and financing policies (IOD, 2011; Atkins and Maroun, 2015):

> Our aim is to integrate environmental, social and governance criteria into all our investment-making decisions, in line with the [Group's] commitment to the United Nations Principles For Responsible Investment (UNPRI) and the Codes for Responsible Investment SA (CRISA).
>
> (Company 21, Integrated Report, 2012)

References to environmental-related or biodiversity-specific codes of best practice were relatively common. In contrast, there were no examples of companies explaining in detail the anthropocentric or deep ecological case for biodiversity management and supporting this with an analysis of the magnitude, likelihood and impact of specific extinction-related risks (Rimmel and Jonäll, 2013; Maroun, 2016; Romi and Longing, 2016). Nevertheless, some companies were reporting on their policies for managing biodiversity, even if this was at a relatively high level. For example:

[Our policy is] not explore or extract resources adjacent to World Heritage listed properties unless the proposed activity is compatible with the World Heritage outstanding universal values.

(Company 5, Sustainability Report, 2012)

Similarly, in explaining their commitment to sustainability, another company reports:

We are committed to identifying technology opportunities to minimise our environmental impact. An important initiative in this area has been the development of a 'biodiversity overlap assessment tool', through which we will be overlaying biodiversity data available from the World Database on Protected Areas (WDPA) with our own site-based data.

(Company 8, Integrated Report, 2012)

The company stops short of providing more specific information on this initiative and exactly how it has been used to inform its operations and any changes to strategy. Nevertheless, there is, at least, some awareness of the need to understand its biodiversity impact and report this to stakeholders. In addition, general policy disclosures or position statements were usually complemented by some information on actions/initiatives taken to protect endangered species. This was provided in conjunction with details on operations with high biodiversity impact, including affected species. For example, one company was able to explain its policy on biodiversity, report on action taken to address biodiversity loss and include quantified measures and time frames:

[The company] adopted a Biodiversity Management Standard in 2014 and operations were required to comply within two years. All operations are required to have an appropriate Biodiversity Action Plan in place no later than 2016.

(Company 30, Sustainability Report, 2015)

The company explains that:

Our Biodiversity Management Standard is informed by the International Finance Corporation (IFC) performance standard on biodiversity. We also subscribe to the ICMM Position Statement on Mining and Protected Areas which includes a commitment to respect protected areas and an undertaking not to explore or mine on World Heritage properties. We include mitigation measures at all new operations to ensure that no net loss of biodiversity occurs. In areas of critical habitat at new operations, we seek to achieve a net positive impact on biodiversity.

(Company 30, Sustainability Report, 2015)

Although very brief, it provides some insight into performance in terms of this standard and indirect measures specific to two endangered species:

Of the 16-managed operations, three (19%) had such a plan in place at the end of 2015 . . . Two species of mammal at Cerro Vanguardia and three species of bird at AGA Mineração in Brazil are listed on the IUCN Red List as near threatened. Six species of trees at Obuasi are listed as vulnerable.
(Company 30, Sustainability Report, 2015)

There were also examples of companies reporting on conservation projects involving species not affected by their business model which, tentatively, points to some awareness of the importance of species at the deep ecological level (Atkins et al., 2015b, 2018):

The division supports the World Wildlife Fund Rhino DNA Index System or RhoDIS project. Project teams have developed a DNA profiling technique that can identify individual rhino horns. Teams sample rhino across Africa (and soon Asia) so seized horn can be traced to specific poaching incidents. This helps to combat poaching by making it easier to prosecute poachers.
(Company 36, Integrated Report, 2012)

Initiatives aimed at preventing extinction normally involve partnerships with different environmental groups (Atkins et al., 2016a, 2016b). For example:

While we are confident that our current six material issues remain relevant, we re-evaluated the most important issues for our business and our stakeholders in 2015. We commissioned new research on our global context, seeking input from thought leaders and sustainability practitioners and aligning with our business teams. This process has also been informed by our work with United Nations Global Compact (UNGC), World Business Council for Sustainable Development (WBCSD) and WWF, as well as the UN's newly launched SDGs.
(Company 12, Integrated Report, 2012)

There is some impression management evident in the company wanting to ensure that its biodiversity reporting does not result in stakeholders challenging its overall materiality assessment (Atkins et al., 2015c; Cho et al., 2015). Nevertheless, the disclosure also suggests that the company is being proactive in engaging experts to assist with the review of its position on biodiversity. As a second illustration of this type of extinction accounting, consider the following disclosure:

At the end of 2015, our Biodiversity Partnership with three NGOs – Earthwatch Institute, Fauna and Flora International and Tropical Biology Association – concluded after 15 years of collaboration. As a result of the Partnership, biodiversity management has been embedded into our operations and a number of projects continue to thrive. Our commitment to

biodiversity remains an important part of our approach to sustainable agri-culture and our ongoing focus will be on local project-based partnerships.
(Company 1, Sustainability Report, 2015)

It is possible to dismiss these disclosures as appealing to stakeholders' expecta-tions for, at least, some environmental reporting while, at the operational level, few changes are taking place (Higgins et al., 2014; Tregidga et al., 2014). In support of this view, detailed accounts of exactly how biodiversity partner-ships work, quantified measures of performance on anti-extinction projects and explicit statements on how risk assessment and operations are changing are not provided (see Gray et al., 1995; Brown and Dillard, 2014; Cho et al., 2015; Raemaekers et al., 2016). It may, however, be too early to conclude that current trends on extinction accounting are only indicative of impression management. This more optimistic assessment is based on the following:

- Integrated and sustainability reporting were never intended to serve as a substitute for capitalism (Atkins and Maroun, 2015). Despite South Africa's stakeholder-centric corporate governance model, companies are expected to generate returns for providers of financial capital. There is, however, an indication of the importance of the environment and a propensity to report on biodiversity-related issues.
- Integrated thinking and reporting were only recently introduced (2013). It takes time for companies to understand the interconnection between their business models and different types of non-financial capital (including biodiversity) (De Villiers and Alexander, 2014; King, 2016). Nevertheless, there are already some examples of companies articulating biodiversity as a risk factor and explaining how they are attempting to manage these risks, even if these disclosures are not always detailed and clearly interconnected with each part of the value creation process.
- Finally, extinction of species is not easy subject matter for accountants and businessmen to deal with. The concept was only explained in biological terms in the late 1700s and the exact extent to which human behaviour is driving extinction of species remains a debated issue (Atkins and Maroun, 2018). In this context, it will take time for the business community to come to terms with their role in preventing extinction.

Summarising remarks and recommendations

Critical theorists have argued that companies reacted to the sustainability reporting movement only symbolically, providing additional environmental, social and governance disclosures while maintaining an unpublicised atti-tude of business as usual (Bebbington et al., 1999; Solomon et al., 2013; Cho et al., 2015). The same may apply to integrated reporting and, more recently, the calls for additional detail on biodiversity management and prevention of extinction.

Extinction accounting is, however, one of the most recent developments in sustainability accounting and reporting (Atkins and Maroun, 2018). As a result, it may be unreasonable to expect companies to report in detail on their understanding of extinction and the steps they are taking to prevent the loss of species. This is especially true given that extinction accounting is largely a theoretical construct. With the exception of the details provided by the GRI, there is little professional guidance on exactly what and how companies should report on extinction-related issues (Atkins et al., 2015b; GRI, 2016). Perhaps for this reason, most of the disclosures on extinction of species deals with relatively descriptive reporting elements including references to codes of best practice and high-level discussion on conservation projects, including partnerships with various environmental groups, as shown in Figure 9.4 (see also Adler et al., 2018; Usher and Maroun, 2018).

We can choose to see the low disclosure score (Figure 9.2) and emphasis on more descriptive elements of the extinction accounting framework (Figures 9.3–4) as symptomatic of impression management or a lack of interest in biodiversity. Alternately, we can be more optimistic and see the current reporting trends as an indication that some companies have started to understand and contextualise the need for biodiversity management and reporting on their efforts to prevent extinction. In this context, weaknesses in the existing extinction accounting practices become opportunities for the academic community to shed light on how to tackle extinction at the corporate level. Areas for future research include the following:

- Developing a framework to help companies understand better the deep ecological and anthropocentric case for protecting biodiversity.
- Compiling case studies – probably in conjunction with the scientific community – to illustrate exactly how companies can access scientific research on extinction, interpret it in the context of their business and identify extinction-related issues which may be relevant for their business model.
- Engaging with different stakeholders (including institutional investors) to determine how they use environmental information included in integrated and sustainability reports and what additional information can be included.

▪ Bidiversity risk statement   ▪ Partnerships   ▪ Action plans   ▪ Species reporting   ▪ Reporting codes

Figure 9.4 Total disclosures by theme

- Finally, accounting researchers need to support the largely theoretical work on integrated and sustainability reporting with case-specific information on precisely *how* different reporting frameworks can be applied to construct an extinction account. This should include details on what should be included in an extinction account, how to explain the interconnection between the extinction accounting and other parts of the organisation and exactly how an extinction account may look.

The long-term outcome is fairly clear. Left unchecked, our unprecedented population growth and consumption of natural resources will drive many species, including *Homo sapiens*, extinct (Gray and Milne, 2018). We can choose to be critical and either see accounting as a purely economic construct which has nothing to do with the environment or as a means of defending the financial -centric status quo which is destroying the planet. Alternately, the accounting academic can be more proactive. The vast calculable infrastructure of the 'accounting craft' has been used to order and articulate the exceedingly complex capital market process, discipline the individual manager and drive the development of the contemporary organisation (Burchell et al., 1980; Hopwood, 1987; Fogarty, 1992). Perhaps the same technologies of accounting can be modified to help save the earth?

Notes

1 In alphabetical order: buffalo, elephant, leopard, lion and rhinoceros.
2 Approximately USD6 billion.

References

Adams, C. A. and Frost, G. R. 2008. Integrating sustainability reporting into management practices. *Accounting Forum*, 32 (4), 288–302.

Adler, R., Mansi, M. and Pandey, R. 2018. Biodiversity and threatened species reporting by the top Fortune Global companies. *Accounting, Auditing and Accountability Journal*, in press.

Atkins, J. and Maroun, W. 2015. Integrated reporting in South Africa in 2012: perspectives from South African institutional investors. *Meditari Accountancy Research*, 23 (2), 197–221.

Atkins, J. and Maroun, W. 2018. Integrated extinction accounting and accountability: building an ark. *Accounting, Auditing and Accountability Journal*, 31 (3), 750–786.

Atkins, J., Atkins, B., Thomson, I. and Maroun, W. 2015a. 'Good' news from nowhere: imagining utopian sustainable accounting. *Accounting, Auditing and Accountability Journal*, 28 (5), 651–670.

Atkins, J., Barone, E., Gozman, D., Maroun, W. and Atkins, B. 2015b. Exploring rhinoceros conservation and protection: Corporate disclosures and extinction accounting by leading South African companies. *Meditari Accountancy Research Conference*. University of Bolognat, Folrli, Italy.

Atkins, J. F., Solomon, A., Norton, S. and Joseph, N. L. 2015c. The emergence of integrated private reporting. *Meditari Accountancy Research*, 23 (1), 28–61.

Atkins, J., Barone, E., Maroun, W. and Atkins, B. 2016a. Bee accounting and account-ability in the UK. In K. Atkins and B. Atkins (eds) *The Business of Bees: An Integrated Approach to Bee Decline and Corporate Responsibility.* Sheffield, UK: Greenleaf Publishers.

Atkins, J., Barone, E., Maroun, W. and Atkins, B. 2016b. From the Big Five to the Big 4? Exploring extinction accounting for the rhinoceros. *In:* GARI Conference, Henley on Thames, United Kingdom.

Atkins, J., Maroun, W., Atkins, B. C. and Barone, E. 2018. From the Big Five to the Big Four? Exploring extinction accounting for the rhinoceros. *Accounting, Auditing and Accountability Journal*, 31 (2), 674–702

Bebbington, J., Gray, R. and Owen, D. 1999. Seeing the wood for the trees: Taking the pulse of social and environmental accounting. *Accounting, Auditing and Accountability Journal*, 12 (1), 47–52.

Brown, J. and Dillard, J. 2014. Integrated reporting: On the need for broadening out and opening up. *Accounting, Auditing and Accountability Journal*, 27 (7), 1120–1156.

Burchell, S., Clubb, C., Hopwood, A., Hughes, J. and Nahapiet, J. 1980. The roles of accounting in organizations and society. *Accounting, Organizations and Society*, 5 (1), 5–27.

Cho, C. H., Laine, M., Roberts, R. W. and Rodrigue, M. 2015. Organized hypoc-risy, organizational façades, and sustainability reporting. *Accounting, Organizations and Society*, 40, 78–94.

Christian, J. 2016. *Bombus terrestris.* A personal deep ecological account. In K. Atkins and B. Atkins (eds) *The Business of Bees: An Integrated Approach to Bee Decline and Corporate Responsibility.* Sheffield, UK: Greenleaf Publishers.

Cowton, C. J. and Dopson, S. 2002. Foucault's prison? Management control in an automotive distributor. *Management Accounting Research*, 13 (2), 191–213.

Cuckston, T. 2018. Making extinction calculable. *Accounting, Auditing and Accountability Journal*, in press.

Daly, B. and Friedmann, Y. 2016. *Red Data Book of the Mammals of South Africa: A Conservation Assessment.* Available: www.nationalredlist.org/files/2012/11/red-data-book-mammals-south-africa-conservation-assessment.pdf [Accessed 5 May 2017].

De Villiers, C. and Alexander, D. 2014. The institutionalisation of corporate social responsibility reporting. *The British Accounting Review*, 46 (2), 198–212.

Department of Environmental Affairs. 2017. Rhino poaching statistics update [Online]. Available: www.environment.gov.za/projectsprogrammes/rhinodialogues/poaching_statistics [Accessed 7 November 2017].

Dillard, J. and Reynolds, M. 2008. Green Owl and the Corn Maiden. *Accounting, Auditing and Accountability Journal*, 21 (4), 556–579.

EWT. 2016a. Cycad fact sheet. Available: www.ewt.org.za/species%20factsheets/Cycad%20poster%20A1.pdf [Accessed 2 May 2017].

EWT. 2016b. *Integrated Report 2015–2016.* Available: www.ewt.org.za/conreports/2016/book.swf [Accessed 6 May 2017].

EWT. 2016c. Reassessing the Red Data List of Mammals for South Africa. Available: www.ewt.org.za/scientific%20publications/Red%20Data%20List.pdf.

EWT. 2016d. Wild Dog fact sheet. Available: www.ewt.org.za/species%20factsheets/Wild%20Dog.pdf [Accessed 2 May 2017].

Fogarty, T. J. 1992. Organizational socialization in accounting firms: A theoretical framework and agenda for future research. *Accounting, Organizations and Society*, 17 (2), 129–149.

Gallhofer, S., Haslam, J. and Yonekura, A. 2015. Accounting as differentiated uni-versal for emancipatory praxis: Accounting delineation and mobilisation for emancipation(s) recognising democracy and difference. *Accounting, Auditing and Accountability Journal*, 28 (5), 846–874.

Gray, R. and Milne, M. J. 2018. Perhaps the Dodo should have accounted for human beings? Accounts of humanity and (its) extinction. *Accounting, Auditing and Accountability Journal*, in press.

Gray, R., Walters, D., Bebbington, J. and Thompson, I. 1995. The greening of enterprise: An exploration of the (non) role of environmental accounting and environmental accountants in organizational change. *Critical Perspectives on Accounting*, 6 (3), 211–239.

GRI. 2010. GRI reporting in government agencies. Available: www.globalreporting. org/resourcelibrary/GRI-Reporting-in-Government-Agencies.pdf [Accessed 10 February 2017].

GRI. 2016. Consolidated set of GRI sustainability reporting standards (2016). Available: www.globalreporting.org/standards/gri-standards-download-center/?g= ae2e23b8–4958–455c-a9df-ac372d6ed9a8   www.globalreporting.org/reporting/ g4/Pages/default.aspx [Accessed 10 February 2017].

Guthrie, J., Manes-Rossi, F. and Orelli, R. L. 2017. Integrated reporting and integrated thinking in Italian public sector organisations. *Meditari Accountancy Research*, 25 (4), 553–573.

Higgins, C., Stubbs, W. and Love, T. 2014. Walking the talk(s): Organisational narratives of integrated reporting. *Accounting, Auditing and Accountability Journal*, 27 (7), 1090–1119.

Hopper, T. and Macintosh, N. 1993. Management accounting as disciplinary practice: the case of ITT under Harold Geneen. *Management Accounting Research*, 4 (3), 181–216.

Hopwood, A. G. 1987. The archaeology of accounting systems. *Accounting, Organizations and Society*, 12 (3), 207–234.

IOD 2011. *Code for Responsible Investing in South Africa*, Lexis Nexus South Africa, Johannesburg, South Africa.

IRCSA. 2011. Framework for Integrated Reporting and the Integrated Report. Available: www.sustainabilitysa.org [Accessed 5 June 2012].

Jonäll, K. and Rimmel, G. 2016. Corporate bee accountability among Sweedish companies. In K. Atkins and B. Atkins (eds) *The Business of Bees: An Integrated Approach to Bee Decline and Corporate Responsibility*. Sheffield, UK: Greenleaf Publishers.

Jones, M. J. and Solomon, J. F. 2013. Problematising accounting for biodiversity. *Accounting, Auditing and Accountability Journal*, 26 (5), 668–687.

Khisty, C. J. 2006. Meditations on systems thinking, spiritual systems, and deep ecology. *Systemic Practice and Action Research*, 19 (4), 295–307.

King, M. 2012. Comments on: Integrated Reporting and the Integrated Report. International Corporate Governance Conference, Johannesburg, South Africa. 23 October.

King, M. 2016. Comments on: Integrated reporting. GARI Conference, Henley on Thames, United Kingdom. 23 October.

Larrinaga-Gonzalez, C. and Bebbington, J. 2001. Accounting change or institutional appropriation? A case study of the implementation of environmental accounting. *Critical Perspectives on Accounting*, 12 (3), 269–292.

Mansoor, H. and Maroun, W. 2016. An initial review of biodiversity reporting by South African corporates: The case of the food and mining sectors. *South African Journal of Economic and Management Sciences*, 19 (4), 592–614.

Maroun, W. 2016. No bees in their bonnet: On the Absence of bee reporting by South African listed companies. In K. Atkins and B. Atkins (eds) *The Business of*

Bees: An Integrated Approach to Bee Decline and Corporate Responsibility. Sheffield, UK: Greenleaf Publishers.

Maroun, W. and Atkins, J. 2018. The emancipatory potential of extinction accounting: Exploring current practice in integrated reports. *Accounting Forum*, in press.

Maroun, W., Coldwell, D. and Segal, M. 2014. SOX and the transition from apartheid to democracy: South African auditing developments through the lens of modernity theory. *International Journal of Auditing*, 18 (3), 206–212.

Massa, L., Farneti, F. and Scappini, B. 2015. Developing a sustainability report in a small to medium enterprise: process and consequences. *Meditari Accountancy Research*, 23 (1), 62–91.

Melin, A., Rouget, M., Midgley, J. J. and Donaldson, J. S. 2014. Pollination ecosystem services in South African agricultural systems. *South African Journal of Science*, 110 (11/12), 25–33.

Milne, M., Tregidga, H. and Walton, S. 2009. Words not actions! The ideological role of sustainable development reporting. *Accounting, Auditing and Accountability Journal*, 22 (8), 1211–1257.

Raemaekers, K., Maroun, W. and Padia, N. 2016. Risk disclosures by South African listed companies post-King III. *South African Journal of Accounting Research*, 30 (1), 41–60.

Rimmel, G. and Jonäll, K. 2013. Biodiversity reporting in Sweden: corporate disclosure and preparers' views. *Accounting, Auditing and Accountability Journal*, 26 (5), 746–778.

Romi, A. and Longing, S. 2016. Accounting for bees: Evidence from disclosures by US listed companies. In K. Atkins and B. Atkins (eds) *The Business of Bees: An Integrated Approach to Bee Decline and Corporate Responsibility*. Sheffield, UK: Greenleaf Publishers.

Rossouw, G. J., van der Watt, A. and Malan, D. P. 2002. Corporate governance in South Africa. *Journal of Business Ethics*, 37 (3), 289–302.

Russo, I.-R. M., Chimimba, C. T. and Bloomer, P. 2010. Bioregion heterogeneity correlates with extensive mitochondrial DNA diversity in the Namaqua rock mouse, *Micaelamys namaquensis* (Rodentia: Muridae) from southern Africa - evidence for a species complex. *BMC Evolutionary Biology*, 10 (1), 307.

SANBI. 2015a. *Crop Agriculture, Pollination and the Honeybee* [Online]. Available: http://biodiversityadvisor.sanbi.org/wp-content/uploads/2012/11/Crop-Agric-Pollination-and-the-honeybee-Brochure.pdf [Accessed 10 June 2016].

SANBI. 2015b. Honeybees in South Africa – what landowners can do to help. Available: www.sanbi.org/sites/default/files/documents/documents/honbeybees-sa-brochure–28-may-eng-proof.pdf [Accessed 8 May 2015].

SANBI. 2015c. Publications by staff of the South African National Biodiversity Institute (SANBI), 2014–2015, per quarter. Available: www.sanbi.org/sites/default/files/documents/documents/sanbi-staff-publications–2014–2015_0.pdf [Accessed 16 October 2015].

SANBI. 2017a. About SANBI [Online]. Available: www.sanbi.org/about [Accessed 10 June 2016].

SANBI. 2017b. Red List Statistics [Online]. Available: http://redlist.sanbi.org/stats.php [Accessed 10 June 2016].

Solomon, J. 2010. *Corporate Governance and Accountability*, third edition, West Susex, United Kingdom, John Wiley and Sons.

Solomon, J. F., Solomon, A., Joseph, N. L. and Norton, S. D. 2013. Impression management, myth creation and fabrication in private social and environmental reporting: Insights from Erving Goffman. *Accounting, Organizations and Society*, 38 (3), 195–213.

Stubbs, W. and Higgins, C. 2014. Integrated reporting and internal mechanisms of change. *Accounting, Auditing and Accountability Journal*, 27 (7), 1068–1089.

Tregidga, H., Milne, M. and Kearins, K. 2014. (Re)presenting 'sustainable organizations'. *Accounting, Organizations and Society*, 39 (6), 477–494.

Usher, K. and Maroun, W., 2018, A review of biodiversity reporting by the South African seafood industry, *South African Journal of Economic and Management Sciences* 21(1), 1–12

Van Liempd, D. and Busch, J. 2013. Biodiversity reporting in Denmark. *Accounting, Auditing and Accountability Journal*, 26 (5), 833–872.

WWF-SA. 2017. What we do [Online]. Available: www.wwf.org.za/what_we_do/ [Accessed 6 May 2017].

Wynberg, R. 2002. A decade of biodiversity conservation and use in South Africa: tracking progress from the Rio Earth Summit to the Johannesburg World Summit on Sustainable Development. *South African Journal of Science*, 98 (5 and 6), 223–243.

10 Business contributions to extinction risk mitigation for black rhinos in Laikipia, Kenya

Mxolisi Sibanda and Martin Mulama

Introduction

The black rhinoceros (*Diceros bicornis*) has had one of the most dramatic declines in recent times. With an estimated 65,000 in 1960, it declined to 2600 by 1997 as a direct result of mainly game hunting and then poaching linked to increasing demand for its horn in East Asian countries like Vietnam, as well as habitat loss and disease (Emslie and Brooks, 1999; Western and Vigne, 1985). From the verge of extinction in the 1980s there has been a steady increase in numbers due to intensive anti-poaching initiatives, public education and global support to efforts to reduce demand and trafficking to the demand countries. Current estimates of the global population stand at around 5500 scattered in small populations mainly in South Africa, Namibia, Kenya and Zimbabwe. Small populations inherently carry a higher risk of extinction due to generic threats and stochastic changes in survival, environment or reproductive success (Muya et al., 2011). All this means that black rhinos are in a precarious situation and justifiably continue as Critically Endangered (CE) on IUCN's Red List and on Appendix I of the Convention on International Trade of Endangered Fauna and Flora (CITES).

Four ecotypes or subspecies of black rhinos are found across Africa (*D. b bicornis, D. b longipes, D. b michaeli* and *D. b minor*). Kenya is the stronghold of *Diceros bicornis michaeli*, the East African black rhino; and, home to the third largest population of black rhinoceros in the world. The East African black rhino was historically distributed from South Sudan to Ethiopia and Somali, through north central Kenya into Tanzania and Rwanda. Records indicate that in the 1970s Kenya had in excess of 20,000 black rhinos but by the 1980s these had sharply declined to a low of below 400 individuals (see Figure 10.1). Although there has been an increase since then, this has been slow and the species is still under threat.

Today in Kenya, populations are found in mainly protected areas made up of national parks managed by the Kenya Wildlife Services (KWS), reserves under the county governments, private land owned by businesses in the country and lately community conservancies run by communities (see Figure 10.2).

With its savanna ecosystems rich in large mammals, Kenya is a prime tourist destination popular for safari. Tourism makes up 12% of the country's gross

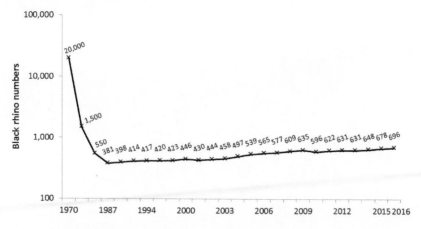

Figure 10.1 Black rhino numbers in Kenya from 1970 to 2016 showing the sharp decline in the 1970s and slow recovery from the mid-1980s

domestic product derived from the sector. The rhino occupies prime place among the tourist attractions that include all the big five game as well as the country's pastoralist cultures typified by the Masaai and Samburu. About forty-nine percent (49%) of the rhino population is found in government owned national parks and reserves and the private lands contain 42% of the population spread on the Laikipia plateau, bar one, in central Kenya, north of Nairobi. The Laikipia landscape is defined by open grassy plains, high altitude plateaus, acacia bushland and forested valleys and kopjes. It stretches from the foot of Mount Kenya running on its eastern side to the edge of the Great Rift Valley.

This chapter traces the history of contributions of private business in Kenya's Laikipia region to black rhino conservation, identifying the specific contributions based on notable achievements that the private land conservancies have bagged in the past few decades and highlights some potential ways of further developing such contributions through a wider practice of extinction accounting in the country.

Laikipia and the rise of black rhinoceros conservation

The Laikipia plateau, at about 1800m above sea level, covers about 9700km^2 on the equator characterised by moderate temperatures and relatively low rainfall varying from 400mm in the northern parts to 900mm per annum nearer the equator. Consequently, rainfall is the limiting factor to land use; and, together with the soils has led to three basic vegetation types in the area: woodland dominated by whistling thorn acacia (*Acacia drepanalobium*); savanna dominated by perennial grasses punctuated by widely spaced trees and shrubs; and bushland with patches of perennial grasses (Kinnaird and O'Brien, 2012).

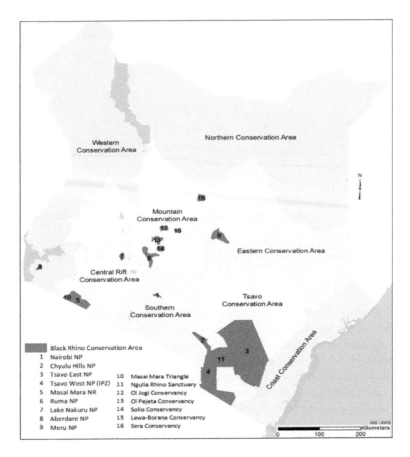

Figure 10.2 Black rhino conservation areas in Kenya

Thus the area's economy is dominated by grazing or ranching in the form of livestock farming, with heads of cattle including the prized Boran, wildlife ranching, and mixed livestock–wildlife ranching with small holder agriculture marginal. Commercial horticulture and wildlife based tourism is also practised. The vegetation and climatic conditions have enabled diverse wildlife to thrive in the area leading to a growing tourism industry in Laikipia County. The wildlife in Laikipia include herbivores and some carnivores like elephants, rhinoceros, hartebeest, oryx, eland, giraffe, buffalo and lions, cheetahs, leopards and hyenas. Several of these are listed on the IUCN Red List as either Vulnerable (e.g. lion) or Critically Endangered (e.g. elephants and rhinoceros). A 2013 study by Laikipia Wildlife Forum revealed that mixed ranches generate at least KSh2 billion per year, employ 3–15 people per 1000 acres and generate significant tax payments of at least KSh180 million per year in addition to the environmental benefits. Environmental benefits for the mixed ranch (and pure wildlife based tourism) model in Kenya include ecosystem services like soil erosion control, soil formation, water retention and regulation, pollination, recreation which have been estimated at KSh9.7 billion.

These benefits accrue to an estimated human population in Laikipia County of 400,000 made up of Kikuyu, Meru, Maasai, Samburu, Turkana and people of European and Indian descent. The mix of culture and wildlife has been the mainstay of the growing tourism ventures in the area.

At the height of the poaching crisis, as evidence pointed to corrupt tendencies in game hunting concessions, the government of Kenya decided to ban consumptive hunting (Somerville, 2016). However that decision led to increased poaching such that by 1984 the black rhinoceros was on the verge of extinction in the country. The dire situation for black rhinoceros led to the development of the concept of rhino sanctuaries. Rhino sanctuaries are secure fenced areas that were initially planned to accommodate 30 to 40 herds of black rhinoceros. The perimeter fences tend to be semi-permeable allowing wildlife other than rhinoceros. Once the concept had been adopted as government policy the private land ranches in Laikipia were among the first to adopt this model in Kenya.

For example, Solio Game Reserve owned in 1970s by Courtland Parfet stocked black rhinoceroses and a combination of effective policing and the myth of man-eating lions in his ranch seem to have kept poachers away from Solio (Miller, 1987). Starting with an initial 23 black rhinos the population in

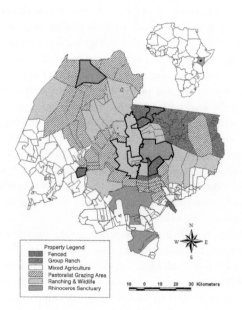

Figure 10.3 Land use in the Laikipia plateau (map taken from Kinnaird and O'Brien, 2012)

Solio increased to an estimated 85–90 by 1986. From this population a new one was established in Lake Nakuru (25–30 animals). The importance of the ability to draw on a private land rhino sanctuary like Solio to build not only the population of black rhinos in the ranch itself but country-wide cannot be overestimated.

Despite the clear state ownership of black rhinoceros in Kenya and the business case for keeping black rhinoceros for eco-tourism, the private land ranches in Laikipia have been staunch supporters of the rhino sanctuary model, and by extension averted black rhinoceros extinction. Over time there has been an increase in development of the rhino conservation areas with six such now established in Laikipia. These are Borana, Lewa, Solio Game Reserve, Ol Pejeta and Sera. These were mostly driven by relatively wealthy private business individuals including Colin Francombe, David and Delia Craig, Ian Craig and Anna Merz among others. These efforts have been vital in delivering real and tangible benefits for black rhinoceros beyond philanthropic accounting. Such tangible benefits for black rhinoceros include provision of new habitats, investment into monitoring and security; ensuring growth in black rhino populations through improved biological management; and innovating in conservation-tourism models that are now being taken up in other places.

Contributions of private land rhino sanctuaries

New habitat

One of the key constraints to the recovery of the East African black rhino is decreasing secure habitat enabling new individuals to thrive. The decreasing extent and quality of appropriate habitat is directly due to increased competition for land for different land use purposes including agriculture and infrastructure development. Black rhinoceros generally require large areas as home range with estimates varying depending on the condition of the habitat. In Laikipia this has been estimated at between 2–54 km^2 with some level of overlap reported. Clearly the private land sanctuaries have provided welcome contributions to this quest for the expansion of range for the black rhinoceros. Using the size of the ranches with established rhino conservation areas in Laikipia about 4632km^2 has been added which is about 46% of the whole county (see Table 10.1). Such new habitat has come with other costs for the private ranches such as monitoring and managing invasive plants, provision of water, secure fencing and in some cases installing watch towers among other costs.

There are already efforts in Laikipia to bring down fences so as to allow rhinos and other wildlife to freely roam across adjacent properties as exemplified by Lewa and Borana ranches which has resulted in a combined area growth of 36% from the original extent of these two separate ranches. The two properties have also made efforts to procure new land to enable such expansion. These efforts are important as fragmentation of habitat limits reproductive success of black rhinoceros.

Table 10.1 Size of rhino ranches in Laikipia

Ranch	Size (km^2)	Initial black rhino population
Solio	57	23
Lewa Downs	396	15
Borana	130	11
Ol Jogi	235	7
Ol Pejeta	364	23
Sera	3450	10
	4632	**89**

Growth in black rhino populations through improved biological management

Amin and others (2006) highlighted that reproductive capacity of Kenya's eastern Black Rhinoceros meta-population had a growth of less than 5%. They posited that this could easily be increased with correct biological management of populations. From the early 1980s, private ranches have made significant contribution to the overall growth of the Kenyan black rhinoceros meta-population. This has been largely as a result of growth beyond their ecological carrying capacity for rhinos from their relatively small founder populations (see Table 10.1) thereby enabling translocations to be done. It is well accepted that such translocations are a key component of any successful rhino recovery project in Africa (Brett, 1998). Between 1984 and 1995, Solio has had 61 black rhinoceros translocated from the game reserve to other areas in Kenya including state parks. This was about five times the original founder population that had been brought into Solio (ibid.). Being able to act as sources for black rhinoceros translocations has not held back the growth in Laikipia's conservancies. Today the private rhino conservation areas in Laikipia hold 49% of Kenya's black rhinoceros population. Ol Pejeta, a key conservancy in Laikipia, now boasts the largest number of black rhinoceros in the country with 115 animals.

Investment in security

Trade in illegal wildlife products is estimated at USD19 billion; and, the rhino horn obtained through poaching is a part of that. Consequently any efforts to make sure that black rhinoceros survive require significant investment into monitoring and security. With poaching becoming a sophisticated and well organised criminal activity private land sanctuaries in Laikipia have established well trained and equipped ranger teams and intelligence networks with communities and law enforcement agencies. It is these ranger teams that are on the frontline of foiling poaching attempts and if necessary engaging armed poachers. When intrusions occur response has to be rapid and appropriate which often involves use of aircraft, ground vehicles and tracker dogs.

As part of the Kenya–wide Black Rhinoceros Strategy, efforts are being made to ear notch all rhinos and where possible fit them with microchips. Operations to do this are expensive as they need helicopters, darting chemicals, manpower and huge logistic support. While support through conservation organisations all rhino conservation areas have to invest resources into making sure that these operations succeed.

As an indicator of the kind of investment that private land rhino sanctuaries have to make to achieve this, in 2017 Ol Pejeta reported that 65% of their annual conservation budget goes towards anti-poaching activities.

Developing a viable business model that mitigates extinction

One of the key contributions of the Laikipia rhino sanctuaries has been the development of a business model that generates returns while contributing to extinction mitigation for black rhinoceros. This is a vital contribution in a country where social development needs are primary. At the forefront of this effort have been Ol Pejeta and Lewa. Ol Pejeta's story is particularly inspiring as it evolved from private ownership into a wholly Kenyan enterprise through collaboration with an international conservation charity, Fauna and Flora International (FFI) and a donor who supported the purchase of the land and put down the initial investment into the conservancy.

This was a first for Kenya with potential for adoption by others elsewhere. The capacity of the conservancy to break even and deliver impact on rhinoceros numbers has made the model the envy of many. It also ensured that social benefits for communities were tangible which has over time earned the respect and support of the local communities. While Lewa is still maintained as a private entity it has worked with the communities thereby generating social dividends and importantly support from communities. Through this demonstration of success and commitment to social development communities have also brought their land holdings together to form conservancies with Sera being a prime example of this. Projections are that there will be 3–4 times more visitors to Kenya with potential for the Laikipia– Samburu landscape top of the list.

Institutionally this has found form through organised platforms such as the Association of Private land rhino sanctuaries and Laikipia Forum who are strong voices for the work that the Laikipia sanctuaries model.

Extinction accounting and businesses in Kenya: going forward

Primarily businesses exist to generate returns for investors and owners. However with the reality of a sixth mass extinction underway due to human activity, the moral and social impetus for businesses to genuinely devote resources, financial and otherwise, to mitigating extinction has strengthened. This is encouraged by the Global Reporting Initiative (GRI) leading to businesses around the world beginning to earnestly embrace extinction accounting (Maroun and

Atkins, 2018). While corporate social responsibility (CSR) has arguably been in existence for over 50 years, extinction accounting is fairly new as a concept.

Ranching businesses in Laikipia should perhaps be regarded as already being on that journey as they have had concern for the black rhinoceros for decades. Perhaps due to escalating and ugly poaching, Kenya as a country became aware of the imminence of extinction for black rhinoceros which rallied businesses such as the ranches in Laikipia into action. Those actions seem to have gone beyond compliance to Kenya's conservation laws or the need for social acceptance to levels where businesses are seeing the potential to make a significant difference through reducing extinction risk. Reading through the annual reports and websites pages of all the rhino conservancies described in this paper black rhino conservation is highlighted as an important part of their existence.

Lately this has started to go beyond the vested interests of conservationists and business people to be embraced by communities who are creating conservancies for both social development and black rhino conservation. The link is strong for conservancies that have mixed livestock and wildlife ranching but not yet there for other businesses types. In fact research by Muthuri and Gilbert (2011) indicates that other big Nairobi Stock Exchange listed businesses in Kenya have low regard for biodiversity conservation in their corporate social responsibility reporting.

The case for the application of extinction accounting in Kenya is arguably incontrovertible. There is a need to popularise the potential that exists for the wider business community including international businesses that operate in Kenya. The Nairobi Stock Exchange (NSE) has at least 64 companies listed on it covering telecommunications and technology, manufacturing, banking, insurance, commercial services and investment that can make a contribution to the conservation of black rhinoceros and other extinction species in the country. Environmental NGOs, media and professional bodies like GRI can exert normative influence on some, if not all, of these companies to make a meaningful contribution to Kenya's wildlife heritage and avert further extinctions. Companies that already have stakeholders fully supportive of extinction risk reduction such as those with international headquarters in North America and Europe should lead the way in this. Prominent and wealthy individuals with business interests and links to the country should also be active in this endeavour.

There is also a need for the government of Kenya to incentivise the adoption of GRI reporting in the country which includes extinction accounting. The clear emphasis on much CSR reporting as highlighted by Muruthi and Gilbert, 2011, is around community issues that are of national concern like HIV-AIDS and health. Making wildlife extinction a priority would certainly ratchet its importance in the corporate sector. Kenya has in some way taken decisive actions for the benefit of wildlife such as the ban on consumptive hunting in 1997 and encouraging contributions to extinction mitigation would only be in order.

Atkins et al. (2018) and Maroun and Atkins (2018) suggest elements of an extinction reporting framework that companies willing to go on this journey should consider. It covers six parts from describing the extinction accounting context, reporting focused actions, partnerships, assessment and evaluation against local and global targets to accounts of mitigation, planned future actions and risk exposure.

In a world in the midst of an unprecedented extinction crisis this kind of framework needs to be promoted, adopted and celebrated by all, including in Kenya. We must by all means avert the extinction of the majestic black rhinoceros which is certainly imminent if business, conservationists, communities and governments of the world do not act now (Atkins et al., 2018).

References

Amin, R., Okita-Ouma, B., Adcock, K., Emslie, R.H., Mulama, M. and Pearce-Kelly, P. (2006) An integrated management strategy for conservation of eastern black rhinoceros in Kenya. *International Zoo Yearbook* 40: 118–129.

Atkins, J. F., Maroun, W., Atkins, B. C. and Barone. E. (2018) From the Big Five to the Big Four? Exploring extinction accounting for the rhinoceros. *Accounting, Auditing & Accountability Journal* 31(2): 1–31.

Brett, R. (1998) Mortality factors and breeding performance of translocated black rhinos in Kenya: 1984–1995. *Pachyderm* 26: 69–82.

Emslie, R. and Brooks, M. (1999) *African Rhino: Status Survey and Conservation Action Plan*. Gland, Switzerland: IUCN/SSC African Rhino Specialist Group.

Kinnaird, M. and O'Brien, T. (2012) Effects of private-land use, livestock management, and human tolerance on diversity, distribution, and abundance of large african mammals. *Conservation Biology* 26(6): 1026–1039.

Maroun, W. and Atkins, J. F. (2018) The emancipatory potential of extinction accounting: Exploring current practice in integrated reports. *Accounting Forum*. In press.

Miller, R. E. (1987) Black rhinoceros conservation in Kenya: A field SSP. Paper presented to AAZPA Great Lakes Regional Meeting, St Louis, MO, USA.

Muthuri, J. N. and Gilbert, V. (2011) An institutional analysis of corporate social responsibility in Kenya. *Journal of Business Ethics* 98(3): 467–483.

Muya, S. M. *et al.* (2011) Substantial molecular variation and low genetic structure in Kenya's black rhinoceros: implications for conservation. *Conservation Genetics* 12: 1575–1588.

Somerville, K. (2016) *Ivory: Power and Poaching in Africa*. Oxford: Oxford University Press.

Western, D. and Vigne, L. (1985) The deteriorating status of African rhinos. *Oryx* 19(4): 215–220.

11 Extinction accounting by the public sector

South African National Parks

Michael Büchling and Warren Maroun

Introduction

At both the deep ecological and anthropocentric level, organisations have a clear role to play in protecting the environment (Jones and Solomon, 2013). They have, however, been slow to respond to suggestions from reporting institutions, non–governmental organisations and civic society to provide detailed accounts on biodiversity loss and extinction in their annual, integrated or sustainability reports (see, for example, Rimmel and Jonäll, 2013; Mansoor and Maroun, 2016; Romi and Longing, 2016). This is confirmed by a recent survey by KPMG (2017) of reporting trends by 4900 companies in multiple jurisdictions which shows that organisations are aware of issues such as climate change, water risks and loss of biodiversity but do not regard these as material business considerations.

The continuing centrality of financial imperatives is often cited as the primary reason for a lack of commitment to and awareness of environmental sustainability (see, for example, Gray, 2006; Milne et al., 2009; Tregidga et al., 2014). However, even when companies are keen to champion sustainability, understanding the scientific evidence on environmental problems and how to effect change is no easy task (Maroun, 2016). Having to explain this in a sustainability or an integrated report in a manner which stakeholders can understand is, arguably, even more difficult. Nevertheless, there are early indications that some companies are beginning to tackle otherwise complex scientific issues in their corporate reports. For example, Atkins et al. (2016) show how companies in the UK have started to grapple with the decline in pollinator populations. They are accessing, interpreting and referring to biological research to make consumers and investors aware of the material social, environmental and economic impact which the extinction of insect species (such as the honey bee) can have on society and on the planet. Similarly, while the extent of reporting may be poor (Mansoor and Maroun, 2016), several South African companies are taking the initiative to deal with issues such as decline of fish stocks, deteriorating soil quality and the threat of extinction of the rhinoceros (Usher and Maroun, 2018; Atkins et al., 2018) in a manner which suggests that attitudes to the environment are beginning to change.

Even if these emerging forms of what this book refers to as 'extinction accounting' grow in recognition, corporate accounts of extinction will be inherently limited because they focus on the impact which a particular company has on biodiversity mass. It is unlikely that this will be sufficiently broad to capture changes in important biodiversity measures across multiple biomes or at a national level. If extinction accounting is to live up to the potential outlined in this book, the narrow focus on private sector reporting needs to be complemented by a form of biodiversity consolidation accounting which reports on extinction indictors for different industries, environmental regions and globally. To date, however, the prior research on biodiversity reporting (Jones and Solomon, 2013), ecological accounts (Russell et al., 2017) and extinction accounting (Atkins and Maroun, 2018) is limited to the individual reporting entity. To explore the possibility for a broader scope of these emerging forms of accounting, this chapter considers how extinction accounting can be applied by the South African National Parks (SANParks) as part of a broad commitment to conserve species and to save some of the last pristine wilderness areas in Africa.

The South African National Parks

In 1910 the then Union of South Africa placed responsibility for the administration of game reserves and general wildlife in an environmental administration body based in the Transvaal Province. In 1912 Stevenson-Hamilton (one of the forefathers of what is today the world-famous Kruger National Park) was able to have large areas of land, located between the Sabi and Olifants Rivers and Letaba and Shingwedzi Rivers, recognised as national parks. By 1926, the National Parks Bill was tabled in Parliament, leading to the establishment of the first Board of South African National Parks (SANParks, 2017).

The period coinciding with democracy in South Africa has seen significant developments. The National Parks Act was repealed and, in 2003, the *Environmental Management: Protected Areas Act* (EMPAA) was promulgated. The purpose of the legislation is to ensure the 'protection and conservation of ecologically viable areas representative of South Africa's biological diversity and its natural landscapes and seascapes' (EMPAA, 2003). To achieve this objective, land under management by SANParks was increased by over 700,000 hectares.[1] As at the end of 2016, SANParks was responsible for managing and protecting over 4millon hectares of land divided into 21 national parks (SANParks, 2015, 2016).

'Much of this expansion programme has been geared towards the anticipation of the impacts of climate change' on both flora and fauna (SANParks, 2016, p. 6). Expansion of areas under conservation has been complemented by a concerted effort to carry out important environmental research, create employment opportunities for poor communities and encourage local and international tourism to ensure the financial sustainability of the national parks (SANParks, 2015, 2016). As a result:

SANParks has gone from strength to strength to the point today where SANParks is recognised as a world leader in conservation and protected area management. This is evident within the national conservation discourse, and at international conferences where SANParks is often used as a point of reference in relation to best practice in the management and development of protected areas.

(SANParks, 2016, p. 6)

As a state-owned entity, SANParks is required to prepare an annual report which provides government (and the public) with an account of how well the organisation has performed in terms of environmental, financial and social indicators. As one of the custodians of South Africa's biodiversity, the emphasis is not on the maximisation of financial returns. Instead, SANParks' mission is:

to develop, expand, manage and promote a system of sustainable national parks that represents biodiversity and heritage assets, through innovation and best practise for the just and equitable benefit of current and future generations.

(SANParks, 2016, p. 7)

By reporting on how this objective is being achieved, SANParks offers an indication of a type of extinction accounting at the national level. This can be used to provide a more complete view of changing trends in number of species found in South Africa and their population sizes. It can also be used to mobilise public action by drawing on accounting's emancipatory potential.

Towards an emancipatory accounting framework

For the purpose of this chapter, the framework developed and applied by Atkins and Maroun (2018) and introduced in chapter two of this book, is used to illustrate the construction of an extinction account by SANParks. This is because this framework is grounded in already existing reporting standards – such as those issued by the GRI and IIRC – and is already being applied (to some extent) by the private sector in South Africa (Maroun and Atkins, 2018) and the UK (Atkins et al., 2016). As a result, it offers an approach to extinction accounting which is grounded in both the emancipatory accounting literature and the practical experiences of professional accountants. As there is a full exposition of a hybrid emancipatory extinction accounting framework in chapter two, we do not repeat that discussion here but move straight on to applying the framework to the South African public sector context in relation to national parks. The model presented in chapter two was developed for the private sector where companies need to balance financial objectives with mitigating environmental impact and risk. The principle that a complete account of extinction includes detailed reporting on context; actions taken to address the threat of extinction and post-implementation review of conservation initiatives are, however, equally relevant in the public sector. To illustrate this, the annual reports of SANParks are reviewed to show how one of the world's largest environmental management bodies is providing a detailed account of extinction risk and prevention.

Data collection and analysis

Content analysis is used to collect and analyse data from SANParks' 2015 and 2016 annual reports. These are publicly available and were read several times by the researchers to gain a sense of their overall structure and content. Once this was complete, the reports were systematically coded. Examples dealing with each element in the extinction accounting model were identified and used to construct a view on how SANParks is reporting on the risks posed by extinction and the steps taken to prevent it. For this purpose, the researchers did not use single words or sentences as the unit of analysis but images, sub-sections and themes in the reports which best illustrated each of the extinction accounting model's elements (adapted from Krippendorff, 1989). As the data collection deals only with SANParks' 2015 and 2016 reports to show how extinction accounting can be applied by environmental organisations, the frequency of disclosures has not been tracked.

Extinction accounting by South African National Parks

The 2015 and 2016 reports open with an explanation of SANPark's primary objective is framed in ecological terms:

> SANParks' main purpose is the conservation of a representative system of biodiversity, landscape, encompassing fauna, flora, geological structures and unique scenery within the national park under its management authority. SANParks *does not focus on traditional natural resource management* of species, but rather on *ecosystem management and ecological integrity* within the national park. SANParks can intervene in ecosystems responsibly and sustainably, but it focuses management on *complementing natural processes* (e.g. floods, fires and disease outbreaks) *under a minimum interference philosophy*. SANParks does not manage for the reproduction of biodiversity, but for biodiversity representivity and complementarity *that promote resilience and ensure ecosystem integrity*. SANParks acquired the majority of biodiversity at no cost to SANParks.
>
> (SANParks, 2015, p. 149; emphasis added)

Reporting is multi-dimensional. Economically, SANParks needs to ensure that it is financially sustainable. As a result, it includes metrics such as income-to-cost ratios and revenue from tourism as key performance indicators. These are, however, complemented by an extensive list of performance targets dealing with, for example, hectares of land rehabilitated, number of species interventions and cultural heritage projects (SANParks, 2015, 2016). These issues are dealt with in a number of sections in the annual reports, namely:

- general information about SANParks, which includes details about the organisation's structures, mandate and policy statements;
- a situation analysis summarising financial performance;
- a review of strategic outcomes and performance against planned targets;
- a report on conservation services;
- details on tourism development, marketing and cooperative services;
- socio-economic review;
- an outline of operations;
- details on corporate governance and regulatory compliance;
- a report on human capital management; and
- financial statements.

Collectively, the different sections in the 2015 and 2016 reports give a detailed overview of how SANParks recognises the important role it plays in protecting biodiversity, the steps being taken to prevent extinction of species and how well its conservation initiatives are performing. Each of the elements of the extinction accounting model is presented below.

Element 1: extinction in context

SANParks reports on the size and location of each of the national parks under its supervision. Figure 11.1 is included in its annual reports and is useful for giving stakeholders an understanding of the scope of the organisation's operations. There are also details on the different types of biodiversity in South Africa which are shown in Figure 11.2.

The disclosures could be improved by superimposing the location of national parks (Figure 11.1) on the biodiversity map (Figure 11.2). Nevertheless, the reader is given an idea of the location of key biomes. This high level reporting is also supported by a detailed narrative on each national park which includes climate, different species and how SANParks is managing relevant biodiversity issues. For example, the following deals with the Kruger National Park:

> The average KNP rainfall is currently below that of the 1991/92 drought, the most severe drought on record for the KNP. The average rainfall during December 2015 was 16,7 mm versus the long-term average of 91,7 mm. If these conditions continue (and according to long-term forecasts, it will) it will probably cause significant declines in the bloated populations of elephant, buffalo and hippo.
>
> (SANParks, 2016, p. 96)

The relevance of changes in the populations of these species are discussed. The report includes detail on population sizes, how these are changing and how

Figure 11.1 Map of SA National Parks
Source: SANParks (2016, p. 16)

data are being collected. For elephants, in particular, because of the material impact which elephants can have on biodiversity in sensitive areas, SANParks discusses how it tracks population numbers:

> The organisation collates aerial survey data since 1998 and conduct an aerial total count using a helicopter observation platform during 2015. A minimum of 17 086 elephants lived in Kruger National Park during 2015, changing at 4.2% (95% CI: 1.1–7.3%) per annum over the last generation of elephants, compared to 6.5% annual population growth noted during the intensive management era . . . Authorities should continue to evaluate the demographic responses of elephants to landscape scale interventions directed at restoring the limitation of spatial variance in resource distribution on elephant spatio-temporal dynamics and the consequences that may have for other conservation values.
>
> (SANParks, 2016, p. 96)

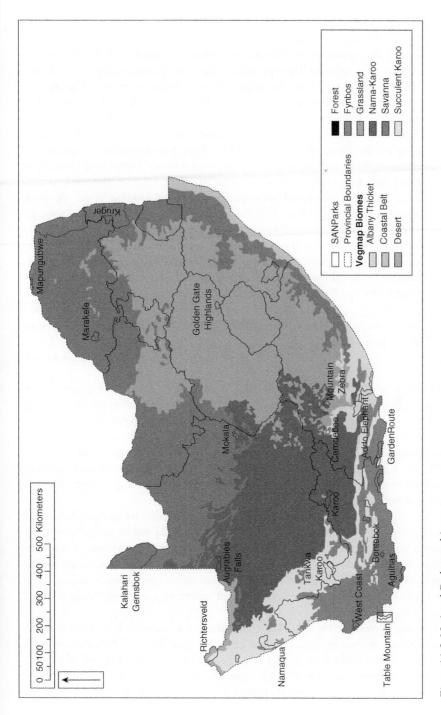

Figure 11.2 National Parks per biome

Source: SANParks (2015, p. 14)

Other examples of conservation projects deal with species affected by poaching. The most notable case is the rhinoceros, which, due to unprecedented levels of poaching, is at risk of becoming extinct.

> SANParks embraces an integrated approach aligned with South Africa's Rhino Management Strategy that seeks to maintain persistent black and white rhino populations throughout their distribution ranges. *The approach identifies that rhinos may play key roles in providing opportunities to improve people's livelihoods through aesthetic, ecological and economic values.* Rhino poaching, however, impacts on SANParks achieving these objectives. At the beginning of the financial year, SANParks rhino population was estimated at between 8991 and 10,305 animals in seven national parks comprising both black and white rhino. At the close of the financial year, the rhino population was best estimated between 8573 to 9984 animals across all seven national parks. In the case of the rhino population in Kruger National Park, the combination of poaching and natural deaths (12%) exceeded the annual birth rate (10.7%) recorded during the reporting period. For the period under review, SANParks lost 878 rhinos due to poaching, with Kruger National Park being the most affected national park. This is 42.8% (from 615 to 878) more poached animals when compared to the same period of the previous financial year. For the same reporting period, a total of 178 suspects were arrested in the Kruger National Park in relation to rhino poaching.
>
> (SANParks, 2015, p. 14, emphasis added)

This type of detailed narrative reporting quantifies the number of animals being lost to poachers and gives comparative information to reveal trends in poaching statistics. The disclosure also offers a case for wanting to protect the rhinoceros. In addition to the mandate to conserve biodiversity, SANParks recognises the key role which this species plays in a social or cultural context (Atkins et al., 2015b). This deep ecological perspective is complemented by reminding stakeholders that the loss of the rhinoceros can have a financial implication although this cannot currently be quantified.

Overall, reporting on specific species, biodiversity by geographical area and the state of conservation at different national parks is important for providing context. The disclosures give the reader an overview of the ecological/biological issues and where and how these are being managed. This in turn, provides an understanding of what the organisation is doing, how it is carrying out different operations and where its efforts are being focused (see Cuckston, 2017).

It may, however, be argued that SANParks can do more to explain the role of different species in the ecosystem and why their loss will pose risks in both ecological and anthropocentric terms. For example, while the risk of extinction of the rhinoceros is dealt with explicitly, the 2015 and 2016 annual reports are based on the assumption that the need to protect biodiversity, backed by legal mandate to do so, is sufficient. It may, however, be possible to gain additional support for conservation projects from key stakeholders if the moral, ethical or social duty to protect species is made explicit (see Christian, 2016; Russell et al., 2017) While deep ecologists may object, clarifying the significant financial impact of losing key species may also be a useful tactic for driving an anti-extinction agenda (Atkins and Maroun, 2018).

Elements 2 and 3: reporting on actions and partnerships

For extinction accounting to be emancipatory, it needs to explain how extinction prevention policy translates into specific actions to reverse extinction trends and the results of any conservation or environmental initiatives on rates of species loss (see Atkins et al., 2015a; Gallhofer et al., 2015). The earlier example of rhinoceros poaching is used to illustrate how Elements 2 and 3 of the extinction accounting model are addressed in the SANPark's annual reports.

In 2015, the following is reported:

> The roll-out of the SANParks Rhino Management Strategy and the NATJOINTS Priority Committee 'Operation Rhino' initiatives will continue to receive priority, particularly in the Kruger National Park as the most affected area. Furthermore, SANParks will enhance its participation in 'Operation Pyramid' that is led by the Department of Home Affairs, in the border control environment.
>
> (SANParks, 2015, p. 63)

The disclosure points to a collaborative effort between SANParks and other organs of state to combat poachers. It also shows that SANParks has developed a policy for managing the risk of losing the rhinoceros. However, the level of detail for this type of reporting to be seen as emancipatory is lacking and should be contrasted with the following outline of efforts to protect the rhinoceros in the 2016 annual report:

'For the period under review, the following was achieved:

a) Rhino compulsory interventions: Programme that provides rhino security continued in all national parks that have rhinos. The number of rhino poached per day remained stable even though poaching activities per day increased.

b) Rhino biological management interventions: Internal translocations of rhino in Kruger National Park out of poaching hot-spots, to the Intensive Protection Zone (IPZ) continued and five individuals are constantly being monitored.

c) Rhino long-term sustainability interventions: SANParks' participation in the DEA' Commission of Inquiry tasked with assessing the feasibility of trade in rhino horn, as part of the strategic responses of South Africa to curb rhino poaching was completed in January/February.

d)   Rhino game-changing interventions: A pledge made by SANParks in support of the country's wildlife economy resulted in a document to guide SANParks' contribution towards a community-based wildlife economy. The document outlines the desired outcome, the key factors for consideration to achieve this outcome and various organisational risks for consideration.

e)   Rhino population census: Census and analyses for Kruger and Marakele National Parks were completed. Ground-based monitoring of individual rhino and registration records for Mapungubwe, Mokala, Addo Elephant, Mountain and Karoo National Parks have been completed.

f)   Elephant impact interventions: Management protocol completed. Experimental testing continued in Addo Elephant and Kruger National Parks (SANParks, 2016, p. 35).

In the authors' views, this is a good example of the type of action-orientated reporting which characterises an extinction accounting framework. SANParks is addressing poaching in multiple locations and is relying on a combination of long-term policy reform focused on the wildlife economy, and specific interventions (such as a census and animal translocations) to mitigate the risk of extinction. This is complemented by a number of partnership-based initiatives such as collaboration with leading South African retailers, financial service providers and civil society groups to raise funds needed for conservation and public awareness about the plight of the rhinoceros (Atkins et al., 2018). Steps have also been taken to collaborate with other conservation bodies to deal with poaching at a regional level (rather than only at specific national parks):

> There has been significant progress in formalising and implementing the alliance partnerships in support of a regional effort to combat the rhino-poaching threat and to support efforts in . . . the KNP. Game Reserves United (GRU), the Greater Kruger Environmental Protection Foundation (GKEPF), Mozambique Lebombo Concessions (MLC) and the Nkomati Interest Group continue to evolve and have become key role players in the regional rhino campaign.
>
> (SANParks, 2016, p. 100)

This type of action-orientated reporting is not limited to high profile species. For example, the 2015 and 2016 reports deal in detail with the threat which invasive plants pose to local biodiversity and the steps taken to mitigate the environmental risks:

> the exotic red claw crayfish (*Cherax quadricarinatus*) was reported at the Van Graan Dam along the borders of the KNP [Kruger National Park] during January 2016. SANParks, in collaboration with MTPA [the Mpumalanga Tourism and Parks Agency] and SANBI [the South African National Biodiversity Institute], have initiated a research project to determine the extent of the distribution of the invasive crayfish in the Crocodile

River and to compile a management plan to control its distribution. A management brief and tabling of a Threshold of Potential Concern has been tabled at the KNP Conservation Management Committee. Strategic adjustments were made in the way in which the clearing of invasive alien plants is done in KNP. The focus has shifted to the perennial rivers in the KNP, with one team on each river undertaking the clearing and mapping/monitoring of invasive alien plants. Increased focus to clear invasive alien plants outside the park on river systems that enter the KNP have been initiated. Twenty-six invasive alien plants have been prioritised (as per the CSIR and various workshop recommendations). Famine weed is getting special attention.

(SANParks, 2016, pp. 96–97)

The disclosure is species-specific and gives stakeholders background on the areas affected. There is also detail on the partnerships formed, the steps being taken to tackle the invasive plants and animals. As with the reporting on rhinoceros poaching, information on action plans is supported by clearly presented post-implementation review of conservation initiatives discussed below.

Elements 4 and 5: analysis and reflection

There is evidence of SANParks reviewing and reporting on the successes and failures of its anti-extinction projects. For example, Figure 11.3 shows how efforts taken to deal with the threat posed by invasive species are being assessed by management. The report includes a clear indication of target versus actual performance and favourable/unfavourable variances.

DELIVERABLES	PLANNED	ACTUAL	PERCENTAGE
Beach Clean up			
WftC Beach clean-up (km)	11 726	4 583	39%
Wetlands Rehabilitation			
Cubic meters	13 535	14 926	110%
No of wetlands rehabilitated	20	18	90%
Environmental Monitors			
EMs appointed	1 441	1 660	115%
Alien Vegetation Clearing			
Initial hectares	27 330	31 092	114%
Follow up hectares	196 444	221 947	113%
Working for Ecosystems: Rehabilitation			
Initial rehabilitation (ha)	5 200	13 301	256%
Follow up rehabilitation (ha)	12 394	19 149	155%
Working for Ecosystems: Bush Clearing			
Initial bush clearing	2 607	2 509	96%
Follow up bush clearing	792	840	106%
Total Rehabilitation (Alien vegetation, erosion & bush clearing)			
Initial rehabilitation (ha)	35 137	46 902	133%
Follow up rehabilitation (ha)	209 630	241 936	115%
Eco Furniture Programme			
School desks (SDEs)	279 290	142 720	51%

Figure 11.3 National Parks per biome

Source: SANParks (2016, p. 89)

Results of the anti-poaching missions aimed at protecting the rhinoceros are also dealt with in detail. For example, the following narrative is included as part of the conservation review in the 2016 annual report:

> for the first time in a decade, the poaching situation has stabilised. The number of rhinos poached in the Kruger National Park was 826 in 2015 in comparison to 827 poached in 2014. This has happened despite a significant increase in the number of poaching activities in the Kruger – a positive indication of the effectiveness of current anti-poaching initiatives. Poachers arrested in Kruger National Park amounted to 202, with a further additional 115 in the area adjacent to the park during 2015, making the total arrested in the park and surroundings to 317 individuals. This is a marked increase on the 258 poachers arrested in and around the park in 2014. Firearms seized inside the park in 2015 amounted to 125 and 63 outside the park – 188 compared to the 148 of the previous year . . . SANParks biological management interventions focused on shifting rhinos from high poaching risk areas to safer localities within Kruger National Park, evaluating and initiating several rhino strongholds, and saving rhino orphans left abandoned when their mothers were poached. SANParks captured 34 white rhinos from poaching hotspots and relocated them to safer areas within the park. Eighteen animals were fitted with VHF radio collars provided through funding by the Peace Parks Foundation. Towards the end of 2014, SANParks put out a tender request to potential private owners that could assist in achieving white rhino conservation objectives. Following the assessment of properties and the rhino allocation process, SANParks initiated the translocation of 111 white rhinos during August 2015. SANParks rescued nine rhino orphans during 2015, all of which are being cared for in specialised facilities. None of these orphans has been released back into the wild yet.
>
> (SANParks, 2016, p. 53)

Detailed narrative information on population size, number of arrests and number of animals tagged and relocated is complemented by tables, charts and diagrams which give a clear overview of outcomes. For example, Figure 11.4 shows the effect which park rangers and armed patrols are having on incidences of poaching.

This type of information is reported as part of a review of operations and conservation programmes. It also features as an integral part of SANParks' key performance indicators (KPI). For example, the KPI illustration in Figure 11.5 deals with land rehabilitation (including the removal of alien species). Similarly, in terms of overall management of protected areas, the 'Management Effectiveness Tracking Tool' (a type of balanced score card measure) is referred to (Figure 11.6).

In both cases, SANParks reports the target set for the year and how well it has performed against that target. Importantly, where unfavourable variances

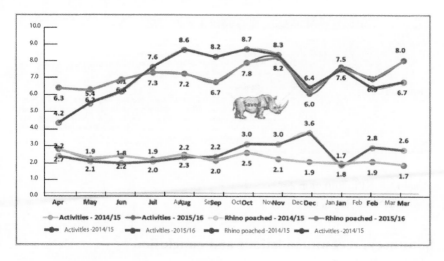

Figure 11.4 Effect of Rangers on poaching
Source: SANParks (2015, p. 35)

are noted, an explanation is provided. This indicates that the annual report is more than just an impression management tool. The fact that biodiversity is addressed at the strategic and operational level and that SANParks reviews and reports on both positive and negative performance shows a genuine commitment to conservation in South Africa.

PERFORMANCE INDICATOR	ANNUAL TARGET	ACTUAL PERFORMANCE
2.2 Total Hectors of Land Rehabilitated/Restored	Initial/New Area = 33 368 ha² Follow-Up Area = 202 694 ha Wetlands = 6 508 m³ (26 sites)	Initial/New Area = 46 902 ha Follow-Up Area = 241 936 ha Wetlands = 14 962 m³ (18 sites)
Performance Analysis	The initial area rehabilitated was 13 534 ha more (41%) than the target, while the annual follow-up rehabilitation target of 202 694 ha was exceeded with 39 242 ha or 19%. For the full year, of the planned 6 508m³ wetlands, rehabilitation was exceeded by 229% with 14 962m³ rehabilitated. This programme only started in October as opposed to April 2015 after delays in transferring of the implementation responsibilities from the South African National Biodiversity Institute (SANBI) to the Department of Environmental Affairs (DEA), and then to SANParks. Work was done on 18 wetlands in the participating parks. The increase in cubic meters is related to environmental factors in that structures had to be re-designed following floods after the original designs were made, and alternative activities had to be done in other areas, since no work could be done in the Stolsnek area of Kruger National Park due to the rhino-poaching situation. **Reasons for variance** The deployment of an experienced programme manager to assist with the rehabilitation projects was key over achievement of the planned targets. All the rehabilitation programmes, i.e. alien invasive vegetation clearing, land restoration and bush clearing performed and achieved and/or exceeded planned targets.	
Planned Improvement/ Corrective Actions	No further intervention needed. All rehabilitation projects performed excellently during the past year, taking into consideration the capacity challenges and the late start of the Wetlands programme. Appointments of critical staff are in process.	

Figure 11.5 KPI illustration 1
Source: SANParks (2016, p. 33)

PERFORMANCE INDICATOR	ANNUAL TARGET	ACTUAL PERFORMANCE
2.1 METT Score	70,0%	71%
Performance Analysis	The METT-SA is designed as an assessment tool to measure trends that determine how effectively protected areas are managed. The SANParks bi-annual METT-SA assessment was completed for all 19 parks in February and March 2016. SANParks submitted the METT report to DEA in early May 2016. The assessment showed that SANParks has achieved an average score of 71%. **Reasons for variance** The difference between the annual target and actual performance is not material enough to make any meaningful conclusion other than just to indicate that park management attended to the implementation of the corrective measures identified through the METT assessment and audit for their specific parks respectively. It should be noted that the score achieved; however, falls within the same classification of effectiveness. In terms of the METT-SA methodology, a score of 67% and above constitute sound management effectiveness.	
Planned Improvement/ Corrective Actions	No corrective measures are required at this stage.	

Figure 11.6 KPI illustration 2
Source: SANParks (2016, p. 32)

Summary, recommendations and conclusion

Overall, SANParks provides a detailed review of efforts being taken to prevent the extinction of species. Its 2015 and 2016 annual reports cover each of the aspects included in Element 6, which should be incorporated in a corporate report.

Stakeholders are provided with an overview of the location of national parks, the country's key biomes and the information on different types of conservation initiatives at South Africa's national parks. This is complemented by disclosures on specific species and the nature of environmental issues being dealt with, which gives the annual reports context. In addition to information on different species, there are detailed examples of policies, plans and actions being taken to combat extinction. Steps taken to address the risks posed by invasive plant and animal species and to combat rhinoceros poaching are two examples. In each case, narrative and diagrammatic reporting is used to explain the location, nature and magnitude of the environmental challenge and how SANParks is working to protect biodiversity. Importantly, the annual reports include detailed statistics on how well the organisation has performed in terms of clearly defined (and transparently reported) targets.

Given that extinction accounting is an emerging practice, there are areas for improvement. Most of the detail on extinction trends and prevention methods is focused on high profile species. This is to be expected. The plight of animals, such as the rhinoceros, has been covered extensively by the popular press with the result that there is significant public pressure to explain how SANParks is protecting this iconic member of the Big Five. The rhinoceros also provides an opportunity to raise much needed funding. This is not inconsistent with an emancipatory extinction accounting ethos. Responding to stakeholders' expectations for detail on specific species or using the accounting system to raise money for conservation is a key part of protecting biodiversity. Care must, however, be taken to ensure that details on other ecologically important flora and fauna is not omitted and that the completeness of the extinction account is not compromised.

Related closely to this, SANParks stops short of giving an overview of how plant and animal populations and ranges have changed in total. Reporting on the 'inventory' of natural capital by type of species, geographical region and IUCN categorisation would be useful for explaining the biodiversity resources which SANParks is responsible for managing, the level of extinction risk and the *consolidated* effect of conservation initiatives (see Ceballos et al., 2017; Cuckston, 2018), This can also be used to organise reporting on different conservation projects (including partnerships with NGOs). The aim is to provide a multi-dimensional account of conservation efforts, KPI's and material outcomes according to the level of extinction risk. A possible approach for organising this type of extinction risk and response report is outlined in Figure 11.7.

Extinction accounting needs to give stakeholders context (Element 1) and make a clear connection between the types of species, population sizes and the corresponding action to protect biodiversity (Elements 2 and 3) (Atkins and Maroun, 2018). Drawing on the earlier research on biodiversity reporting, the first dimension of the proposed risk response matrix gives detail on the total number of species under protection and their population sizes (see Jones, 1996). SANParks would also explain its policy for managing extinction risk and summarise material conservation programmes including the extent to which these rely on stakeholder partnerships (such as those with researchers, NGO's or the private sector). This would be complemented by outlining each programme's objectives and KPIs (see Maroun and Atkins, 2018).

Dimension 2 builds on the relatively descriptive reporting in Dimension 1 by providing a measurable assessment of extinction (Cuckston, 2018). Using, for example, the IUCN categorisation, species can be grouped according to the increasing risk of extinction. Disclosures would include, for example, the number of species per risk category, population sizes, changes in population and ecological function. This would be cross-referenced to detailed policies, plans and actions aimed at preventing extinction. It is important to show how the investment in conservation projects, number of stakeholder partnerships and level of research is directly proportionate to the extinction risk. Details on the positive and negative outcomes of anti-extinction efforts should also be provided and aggregated according to extinction risk.

The third dimension is a type of consolidated extinction account. Information from Dimension 2 would be aggregated to provide an overview of the extinction trends at the geographical or biome level (Cuckston, 2017). Examples of Dimension 3 disclosures include: increases or decreases in the range of endangered plant and animal species; population changes per national park; total investment in conservation projects per biome and the number of KPI's which have or have not been achieved per group of species and by region.

Finally, the extinction risk response matrix can be used to show where conservation projects and have succeeded or failed for individual species or

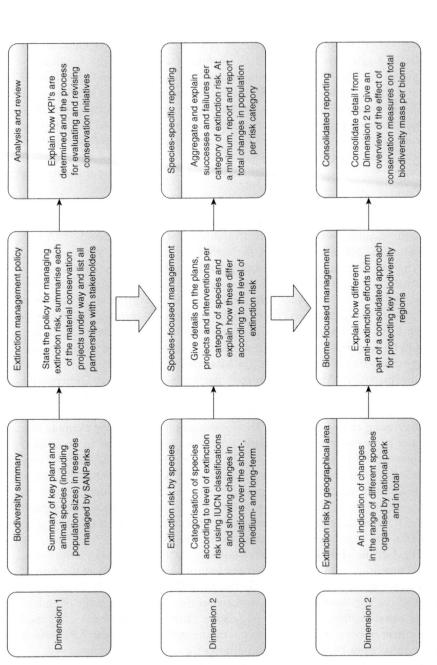

Figure 11.7 Extinction risk versus response matrix

in different locations. This should be taken into account by management at SANParks when planning future interventions (Elements 4 and 5) and reporting to stakeholders (Element 6). Any insights from post-implementation review can be used to provide a detailed account of how policies and KPIs are being revised and the steps being taken to improve existing projects or introduce new initiatives which will reverse extinction trends. In this way, reporting on the toss of species becomes emancipatory. In addition to the descriptive information typically provided in biodiversity reports, stakeholder are provided with a measurable assessment of extinction risk, an explanation of what is currently being done to protect species and an indication of how resources will be used in the future to protect life on earth.

Note

1 This was the result of the establishment of new national parks including Agulhas National Park, Camdeboo National Park, Garden Route National Park, Mapungubwe National Park, Mokala National Park, Namaqua National Park and Table Mountain National Park.

References

Atkins, J. and Maroun, W. 2018. Integrated extinction accounting and accountability: building an ark. *Accounting, Auditing and Accountability Journal*, 31 (3), 750–786.

Atkins, J., Atkins, B., Thomson, I. and Maroun, W. 2015a. 'Good' news from nowhere: imagining utopian sustainable accounting. *Accounting, Auditing and Accountability Journal*, 28(5), 651–670.

Atkins, J., Barone, E., Gozman, D., Maroun, W. and Atkins, B. 2015b. Exploring rhinoceros conservation and protection: Corporate disclosures and extinction accounting by leading South African companies. Meditari Accountancy Research, Forli, Italy, 2 July.

Atkins, J., Barone, E., Maroun, W. and Atkins, B. 2016. Bee accounting and accountability in the UK. In K. Atkins and B. Atkins (eds), *The Business of Bees: An Integrated Approach to Bee Decline and Corporate Responsibility*. Sheffield: Greenleaf Publishers.

Atkins, J., Maroun, W., Atkins, B. C. and Barone, E. 2018. From the Big Five to the Big Four? Exploring extinction accounting for the rhinoceros. *Accounting, Auditing and Accountability Journal*, 31(2), 674–702.

Ceballos, G., Ehrlich, P. R. and Dirzo, R. 2017. Biological annihilation via the ongoing sixth mass extinction signaled by vertebrate population losses and declines. *Proceedings of the National Academy of Sciences*, published online ahead of print 10 July 2017.

Christian, J. 2016. *Bombus terrestris*. A personal deep ecological account. In K. Atkins and B. Atkins (eds), *The Business of Bees: An Integrated Approach to Bee Decline and Corporate Responsibility*. Sheffield: Greenleaf Publishers.

Cuckston, T. 2017. Ecology-centred accounting for biodiversity in the production of a blanket bog. *Accounting, Auditing and Accountability Journal*, 30(7), 1537–1567.

Cuckston, T. 2018. Making extinction calculable. *Accounting, Auditing and Accountability Journal*, in press.

Gallhofer, S., Haslam, J. and Yonekura, A. 2015. Accounting as differentiated universal for emancipatory praxis: Accounting delineation and mobilisation for emancipation(s) recognising democracy and difference. *Accounting, Auditing and Accountability Journal*, 28(5), 846–874.

Gray, R. 2006. Social, environmental and sustainability reporting and organisational value creation? Whose value? Whose creation? *Accounting, Auditing and Accountability Journal*, 19(6), 793–819.

Jones, M. J. 1996. Accounting for biodiversity: A pilot study. *The British Accounting Review*, 28(4), 281–303.

Jones, M. J. and Solomon, J. F. 2013. Problematising accounting for biodiversity. *Accounting, Auditing and Accountability Journal*, 26(5), 668–687.

KPMG. 2017. The road ahead. The KPMG Survey of Corporate Responsibility Reporting 2017. Available: https://assets.kpmg.com/content/dam/kpmg/xx/pdf/2017/10/kpmg-survey-of-corporate-responsibility-reporting-2017.pdf [Accessed 20 November 2017].

Krippendorff, K. 1989. Content Analysis. In G. Barnouw, W. Gerbner, T. Schramm, L. Worth and L. Gross (eds), *International Encyclopedia of Communication*. New York: Oxford University Press.

Mansoor, H. and Maroun, W. 2016. An initial review of biodiversity reporting by South African corporates: The case of the food and mining sectors. *South African Journal of Economic and Management Sciences*, 19(4), 592–614.

Maroun, W. 2016. No bees in their bonnet: On the Absence of bee reporting by South African listed companies. In K. Atkins and B. Atkins (eds), *The Business of Bees: An Integrated Approach to Bee Decline and Corporate Responsibility*. Sheffield: Greenleaf Publishers.

Maroun, W. and Atkins, J. 2018. The emancipatory potential of extinction accounting: Exploring current practice in integrated reports. *Accounting Forum*, in press.

Milne, M., Tregidga, H. and Walton, S. 2009. Words not actions! The ideological role of sustainable development reporting. *Accounting, Auditing and Accountability Journal*, 22(8), 1211–1257.

Rimmel, G. and Jonäll, K. 2013. Biodiversity reporting in Sweden: corporate disclosure and preparers' views. *Accounting, Auditing and Accountability Journal*, 26(5), 746–778.

Romi, A. and Longing, S. 2016. Accounting for bees: Evidence from disclosures by US listed companies. In K. Atkins and B. Atkins (eds), *The Business of Bees: An Integrated Approach to Bee Decline and Corporate Responsibility*. Sheffield: Greenleaf Publishers.

Russell, S., Milne, M. J. and Dey, C. 2017. Accounts of nature and the nature of accounts: Critical reflections on environmental accounting and propositions for ecologically informed accounting. *Accounting, Auditing and Accountability Journal*, 30(7), 1426–1458.

SANParks 2015. *Annual Report 2014/2015*. Pretoria: SANParks.

SANParks 2016. *Annual Report 2015/2016*. Pretoria: SANParks.

SANParks. 2017. *SANParks: brief history [Online]*. Available: www.sanparks.org/about/history.php [Accessed 23 January 2018].

Tregidga, H., Milne, M. and Kearins, K. 2014. (Re)presenting 'sustainable organizations'. *Accounting, Organizations and Society*, 39(6), 477–494.

Usher, K. and Maroun, W., 2018, A review of biodiversity reporting by the South African seafood industry, *South African Journal of Economic and Management Sciences*, 21(1), 1–12.

III.2

Extinction accounting in Europe and Scandinavia

12 Extinction accounting in European zoos

Reporting practice of conservation programmes to protect animals from extinction

Gunnar Rimmel

This chapter reviews the way in which European zoos and aquariums report on their contribution to protect animals from extinction through regulated breeding programmes. Without these types of effort, fewer species would be alive today. What would the future be like without the sea otter, California condor, or the Przewalski's horse? The zoo and aquarium community has a large potential through conservation programmes to protect animals from extinction. Certainly, preserving individual species through captive breeding is not enough to protect global biodiversity, as conservation of ecosystems is the key to survival of our planet's wildlife.

> Although ecosystem health should be a conservation priority, a recent evaluation of the status of the world's vertebrates (5) noted that captive breeding played a major role in the recovery of 17 of the 68 species whose threat level was reduced.[1]

The quote above shows that Zoos do play a vital role in conservation of species preventing endangered species from becoming extinct. This reflects the first World Zoo Conservation Strategy that the World Association of Zoos and Aquariums (WAZA) initiated in 1993 stating that "conservation is being seen as the central theme of zoos, and zoos should thus further evolve into conservation centres".[2] Reflecting the WAZA conservation strategy, an increasing number of zoos and aquariums have recognised that the real challenge of biodiversity conservation is saving wild species and habitats. Captive breeding and reintroduction programmes are facilitators to reduce the biodiversity loss effects for specific endangered species. Therefore, captive populations require to be self-sustainable and this can be obtained by intensive population management focusing on retention of genetic diversity maximisation, upholding demographic stability, and decreasing adaptation to captivity.[3] Even on a political level, the importance of zoos and aquariums have been acknowledged by the European Union through issuing in 2015 the EU Zoos Directive Good Practices,[4] which illustrates examples of efforts that European Zoos should undertake to face the challenges of biodiversity crisis by engaging in conservation programmes, as well as to inform and report such efforts to their external stakeholders.

The biodiversity crisis, with all its effects on species and habitats, is no longer only the focus of research by zoologists and ecologists, but has also found increasing acceptance within corporate sustainability accounting. During the past years, a number of accounting academics have introduced a new stream of research to the field of accounting focusing on accounting for biodiversity.[5] The emergent studies on accounting for biodiversity highlighted that our planet currently faces sixth period of mass species extinction,[6] which can be linked to financial accounting calculations[7] and will be exposed in corporate reporting.[8]

Multinationals have only recently started to disclose information on extinction in corporate reports with the intention to contribute to a sustainability and express corporate willingness to change. Consequently, extinction accounting is concerned with the aspiration to prevent species from extinction, which will lead to disclosure of information relating to conservation activities.[9] Despite the fact that multinationals started to disclose non-financial information on conservation programmes,[10] they are unlikely to have the professional knowledge on conservation practice that zoos and aquariums have. According to the EU Zoo Directive, corporate annual reports should be produced by zoos and aquariums to inform their stakeholders. These annual reports should contain non-financial disclosures about preservation efforts drawing attention to affect the risk of extinction.

The focus of this chapter is largely, although not exclusively, on reporting practice by European Zoos, exploring the ways in which they inform their stakeholders about their preservation efforts. A short historical summary of the evolution of zoos illustrates the change in nature of operations in the context of evolving biodiversity conservation policy. The aim and scope of the Zoos Directive is outlined. The chapter will include a review of the current state of reporting practice by European zoos on their contribution to biodiversity conservation and their efforts to prevent species from extinction. The empirical part of this chapter applied a mixed-method approach to go beyond analysing the quantity of the current state of zoos reporting with open-ended interviews of zoo management in four EU member states regarding the importance of the Zoo Directive for reporting practice. Finally, based on the empirical findings, a discussion is made towards future prospects of Extinction Accounting in European Zoos.

The historical evolution of zoos

The Encyclopædia Britannica provides the following definition: "Zoo, also called zoological garden or zoological park, place where wild animals and, in some instances, domesticated animals are exhibited in captivity."[11] The word zoological garden stems from the Greek zōon (ζῷον, "animal") and lógos (λόγος, "study"), a garden to study animals. The London Zoological Gardens in Regent's Park opened in 1828 by the Zoological Society of London and used the abbreviation "zoo" for the first time.[12]

The earliest zoos were established in Hierakonpolis the capital of ancient Egyptian around 3500 BC, as archaeologists discovered in 2009 the remains of zoological garden or exotic menagerie including two elephants, three hippos, eleven baboons, and six wildcats.[13]

Collections of captive animals were not uncommon in ancient empires. The first known menagerie that was open to the public was in Alexandria. By the 4th century BC the Greek Empire expanded and exotic animals were send back to Greek cities as public spectacles and the development to study animals, which led to the first classifications of species. During medieval times kings and emperors were making gifts of exotic animals for their private collections, like King John I held his collection in the Tower of London.[14]

The modern zoos in Europe that were opened to public started to be established during the 18th and 19th centuries. The oldest zoo in the world is Vienna's Tiergarten Schönbrunn in Austria that transformed from the private menagerie of the imperial family to a public zoo in 1765.[15] A growing interest in zoology led to the development of modern zoos in Europe. In 1907, Carl Hagenbeck founded Tierpark Stellingen, which was the first zoo that displayed captive animals in open enclosures surrounded by moats. It was common at that time to keep animals in barred cages. This new panorama system using hidden moats made it possible to display mix of species that appeared to be together in one landscape.[16]

Zoos were transformed from private collections of kings and emperors in barred cages into panorama exhibits replicating natural habitats for behavioural patterns. However, the modern zoo faced severe criticisms in the 1970s regarding animal welfare, which varied extensively between zoos. Also moral concerns were uttered by organisations like the World Wildlife Fund (now World Wide Fund for Nature; WWF) or the Born Fee Foundation that wild caught animals do suffer during the transition from being free and wild to captivity, which led to high death rates during the first months of captivity. Consequently, zoos started to change their concept from simply exhibition of animals towards being concerned with animals' welfare and needs.

A further push in the evolution of zoos is the response to the increasing awareness of climate change and its impact on wild animals. The loss of biodiversity expressed as consciousness to protect wild animals and their habitats raised also the awareness about animal welfare in zoos.

The biodiversity crisis has been acknowledged in a number of transnational and national policy documents that draw attention to the importance of biodiversity for conversation and reporting. The United Nations Environment Programme (UNEP) started the Ad Hoc Working Group of Experts on Biological Diversity to investigate the demand for an international convention on biological diversity, which at the Rio "Earth Summit" in 1992 led to the establishment of the Convention on Biodiversity (CBD).

The zoo community organisations followed this development, as the predecessor of WAZA together with WWF and the International Union for the Conservation of Nature (IUCN) developed "The World Strategy for Conservation in Zoos and Aquaria".[17] The European Association of Zoos and Aquaria (EAZA), which is an organisation for the European zoo and aquarium community, proposed a fundamental change in the role of modern zoos to become active conservation centres. In the EAZA Strategic Plan 2013–2016[18] the EAZA's mission was directed towards education, research and captive breeding and reintroduction programmes to advance its professional quality to educate the public, contribute to scientific research and towards the conservation of global biodiversity.

Therefore, the evolution of modern zoos has led to a role that goes well beyond merely recreational activities for society to a vital part in biodiversity conversation.

The Zoos Directive legislating zoos' keeping of wild animals

Although modern zoos have a long history, it is rather recently that zoos have become subject to legislation. The European Commission had initiated a study about the conditions in zoos and their legal framework in the different EU Member States. The European Survey of Zoological Collections[19] was published in 1988. The findings in the report led to that the European Commission made a commitment to develop a proposal regarding the protection of animals in zoos. This proposal for a Zoo Directive draft recognised the role that zoos could play in species conservation, scientific research and education. The Zoo Directive draft acknowledged also animals trading for zoos purposes and proposed legislation to safeguard that zoo animals were kept under conditions suited to their behavioural and physiological needs received high standard of veterinary and are taken care of by trained staff.[20]

First in 1999, became the Council Directive 1999/22/EC relating to the keeping of wild animals in zoos[21] (Zoos Directive) endorsed after almost a decade from the European Commission's commitment regardless the support of the European Parliament and the Committee on the Environment, Public Health and Consumer Protection.

The Zoos Directive just two pages long, containing a preamble and nine Articles. According to the preamble the Zoos Directive purpose is to provide a common basis for EU Member States' legislation for licensing and inspection of zoos, keeping of animals in zoos, as well as training of staff and education the public.

The preamble of the Zoos Directive mentions that the directive is framed by the following EU legislation:

- Council Regulation (EEC) No 338/97;[22]
- Council Directive 79/409/EEC (Birds Directive);[23] and
- Council Directive 92/43/EEC (Habitats Directive).[24]

The Zoo Directive preamble starts with Council Regulation (EEC) No 338/97 on the protection of species of wild fauna and flora by regulating trade therein, which specifies the requirements, procedures and required documents for import, export and re-export of endangered live and death species. It contains the procedures for obtaining trade certificates to ensure compliance as well as sanctions by Member states in case of violation internal EU trade of endangered species. Council Regulation (EC) No 338/97 is at the European level the Basic Regulation of the Convention on International Trade in Endangered Species of Wild Flora and Fauna (CITES), which has the purpose to protect that no species of wild fauna and flora becomes or remains subject to unsustainable exploitation because of international trade.

The EU's nature conservation policy is based on two main pieces of legislation, the Council Directive 79/409/ECC (Birds Directive) on the conservation of wild birds and the Council Directive 92/43/EEC (Habitats Directive) on the conservation of natural habitats and of wild fauna and flora. While the Birds Directive aims for the long term conservation of all wild bird species in the European Union, the Habitats Directive aims to protect all wild species listed in the annexes of the Directive. The Birds Directive is the oldest piece of EU legislation on the environment and one of its cornerstones. Both directives are intertwined as habitat loss is regarded to be one of the biggest threats to the wild bird conservation efforts.

The Zoo Directive preamble proclaims that in order that zoos contribute to biodiversity conservation consistent with Article 9 of the Convention on Biological Diversity (CBD) action is needed at EU level. Zoos can play a valuable role in biodiversity conservation by adopting measures for *ex situ conservation*. Ex situ conservation is the process of protecting endangered species outside its natural habitat.

The EAZA is the only organisation that is specifically mentioned in the Zoo Directive as an example that has developed guidelines for the care and accommodation of animals in zoos. According to the Zoos Directive the definition of "zoo" are permanent establishments where animals of wild species are kept for exhibition to the public for seven or more days a year. Circuses and pet shops are excluded from the zoo definition, as well as exemption granted by Member States' competent authorities like less significant numbers of animals kept for display to the public.

Member States have to assign competent authorities which have the discretion to adopt measures for licensing and inspection of existing and new zoos in order to ensure that the requirements of the Zoo Directive are fulfilled.

Studying the reporting practice of conservation programmes to protect animals from extinction

In order to study how and conservation programmes have been reported by zoos in Europe it was necessary to obtain a valid number of zoos in Europe. However, the number of zoos in Europe is relatively difficult to determine, as there is no official aggregated database or statistics available by the European

Union's institutions. According to animal rights activists' organisations like The Born Free Foundation there are 3,500 zoos existing in Europe. However, this number of 3,500 zoos was not possible to verify, as The Born Free Foundation did not provide lists or statistics.

Unlike corporate annual report databases, there is no official EU Zoo database available. Even on a EU member state level, Competent Authorities in Bulgaria, Cyprus, England, Germany, Italy, Poland and Portugal do not maintain a national database of zoos.[25] EAZA has developed an accreditation programme for its members, which includes compliance with national and international legislation regarding animal and plant acquisition, possession and transport. While EAZA has no accessible database or downloadable membership list for non-members, EAZA has an interactive map on their website that makes it possible to locate EAZA members as a verifiable source.[26] The EAZA interactive map shows the location of all full, associate and temporary members of EAZA, as well as candidates for EAZA membership, by clicking on placemarkers to find the name of the institution and the link to its website.

To collect suitable data for this study, 277 websites of EAZA members were accessed manually in January 2016 covering 29 countries, whereas Malta and Cyprus had no zoo or aquarium that were EAZA members. Thereafter, all EAZA member websites were examined in order to determine whether it would be possible to collect data from European zoos that could be comparable. For this study European zoos are those (including aquariums) within the European Union's member states including Norway, which is part of Scandinavia and member of the European Free Trade Association (EFTA).

For the data collection for this study, no difference had been made regarding the membership status of the EAZA, as they have three types of membership being, full, temporary or candidate members. Since the EU Zoo Directive *Good Practices Document*[27] advocates that corporate reports should be produced by zoos, all websites were initially examined as to whether corporate reports were made publicly available.

The distribution of 277 accredited EAZA members illustrated in Figure 12.1 showed that Germany (17%), United Kingdom (16%) and France (16%) are making up almost half (49%) of the zoos and aquaria in sample. Thereafter follow Netherlands (6%) and Spain (6%), the Czech Republic (5%) as well as Denmark (4%), Poland (4%) and Sweden (4%). The remaining 19 countries Austria, Belgium, Bulgaria, Croatia, Cyprus, Estonia, Finland, Greece, Hungary, Ireland, Latvia, Lithuania, Luxembourg, Malta, Portugal Romania, Slovakia, Slovenia and Norway have aggregated 22% of the Zoos and Aquaria in the sample.

Annual reports and conservation disclosure by European zoos

In the early stages of gathering data, I identified the membership status for each of the 277 accredited EAZA members held (see Table 12.1). I also noted what category Zoo, Aquarium or Zoo/Aquarium organisations belonged to. At the

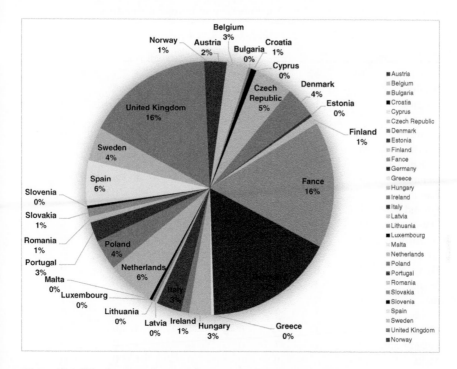

Figure 12.1 Distribution of zoos and aquaria in European countries

same time it was felt necessary to check on each organisation's website whether they also held WAZA membership. The WAZA is the unifying organisation for the world zoo and aquarium community with more than 300 members zoos and aquariums from around the world. WAZA and EAZA are independent from each other and WAZA is not the head organisation of regional organisations like EAZA.

However, from the 277 organisations in this study 105 organisations were doubly accredited as they also were WAZA members. From the 277 EAZA members the distribution in the three categories[28] were 264 full members, 8 temporary and 5 candidates. Temporary EAZA membership is granted to zoos and aquariums that do not yet meet the standards required for full membership of EAZA, but are. These institutions will be considered as being capable of reaching full membership within a one to two year timeframe. EAZA candidate membership are allowed for zoos under construction and so far have not been open to the public. These organisations are working towards compliance with EAZA accreditation standards. The majority of the sample in this study were zoos (90.6%); 7.5% organisations of this study were aquaria, and only 1.9% were organisations that were both zoo and aquarium.

While gathering data gathering, the research identified where the organization made conservation information available, which could be as communication on

Table 12.1 Distribution of EAZA membership in European countries

Country	WAZA	EAZA	EAZA full	EAZA temporary	EAZA candidate	Zoo	Zoo/ Aquarium	Aquarium
Austria	6	6	6	0	0	4	1	1
Belgium	2	8	7	1	0	8	0	0
Bulgaria	0	1	0	0	1	1	0	0
Croatia	1	2	1	0	1	2	0	0
Cyprus	0	0	0	0	0	0	0	0
Czech Republic	6	14	13	1	0	14	0	0
Denmark	4	11	11	0	0	8	0	3
Estonia	1	1	1	0	0	1	0	0
Finland	1	3	3	0	0	3	0	0
France	11	45	44	1	0	39	0	6
Germany	32	47	45	2	0	45	2	0
Greece	1	1	1	0	0	1	0	0
Hungary	2	8	7	1	0	8	0	0
Ireland	1	3	3	0	0	3	0	0
Italy	1	9	9	0	0	8	0	1
Latvia	0	1	1	0	0	1	0	0
Lithuania	0	1	0	0	1	1	0	0
Luxembourg	0	1	1	0	0	1	0	0
Malta	0	0	0	0	0	0	0	0
Netherlands	5	17	17	0	0	15	1	1
Poland	8	11	11	0	0	11	0	0
Portugal	2	7	7	0	0	4	1	2
Romania	0	2	0	0	2	2	0	0
Slovakia	2	3	3	0	0	3	0	0
Slovenia	1	1	1	0	0	1	0	0
Spain	5	16	15	1	0	11	1	4
Sweden	6	11	11	0	0	11	0	1
United Kingdom	12	45	44	1	0	44	1	1
Norway	1	2	2	0	0	1	0	1

the website, in annual reports or corporate social responsibility (CSR) reports as illustrated in Table 12.2.

Although the Zoo Directive *Good Practices Document*[29] as well as EAZA recommends to provide information on websites it seems that this is largely locally focused on national languages. Only 65% of the 277 organisations provided English versions of their websites. The Swedish Zoo Skansen provided 10 different language versions for their visitors to get informed about the zoo.

Further inquiries were made examining the 277 EAZA member websites regarding information about conservation efforts within the zoo (e.g. breeding programmes, endangered species programmes, studbooks or regional

Table 12.2 Communication, reports and conservation disclosure

Country	Website	Conservation information	Annual report	CSR report	English language
Austria	6	0	2	0	4
Belgium	8	0	0	0	6
Bulgaria	1	0	0	0	1
Croatia	1	0	0	0	1
Cyprus	0	0	0	0	0
Czech Republic	14	3	6	0	10
Denmark	11	6	5	0	10
Estonia	1	1	0	0	1
Finland	1	0	0	0	1
France	45	2	0	0	20
Germany	47	4	1	0	19
Greece	1	1	0	0	1
Hungary	8	0	1	0	5
Ireland	3	0	0	0	3
Italy	9	0	0	0	7
Latvia	1	0	1	0	1
Lithuania	1	0	1	1	0
Luxembourg	1	0	0	0	0
Malta	0	0	0	0	0
Netherlands	17	0	2	1	12
Poland	11	0	0	0	6
Portugal	7	0	0	0	4
Romania	1	0	0	0	0
Slovakia	3	0	0	0	1
Slovenia	1	0	0	0	0
Spain	16	0	0	0	11
Sweden	12	4	2	0	10
United Kingdom	46	34	4	0	46
Norway	2	0	0	0	1

collection plans). 54 zoos were found to mention on their websites that they are engaged in conservation programmes However, the majority of these 54 zoos provided information about conservation efforts only at a very vague level without any further detailed information or the possibility to read specifically about what their conservation efforts were. Many zoos and aquaria barely present any facts about their conservation efforts at all providing just marketing information for interested visitors such as that describing high profile animals, entrance fees and opening hours.

The Zoo Directive *Good Practices Document*[30] provided best practice examples of how to provide annual reports and information about CSR efforts. However, only 25 members provided annual reports on their websites. Only two zoos in Lithuania and the Netherlands provided separate CSR reports.

Eight annual reports were in English. With the help of native speakers, the remaining 17 annual reports were read in seven national languages to determine whether these reports contained disclosures about preservation efforts illustrating extinction accounting or using IUCN categories drawing attention to affect the risk of extinction. In contrast to listed companies, European zoos and aquaria tend not to provide corporate information. Financial information of relevant preservation information is seldom made available.

After having examined 277 EAZA members, there was only one zoo that provided an annual report containing financial statements and detailed information about the zoo's operations and conservation activities to prevent species from extinction. The Swedish zoo Nordens Ark has exclusively focused its operations on the conservation of threatened species, and is the only zoo in Europe to do so. Nordens Ark has an annual report comparable to those of companies, containing financial statements and notes, as well as a detailed review of their history, narratives about their projects and animals, as well as many specific biodiversity disclosures.

To sum up, after having read the EU Zoos Directive *Good Practices Document*,[31] The World Zoo Conservation Strategy[32] and the EAZA Strategic Plan 2013–2016[33] it was not expected that zoos in Europe are opaque in the information about conservation programmes.

The importance of the Zoo Directive and *Good Practices Document* for zoos' reporting practice

In order to examine the reporting practice of Zoos to illustrate their efforts in conservation and prevent species from extinction it seemed important to get insights from zoo managers (CEOs) on how they view the importance of the Zoo Directive and the Zoo Directive *Good Practices Document*. Four zoo managers from zoos that provided websites and annual reports that contained detailed information on their conservation efforts. These four managers required the interviews to be anonymised, so that they could speak openly without themselves or their zoos being identifiable. The four interviewees manage zoos in Austria, Denmark, Germany and Sweden. The interviews were recorded and varied in duration between 35 minutes to 2 hours. The open-ended interview guide focused on biodiversity, conservation, reporting and legislation. During the interviews it became apparent that reporting and information about conservation programmes benefitted from the animal records and biodiversity measures required by international conservation programmes. Since this information is already available for the zoo management had decided that this existing information could easily be made available as detailed disclosures in annual reports to inform interested parties about their conservation efforts. All interviewees mentioned that they had not received external requests or demands to make this kind of information available, so there was no external pressure from stakeholders. Research by Burritt and Schaltegger had discussed this issue that sustainability reporting can develop as a pragmatic inside-out approach as a result of internal or external pressures or of opportunities.[34]

The interviewees were asked, "What role does the EU Zoos Directive and the *Good Practices Document* play for your way of reporting?" to determine the impact that regulation might have in shaping reporting practice in the industry. It was pointed out that both the Zoos Directive and the *Good Practices Document* are very helpful and appreciated among those zoos that foster scientific work by zoos. However, it was pointed out that zoos as an industry is quite vulnerable, as there are operators mainly focusing on entertainment and not on animal welfare, as well as there are dodgy actors who create problems for serious zoos that might to have to turn down exhibition that might be highly profitable, but oppose their work towards conservation to prevent species from extinction.

It was uttered that these problems are partly due to the lack of understanding from policy makers in the EU, which is reflected in the fact that it took very long until the Zoo Directive was put into action. Some of the interviewees mentioned that official representatives from the EU thought that the Zoo Directive was too small as it is a very specialised business that already had some effective regulation in other directives.

However, all interviewees stressed that they would appreciate even harder regulations that urge zoos to publish reports that are comparable within the industry. Further, they mentioned that annual reports about zoos operations and engagement in conservation and breeding programmes could lead to improve the zoo community as a whole.

Currently there seems to be rather weak enforcement of the Zoo Directive in many EU member states, which could be due to the proximity of local competence authorities for issuing licenses for zoos. It was stated that local competence authorities often take the recreational aspects and effects for local businesses into consideration, which might not be consider improvement for animal welfare or conservation efforts of zoos. Therefore, increased requirements for zoos to keep proper animal records and operation reports should be in the interest of competent authorities for granting zoo licences, as those zoos who are already involved in conservation programmes would have no problem to provide such information due to the requirements of international conservation programmes demand accurate data. According to the opinion of the interviewees it would therefore not difficult to produce annual reports, which could be made public on zoos websites as well. However, stronger requirements and enforcement would raise the bar for those zoos that just due the minimum to fulfil requirements for obtain a licence or accreditation in associations.

Discussion

In the introduction to this chapter it was stated that zoos do play a vital role in conservation of species preventing endangered species from becoming extinct. But do they really? Examining the current reporting practice by European zoos to inform their stakeholders about their preservation efforts the genuine contribution to extinction prevention by zoos might be called into question, as this study showed that only a minority of zoos provide detailed information about their conservation strategy. In that sense it could be argued that out of the low level of information made available by zoos to interested external stakeholders, WAZA's World Zoo Conservation Strategy conservation that zoos evolved into conservation centres has not been communicated properly. Rather disappointingly, this study illustrated that the zoo community are not explaining in disclosures the ways in which zoos and aquariums have acknowledged that the real challenge of biodiversity conservation is saving wild species and habitats. Surprisingly, little information is provided on websites or annual reports how zoos actively contribute through captive breeding and reintroduction programmes, which are facilitators to reducing biodiversity loss effects for specific endangered species. However, those zoos that have provided detailed information on their websites and in their annual reports showed that they actually contribute a great deal to retain captive populations towards self-sustainability by intensive population management, maximising genetic diversity and protecting endangered species in ex situ conservation programmes from becoming extinct.

At a political level the European Union acknowledged the importance of zoos and aquariums have been by through issuing the Zoos Directive and publishing the Directive's *Good Practices Document*. However, as the interviews revealed there seems to be a lack of enforcement by national competent authorities, which might explain the lack of reports and detailed information by EAZA members. From that perspective, it could be reasoned that the Zoos Directive in its current state fails its intentions. Further, it could be argued that the Zoos Directive in its current state fails its intentions. Earlier studies on biodiversity reporting showed that companies that disclosed limited and biased biodiversity information, raised concerns for stakeholders.[35] Previous accounting research that focused on biodiversity disclosures in listed companies showed that companies provide only limited disclosures[36] Consequently, this study obtained similar results. The difference is that listed companies neither do not have a professional interest in conservation nor the professional knowledge on managing conservation programmes to safe species from the threat of extinction.

Maybe zoos could learn from listed companies' communication about their operations as they disclose narrative information in their annual reports? For zoos there is much to gain, as they can demonstrate that their operations are a vital part that contributes to conservation programmes. Conservation programmes need the scientific expertise from zoos, as successful conservation programmes have the capability to change the rate of mass extinction as successful programmes for the Sea otter, California condor, or the Przewalski's horse illustrate.

Notes

1 D.A. Conde et al., "An emerging role of zoos to conserve biodiversity", *Science* 331 (2011): 1390.
2 World Association of Zoos and Aquariums (WAZA). *Executive summary of the world zoo conservation strategy: The role of the zoos and aquaria of the world in global conservation.* Gland: WAZA, 1993, p. 3.

3 T. Gilbert, "The sustainability of endangered species under intensive management: the case of the scimitar-horned oryx *Oryx dammah*", University of Southampton, Centre for Biological Sciences, PhD thesis.
4 EU Zoos Directive, *Good Practices Document*, 2015, accessed 6 January 2016. http://ec.europa.eu/environment/nature/pdf/EU_Zoos_Directive_Good_Practices.pdf.
5 M. J. Jones, "Accounting for biodiversity: A pilot study", *British Accounting Review* 28 (1996): 281–303; M. J. Jones and J. F. Solomon, "Problematising accounting for biodiversity", *Accounting, Auditing & Accountability Journal* 26 (5) (2013): 668–687.
6 TEEB (2008), "Economics of ecosystems and biodiversity report", accessed 23 April 2016. www.teeb.org.
7 T. Cuckston, "Bringing tropical forest biodiversity conservation into financial accounting calculation", *Accounting, Auditing & Accountability Journal* 26 (5) (2013): 688–714.
8 G. Rimmel and K. Jonäll, "Biodiversity reporting in Sweden: corporate disclosure and preparers' views", *Accounting, Auditing & Accountability Journal* 26 (5) (2013): 746–778.
9 J. Atkins, W. Maroun, B. Atkins and E. Barrone, "From the Big Five to the Big Four? Exploring Extinction Accounting for the Rhinoceros", *Accounting, Auditing & Accountability Journal*, 31 (2) (2018): 1–31.
10 J. Atkins, "How can corporate narrative reporting prevent extinction?", *The Corporate Report* (2016): 39–43.
11 Encyclopædia Britannica, "Zoo", Accessed 6 March 2017, www.britannica.com/science/zoo.
12 Zoological Society of London, "Landmarks in ZSL history", Accessed 6 March 2017, www.zsl.org/about-us/landmarks-in-zsl-history.
13 M. Rose, "World's first zoo – Hierakonpolis, Egypt", *Archeology*, 63 (1) (2010).
14 V. Croke, *The modern Ark: The story of zoos: Past, present & future*, Diane Publishing Company (1997).
15 K. Polinger-Foster, "The earliest zoos and gardens", *Scientific-American* 281 (1999): 48–55.
16 N. Rothfels, *Savages and Beasts: The Birth of the Modern Zoo*, Johns Hopkins University Press, Baltimore, MD (2002).
17 WAZA, *Executive summary of the world zoo conservation strategy*.
18 EAZA Strategic Plan 2013–2016 – EAZA moving forward in the UN decade of Biodiversity, accessed 6 March 2017, www.eaza.net/assets/Uploads/Strategies/2013-2016-EAZA-Strategy-low-res-version2.pdf.
19 W. Travers and R. Straton, *European Survey of Zoological Collections: Final Report*, EEC Contract No 6681 (87)07, 31 August 1988.
20 Proposal for a Council recommendation relating to the keeping of wild animals in zoos (COM(95)0619-C4-0103/96-95/0333(SYN)).
21 Council Directive 1999/22/EC relating to the keeping of wild animals in zoos, accessed 13 May 2016, http://eur-lex.europa.eu/LexUriServ/LexUriServ.do?uri=OJ:L:1999:094:0024:0026:EN:PDF.
22 Council Regulation (EC) No 338/97 of 9 December 1996 on the protection of species of wild fauna and flora by regulating trade therein, accessed 13 May 2016, http://data.europa.eu/eli/reg/1997/338.
23 Directive 2009/147/EC of the European Parliament and of the Council of 30 November 2009 on the conservation of wild birds, accessed 7 January 2016, http://eur-lex.europa.eu/legal-content/en/TXT/?uri=CELEX%3A32009L0147.
24 Council Directive 92/43/EEC of 21 May 1992 on the conservation of natural habitats and of wild fauna and flora, accessed 7 January 2016, http://eur-lex.europa.eu/legal-content/EN/TXT/?uri=celex%3A31992L0043.

25 The Eu Zoo Inquiry 2011 – An evaluation of the implementation and enforcement of EC Directive 1999/22, relating to the keeping of animals in zoos. Report Findings and Recommendations, accessed 17 January 2016, http://endcap.eu/wp-content/uploads/2013/02/EU-Zoo-Inquiry-Report-Findings-and-Recommendations.pdf.
26 Where are EAZA Members located? Accessed 17 January 2016, www.eaza.net/#map_home.
27 EU Zoos Directive, *Good Practices Document*.
28 EAZA membership categories, accessed 6 January 2016, www.eaza.net/members/eaza-membership.
29 EU Zoos Directive, *Good Practices Document*.
30 Ibid.
31 EU Zoos Directive, *Good Practices Document*.
32 WAZA, *Executive summary of the world zoo conservation strategy*.
33 EAZA Strategic Plan 2013–2016.
34 R.L. Burritt and Schaltegger, S. "Sustainability accounting and reporting: fad or trend?", *Accounting, Auditing & Accountability Journal* 23 (2010): 829–846.
35 O. Boiral "Accounting for the unaccountable: biodiversity reporting and impression management", *Journal of Business Ethics* 135 (2016): 751–768.
36 J. Atkins, Gräbsch, C., and Jones, M. J. "Corporate biodiversity reporting: exploring its anthropocentric nature" in M. Jones (ed.), *Accounting for biodiversity*, Routledge, Oxon, (2014): 215–244; D. Van Liempd and Busch, J. "Biodiversity reporting in Denmark", *Accounting, Auditing & Accountability Journal* 26 (5), (2013): 806–832.

References

Atkins J., "How can corporate narrative reporting prevent extinction?", *The Corporate Report* (2016): 39–43.
Atkins J., Gräbsch, C., and Jones, M. J. "Corporate biodiversity reporting: exploring its anthropocentric nature", in M. Jones (ed.), *Accounting for biodiversity*, Routledge, Abingdon, (2014): 215–244.
Atkins J., W. Maroun, B. Atkins and E. Barrone, "From the big five to the big four? Exploring extinction accounting for the rhinoceros", *Accounting, Auditing & Accountability Journal*, 31 (2) (2018): 1–31.
Boiral O. "Accounting for the unaccountable: biodiversity reporting and impression management", *Journal of Business Ethics* 135 (4) (2016): 751–768.
Burritt R.L. and Schaltegger, S. "Sustainability accounting and reporting: fad or trend?", *Accounting, Auditing & Accountability Journal* 23 (7) (2010): 829–846.
Conde, D. A., N. Flesness, F. Colchero, O. R. Jones and A. Scheuerlein "An Emerging Role of Zoos to Conserve Biodiversity", *Science* 331 (2011): 1390–1391.
Council Directive 1999/22/EC relating to the keeping of wild animals in zoos. Accessed 13 May 2016, http://eur-lex.europa.eu/LexUriServ/LexUriServ.do?uri=OJ:L:1999:094:0024:0026:EN:PDF
Council Directive 92/43/EEC of 21 May 1992 on the conservation of natural habitats and of wild fauna and flora. Accessed 7 January 2016, http://eur-lex.europa.eu/legal-content/EN/TXT/?uri=celex%3A31992L0043
Council Regulation (EC) No 338/97 of 9 December 1996 on the protection of species of wild fauna and flora by regulating trade therein. Accessed 13 May 2016, http://data.europa.eu/eli/reg/1997/338/
Cuckston, T. "Bringing tropical forest biodiversity conservation into financial accounting calculation", *Accounting, Auditing & Accountability Journal* 26 (5) (2013): 688–714.

Croke V. *The modern Ark: The story of zoos: Past, present & future*, Diane Publishing Company (1997).

Directive 2009/147/EC of the European Parliament and of the Council of 30 November 2009 on the conservation of wild birds, Accessed 7 January 2016, http://eur-lex.europa.eu/legal-content/en/TXT/?uri=CELEX%3A32009L0147

Encyclopædia Britannica. Definition Zoo. Accessed 6 March 2017, www.britannica.com/science/zoo

EAZA membership categories. Accessed 6 January 2016, www.eaza.net/members/eaza-membership/

EAZA Strategic Plan 2013–2016 – EAZA moving forward in the UN decade of Biodiversity. Accessed 6 March 2017, www.eaza.net/assets/Uploads/Strategies/2013-2016-EAZA-Strategy-low-res-version2.pdf

EU Zoos Directive – *Good Practices Document*, 2015. Accessed 6 January 2016. http://ec.europa.eu/environment/nature/pdf/EU_Zoos_Directive_Good_Practices.pdf

Gilbert, T. The sustainability of endangered species under intensive management: the case of the scimitar-horned oryx *Oryx dammah*, University of Southampton, Centre for Biological Sciences, PhD thesis.

Jones, M. J. "Accounting for biodiversity: A pilot study", *British Accounting Review* 28 (1996): 281–303.

Jones M. J. and J. F. Solomon, "Problematising accounting for biodiversity", *Accounting, Auditing & Accountability Journal* 26 (5) (2013): 668–687.

Polinger-Foster K. "The earliest zoos and gardens", *Scientific-American* 281 (1999): 48–55.

Proposal for a Council recommendation relating to the keeping of wild animals in zoos (COM(95)0619-C4-0103/96-95/0333(SYN))

Rimmel, G. and K. Jonäll. "Biodiversity reporting in Sweden: Corporate disclosure and preparers' views". *Accounting, Auditing and Accountability Journal* 26 (2013): 746–778.

Rose M. "World's first zoo:- Hierakonpolis, Egypt", *Archeology*, 63 (1) (2010).

Rothfels N. *Savages and beasts: The birth of the modern zoo*, Johns Hopkins University Press, Baltimore, MD (2002).

TEEB (2008), "Economics of ecosystems and biodiversity report". Accessed 23 April 2016. www.teeb.org

THE EU ZOO INQUIRY 2011 – An evaluation of the implementation and enforcement of EC Directive 1999/22, relating to the keeping of animals in zoos. Report Findings and Recommendations. Accessed 17 January 2016, http://endcap.eu/wp-content/uploads/2013/02/EU-Zoo-Inquiry-Report-Findings-and-Recommendations.pdf

Travers W. and R. Straton, *European survey of zoological collections: Final report*, E.E.C. Contract No 6681(87)07, 31 August 1988.

Van Liempd D. and Busch, J. "Biodiversity reporting in Denmark", *Accounting, Auditing & Accountability Journal* 26 (5), (2013): 806—832.

Where are EAZA Members located? Accessed 17 January 2016, www.eaza.net/#map_home

World Association of Zoos and Aquariums (WAZA). *Executive summary of the world zoo conservation strategy: The role of the zoos and aquaria of the world in global conservation*, Gland: WAZA, 1993.

Zoological Society of London. *Landmarks in ZSL History*. Accessed 6 March 2017, www.zsl.org/about-us/landmarks-in-zsl-history.

13 An RSPB perspective on extinction and extinction prevention

How is the RSPB collaborating and partnering with business to prevent extinction?

Vanessa Amaral-Rogers

The Royal Society for the Protection of Birds (RSPB) was formed in 1889 to counter the growing trade in feather plumes for ladies' hats. In the 1880s, the UK was importing feathers from all manner of exotic birds across the world, for a fashion which was leading to the destruction of many species.

Plumes from birds of paradise, parrots and hummingbirds were just a select few of the species targeted. Even native birds were under threat: herons, kingfishers, owls and egrets were all being harvested – the great crested grebe (*Podiceps cristatus*) was almost driven to extinction by 1860 as its feathers were used as a fur substitute for boas and mitts.

In its earliest days, the society entirely consisted of women with the aim of campaigning for better protection of birds. After gaining support from a number of influential figures, including the leading ornithologist at the time – Professor Alfred Newton – it received its Royal Charter in 1904.

The RSPB quickly grew to encompass other environmental aims and is now the largest nature conservation charity in the UK. Its membership consists of over 1.2 million members. In the 2016/2017 financial year, nearly £100 million was spent towards saving nature (RSPB 2017a).

As a large charity, working with businesses offers numerous benefits. Corporate sponsorship, such as the much-enjoyed Bird & Wild coffee, not only delivers financial support but also achieves conservation outputs in other countries.

The RSPB is able to offer advice to thousands of family farms about nature-friendly farming every year and enter a number of partnerships which support conservation management. In this chapter we will be investigating some examples of where partnerships with the private sector have benefited the environment and nature, and potentially prevented extinctions in doing so.

Albatross task force

Albatrosses are the most threatened group of seabirds in the world. With only 22 species, 15 are currently threatened with extinction (IUCN 2018). The key threat is that the birds are constantly in conflict with fishing vessels. Squid and fish are used to bait the longline hooks, or discarded as waste and so birds are attracted to the fishing vessels from miles away by the smell.

The temptation for an easy meal lures many to their death as they are either struck by a trawl cable or caught on the longline hook and drowned, a term known as seabird bycatch. Rough estimates had placed an albatross death at every five minutes. These are particularly long-lived birds, but they do not breed until they are at least ten years old. Albatrosses then only raise one chick every one or two years meaning that this rate of mortality was unsustainable.

The problem of their decline was identified back in the late 1980s and since then scientists had been working with fishery managers across the world to develop creative solutions to the problem. However, there was a critical gap between the results of their findings and the science, how to disseminate it to the people working at sea and how to make the policy makers listen.

Thus, the creation of the Albatross Task Force came about. In 2005, the RSPB and BirdLife International brought together an international team of seabird experts tasked with the job of acting as liaison between the fishing industry and science. Their remit was to work with fisheries which had a known impact on albatrosses, as well as other vulnerable seabirds. This included the petrels and shearwaters which would visit fishing vessels to scavenge for an easy meal from the nets and drown.

They were to demonstrate how seabird bycatch mitigation measures can reduce these detrimental impacts, and to improve the conservation status of these threatened seabirds by reducing bycatch in targeted fisheries.

Work began in 2006 in South African fisheries. Since then, the task force now works in eight countries throughout Africa and South America (RSPB and BirdLife International 2017). The team is made up of international practitioners, each trained in seabird bycatch mitigation measures. They are hosted by a local conservation organisation, or by the BirdLife partner in that country.

Ten target fisheries were initially identified which were known to have a high overlap with vulnerable seabirds and were considered to be the deadliest. These were the pelagic longline fisheries in Chile, South Africa, Brazil and Uruguay; the Ecuadorian artisanal demersal longline fleet; the demersal trawl fleets in South Africa, Argentina, Namibia and Chile; and the Namibian demersal longline fishery.

At these hotspots, experimental trials were undertaken in collaboration with the fishermen to identify best practice. Each measure would be unique to that fishery with the aim of reducing seabird bycatch. Measures range from testing equipment which include bird-scaring lines or weighting hooks to drop below the surface of the water.

Mitigation included the simple act of setting lines at night, while educating became an integral part to ensure that compliance with the legislation was achieved. Training ranged from seabird identification to fishermen, to educating children.

Enormous reductions in Shearwater bycatch had been shown in Chile after tests on modified purse seine nets. The nets were being laid at the surface of the water to trap sardines but Shearwaters dive under them to also catch the fish, becoming entangled in the mesh and drowning. A simple design change in the nets led to a decrease in the floating mesh without reducing overall fish catch. This simple measure reduced seabird bycatch by over 98%. The use of lights on gillnets in the Peruvian fisheries had appeared to have almost eliminated seabird, marine mammals and sea turtle bycatch without affecting fishing efficiency.

Adoption and implementation of regulations

One of the additional platforms to ensure the long-term sustainability of bycatch reduction was the introduction of regulation. Of the ten priority fisheries, seabird conservation regulations have been adopted in eight of the ten fisheries.

Securing these regulations to reduce bycatch to negligible levels has been a big step – but work now turns towards supporting implementation and uptake. Bycatch reduction is completely dependent on the uptake from the fishermen themselves although enforcement and compliance are important. This is another part of the role of the Task Force, taking trips out to sea with the fishermen to make sure that rules are being adhered to.

In the demersal longline and trawl fisheries in Namibia, regulations came into effect in 2015. Seabird bycatch mitigation measures had been monitored since then and the difference is positive. Bycatch fell to a minimum compared with the figures prior to the regulations coming into effect.

An Argentinian case study

In Argentina, the Albatross Task Force is hosted by the BirdLife partner Aves Argentinas. Although creating new regulations have been a problem in Argentina, 2017 was a resounding success.

Through open dialogue and support from the National Fisheries Secretariat, the National Institute for Research and Fisheries Development (INIDEP), the Ministry of Environment and Sustainable Development, the University of Mar del Plata (IIMyC-CONICET) and Fundación Vida Silvestre, a draft resolution for the use of bird-scaring lines on Argentinean trawlers was presented for consideration.

The conservation measure requires that bird-scaring lines are used on all vessels by May 2018, preceded by a voluntary adoption period of twelve months. The members of the Federal Fisheries Council unanimously approved the regulation. This was a win for Aves Argentinas as although the main industrial trawl fleet only had 33 vessels, it is responsible for the deaths of over 13,500 black-browed albatross (*Thalassarche melanophris*) a year. Based on experimental results, implementation of this regulation will save over 85% of this figure, a total of over 10,000 birds.

Aves Argentina are also working with a fresh-fish fishery and a mid-water trawl fishery. The fresh-fish fishery is made up of 60 vessels and the initial evaluation identified net entanglement as the main source of seabird bycatch. The nets are hauled over the side of the vessel and left for a long time in the water. The birds come to scavenge and are caught up in the net. Unfortunately, bird-scaring lines would not work as a mitigation measure and so new solutions are being investigated. 95% of the birds caught are diving species such as the great shearwater (*Ardenna gravis*) but also include albatrosses such as the southern royal (*Diomedea epomophora*) and black-browed.

The mid-water trawl fishery only has four ships and most seabird deaths occur as a result of collision with the 'third wire'. This cable is attached to the net and sends an electronic signal when the net is full. Bird-scaring lines have been used successfully in this fishery to reduce bycatch.

Next steps

When the ATF was formed the initial focus was on industrial fleets. These large-scale operations have enormous impacts on seabirds per vessel but have relatively few boats per fleet making engagement much simpler.

As the project has progressed, the task force has turned its attention to new fisheries. The next challenge is also the small-scale fisheries such as the purse seine and gillnet fleets in Chile, Peru and Ecuador. These are a small number of fleets and each boat may only kill a few birds per year. However, each fleet can have thousands of boats which has a considerable impact on seabirds when scaled up and discovering practical solutions will be challenging.

Farming

Agriculture and biodiversity conservation are often viewed as opposing forces, both competing for land and management rights. The human race has doubled over the last forty years and with this figure rising rapidly, is it possible to balance agricultural production with protecting nature? If done sensitively, the two do not have to compete.

A UK case study: cirl bunting

In the UK over 75% of UK land is used for agriculture making it our dominant habitat. However, with an uncertain post-Brexit/post-Common Agricultural Policy future, it is imperative to ensure that farming policies are put into place which support nature.

The RSPB is making the case for farming policies which will create a landscape that supports healthy populations of wildlife by 2030. They're also working with farmers to promote the use of wildlife-friendly farming techniques that will boost struggling farmland bird populations, notably in species such as tree sparrow (*Passer montanus*), turtle dove (*Streptopelia turtur*) and corn bunting (*Emberiza calandra*) which declined by more than 80% between 1970 and 2007 (RSPB 2007).

The cirl bunting (*Emberiza cirlus*) project is a great example of the partnership with the farming sector. This finch-like bird is a close relative of the yellowhammer (*Emberiza citronella*) and was once common across southern England (RSPB undated). However, their numbers plummeted and in 1989 there were only 118 pairs left in the UK, mostly confined to south Devon in coastal farmland between Exeter and Plymouth (Evans 1992).

In 1988, the RSPB began research into cirl bunting ecology to identify the reasons for their decline. The research found that changes in agricultural practices had meant a loss of nesting sites and available food sources which was the most important factor in their numbers disappearing.

In winter, cirl buntings feed in stubble fields on spilt grain and seeds (Evans and Smith 1994), particularly following spring barley with plenty of broad-leaved plants such as annual meadow-grass. They find plenty of foraging opportunities in fallow land and field margins, as well as grain or hay which was used for over-wintering stock.

During the summer, they can be found nesting in scrub and hedges. Thick hedgerows consisting of hawthorn, bramble, gorse and blackthorn, along with pockets of dense shrub are ideal (RSPB 2017b). Cirl buntings feed in grasslands where high numbers of invertebrates, particularly grasshoppers and crickets, provide a high-energy source of food for the chicks (Evans et al. 1997). These unimproved grassland and field margins shelter insects who can over-winter in taller grasses. They may also still forage in arable areas for 'milky grain' to feed their chicks if bad weather means that fewer insects are available.

Unfortunately the two habitats must be close together, as these sedentary birds will only move up to two kilometres between both sites to find weedy stubble sites. During the summer they will usually only travel within 25 metres of their nests to find food.

Several changes eventually led to a decrease in their numbers. As machinery became more efficient, fewer grains would be spilt and so there was less food on the floor; pesticide use has increased significantly which led to fewer invertebrates being available; and a desire for larger field sizes has meant that many ancient or floristically species-rich hedgerows were removed.

Also farms became more specialised; some converted to mainly grass and some to arable. This reduction in mixed farms meant that there were fewer areas where the cirl bunting has both habitats close to each other. Luckily, small-scale traditionally managed farms had stayed the norm in Devon and so these small birds found a stronghold here.

As part of Government agri-environment funding for farmers, the Countryside Stewardship Scheme introduced a special project in 1992. This gave the option for farmers to receive payments if they made special provisions for cirl buntings by cultivating spring barley. By growing this crop within the bunting's natural range and leaving as a weedy stubble until the end of March, the birds would have a valuable food source over winter.

In 1993 a cirl bunting project officer was recruited to work with farmers and landowners and encourage them to take up cirl bunting-friendly measures. The following year, numbers increased slightly to 450 pairs, although these were still restricted to Devon.

However it seemed that measures were working. Cirl bunting numbers were flourishing on land which was under the Countryside Management Scheme. Between 1992 and 1998, the population had jumped by 83%, compared with just 2% on the adjacent land which hadn't been managed (Peach et al. 2001).

Now, this colourful bird is bucking the trend for most other farmland birds. Numbers have jumped by over 800% and 1,079 pairs were recorded in 2016. This mixed farming system has been key to helping recover numbers and more than 200 farmers in the south-west England have taken up the management schemes to manage their land.

Without their hard work, the comeback would not have been possible. However this bird still remains vulnerable. Agri-environment schemes are just one of the many issues that will need to be sorted post-Brexit given the uncertainty around funding for wildlife-friendly measures.

International case study: shade-grown coffee

Coffee is big business and with over ten million bags sold a month, there's a huge global market for this tropical crop (ICO 2018). Traditionally coffee was grown commercially under a diverse and dense canopy of trees. However as global demand grew, new sun-tolerant plants were developed in the 1980s which increased yields through planting at high densities.

This paved the way for monoculture swathes of coffee plantations in place of pristine tropical rainforest. As the plantations supported little vegetation, the diversity of native wildlife was reduced in these habitats.

Shade-grown has become a movement back towards a more traditional way of farming. In it, a canopy of assorted types of shade-giving trees are cultivated to create a forest-like structure under which the coffee grows. Studies show that the structural complexity in the vegetation of a coffee plantation is correlated positively to the number of species found.

These shaded coffee farm habitats provide for a number of animals including mammals (McCann et al. 2003), resident birds (Greenberg, Bichier and Sterling 1997), migratory birds (Bakermans et al. 2012) and invertebrates (Nestel, Dickschen and Altieri 1993) when compared with sun-grown plantations.

Not only can this high-quality matrix provide a diverse habitat, it acts as buffer zone and reduces edge effects (Perfecto et al. 2007). They create biological corridors that promote the migration of wildlife and increases connectivity between the remnant forests in fragmented landscapes (Pineda et al. 2005).

Currently only 2% of the global coffee market is described as 'sustainable' using organic, fair trade and eco-friendly certification (Giovannucci and Koekoek 2003) however this is set to grow in the developing world. In response to this growing trade for more sustainable coffee and a concern for migrating songbirds, the Smithsonian Migratory Bird Centre (USA) developed 'Bird Friendly® Coffee'.

No other coffee in the world is produced as 100% organic and with Shade Grown Certification to ensure that tropical agroforests are conserved. The organic certification also ensures that a healthy soil base is maintained and that no artificial pesticides are used. Producers must recertify every three years to ensure that their products continue to meet the requirements.

Bird & Wild is a UK-based roastery, which is working in partnership with the RSPB to provide Bird Friendly Coffee to the UK market. The coffee is also certified Fairtrade which ensures that producers are paid a fair price for the crop. Not only does the RSPB benefit as 6% of sales are donated to them, but the project protects overseas habitats.

Hen harrier

Working in conservation can also bring its own conflicts; one of the less successful stories is that of the hen harrier (*Circus cyaneus*). These birds of prey are among the UK's most beautiful and yet are the most persecuted. When discussing extinctions, it made sense to acknowledge potential issues, especially here in the UK, when a sector could be driving a species to extermination.

Hen harriers live in open areas with low-lying vegetation. Between March and September, they are found breeding on the upland heather moors in the north of England and Wales, Northern Ireland and Scotland. From October onwards, they move to the lowlands – favouring coastal marshes, fenland and heathland. There is also a small population of non-residents which visit from mainland Europe in the east and south-eat of England.

Hen harriers feed on small birds and mammals and their diet can include red grouse. This brings them into direct conflict with shooting estates which intensively rear grouse for hunting. It is this interaction which is threatening the future of hen harrier populations.

The latest hen harrier breeding survey shows the level of this devastation. In 2016 there were only 545 breeding pairs in the UK (RSPB 2017c). Since 2004, that's a decrease of 39% (204 pairs). Scotland currently has the highest numbers with 460 pairs, although even they have seen a reduction.

The most sombre point is the fate of the hen harrier in England. In 2010 there were only twelve pairs which attempted to breed – in 2016, this dropped to just four pairs. There is enough viable habitat to support three hundred pairs of hen harriers in England.

Hen harriers are fully protected yet are being illegally shot and trapped as a result of grouse moor management. This continuous wildlife crime is preventing populations from recovering. As an environmental charity, the RSPB is not anti-sports shooting unless there is an impact on the conservation status of a species. However, attempting to work with the shooting community will only succeed if the problem is acknowledged.

Whenever issues had been raised regarding intensive grouse moor management, the status quo from grouse moor estates had been to simply deny that there was any problem. This was one of the reasons that the RSPB took the decision to withdraw from the Hen Harrier Action Plan.

The plan was set up by Defra along with other organisations including the Game & Wildlife Conservation Trust, Moorland Association, National

Gamekeepers Organisation, National Parks and Natural England (Defra 2016). The RSPB was originally a member until 2016 when it became clear that the commitments of the action plan were not being delivered and hen harriers were still being persecuted.

The action plan is still in effect and will go ahead without the input from the RSPB and already one of the more contentious suggestions has been set in motion. Natural England have recently issued a licence to remove hen harrier chicks, raise them in captivity and release them back into the wild (Barkham 2018), a move which has been criticised by the RSPB as 'facilitating unsustainable intensive land management which is destroying our uplands'.

The RSPB is now advocating a licensing system similar to one that has been suggested in Scotland. As an example, it will mean that shooting estates which have crimes committed on them will lose their licence to operate. A licensing system would benefit all; it would remove unfair competition from estates engaging in damaging practices as well as driving up environmental standards. It will ensure that all businesses which are operating in a legal manner will have the right to continue and be the first step in helping to protect these iconic birds.

Mining for nature

It may seem surprising that mineral mining can be beneficial for nature, but these sites can become some of the best reserves for wildlife. There are only a finite set of resources and although the use of recycled aggregate is increasing, there is still considerable necessity for quarrying. The positive note is that through sensitive restoration, mineral sites have the potential to enhance biodiversity at the end of their working lives (Davies 2006).

Since working in partnership CEMEX, the building materials company and the RSPB have transformed over one thousand hectares of used quarries into reserves – an area twice as big as the London Olympic Park. These incredible habitats, including heathland, flower-rich grasslands and diverse woodland, have become homes for some of the UK's most threatened species.

With advice from experts at the RSPB, and other environmental organisations such as the Wildlife Trusts and Butterfly Conservation, Cemex have created new habitat deemed as ideal for a number of target species.

These include forty six different birds that had been identified as being at risk of being lost in the UK; species such as the twite (*Carduelis flavirostris*) – a bird which breeds predominantly on moorland – and chough (*Pyrrhocorax pyrrhocorax*), a member of the crow family. Other rare species have also been taken into account such as the water vole (*Arvicola amphibious*) and red squirrel (*Sciurus vulgaris*).

This partnership has allowed the company to balance the needs of their operations by acknowledging that mineral extraction can have an impact on the environment. But while Cemex are supplying concrete, cement, sand and stone, they also have a role to play in protecting and enhancing the natural world.

The partnership began in 2010 and the thousand hectares were originally planned to take ten years to complete – however they were created two years early. Now, fifty sites across England, Scotland and Wales with a diverse range of habitats exist. These include over 100 hectares of heathlands, 190 hectares of water bodies, 600 hectares of grassland and 177 hectares of woodland. Of these, nine are also nature reserves which receive over 750,000 visitors a year.

The first hectare to benefit from the partnership in 2010 was Eversley Quarry, Hampshire in the Blackwater Valley. The quarry had been in operation since the 1970s, providing sand and gravel for construction projects. An extensive community sports facility was created through the Eversley Sports Association on the exhausted quarry land. The adjacent land hundred hectares were converted into a mosaic of different habitats, including the creation of reed beds to encourage bitterns (*Botaurus stellaris*).

The tenth hectare was a clay and limestone quarry in South Warwickshire which provided materials for cement production. Part of the quarry which had been exhausted has been turned into a capped landfill and an area of mosaic grassland created on top. Great crested newts (*Triturus cristatus*) are on the site as well as high numbers of kidney vetch (*Anthyllis vulneraria*). Kidney vetch is the sole food plant for the caterpillar of the rare small blue butterfly (*Cupido minimus*), which is now thriving at the site.

The thousandth hectare was completed in 2017 at Hopwas quarry in Staffordshire. This exhausted sand and gravel quarry has been turned into lowland heath which is in keeping with the neighbouring Site of Special Scientific Interest, Cannock Chase. Heather cuttings containing seeds and other flora have been taken from Cannock and spread over part of the land to encourage new heathland growth.

Businesses and charities have a lot to offer each other and working in partnership can often reap a number of benefits. There can be pitfalls and care has to be taken to ensure that the companies encompass the same values as the charity.

Ensuring that the business supports the vision and mission may seem obvious but unless some of the values are unifying then it's hard to identify the ways that the business can contribute to the success of the organisation. In return, the corporate organisations receive advice which helps prevent extinctions, as well as improving on their green credentials and increasing their market attractiveness.

References

Bakermans, Marja H., Amanda D. Rodewald, Andrew C. Vitz, and Carlos Rengifo. 2012. Migratory bird use of shade coffee: the role of structura and floristic feature. *Agroforestry Systems* 85, no. 1 pp. 85–94.

Barkham, Patrick. 2018. Plan to remove hen harrier chicks and raise them in captivity dismissed as 'nonsense'. *The Guardian*, 17 January. Accessed 10 February 2018. www.theguardian.com/environment/2018/jan/17/plan-to-remove-hen-harrier-chicks-and-raise-them-in-captivity-dismissed-as-nonsense.

Davies, A. 2006. *Nature after minerals: how mineral site restoration can benefit people and wildlife*. Sandy: RSPB.

Defra. 2016. Joint action plan to increase the English hen harrier population. Uplands Stakeholder Forum, Hen Harrier Sub-Group, OGL. Accessed 10 February 2018. www.gov.uk/government/uploads/system/uploads/attachment_data/file/491818/hen-harrier-action-plan-england-2016.pdf.

Evans, Andy. 1992. The numbers and distribution of Cirl Buntings *Emberiza cirlus* breeding in Britain in 1989. *Bird Study* 39, no. 1 pp. 17–22.

Evans, Andy, K. W. Smith, David L. Buckingham, and J. Evans. 1997. Seasonal variation in breeding performance and nestling diet of cirl buntings Emberiza cirlus in England. *Bird Study* 44, no. 1 pp. 66–79.

Evans, D. A., and K. W. Smith. 1994. Habitat selection of Cirl Buntings Emberiza cirlus wintering in Britain. *Bird Study* 41, no. 2 pp.81–87.

Giovannucci, Daniele, and Freek Jan Koekoek. 2003. *The State of Sustainable Coffee: A study of twelve major markets.* Winnipeg: International Coffee Organization and International Institute for Sustainable Development. Accessed 1 February 2018. www.iisd.org/pdf/2003/trade_state_sustainable_coffee.pdf.

Greenberg, Russell, Peter Bichier, and John Sterling. 1997. Bird populations in rustic and planted shade coffee plantations of eastern Chiapas, Mexico. *Biotropica* 29, no. 4 pp. 501–514.

ICO. 2018. Coffee market recovers slightly from December slump. Accessed 10 February 2018. www.ico.org.

IUCN. 2018. The IUCN Red List of Threatened Species. 17 February. www.iucn redlist.org.

McCann, Colleen, Kimberly Williams-Guillén, Fred Koontz, Juan Carlos Martínez Sánchez,, Alba Alejandra Roque Espinoza, and Charles Koontz. 2003. Shade coffee plantations as wildlife refuge for mantled howler monkeys (*Alouatta palliata*) in Nicaragua. *Primates in Fragments* pp. 321–341.

Nestel, David, Franzisca Dickschen, and Miguel A. Altieri. 1993. Diversity patterns of soil macro-Coleoptera in Mexican shaded and unshaded coffee agroecosystems: an indication of habitat perturbation. *Biodiversity & Conservation* 2, no. 1 pp. 70–78.

Peach, Will J., Lucy J. Lovett, Simon R. Wotton, and Cath Jeffs. 2001. Countryside stewardship delivers cirl buntings (*Emberiza cirlus*) in Devon, UK. *Biological Conservation* 101, no. 3 pp. 361–373.

Perfecto, Ivette, Inge Armbrecht, Stacy M. Philpott, Lorena Soto-Pinto, and Thomas V. Dietsch. 2007. Shaded coffee and the stability of rainforest margins in northern Latin America. In *The stability of tropical rainforest margins, linking ecological, economic and social constraints of land use and conservation*, edited by Teja Tscharntke, Christoph Leuschner, Manfred Zeller, Edi Guhardja and Arifuddin Bidin, pp. 227–263. Berlin: Springer.

Pineda, Eduardo, Claudia Moreno, Federico Escobar, and Gonzalo Halffter. 2005. Frog, bat, and dung beetle diversity in the cloud forest and coffee agroecosystems of Veracruz, Mexico. *Conservation Biology* 19, no. 2 pp. 400–410.

RSPB. 2007. The farmland bird indicator. Accessed 4 January 2018. www.rspb.org.uk/our-work/conservation/conservation-and-sustainability/farming/near-you/farmland-bird-indicator.

RSPB. 2017a. *Annual report 2016/2017.* Sandy: RSPB. Accessed 10 February 2018. www.rspb.org.uk/globalassets/downloads/documents/abouttherspb/annual-review-archive/annual-review-2016-2017.pdf.

RSPB. 2017b. Land management for wildlife: Cirl bunting (*Emberiza cirlus*). Accessed 10 January 2018. www.rspb.org.uk/globalassets/downloads/documents/conservation--sustainability/land-management-for-wildlife/land-management-for-wildlife---cirl-bunting.pdf.

RSPB. 2017c. UK hen harrier population suffers decline, according to latest figures. 28 June. Accessed 10 February 2018. https://ww2.rspb.org.uk/our-work/rspb-news/news/443191-UK-hen-harrier-population-suffers-decline-according-to-latest-figures.

RSPB. Undated. The Cirl Bunting Project. Accessed 4 January 2018. www.rspb.org.uk/our-work/conservation/projects/cirl-bunting-project.

RSPB and BirdLife International. 2017. Team highlights, June 2017. Albatross Task Force. Accessed 10 February 2018. www.rspb.org.uk/globalassets/downloads/join-and-donate/appeals/albatross-task-force-annual-report-2016.pdf.

14 Endangered house sparrows and thriving red kites

Do we have useful metrics for sustainability?

Timo Punkari

Introduction

The sight of red kites circling high on sunny days is common in many areas of England, Wales and Scotland. It is somewhat difficult to grasp that these magnificent birds were all but extinct until very recently. At the same time, the familiar chirping of house sparrows has become a more notable occasion, rather than the common feature of agricultural or urban landscape it once was.

This chapter discusses whether the environmental sustainability reporting commonly in use reflects the development of sustainable biodiversity and biotype. We compare the fate of two common birds, the house sparrow and red kite, and use them as examples of environmental reporting challenges. Both species are dependent on cultural landscape used for agriculture, or rather such agriculture that supports their food supply and nesting possibilities. While house sparrow populations have long been in decline, red kite have been successfully reintroduced following near extinction in the UK. The common metrics measure the development of the population, and as an example, currently the RSPB indicator[1] shows Red status to house sparrow, estimated to 5.3 million pairs,[2] and Green status to red kite with just 1,600 pairs.[3] Should the house sparrow population decline trend stop, its status would eventually return to green, even if the population remaining would be minimal compared to the earlier coverage.

It can be argued that the various environmental reporting presented by nature and corporate organisations fails to properly to support sustainable biodiversity. The environmental sustainability reporting of associations and nature organisations is very different to corporate sustainability reporting. In the same time when many companies are telling how they have reduced their environmental impact, the nature organisations are reporting alarming development of both biodiversity and individual species. There does not seem to be many direct links between corporate activity and its impact to nature in environmental reporting, and even more when the development of individual species is reported.

Finally, we discuss how the sustainability reporting and metrics applied could be developed to better reflect the entire biotope effects resulting from the reporting venture activities. Dialogue and co-operation of various actors is also discussed.

Environmental sustainability

When reading about sustainability, changes in biodiversity, and threatened species, there seems to be two worlds very apart. On one hand, corporate sustainability reports and environmental indicators show significant progress, with emissions and waste reducing year on year. On the other hand, environmental organisations and wildlife non-governmental organisations (NGOs), such as the World Wide Fund for Nature (WWF) and the Royal Society for the Protection of Birds (RSPB), provide ample evidence of biodiversity decline, habitat loss and many species becoming threatened or extinct. What is the reason for this contradiction? Is there a catch, one may ask?

The scope and metrics of corporate environmental reporting and environmental indicators used by wildlife NGOs and other actors are different. Corporate reporting is numeric and quantifiable over a short period of time, while wildlife NGOs employ more qualitative indicators and long-term trends when assessing the state of environment.

This chapter discusses whether corporate reporting focuses too heavily on simplified quantitative details when targeting sustainability and conservation of nature, and whether the metrics involved are appropriate for supporting sustainable biodiversity. Further, a novel perspective on the issues of extinction is discussed, by studying two birds, which are closely connected, or dependent on, human action or population: the common house sparrow and red kite. Both species depend on agricultural landscape that supports their food supply and nesting possibilities. Both have also been victims of purported population destruction and harmful substances being infiltrated into their food through human activity.

A comparison between the house sparrow and red kite is particularly interesting, as the population of house sparrows has long been in declined, whereas the red kite has been successfully reintroduced from near extinction in the UK. The common environmental trend metrics measure the development of the population, and as an example, currently the Birds of Conservation Concern (BoCC)[4] indicator allocates Red status to the house sparrow, estimated to 5.3 million pairs,[5] but Green status to the red kite, which have an estimated 1,600 pairs.[6] While red kite are arguably the more threatened species, development of the population make the indicators show this seemingly contradictory status. Should the house sparrow population decline trend stop, its status would turn to amber, even if the population remaining would be minimal compared to the earlier coverage, and could eventually return to green, if the remaining population grew over a defined period of time.

The sustainability reporting and metrics applied by companies which have a direct impact on such agriculture, affecting the biodiversity which supports house sparrows and red kites, cannot be connected to the population development of those species directly or indirectly, as the metrics commonly applied in corporate sustainability reporting are not directly connected to influence on biodiversity or individual species.

Sustainability reporting

Sustainability reporting is the key for any species or biotype development reporting. While the term is familiar to everyone, it has some many facets that presenting one, general and generally accepted definition is difficult. Although the evolution of sustainability and indeed integrated reporting, are discussed in chapter two, this chapter re-examines corporate environmental and sustainability reporting in a different manner in order to lay the basis for the discussion.

Sustainability reporting background

Most national and international definitions of sustainability arise from the 1987 UN definition, in what is commonly known as the Brundtland Report: "Sustainable development is development that meets the needs of the present without compromising the ability of future generations to meet their own needs."[7] Such a definition of sustainability covers naturally anything promoting human rights and wellbeing to conservation of individual species. There is no generally accepted exact definition for the word, and the use of the term is variable from one standard setter, sustainability reporting party or user of such reports.

The word "sustainable" can have different meanings, and in the corporate world it can refer to two interlinked, but profoundly different matters: either how the corporation can create value over long periods of time while maintaining sound principles and methods in creating that value, or how the corporation reports their impact and actions to and within the society and environment.

Consequently, "sustainability reporting" has no universally accepted, or specified content. The largely adopted and applied framework of the Global Reporting Initiative (GRI) defines sustainability reporting as follows:

> A sustainability report is a report published by a company or organization about the economic, environmental and social impacts caused by its everyday activities. A sustainability report also presents the organization's values and governance model, and demonstrates the link between its strategy and its commitment to a sustainable global economy.
>
> Sustainability reporting can help organizations to measure, understand and communicate their economic, environmental, social and governance performance, and then set goals, and manage change more effectively. A sustainability report is the key platform for communicating sustainability performance and impacts – whether positive or negative.
>
> Sustainability reporting can be considered as synonymous with other terms for non-financial reporting; triple bottom line reporting, corporate social responsibility (CSR) reporting, and more. It is also an intrinsic element of integrated reporting; a more recent development that combines the analysis of financial and non-financial performance.[8]

The GRI standards and approach to sustainability reporting are applied within some national sustainability reporting requirements, and many large corporations apply those standards or principles. However, the above definition covers more or less all company activities. Hence it would be very difficult to cover the broad range by one single report or even set of reports, even if the general principles would be generally accepted and observed.

While most corporate definitions of sustainability include a reference to social and economic elements, in many cases accounting practices have focused largely on environmental issues only.

Environmental reporting

As was discussed in Chapter 2, corporate environmental reporting emerged in the late 1980s and early 1990s. Since then it has become a standard part of corporate reporting, even if it has often remained outside the financial statements. Definitions of environmental reporting are perhaps less variable and less comprehensive than those of sustainability reporting, but even there is no generally accepted definition and format of environmental reporting. The European Federation of Accountants (FEE, currently Accountancy Europe) have defined environmental reporting in their discussion paper as follows:

> "environmental reporting" covers the preparation and provision of information, by management, for the use of multiple stakeholder groups (internal and external), on the environmental status and performance of their company or organisation.[9]

Wildlife NGOs and other nature and conservation organisations publish their own environmental reports, such as the IUCN Red List of Threatened Species, or the RSPB's "State of Nature". The IUCN report dates back to 1964, when the environmental movement was becoming active, while the RSPB report has only been published since 2013. Wildlife NGOs' reports are compiled according to the scope defined by the organisation, and using the resources available to the organisation. While corporate environmental reporting is very variable and without any common format, the nature and conservation organisation reports are even more variable and apply different metrics and formats.

The Birds of Conservation Concern 4 reporting (BoCC4), developed by British Birds in partnership with nine wildlife NGOs, has metrics to assess the conservation concern of bird species. As we have seen, the metrics applied can lead to seemingly illogical conclusions.

There is little academic research comparing reporting by wildlife NGOs with corporate environmental reporting. However, it can be seen that there has not been much connection between the reports, and that they are intended for different audiences and to serve different purposes. This does not, however, explain the paradox of improving corporate sustainability while at the same time witnessing a decline in biodiversity. We need to try and find other reasons why this paradox has developed, and if there is anything that could be done to align the different forms of environmental reporting.

One key difference between the purpose of these two forms of reporting is easily perceived: companies report the impact their activity has on the surrounding environment separately from their main reporting, which explains the financial performance and status, whereas wildlife NGOs report how the environment has been changing and where the critical points are, and that reporting directly reflects their scope of activity.

Actors

There are different actors participating in the collection of data and preparation of environmental reports. These actors have notably different roles in corporations from those in wildlife NGOs. Corporate reporting is subject to various audits, and hence there are also different auditors involved. Reporting by wildlife NGOs is not usually audited, even if it attempts to be verifiable.

Wildlife NGO researchers

Data for wildlife NGOs are often collected by volunteers, as is the case with the BoCC4 report.[10] The report itself is commonly collated and compiled by experts in biology and biodiversity. The IUCN report also relies on substantial voluntary work: "IUCN gratefully acknowledges the dedication and efforts of the hundreds of scientists and practitioners who have contributed to the scientific development and practical testing of the IUCN Red List of Ecosystems Categories and Criteria since 2008."[11] This makes it naturally more difficult to manage, co-ordinate and supervise than having the reporting prepared by own staff or paid service supplier.

Corporate environmental reporting managers

Managers responsible for corporate environmental issues tend to hold a risk management position and have an engineering background. Data for the reports are gathered by various measuring equipment or staff reporting. Some measurements are taken continuously, such as emissions of regulated substances, and all data are collated at least monthly and then presented in the monthly reporting reviews. The approach is to provide regular, similar and quantified data fitting with the rhythm of other corporate reporting.

Financial reporting managers

Financial reporting is carried out by the company or group finance director or manager. They typically have the responsibility for putting together the public reporting packages quarterly and annually, unless the group has an investor relations manager, who may be assigned to this task. Sustainability is not part of the financial statements, but sustainability reporting follows the financial reporting schedule, and the internal reporting reviews are planned according to the financial reporting schedules.

Supply chain managers

There is a growing customer interest in the origins and traceability of food and clothing which has encouraged supply chain managers to develop reporting of the supplier base structure and indicate which parts of this are certified (such as tea, cotton, carton packages and other raw materials), as well as which part of the supplier working conditions have been audited, for instance. There is a relatively recent movement towards sustainable supply chain management, including the development of accompanying reporting frameworks.

Sustainability reporting auditors

Corporate sustainability reports are not subject to financial statutory audits, even if the auditors have to check that statutory emissions disclosures are prepared, and that the details are identical to those in the financial statements. There are specific environmental audits, which concentrate more on assessing the process and its viability than on the environmental impacts. Increasing interest in supply chain sustainability management has however also increased interest in assessing how the activity impacts on the environment.

There is remarkably little dialogue or interaction between the corporate and environmental reporting people. Both worlds produce their own reports, apply their own standards and frameworks. There are attempts to break this barrier when wildlife NGOs, such as the RSPB, assist companies to become more sustainable,[12] but there does not seem to be an attempt to match the reporting frameworks and systems. In preparing this paper, I sought an interview with an academic working in biodiversity to ask them about environmental reporting. She clearly knew a great deal about reporting by wildlife NGOs and why the metrics chosen are important, and I was given some valuable ideas. However, when I tried to discuss corporate environmental reporting, she had a very negative perception of corporate activities. She was convinced that companies do not care about biodiversity and that sustainability reports are merely part of their "greenwashing". From the corporate reporting side there was a similar attitude among accountants and auditors, as they do not consider reporting by wildlife NGOs relevant to corporate life, and perceive such reporting as detached from corporate activity.

The lack of dialogue and true willingness to develop common reporting framework for both nature organisations and corporate reporting prevents any progress towards genuine integrated reporting. The IASB, which is the leading organisation in international financial standards (IFRS), could take the lead, but has not been willing to do so. The International Integrated Reporting Council has done much work to create an integrated framework, however, they have not issued standards to follow, and do not have the resources to change the reporting frameworks.

Reporting standards and methods

There is one fundamental difference between environmental reporting by companies and that by wildlife NGOs. Corporate reporting almost always applies a framework issued by an independent third party, such as the GRI or SASB, whereas wildlife NGOs tend to publish reports which use their own structures and methods, such as the IUCN and BoCC4.

In corporate life it is important that all published reports are audited by a third party, and the auditors must be able to verify the reporting structures and metrics. For a company it is always easiest to apply a generally accepted third party framework or set of standards, as there are rules and metrics readily available, and they need not to be audited separately.

Wildlife NGOs promote environmental issues and conservation, and have to create their own reports and metrics, as often there is nothing available from standard setters. Wildlife NGOs' reports are usually not audited, but may comply with academic peer review rules, as Dr Mark Eaton from the RSPB says, "so we can publish the findings both as a scientifically rigorous paper so the facts are there for scrutiny, and as a summary report".[13]

There are statutory environmental reporting requirements for some companies, such as quoted companies, which must report on greenhouse gas emissions for which they are responsible, as required by the Companies Act 2006 (Strategic Report and Directors' Reports) Regulations 2013. However, the Act does not prescribe any method for the reporting. The related guidance recommends that "for effective emissions management and transparency in reporting it is important that you use robust and accepted methods. It is recommended that you use a widely recognized independent standard".[14]

The guidance does not elaborate further on what it considers to be "widely recognised" or "independent". In practice, such guidance will lead to monopoly or oligopoly of one or few standards, as it is easier to use what everyone else is using. Such standards are chosen by the structures, which have been found convenient by the industry. They do comply with the regulation and the guidance; however, there is no control that the chosen framework would best report all the relevant facts.

Standard setters

Most corporate standard setters are private not-for-profit organisations. They are funded by governmental departments, but even more importantly by private companies. For instance, the Greenhouse Gas Protocol lists 68 funding partners on their web pages, of which 42 are large private companies, or foundations run by them.[15] Whether this setup has any material influence on the reporting structure or metrics is beyond the scope of this chapter, but would be an interesting topic for further research.

As discussed above, wildlife NGO use often their own reporting, suited to their interests. There are few standards used widely by organisations other than the issuer itself.

Reporting metrics

Reporting metrics have little in common when comparing reporting by wildlife NGOs to corporate sustainability reporting. There are differences in practically all areas of metrics: length of measuring period, how the metrics are obtained, whether they are quantified or more qualitative, whether they can be used alone or as part of a set of metrics, and how easy it is to compare the measurement between different measured objects.

Wildlife NGO reporting metrics tend to require a number of measurements over a period of time, which may take years, or sometimes even hundreds of years, and the measurements can be collected from different sources in different ways, qualitative assessments being commonly in use, and the results are usually a function of a number of metrics together. Due to the complexity of setting metrics for a certain purpose, using the same metrics for different objects, such as biotypes, species, or natural environments, can be difficult.

Corporate sustainability reporting has commonly quantified metrics taken at a point of time, measured by a measuring device or counting occurrences, which can be reported alone, and which are simple to compare between objects, which can be plants or companies.

Stakeholders

Wildlife NGOs do not usually list the stakeholders, to whom the reporting is directed, but the nature of reporting is often closely connected to the message of the organisation, and purported to create material to enhance the visibility of the organisation and their message.

In corporate reporting, the audience is clearly defined: investors and potential investors. This is also the basis for the EU non-financial information directive, which however has a broader scope. The so-called public interest entities must report their impact in environmental, social and employment, human rights, and corruption and bribery issues.[16] Among other stakeholders, employees, customers and suppliers are often mentioned as specific groups, and the society as a whole. Environment or nature do not count as stakeholders.

Corporate sustainability reporting

Financial reporting is often considered as a natural outcome of standardised accounting which applies values in money. This assumption has been challenged by research, and the objectivity of accounting and financial reporting has been criticised. It seems evident that accounting does not only reflect a reality, it changes how the reality is built,[17] adhering to an ideologically influenced set of values on a variety of actors.

Financial reporting exists mainly for two groups, the investors and the tax collector. The main purpose of any financial reporting is to provide information to current and potential investors. In the International Financial Standards (IFRS) that is pronounced in the framework, which declares that

> The objective of general purpose financial reporting is to provide financial information about the reporting entity that is useful to existing and potential investors, lenders and other creditors in making decisions about providing resources to the entity. Those decisions involve buying, selling or holding equity and debt instruments, and providing or settling loans and other forms of credit.[18]

Management reporting, or the company's internal reporting aims to assess performance and direct the action, usually concentrating on profit and cost issues rather than social, environmental, or any other non-financial targets.[19] This is quite natural, as management performance tends to be assessed and remunerated on the financial performance, either the chosen profit figure (net result, EBIT, EBITDA, non-GAAP adjusted result, etc.), or by growth in the share price, or both. Non-financial issues have an impact on management reporting only as risk factors of possible production loss, penalties payable on breaches of environmental rules and regulations, or reputational risk, which may lead to lower sales, or even boycotts of the company products or services.

Corporate sustainability reporting follows the normal corporate reporting principles, and hence also environmental reporting observes the same underlying principles. These principles are divided by the IASB to fundamental and enhancing qualitative characteristics:

> The fundamental qualitative characteristics are relevance and faithful representation.[20]
>
> Comparability, verifiability, timeliness and understandability are qualitative characteristics that enhance the usefulness of information that is relevant and faithfully represented. The enhancing qualitative characteristics may also help determine which of two ways should be used to depict a phenomenon if both are considered equally relevant and faithfully represented.[21]

If these principles were fully adhered to by companies, all reports would give easily digested, correct, verified information about relevant matters in swiftly produced reports, which could be effortlessly compared to other companies. While this is the governing objective of the IFRS and most local GAAP reporting, companies have created their own measurements, called non–GAAP measures. Criticism on such company chosen measures is increasing, as those IFRS framework characteristics are not met. The US Center for Audit Quality has issued a list of questions for Audit committees to assess the quality of such non-GAAP reporting.[22] These questions have been divided into two groups: comparability and consistency. About consistency they say:

According to a 2014 survey conducted by the University of Washington and the University of Georgia, 27 percent of companies disclosed non-GAAP earnings that excluded one-time losses but did not report adjusted figures for one-time gains.[23]

Questions to ask included:

- Has the company presented this measure before? Has the company stopped presenting certain measures?
- Has the method or nature of the inputs to the calculation changed since the last time presented? If so, why and have the comparable periods been revised consistently?[24]

Comparability questions are introduced by considering the reporting metrics against other companies in the same industry:

There is no authoritative framework that defines the calculation of each non-GAAP measure. This enables the non-GAAP measure calculations to be tailored from one company to the next. The more tailored the calculation, the less comparable the measure may be across an industry. The less comparable the measure, the more confusing it may be to investors.[25]

Such individual reporting could be detected by asking such questions as:

- Do other companies present this measure or similar measures? If not, why is this measure important for this company but not its peers?
- If there are differences from peers, is the disclosure transparent about how the measure is calculated differently than peers?
- Have any industry groups defined standard calculations that companies within the industry could follow in order to present more comparable measures to investors?[26]

Questions about financial reporting consistency and comparability are discussed here at some length, because the same reporting opportunism may also extend to sustainability reporting. Considering that financial reporting has better defined and standardised rules than sustainability reporting, one cannot avoid assuming that sustainability reporting consistency and comparability are even less well-maintained than in the financial reports. On the other hand, financial reporting adjustments are deviations from commonly accepted rules, and can be adjusted back to those rules, such that transparency of the reporting method is maintained.

Corporate sustainability reporting is, on the one hand, an obligation, when such reporting is mandatory, such as greenhouse gas emissions reporting, and on the other hand, a way to convey an image of socially responsible company, which is at least on the same level as its peers. However, as long as sustainability reports are issued separately from the financial statements, they are unlikely to command the same interest from management, investors, or other stakeholders than the financial statements, which are also studied and reviewed by a host of well-paid professional analysts. Those analysts do not necessarily understand, or do not want to understand, sustainability reports, and if they are part of the analysis, it seems that the review is outsourced to specialised sustainability reporting experts.

The sustainability reporting and metrics applied by companies which have a direct impact on agriculture, which in turn influences biodiversity and the ecosystem supporting house sparrows and red kites, cannot be connected to the population development of those species directly or indirectly, as the metrics commonly applied in corporate sustainability reporting are too general in their current form.

Sustainability reporting standards

There are a host of sustainability standards available, for different purposes, from different approaches and by various organisations. There are also frameworks to integrate sustainability reporting and financial reporting into one reporting system, such as the (IIRC) International Integrated Reporting Council framework or the United Nations Sustainable Development Goals (SDGs), which do not contain reporting standards. Compared to reporting by wildlife NGOs, they all have one common major difference: the reporting period and timeframe is aligned to the corporate financial one-year period reporting. The nature organisation reporting has commonly a long reference period, presenting developments or trends over a number of years. Corporate sustainability reporting only presents the emission or waste amounts, or other mostly quantitative data of the reporting period, and corresponding data of the previous period.

We discuss here two widely used standard systems, which have different approaches, to show that choosing the reporting framework has an important influence to the reporting structures and also contents. These two are the GRI (Global Reporting Initiative) and SASB (Sustainability Accounting Standards Board) standards and reporting metrics systems. GRI has been alluded to in Chapter 2, but we provide more detail here on its aim and content.

The GRI reporting framework is most widely used by large companies.[27] It is built on generic standards, which can be used in all industries, and it has an international approach.

The SASB framework is industry specific, so that all industries have their own, adapted standards to reflect the sphere of that industry. It does not attempt to produce international standards, as it purports to serve the US listed companies only.

GRI standards are divided into "universal standards" and "topic-specific standards" (Figure 14.1).[28] The universal standards set the foundation of reporting, describes general disclosures and management approach. The topic-specific standards detail economic, environmental, and social standards.

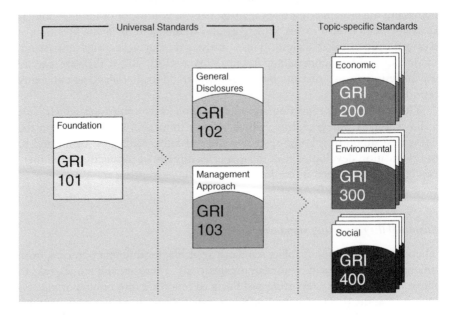

Figure 14.1 Universal standards and topic-specific standards

Because the standards are applicable to all companies, they are comparable between all companies. However, they are generic and do not cater for industry-specific issues.

The SASB reporting framework is built on industry-specific standards. There are 79 industries in 11 sectors, and they all their own standards. The purpose is to "help public corporations disclose financially material information to investors in a cost-effective and decision-useful format."[29]

The standards are first drafted by the SASB staff, and the drafts are then discussed and developed in the industry work groups. I had the honour and pleasure to participate in three of those working groups. The participants were genuinely interested in creating working sustainability standards, which would report the company activity impact in environment, social capital, human capital, business model and innovation, and leadership and governance issues, within the corporate circumstances. However, it was clearly pronounced that the standards are for US listed companies only, and the main stakeholder group are the investors in listed companies. Any suggestion of an issue, which as such was justifiable, was declined, if there were no US listed company, which would meet that specific issue. The advantage of SASB standards is that within an industry the reporting is comparable and concentrates in essential industry issues. However, comparing companies in different industries is more complicated.

Choosing the standard system can have a major impact on what is reported and which metrics are used. Take, say, a chemical company producing pesticides. Applying the GRI standards the company may avoid reporting distasteful details on the impact of its activities, which it could not do when reporting by SASB standards.

As mentioned above, some sustainability reporting is mandatory, such as greenhouse gas emissions reporting, but most sustainability reporting is voluntary. Listed companies and other large EU corporations must now report these issues under the Non-financial information directive, which will certainly put pressure to companies in reporting relevant data. Since most companies, covering all non-listed family companies and for instance most German Mittelstand, which are important in industrial production, are not subject to the directive, their sustainability reporting is either limited to the mandatory reporting, or basic information about the sustainability issues.

Sustainability reporting audits

Auditing sustainability reporting has been a complicated issue, because the financial auditors do not have the necessary competencies to audit sustainability reporting. Since the financial auditors must audit all material within the financial statements, sustainability reporting has been separated from the financial reports – thus the auditors need not audit the sustainability parts. They only need to confirm that the mandatory reporting exists, and that any same information is identical in both financial statements and sustainability reporting. This has made sustainability reporting to be a separate report, and consequently not be important for users of the financial statements.

There are specialised sustainability reporting auditors, who are typically accountants or engineers with interest in the area. Such audits are prepared for the investors, or the same users as the financial statement audits.

Sustainability reporting by wildlife NGOs

Wildlife NGOs and other non-financial sustainability reporting and reporting frameworks exist usually for society, or for a broad stakeholder audience. The United Nations Sustainable Development Goals (SDGs) are connected to all stakeholders, as "All stakeholders: governments, civil society, the private sector, and others, are expected to contribute to the realisation of the new agenda."[30] The IUCN states that the main purpose of their Red List is to "catalogue and highlight those plants and animals that are facing a higher risk of global extinction" and "providing the world with the most objective, scientifically-based information on the current status of globally threatened biodiversity." [31]

Unlike corporate sustainability reporting, which attempts merely to state the impact of the activity, wildlife NGOs reporting aims to raise the alarm on the status of the environment, and to promote action to prevent further deterioration, or improve the situation.

Sustainability reporting standards

There are a vast number of various reporting frameworks and methods in use by the reporting organisations. While the corporate sustainability reporting has clearly defined standards and standard frameworks, the nature organisation methods cannot be called standards in the same sense of the word. These frameworks and methods are more extensive and require data collection from different sources, and processing of that data to usable form.

The IUCN reports have five different criteria to consider, and each of them have extensive instructions, how data should be collected and processed for these criteria (see Table 14.1).[32]

The BoCC4 classification of birds to red, amber, and green status has nine different criteria to consider. Amber classification, as an example, is given, when most of the criteria below are met:[33]

- Species with unfavourable conservation status in Europe (SPEC = Species of European Conservation Concern).
- Historical population decline during 1800–1995, but recovering; population size has more than doubled over last 25 years.
- Moderate (25–50%) decline in UK breeding population over last 25 years, or the longer-term period.
- Moderate (25–50%) contraction of UK breeding range over last 25 years, or the longer-term period.
- Moderate (25–50%) decline in UK non-breeding population over last 25 years, or the longer-term period.
- Rare breeder; 1–300 breeding pairs in UK.

Table 14.1 IUCN report criteria

Criterion		Purpose
A	Reduction in geographic distribution.	Identifies ecosystems that are undergoing declines in area, most commonly due to threats resulting in ecosystem loss and fragmentation
B	Restricted geographic distribution.	Identifies ecosystems with small distributions that are susceptible to spatially explicit threats and catastrophes
C	Environmental degradation	Identifies ecosystems that are undergoing environmental degradation
D	Disruption of biotic processes or interactions	Identifies ecosystems that are undergoing loss or disruption of key biotic processes or interactions
E	Quantitative analysis that estimates the probability of ecosystem collapse	Allows for an integrated evaluation of multiple threats and symptoms, and their interactions

- Rare non-breeders; less than 900 individuals.
- Localised; at least 50% of UK breeding or non-breeding population in 10 or fewer sites, but not applied to rare breeders or non-breeders.
- Internationally important; at least 20% of European breeding or non-breeding population in UK (northwest European and East Atlantic Flyway populations used for non-breeding wildfowl and waders respectively).

As these two classification standards show, the result requires much data collection over a long period of time and processing the collected data, and also judgment from the organisation to weigh up different criteria. Referring to the assessment periods and reference dates, the IUCN reference point is around 1750, or when the industrial revolution took place. The trend analyses are performed over 25 or 50 years' development.

Criticism of reporting methods and results

There has been criticism around the transparency and accountability of reporting by wildlife NGOs. Since the data are collected from a number of different sources, and sometimes by a large number of people, the consistency and comparability of the data, and subsequently the results obtained, has been queried. Also, the more or less subjective criteria can lead to results which do not satisfy all users' expectations. After the IUCN faced some serious criticism at the end of 1990s, it has improved transparency of its methods and processes. The main issue around the IUCN criticism at that time concerned data quality and documentation of the assessment of the status of a species, and one critic suggested that the species without sufficient documentation would be classified as "data deficient", which would exclude the species from having any status at all.[34] What is remarkable about the problem is that it lies directly in the heart of the reporting system and methods. If the raw base data and the documentation made on the data cannot be trusted, credibility of the entire framework is jeopardised. If this is compared to the IASB reporting fundamental qualitative characteristics of relevance and faithful representation discussed above, both characteristics seem have to be lacking.

Reporting on species living in agricultural and cultured landscapes

Cultured landscapes, such as agricultural land and urban spaces, are habitats that are directly under human activity, and they change when that activity changes. There has been substantial discussion about the ways in which agriculture has changed and how the move to more intense and effective production has reduced biodiversity. Urbanisation changes the landscape, when new areas are taken for bigger cities, but the change urbanisation causes is much wider, ranging from emptying countryside in developed countries to changing structures and nature of cities. In developing countries, shantytowns create new biotypes and in rich cities maintaining the buildings in immaculate condition, and yards and parks clean and managed, reduce natural nesting places and food sources.

Which cultural biotypes should we conserve in this continuous development, and which point of time do we use as an anchor against which to gauge change? These are questions which have attracted relatively little attention in spite of their importance as a fundamental basis for any environmental reporting of cultural biotypes and species living in them. The IUCN's reference year is 1750, or around the time when the industrial society emerged and industrial-scale exploitation of ecosystems started.[35] While this seems a reasonable reference point, at least many European countries had already been largely exploited by humans by that time: Forests had been cut and land taken for agriculture, and large cities existed since Graeco-Roman times.

This creates a certain difficulty in finding a reference point before major human involvement for those species, which live in agricultural or urban environments, such as the house sparrow. The population when land was covered by forests, could be another reference point. Apparently the English forests had already been felled 3000 years ago, and agriculture was intense by Bronze Age: "Even in supposedly backward counties such as Essex, villa abutted on villa for mile after mile, and most of the gaps were filled by small towns and the lands of British farmsteads."[36]

Species living close to humans are said to have commensal relationships with humans. Commensalism is defined as an interaction between two species in which one species benefits from the relationship while the other is unaffected by it.[37] This relationship is naturally changing as human activity changes, and thus defining reference points for reporting is complicated.

Comparing the house sparrow populations of England and Germany in any chosen year of modern history seems to be more or less flawed, because England was already densely populated and land cleared for cultivation, while large parts of Germany have been sparsely occupied and covered by forests. Hence the distribution of house sparrow would be unlikely to be similar, and the development, too: In England it could be that there was saturation of house sparrow populations in some areas, when the populations were strongly increasing in Germany because of more land was taken for cultivation. Any reference year before the modern collection of data started requires statistical methods to estimate the population. The IUCN guide sets methods for such analysis:

> In parts of the world where industrial-scale exploitation of ecosystems commenced earlier or later than 1750, it is justifiable to assess historical declines with a different baseline. Distribution models with environmental predictors may be used to estimate historical declines based on the difference between the current state of an ecosystem and its expected state in the absence of industrial-scale anthropogenic effects. Such approaches are most useful in regions where landscape-scale change did not occur before the industrial era.[38]

This principle might push the English reference date back very far, depending on how the "industrial-scale" effects are understood.

To overcome the historical reference date problem, IUCN applies also the 50-year change rules. Changes are assessed over the past 50 years, over future 50 years, and over any 50 years period, including the past, present and future.[39] Applying 50-year rules is certainly easier and allows the use of collected data to estimate the already observed population changes and expected future development. While the 50-year ranges and historical reference dates fit to IUCN and the same principle can be applied by other nature and conservation organisations, it does not agree with the corporate reporting principles and methods. The common financial reporting time frame is about two years: the current reporting year and the previous year are presented as comparative information. Public future oriented reporting does not really exist, as any budgets or plans made are internal documents, and even those cover usually the next five years only. Environmental reporting, however, sometimes gives details about the changes over a longer period of time, notably when the emissions or other impacts on the environment can be compared to such a reference date, when those impacts were bigger. There are usually targets for the future, often given as proportional changes, such as reducing the CO_2 emissions by 15% in three years.

How companies affect species within cultured landscape is beyond the scope of corporate environmental reporting. Companies may report how they manage land areas which they use, or protect birds and other animals and plants in areas they use, as well as they emissions but there is little analysis of how their products and services influence nesting possibilities and food sources in agricultural land or urban areas. As an example, a construction company building houses and blocks of flats could report how the bird, bat and insect nesting possibilities have been taken into account in the design of buildings and planting bushes and shrubs, which would also provide feeding sources by hosting the species necessary in the food chain. Too well maintained buildings and neat gardens reduce nesting and feeding possibilities and result in population losses, as the report from German house sparrow counts show. In Munich, the richest of large German cities, the reference house sparrow count of Landesbund für Vogelschutz (LBV) is just 0.9 in Munich, compared to 1.5 in Hamburg, and 7 in Berlin. The local project manager, Ms Sofia Engel, says that the city is too rich, people instantly repair any cracks and keep the facades in immaculate condition, so that there are no nesting places for birds.

> In Munich, only 0.9 house sparrows were counted by an observer. "That's ridiculously little," says Engel. To compare: in Berlin there were seven and in Hamburg at least 1.5 observations.
>
> "The better shape a building is, the harder it is for birds to find nesting places," says Engel. In Munich, the problem for the birds is that the city is too rich. People renovate their houses and make facades watertight, spending a lot of money. "Every crack is filled, so that no draught can get through," says Engel.[40]

How to report the connection of otherwise positive development and its adverse impacts to certain habitats and species could probably be solved. Statistical models could be created to estimate the rate of impact when the income per capita increases. However, it would be much more complicated to assess the trade-off between buildings in better condition and loss of nesting places of some species.

Conserving cultured landscapes

The EU Birds and Habitats Directive governs mainly vulnerable species in natural state areas, however, the directive should apply to all bird species. Articles most relevant to cultural landscape species require member countries to maintain populations of all wild bird species across their natural range (Article 2), preserve, maintain or re-establish a sufficient diversity and area of habitats for birds, inside and outside protected areas (Article 3), prohibit large-scale non-selective means of bird killing (Article 8), and monitor habitats and species (Article 11).[41]

There are many areas in the directive, which require interpretation, and may cause disagreement. The terms, "to maintain populations" and "across their natural range", involve defining the reference point in time, as the population size and range change over time. In cultural landscapes defining "natural range" is problematic, as should one refer to the agricultural and urban areas in 1750 (the IUCN reference year) or any other year, or should the current cultural landscapes be taken as the natural range of any given point of time, as discussed above.

Some meadows and fields are maintained to keep them as they were for small-scale agriculture and farming, even when the cattle would have been withdrawn from the area. Such activity certainly contributes to the conservation of those habitats, however, it could be argued that artificial maintenance of abandoned meadows and fields is not sustainable, as it requires such constant human action, which is not anymore supported by the farming community.

Agricultural land use is moving to increasingly effective use of resources and low waste, which reduces he food supply of birds and rodents, and thus has a direct impact of populations of those species and their predators. The latest development is called precision agriculture (PA), which is an approach to farm management that uses information technology (IT) to ensure that the crops and soil receive exactly what they need for optimum health and productivity. The goal of PA is to ensure profitability, sustainability and protection of the environment. Agricultural control centres provide farmers with the ability to identify fields that require treatment and determine the optimum amount of water, fertilisers and pesticides to apply. This helps the farmer to avoid wasting resources and prevent run-off, ensuring that the soil has just the right amount of additives for optimum health, while also reducing costs and controlling the farm's environmental impact.[42]

The more resources the PA saves, the more sustainable and environment friendly it is considered. However, this pursuit of more efficiency has led to more monoculture (i.e. cultivation of only one crop). In Continental Europe the crop is increasingly maize, which is thick, tall, and prevents any other plants growing. In Germany the area of maize fields has tripled in thirty years, while the agricultural land are has not significantly increased.[43] At the same time, the area of uncultivated fields has reduced. The EU agricultural policy supported and also required maintaining some of the total farming area uncultivated during 1988–2007. While the purpose was to reduce agricultural products overproduction, the policy also maintained part of the fields uncultivated, and thus growing natural grass, flowers and other plants. Besides the multitude of plants, those rather bare areas are necessary for many insects, small mammals and birds, and when they thrive, also the predators of those species prosper.

Open, uncultivated areas may be incorporated within nature protection sites, created to protect vulnerable species may also benefit common species. According to RSPB, common species are also faring better, with higher populations inside Natura 2000 sites.[44] In reference to reporting, development of monoculture agriculture could be deducted by comparing the EU agricultural reports measuring areas of cultivation of different crops. It is more difficult to connect sustainability reporting to such development, as the more efficient production of crops is considered also more sustainable and environmentally friendly. What may be good for reducing water and other resource use can in the same time be harmful to biodiversity, penalising those species, which are dependent of the waste of those resources.

House sparrow and red kite population change

When we think about the cultural landscape required by our two key species, the house sparrow and red kite, the area of suitable habitat is not an issue. House sparrows thrive on agricultural and urban landscapes, which are abundant, and the red kite needs open landscape, such as agricultural fields, with some trees for nesting, which are also common landscape. Consequently, habitat loss or increase cannot explain the changes of populations of these two species.

Population change

The BoCC4 reporting estimates the status of UK bird species, and it states that the population of the house sparrow has declined severely, and the status is Red, while the population of red kite is increasing, and the status is Green. Taking into account that there are still millions of sparrows and just a few thousand kites, one could argue that the picture is incomplete.

The UK house sparrow population is estimated to have dropped by 71 per cent between 1977 and 2008 with substantial declines in both rural and urban populations.[45] Similar developments have been reported in Continental Europe, too. However, there are still 5.3 million pairs around the UK.[46]

The UK red kite population has risen from being close to extinction to almost 2,000 pairs.[47] The populations have also increased in other countries. Central Europe holds the majority (50% of all breeding pairs) of the global population, which is concentrated in Western Europe.[48]

Both species have been and still are victims of human activities. The red kite was hunted and its nests were destroyed before the bird was protected. However, even today the red kite is subject to illegal persecution, accidental secondary poisoning by rodenticides and electrocution on power lines.[49] Also, wind farms kill red kites, which are hit by the wind turbine blades. Red kites are the second most frequently reported species in relation to collisions with wind turbines in Germany.[50] The house sparrow has a long history of being a victim of "pest management", or reducing population size, developing pest avoidance of seeds or crops, and frightening pests away from sensitive areas. Most of the pest management work on sparrows has focused on the first two methods.[51] Even if the house sparrow would not be persecuted as widely as in past, it does not have any protection against methods the reduce waste, or pest avoidance arrangements.

The absolute population numbers do not necessarily provide a true picture, as house sparrows live in colonies and red kites in pairs. In the same area the potential number of house sparrows is much higher than that of red kites. That is why the IUCN reference point is in 1750, or before the human industrial impact to the nature. However, even that has its limitations, as the human industrial activity has helped the house sparrow populations to increase by providing more food as agricultural waste, and more nesting places in farms, towns and cities, before the current efficient and intense agriculture took over the traditional ways. The red kite has probably also benefitted from industrial agriculture, as the waste supported more rodents and thus offered more abundant feeding opportunities.

There is some German research about the potential distribution of the red kite, should it populate all the potential habitats. The model is very extensive, requiring much work:

> An extensive data set was used for modelling comprising a sample size of 2,625 Red Kite breeding sites, high-resolution land-use data (10 m × 10 m) and climatic as well as topographic variables.[52]

Such extensive models are perhaps not practical for application to most species, such as house sparrows, which live in tight colonies. However, this type of measuring might be useful to estimate the current population size compared to the potential population. In the German study the outcome was that not all suitable habitats were occupied by the species and thus the species distribution seems not to be in equilibrium with its environment. This study provides an example of how reporting on the status of individual species could be developed. It would also link the habitat loss to the population development, as the result may be that a declining species fully occupies all the available habitats, if such habitats are disappearing.

Detecting key factors and metrics for relevant reporting

The metrics of population change are basically simple: take the population in the reference year, and compare the figure to that of the current year. This simple calculation will give a quantified result to present in the report. As we have already discussed, the picture is not that simple, and in the constantly changing world the simple difference of population numbers does not tell much about the factors and circumstances behind the development.

The decline of house sparrow populations has been explained by the change in agriculture. While the reasons for this decline have yet to be identified, despite intense public interest in the matter, the agricultural intensification seems to be at least one of the key factors:

> Key changes resulting from agricultural intensification that are likely to have reduced winter food supplies for house sparrows in recent decades are the switch from spring sowing of cereals to autumn and an increase in bird-proof storage of grain and other animal-feed stocks.[53]

Agricultural intensification is a general term covering a host of various issues, which can be challenging to identify and even more demanding to explain or quantify. As the research result above show, such diverse factors as moving the sowing from spring to autumn and increasing bird-proof storage can have significant impact to the population. House sparrow population development has the additional complexity, as the species also thrives in urban habitats.

The recovery of the red kite population is perhaps easy to describe. The RSPB explains that "following the legal protection of the species and EU-funded reintroduction projects, the red kite is now a bird of the wider countryside."[54] There are a number of similar birds of prey "success stories", which seem to have a few common points: legal protection to end human persecution by hunting and nest destruction, better breeding results because of cessation in use of toxic pesticides accumulating in the food chain, and well organised reintroduction projects. The peregrine falcon is probably the best-known example of such stories.

The peregrine was one of the illustrious birds in a key book bringing the dangers of using DDT to the public at large in the 1960s – *Silent Spring* by Rachel Carson[55] – and the subject of the book *The Peregrine*, by John Alec Baker a little later. At that time the effects of chemicals were sometimes easier to detect, as birds "die on their backs, clutching insanely at the sky in their last convulsions, withered and burnt away by the filthy insidious pollen of farm chemicals", as Baker writes in his book.[56] The movement to stop using DDT also resulted in environmental legislation to take progressive steps to protect nature. That progress has practically ended any clearly visible direct consequences of harmful chemicals, and the impacts are now more indirect or slow to develop or both. Climate change is a prime example of such development, in which the connection between the CO_2 emissions to decline of habitats and species is both slow and indirect.

It can be argued that indirect impact and slow changes make defining appropriate key factors and metrics very complicated, and also delay the reaction to the results too late. When the factors are being tested and the connection confirmed, it could already be too late to change the course of development. Agricultural development, which has a direct impact on both house sparrow and red kite populations, has been gradual and different factors have moved in opposing directions. While the use of most toxic pesticides and herbicides has decreased, and thus reduced the accumulation of toxic substances in birds, moving to more industrial large-scale farming with monoculture fields and better waste management has reduced the feeding and breeding possibilities. As discussed above, such long reporting periods and references work for sustainability reporting by wildlife NGOs, but are inconsistent with corporate reporting, which presents current and previous years only. Measuring even some of the identified factors can take significant time and effort, and also require a long research period to be statistically valid, which reduces the possibilities of regular measuring arrangements.

Without more extensive discussion, a conclusion can perhaps be drawn: the simple population change from the reference year to the current year is the best available metric, as measuring the host of factors influencing populations would us excessive resources rendering it impractical. To extend the reporting, some readily available statistics could be disclosed to serve as simple proxies of agricultural intensification. As an example, statistics of farmland use could be published, to show the crop distribution and the proportion of uncultivated land constituting the total agricultural land. Nevertheless, any reporting always carries the risk of becoming authoritative in the sense that because they are reported, only those issues would be followed and other factors would remain without much attention. Other possibilities include such reports as estimating the occupation rate of individual species in its potential habitats, as discussed above, which would link the reporting to habitat loss.

Possible ways to develop sustainability reporting

We have discussed sustainability reporting by wildlife NGOs, and more precisely, the environmental reporting which it contains. The discussion has revealed that there are two different, and contradictory, reporting worlds, which have little in common with each other and which have little interaction. Dialogue between wildlife NGOs and environmental researchers, and corporate reporting preparers is minimal. Integrating financial and sustainability reporting into one common reporting framework is being promoted by a number of organisations, however, the pace is slow and probably would not solve the paradox of improving impact presented in corporate reports and declining development in wildlife NGO reporting, because the frameworks are fundamentally different.

From the discussion it seems that these reporting frameworks need to approach each other. The corporate sustainability reporting should shift to incorporating more long-term impacts and trends. As many companies have collected data for years, they should have data available for long-term reporting. Also, corporate sustainability reporting could be developed to cover the impact analysis of their products and services. If it is possible to have the supply chain sustainability reported and audited, it should be also possible to create a reporting framework on the product and service impact analysis in such a way, that there would be a direct connection between the product and the impact. Reporting greenhouse gases is doubtless useful, however, it does not tell us the impact on temperature and further impacts on habitat resulting from temperature increases. Furthermore, habitat changes will affect individual species. Research exists on all these issues, so creating the appropriate metrics and reporting framework should be possible. Then a company could report that their emissions would increase temperature by n units over m years, units chosen so that they make sense to users. A description of the temperature increase could be incorporated into the reporting. A further step would be presenting the same information about which are the impacts of their products to environment.

Wildlife NGOs could develop more transparent and point in time reporting metrics, the same way companies are reporting their financial and sustainability information. These would be in addition to trend based reports. Such reports could be for instance some proportional reports, house sparrows by agricultural land area, or even more precisely, house sparrows by acre of wheat field and corn field, or number of red kites lost in power line and wind turbine accidents. These reports should be available swiftly to be comparable to the financial statements, preferably matching the corporate reporting issuance schedule after the period end. Any metrics which could be used by companies directly would link the corporate reporting to the nature organisation reporting and goals.

All reporting needs explanatory comments, so the reporting metrics alone does not improve the user understanding about the meaning of a reported data. Explanations could also be prepared and at least partly standardised to reduce the time spent to produce the reporting.

For cultured landscapes the reporting could take more into account the development of the cultural land, agricultural and urban, and also the human population there. In Europe the total population is rather stagnant, however, the population is concentrating in bigger cities and countryside is becoming less populated. When there are less people, there is also less human waste available for feeding, which may have an impact to such species as the house sparrow. Urban areas, on the other hand, attract some species, so house sparrow populations may increase in those areas. Those species that need open spaces and fields, such as red kites, would have to move away when cities expand, which may have an impact on the distribution of the species.

To conclude, it is evident that environmental reporting within sustainability reporting is such a multifaceted area that creating one simple reporting framework linking wildlife NGOs and corporate life is challenging. More research and dialogue among the many actors would be necessary to build such links.

Notes

1 BTO (2015).
2 RSPB (undated a).
3 RSPB (undated b).
4 BTO (2015).
5 RSPB (undated a).
6 RSPB (undated b).
7 WCED (1987).
8 Global Reporting Initiative (undated).
9 FEE (2000).
10 RSPB (undated e).
11 IUCN (2016).
12 RSPB (undated d).
13 RSPB (undated e).
14 Department for Environment, Food and Rural Affairs (2013).
15 Greenhouse Gas Protocol (undated).
16 European Parliament and of the Council. Directive 2014/95/EU on the Disclosure of Non-financial and Diversity Information.
17 Hines (1989); Morgan (1988).
18 IFRS (2018), OB2.
19 Scapens (1994).
20 IFRS (2018), QC5.
21 Ibid., QC19.
22 Center for Audit Quality (2016).
23 Ibid.
24 Ibid.
25 Ibid.
26 Ibid.
27 KPMG (2017).
28 Global Reporting Initiative (undated).
29 Sustainability Accounting Standards Board (undated).
30 United Nations (undated).
31 IUCN (undated).
32 IUCN (2016).
33 RSPB (undated c).
34 Mrosovsky (1997).
35 IUCN (2016).
36 Rackham (1986).
37 Anderson (2006).
38 IUCN (2016).
39 Ibid.
40 Die Welt (2018); translated by chapter author.
41 European Parliament and of the Council. Directive 2009/147/EC on the Conservation of Wild Birds.
42 Whatis.com (undated).
43 Die Welt (2017).
44 RSPB (2016).
45 RSPB (undated a).
46 Ibid.
47 RSPB (2016).
48 Heuck et al. (2013).

49 Wotton, S.R. et al. (2002).
50 Hötker et al. (2017).
51 Anderson (2006).
52 Heuck et al. (2013).
53 Hole et al. (2002).
54 RSPB (2016).
55 Carson (1962).
56 Baker (1967).

References

Anderson, T. (2006) *Human Commensalism and Pest Management: Biology of the Ubiquitous House Sparrow: From Genes to Populations.* Oxford: Oxford University Press.
Baker, J. A. (1967) *The Peregrine.* New York: Harper & Row.
BTO (2015) Birds of Conservation Concern 4: the Red List for Birds. Retrieved from www.bto.org/science/monitoring/psob.
Carson, R. (1962) *Silent Spring.* Boston, MA: Houghton Mifflin.
Center for Audit Quality (2016) *Questions on Non-GAAP Measures.* Washington, DC: Center for Audit Quality.
Department for Environment, Food and Rural Affairs (2013) *Environmental Reporting Guidelines: Including Mandatory Greenhouse Gas Emissions Reporting Guidance.* London: Department for Environment, Food and Rural Affairs.
Die Welt (2017) Deutschland ist viel zu grün. *Die Welt,* 7 September.
Die Welt (2018) Nirgends haben es Vögel so schwer wie hier. *Die Welt,* 25 January.
Global Reporting Initiative (undated) Sustainability Reporting. Retrieved from www.globalreporting.org/information/sustainability-reporting/Pages/default.aspx
Greenhouse Gas Protocol (undated) Funders. Retrieved from www.ghgprotocol.org/funders.
FEE (2000) *Towards a Generally Accepted Framework for Environmental Reporting.* European Federation of Accountants (FEE).
European Parliament and of the Council. Directive 2009/147/EC on the Conservation of Wild Birds.
European Parliament and of the Council. Directive 2014/95/EU on the Disclosure of Non-financial and Diversity Information.
Heuck, C. et al. (2013), The Potential Distribution of the Red Kite in Germany. *Journal of Ornithology* 154: 911–921.
Hines R. D. (1989) Financial Accounting Knowledge, Conceptual Framework Projects and the Social Construction of the Accounting Profession. *Accounting, Auditing & Accountability Journal* 2(2): 72–92.
Hole, D. G. et al. (2002) Widespread Local House-Sparrow Extinctions. *Nature* 418: 931–932.
Hötker, H. et al. (2017) Red Kites and Wind Farms – Telemetry Data from the Core Breeding Range. In J. Köppel (ed.), *Wind Energy and Wildlife Interactions.* New York: Springer.
IFRS (2018) Conceptual Framework. Retrieved from www.ifrs.org/projects/2018/conceptual-framework.
IUCN (2016) *Guidelines for the Application of IUCN Red List of Ecosystems Categories and Criteria.* Gland: IUCN.
IUCN (undated) Introduction. Retrieved from www.iucnredlist.org/about/introduction.

KPMG (2017) *The Survey of Corporate Responsibility Reporting 2017*. London: KPMG.

Morgan G. (1988) Accounting as Reality Construction: Towards a New Epistemology for Accounting Practice. *Accounting, Organizations and Society* 13(5): 477–485.

Mrosovsky, N. (1997), IUCN's Credibility Critically Endangered. *Nature* 389: 436.

Rackham, O. (1986). *The History of the Countryside: The Full Fascinating Story of Britain's Landscape*. London: Dent.

RSPB (undated a) House Sparrow. Retrieved from www.rspb.org.uk/birds-and-wild life/wildlife-guides/bird-a-z/house-sparrow.

RSPB (undated b) Red Kite. Retrieved from www.rspb.org.uk/birds-and-wildlife/ wildlife-guides/bird-a-z/red-kite.

RSPB (undated c) UK Conservation Status Explained. Retrieved from www.rspb.org. uk/birds-and-wildlife/wildlife-guides/uk-conservation-status-explained#8vXWG zKPZSqTr0bC.99.

RSPB (undated d) Corporate Supporters. Retrieved from www.rspb.org.uk/join-and-donate/join-us/corporate-supporters.

RSPB (undated e) The Story Behind the Red List. Retrieved from www.rspb.org.uk/ birds-and-wildlife/wildlife-guides/uk-conservation-status-explained/#8Lh9D8LZ RMPFKlpe.99.

RSPB (2016) *Defend Nature*. Sandy: RSPB.

Sustainability Accounting Standards Board (undated) Retrieved from www.sasb.org.

Scapens, R. W. (1994) Never Mind the Gap: Towards an Institutional Perspective of Management Accounting Practices. *Management Accounting Research* 5(3–4): 301–321.

United Nations (undated) Sustainable Development Goals. Retrieved from www. un.org/sustainabledevelopment/development-agenda.

Whatis.com (undated) Retrieved from http://whatis.techtarget.com/definition/preci sion-agriculture-precision-farming.

World Commission on Environment and Development (1987) *Our Common Future*. Oxford: Oxford University Press.

Wotton, S.R. et al. (2002), Breeding Status of the Red Kite Milvus Milvus in Britain in 2000. *Bird Study* 49(3): 278–286.

15 Deforestation risk and the tissue industry in Italy

Silvio Bianchi Martini, Federica Doni and Antonio Corvino

Introduction

Over the past few decades, the protection of our planet's natural resources and the risk of species extinction have become increasingly crucial matters not only for scientists, ecologists and conservationists but also for governments, economists, managers, accountants, investors and financial analysts. Recently, several studies have highlighted the key role of accountants – especially environmental accountants – in preserving natural resources and developing new tools to help companies to evaluate, disclose and account for their role in the preservation of species and natural ecosystems.

The focus of this chapter is to assess how accounting and narrative reporting can support companies to reduce the risk of deforestation within the tissue industry. In more detail, we aim to identify companies' strategies and policies aimed at preventing the risk of species extinction in plant life. Hence, our central question is: what is the role of accounting and narrative disclosures in corporate strategy put in place by the players working in the tissue industry?

Background: deforestation risk and forest certifications

The latest IPCC climate change report (IPCC, 2014) highlights the impacts of environmental issues due to the rising atmospheric concentration of anthropogenic greenhouse gas (GHG) emissions, including methane (CH_4), nitrous oxide (N_2O) and, in particular, carbon dioxide (CO_2). The latter has reached unprecedented levels, despite several initiatives designed to reduce emissions and limit global climate change. The IPCC report emphasizes that the presence of those particles determines oceanic and atmospheric warming, rising sea levels and acidification, and the polar ice and snow melt since the mid-20th century (IPCC, 2014). If industrial activities and population growth continue at their current levels, the concentration of GHG emissions into the atmosphere will further increase, with attendant deleterious and pervasive effects on global health, mainly due to air and water pollution.

However, further environmental stresses upon global populations – both human and non-human – have arisen because of continuing deforestation and general land degradation. While concerns about land degradation have direct implications for agriculture productivity – by threatening to reduce global food production by up to 12% by 2030 – deforestation threatens the lives and livelihoods of an estimated 1.6 billion people, who benefit from forest assets such as food, clothing, natural remedies and housing (FAO, 2016). Since the 1990s, the global forest area declined by nearly 130 million hectares, most commonly in tropical regions. Despite some successes in deforestation reduction and improvements in land-use management, if current trends are not reversed forest decline will continue, resulting in the loss of almost 200 million hectares by 2030, and threatening the extinction of countless species of plants and animals (Shah, 2014). Biodiversity in general, including marine species and indigenous populations, is under threat because of the rapid change in the world's climate and environmental degradation.

Climate change increasingly impacts upon social issues, such as inequality, poverty and health problems. Although the global economic effects of climate change are still uncertain, the priority to scale up climate change mitigation and adaptation policies is clear; anthropogenic impact has already created circumstances that may be difficult to reverse, thereby greatly affecting future generations, despite a large net removal of CO_2 emissions from the atmosphere (IPCC, 2014) and actions to limit warming to below 2°C, relative to pre-industrial levels.

To give some context, around 31% of the land area on our planet is covered by forests, which offer homes for people and wildlife and provide vital oxygen: "Many of the world's most threatened and endangered animals live in forests, and 1.6 billion people rely on benefits forests offer, including food, fresh water, clothing, traditional medicine and shelter" (WWF, 2018). Nevertheless the benefits provided by forests are threatened by the risk – and reality – of deforestation which can be determined by different events, such as fires, clear-cutting for agriculture, ranching and development, unsustainable logging for timber, and degradation due to climate change, leading to ever more areas of forests under threat[1] with growing negative effects for a wide range of animal and plant species. Moreover, forests are crucial in the process of mitigation of climate change, deriving from their function in soaking up dioxygen carbon. However, deforestation can substantially decrease this carbon sink role and about 15% of all GHG emissions can be derived from deforestation. This phenomenon is more frequent in the tropical rainforests, where much of world's biodiversity is to be found.

Forest biodiversity is rapidly being lost due to deforestation, fragmentation and degradation of forests (Ndidi and Suleiman, 2009). Some organizations, such as WWF, are working to defend forests through the promotion of protected areas management and sustainable forestry. Given that forests are the largest storehouse of carbon after the oceans, reducing deforestation and forest degradation must constitute a significant element of any solution to the global climate change problem. WWF is carrying out different actions to ensure that the new climate change deal offers incentives to reduce emissions from deforestation and land degradation, and to develop national and regional approaches that tackle forest-based emissions and benefit local communities. From this perspective, collaboration between governments, NGOs, communities, companies and investors plays a crucial role in developing certification of responsible forest management practices, in combating illegal logging, in reforming trade policies and protecting forested areas.

At the European level, the Paris Agreement (2015) pointed out the critical role of the land use sector in reaching long-term climate mitigation objectives. This initiative is in line with the general approach to commit all sectors to the EU's 2030 emission reduction target, including the land use sector. In July 2016, the European Commission presented a legislative proposal to integrate GHG emissions, land use-change and forestry (LULUCF)[2] into the 2030 climate and energy framework. This proposal aims to establish "a binding commitment for each Member State to ensure that accounted emissions from land use are entirely compensated by an equivalent removal of CO_2 from the atmosphere through action in the sector, what is known as the "no debt rule". Although Member States undertook this commitment under the Kyoto Protocol up to 2020, the proposal preserves the commitment in EU law for the period 2021–2030 (EU, 2018). This proposal tries to simplify the current accounting procedure methodology under the Kyoto Protocol, and it sets a new EU governance process for controlling how Member States calculate emissions and removals from actions in their forests and agricultural land use.

One of the most important initiatives to increase consumer awareness and emphasize concern about deforestation and land degradation was the foundation (1993) of the Forest Stewardship Council (FSC). FSC (https://ic.fsc.org/en) includes "a broad-based coalition of environmental organizations, timber trade associations, indigenous peoples' representatives, academics and NGOs from 25 countries" (Elad, 2014). The FSC provides leadership in promoting good forest management through a set of ten principles (FSC, 2015) covering tenure and use rights and responsibilities, community relations and workers' rights, benefits from the forest, environmental impact, management planning, monitoring and assessment, maintenance of high conservation value forests and plantations. These principles show an approach based on the triple bottom line used by companies to manage sustainability issues. Indeed, FSC Principles 1–4 concern social issues (for example, protection of customary rights of indigenous people), principle 5 highlights economic issues of exploration forest companies and lastly, Principles 6–10 refer to environmental or eco-efficiency matters.

The integration of these three pillars within the FSC certification approach can combine the concept of auditing with sustainability disclosure (Swift et al., 2000; Elad, 2014). This scheme seeks to align the statutory financial audit with forest stewardship audit. However, the same difficulties about the credibility and transparency of financial statements issued by financial audit procedures arise in the context of forest stewardship audits. The mere compliance with the ten FSC principles would not ensure that forests are "well managed" (Elad, 2014). The concept of "well managed" led to different definitions and the development of several eco-labelling and certification models around the world. This situation highlights the absence of an agreement on a common definition of forest certification, revealing a schism between the two major global certification schemes FSC and the Programme for the Endorsement for Forest Certification (PEFC; www.pefc.org).

Although the PEFC's public disclosure requirements are less rigorous than those of the FSC, there is a low perception about the credibility of these certifications. Some scholars have pointed out that certified forests do not necessarily mean sustainably managed forests (Kuijik et al., 2009) and in some cases forest certification has been used to green-wash damaging forestry practices (Elad, 2014). The certification stewardship principles as well as audit standards cannot ensure a robust tool to monitor and report biodiversity and extinction of plant species (Swift et al., 2000).

Given the need to increase the credibility of forest management practices, accounting, accountability and narrative disclosure are playing an increasingly essential role. Indeed, over the last decade, accounting for biodiversity has been variously defined by accounting scholars and explored in different contexts (Gray, 1992; Jones, 1996; 2010; Jones and Matthews, 2000; Jones and Solomon, 2013). New developments in accounting for extinction of species are seeking to find ways through accounting of preserving biodiversity and species (Atkins and Atkins, 2016; Atkins and Maroun, 2018; Maroun and Atkins, 2018; Atkins et al., 2018).

From this perspective, our research question aims to explore how extinction accounting (EA) can play a relevant role in the formulation of corporate strategy. Specifically, our main purpose is to apply empirically the newly established theoretical framework (Atkins and Maroun, 2018) by examining in-depth three large and relevant companies operating in the tissue industry, namely Sofidel Group, SCA and Kimberly-Clark Corporation.

Research methodology and design

To this end, the pillars of our qualitative analysis are:

a) application of the emancipatory framework for extinction accounting and accountability (henceforth, EFEAA) developed by Atkins and Maroun (2018); and

b) use of the case study research approach, as the focus is on analytical rather than statistical generalizations (Eisenhardt, 1989; Ryan et al., 2002; Yin, 2008).

It should be noted that the EFEAA rests on the tenet that EA stimulates organizational change, significantly affecting corporate strategy formulation. Although GRI Framework and standards (see www.gri.org) and the IIRC framework could be integrated with the aim of improving environmental disclosure policy, the EFEAA aims to go further than mere reporting activity, since it compels the top management team to opt for an integrated thinking approach which underpins integrated reporting, with the objective of changing practice (Atkins and Maroun, 2018). In so doing, EA can represent a distinctive feature of the firm's mission and strategy and should lead to extinction prevention.

Drawing upon Atkins and Maroun (2018), the key elements of the EFEAA are reported below:

1 a proactive and progressive emancipatory accounting;
2 integrated thinking;
3 a moral and/or business imperative for preventing extinction;
4 motivations;
5 drivers; and
6 outcomes.

From an operating standpoint, such key elements will be applied to our three case studies in order to respond to a dashboard of questions suggested by Atkins and Maroun (2018). Our qualitative analysis mainly uses secondary data collected from the following sources:

• annual report;
• sustainability and integrated reports;
• management letters; and
• website documents.

The time frame covers the three-year period 2014–2016. Data collection activity was carried out during the second six months of 2017.

At this early stage, the empirical study could be enhanced by integrating the dataset with other information amenable to the internal documents (i.e. strategic maps, slides shared during the internal meetings, etc.) and interviews with some key members of the top and middle management team.

In order to safeguard the reliability of findings, the steps established by the research group composed of three members (namely one supervisor and two seniors) are shown in Table 15.1.

Table 15.1 Steps for the validity of findings

Type of validity	Steps
Internal validity	• Literature review • Analysis of relevant theoretical frameworks • Selection of the theoretical framework formulated by Atkins and Maroun (2018)
External validity	• Selection of the case study most appropriate for the qualitative study • In-depth details of the case company selected
Reliability	• Case study database • Description of data collection process • Triangulation of secondary data sources

The tissue industry

The analysis of the tissue industry takes root in the fact that it is built upon a significant consumption of raw materials and has a huge impact on environment, such as water, pulp paper and timber. The portfolio products include toilet paper, kitchen roll, paper handkerchiefs, facial tissues, wet wipes and paper napkins. More broadly, the tissue embraces a part of the paper industry and is categorized in two main segments:

1) consumer tissue; and
2) away from home (AFH) tissues.

Tissue is a capital-intensive industry, given that the building of new plant requires an investment of around 60–80 million euros. Today, this industry has interesting potential opportunities for growth, especially when a company is able to compete in different domestic contexts and to develop an innovative product with higher performance than those of its rivals. Intriguing market opportunities emanate from United States (US) while, in the European arena, the competitive rivalry is truly strong in Italy, France and Spain (PPI, 2017). Over the last three years, the pulp and, in general, the energetic commodities recorded remarkable price reductions, as a consequence of the economic slowdown in the emerging economies. Therefore, the incumbent advantage is the possibility to increase financial performance and to better feed the value creation process.

In this empirical study, we focused on the deforestation risk tied to the production of timber and on the firm actions specified from the perspective of EA. Such production coupled with palm soil, soya and cattle provokes the depletion of several hectares in the tropical forest (Global Canopy, 2017b). It is a risk of great relevance to the safeguarding of the natural ecosystem, in terms of the following items:

a) water cycle regulation;
b) soil fertility;
c) carbon sequestration and storage;
d) soil erosion prevention;
e) pollination; and
f) fresh water, food, fibre and habitat.

WWF envisages that by 2030 the deforestation area could be equivalent to nearly half the size of the Brazilian Amazon (Global Canopy, 2017b).

Given that other risky deforestation areas are in Latin America, South East Asia and Central and Eastern Africa, some international bodies have promoted guidelines and agreements meant to foster zero deforestation commitments, such as the Consumer Goods Forum, the New Declaration on Forests (Global Canopy, 2017a) and the CDP Forest Program. Furthermore, it is worthwhile mentioning the Paris Agreement and, in 2015, the decision to adopt the Sustainable Development Goals (SDGs) taken by the world leaders to the United Nations. Firms have to tackle a new challenge for which their strategic goals should be consistent to the SDGs in order to reduce their environmental footprint. Indeed, deforestation affects a turnover equal to around 941 billion dollars (CDP, 2017). Two years later, in the European context, CDP highlights a gap between some regions, such as France, and the Central and Eastern European countries (ibid.).

Forest management can be considered a concern common to the 17 SDGs, as there is a relevant impact on both Responsible Consumption and Production (SDG 12) and Climate Action (SDG 13). Deforestation is recognized as one of the pivotal determinants of GHG emissions and, more broadly, climate change. Given such relevance, among the 17 SDGs, SDG 15 – named "Life on Land" – focuses on forest management and stimulates firms to assess deforestation risk as part of their strategic approach. Specifically, the top management team should oversee specific operational, reputational and regulatory risks.

Sample selection

The case studies analysed have been selected among the key players firms in the tissue industry who have gained significant visibility in international markets and who, at the same time, hold a brands portfolio particularly appreciated by "business-to-business" customers, such as GDO, and "business-to-consumer" clients, such as the Public Administration, in the case of the AFH segment.

In addition, interesting elements of uniqueness can be seen in one of the companies analysed (i.e. SCA group), because it is an entrepreneurial entity strongly integrated from "upstream" to "downstream" in the tissue sector. In other words, it is one of the few companies that own hectares of forests grown for the production of raw materials to be used in the production of items related to the tissue segment.

Focusing on Sofidel, on the other hand, an element of uniqueness resides in the ownership structure that is characterized by the presence of two families, each holding a 50% stake in the company. Although this could be seen as a source of potential conflict and consequent management "paralysis", Sofidel has transformed from a small company operating only in the paper district of Lucca to an international player. We now turn to providing a brief description of the salient facts and features of the three large companies analysed.

Case study 1: Sofidel

The Sofidel Group (www.sofidel.com) was founded in 1966. After 50 years of activity, it is now one of the world leaders in the tissue paper production for hygienic and domestic use: toilet paper, kitchen towels, paper tissues, paper handkerchiefs and so on.

From its headquarters in Porcari, in Italy, Sofidel manages and coordinates the business activities of 19 companies distributed in Europe and the US.

These are paper mills for the production of tissue paper rollers, paper converters that make finished products, integrated systems (paper mills and paper converting) and offices that deal in sales, logistics and services. The paper production process is highly energy intensive and thus significantly affects planetary resources namely: forests, atmosphere and water.

The Group has therefore committed to reducing its environmental impacts through innovative strategies and technologies, which limit CO_2 emissions, respect the forest resource through the application of strict procurement policies and use water carefully.

Sofidel was the first Italian company, and the first at a global level in the tissue industry, to join the international WWF Climate Savers programme, based on the voluntary definition of consistent plans to reduce carbon dioxide emissions (see www.sofidel.com). In paper production, Sofidel mainly uses virgin pulp. Hence, the Group has implemented strict procurement policies regarding raw materials from forest resources. It usually selects suppliers who comply with the main forest preservation schemes. Almost all (around 99.7%) of the Group's virgin pulp comes from sources certified according to PEFC, FSC, FSC Controlled Wood and SFI standards. The consumer brands comprised in Sofidel's portfolio are Regina, Softis, Kitten Soft, Nalys, Yumi, Soft&Easy, Sopalin, Le Trèfle, Nouvelle, Thirst Pockets, Cosynel, Volare, Onda, Lycke and Forest. In the AFH and private label segments, Sofidel brands are respectively Papernet and Nicky.

Case study 2: SCA

SCA Hygiene Products AB (www.sca.com) manufactures and markets hygiene and forest products in Sweden and internationally. The company is based in Gothenburg, Sweden. SCA Hygiene Products AB operates as a subsidiary of Svenska Cellulosa Aktiebolaget (SCA). The core of business activities is SCA's vast forest holdings in northern Sweden, 2.6 million hectares of forest land, almost the area of Belgium. This is the largest private forest holding in Europe. Using this unique resource, SCA has built a well-invested industry, developed to create the highest possible value from the forest, a resource-efficient industry where the entire tree is used to create value. Its products include solid-wood products, pulp, kraftliner, publication papers and renewable energy. SCA's products are manufactured from raw materials grown in responsibly managed forests with respect for the ecological system and biological diversity. SCA's forest management is certified according to both FSC and PEFC. Hence, SCA complies with the guidelines for responsible forestry. In the personal care segment – equivalent to 29% of SCA's net sales generated in 2016 – the portfolio is composed of: Libero, Libresse, Nosotras, Saba and TENA. In the tissue segment – equivalent to 57% of SCA's net sales produced in 2016, its own brands are: Lotus, Regio, Tempo and Zewa. The remaining 14% of SCA's net sales are amenable to forest products.

Case study 3: Kimberly-Clark

Kimberly-Clark Corporation (www.kimberly-clark.com) was founded in 1872 and is headquartered in Dallas, Texas. It manufactures and markets personal care, consumer tissue, and professional products worldwide. It operates through three segments: Personal Care, Consumer Tissue, and K-C Professional. The Personal Care segment provides disposable diapers, training and youth pants, swimpants, baby wipes, feminine and incontinence care products, and other related products under the Huggies, Pull-Ups, Little Swimmers, GoodNites, and other brand names. The Consumer Tissue segment provides facial and bathroom tissues, paper towels, napkins, and related products under the Kleenex, Scott and other brands. Its policy statement, adopted in 2011, is "to design, manufacture and deliver its products and to operate its business in a way that protects the biosphere and promotes the sustainable use of natural resources upon which our businesses and stakeholders depend, including forests, water supplies and energy resources" (Kimberly-Clark, 2011). In particular, the fiber procurement policy aims to promote sustainable forest management practices by the Corporation's wood fiber suppliers that are economically viable, environmentally responsible and socially beneficial by considering supplier performance in the selection process (Kimberly-Clark, 2009).

Results

From our qualitative content analysis of secondary sources we find some interesting results. It is clear that EA plays a relevant role in the firm's strategic business plan, because the attempt to evaluate and report the impact of the absence of specific species (Atkins and Maroun, 2018) emerges from the disclosure of their common approach to "doing business".

From the analysis of the corporate reports, especially the section focused on vision and mission, we can summarize the following results. The guiding principle of Sofidel's approach can be summarized in the expression "Less is More", in other words the company seeks to obtain the maximum, in terms of values, products and services, while minimizing its "footprint", in terms of consumption of natural resources (Sofidel, 2013, p. 17).

The mission declared by SCA is "To sustainably develop, produce, market and sell value-added hygiene and forest products and services". Furthermore, one of the main strategic objectives disclosed in the last sustainability report is the following statement: "Contribute to a sustainable and circular society" (SCA, 2016, p. 8).

In Kimberly Clark, the mission is focused on emphasizing a steady commitment to safeguarding natural resources that are "consumed" in the production process. In this regard, the first paragraph in the Introduction of the 2014 sustainability report states that "Our mission to provide the essentials for a better life includes our commitment to protect the environment. It's difficult to imagine anything more essential than clean air, clean water and a healthy environment" (Kimberly-Clark, 2014, p. 26).

Given this empirical evidence, we can emphasize that stage no. 7 of the framework proposed by Atkins and Maroun (2018, table 2) with specific reference to the integration of EA into corporate strategy, is present in the reporting, because the priority to evaluate and, even more, to constantly strive to minimize the impact of the use of natural resources, of forests in particular in the tissue industry, is now a fundamental element of the three companies' vision and mission. This common approach, as known, can represent the "compass" in the definition and development of a company's strategic plan.

This integration can emerge not only in the development step of the corporate strategy but also in the implementation step. In these terms, it is interesting to highlight how the corporate governance model is characterized by the provision of specific committees and / or the presence of specific managerial functions that are able to support EA or sustainable management practices for EA.

Focusing on Sofidel, for instance, the Board of Directors puts in place a pervasive control on corporate social responsibility. On an operational level, it constantly relates to a CSR Director who, in turn, coordinates the CSR Committee.

In Kimberly-Clark, it is worth highlighting the establishment of the Sustainability Advisory Board that includes independent directors with high CSR skills and offers supervision to the CEO, the Executive Leadership Team and the Global Sustainability Team.

From the analysis of SCA, we highlight that the governance model includes the presence of the Environmental Committee and the Social Responsibility Committee. Both are concerned with outlining the principles and implementing the group's CSR policies.

More broadly, it is reasonable to believe that similar configurations of the corporate governance model can contribute to increasing the sensitivity to the protection and measurement of the harmful effects related to the extinction of species that is equivalent to deforestation in the specific context of the tissue industry,

Stage no. 7 of the aforementioned framework, however, can be considered partially satisfied from our findings on the EA disclosures in sustainability or integrated reports. In fact, it should be noted that, in two out of three of the case studies analysed, the environmental and economic risks of deforestation have been disclosed in the sustainability report.

We must also highlight that all three companies have taken the appropriate actions, consistent with stage 2 of the EFEAA, to limit their environmental footprint and consequently the risk of deforestation through the traceability and certification of raw materials (i.e. FSC and PEFC) as well as the ethical control of the supply chain.

Focusing specifically on traceability, SCA has developed a database through which it is possible to check the suppliers, the geographical area of origin and the species of timber, the distinctive characteristics of the cellulose and the data on the life cycle of the tree. In order to prevent the risk of deforestation and biodiversity protection, SCA manages five conservation parks covering a geographical extension of more than 10,000 hectares, exclusively for forest use.

In terms of supply chain monitoring, in 2016, thanks to the "TenP" project (Ten Principles), Sofidel launched the "Sustainable Supply Chain Self-Assessment Platform", in order to measure the environmental and social sustainability performance of its own providers.

Consistent with stage no. 3 of the EFEAA, it is insightful to note that in the three case studies analysed there is evidence from the disclosures of strong collaboration with international organizations dedicated to the protection and safeguard of the environment, such as Greenpeace, WWF, Global Compact, etc. Moreover, these organizations promote international awards and recognitions that constitute additional elements to consolidate the corporate image of the winners. In the tissue industry, in general, the awards concern market leadership in responsible fiber sourcing and in forest protection.

Lastly, in accordance with stage no. 4 of the EFEAA (Atkins and Maroun, 2018), it should also be noted that, in 2016, SCA planted about 37 million new seedlings in its forests. Kimberly-Clark, furthermore, in 2014, celebrated the 30th anniversary of the "Keep Korea Green" project which involved the planting of about 50 million trees. The uniqueness of this project lies in the fact that every Korean married couple is invited to plant a tree, in order to make the family aware of the protection of the environment for their children and, in general, for the next generations. Finally, Sofidel no longer uses raw material derived from Indonesian and Sumatra wood, because the forest heritage has become depleted in over fifty years by more than 40% while illegal cutting is around 70%.

Conclusion

Recent trends in environmental matters, especially the risk of land degradation and extinction species and the loss of forest biodiversity, require a relevant commitment by companies through the adoption of new frameworks for reporting on these topics (Atkins and Maroun, 2018). Organizations must consider the impact of their business activities on natural ecosystems as well as adopting preventative measures and promoting anti-extinction initiatives. Moreover, organizations must review the effectiveness of these activities. In particular, with reference to the tissue industry, the features of the paper production require a strict compliance with several principles (i.e. FSC, PEFC). Nevertheless, this compliance cannot ensure the effectiveness of sustainable forestry practices (Elad, 2014).

Given these premises, this chapter provides empirical evidence about the tissue industry applying the theoretical extinction accounting framework for narrative reporting on extinction-related issues. We selected three large companies and we carried out a multiple case studies analysis. In more detail, we have shown that the three companies analysed are acting in accordance with stages no. 2, 3, 4 and 7 of the EFEAA. These companies are controlling their supply chain management through traceability. Moreover, they are involved in relevant international initiatives in safeguarding natural resources and they usually obtain important awards for their socially responsible actions. In addition, one out of the three companies investigated discloses the whole process of extinction accounting into corporate strategy and integrated reporting in a holistic manner without separate disclosures on stand-alone reports or on a company website.

In summary, our main findings highlight that the tissue industry plays an effective role in overcoming or reducing deforestation risk by monitoring its environmental impact, adopting sustainable corporate governance practices and aligning itself to relevant initiatives for preventing land and forest degradation.

Notes

1 "We're losing 18.7 million acres of forests annually, equivalent to 27 soccer fields every minute" (WWF, 2018).
2 Human activities impact terrestrial sinks, through land use, land-use change and forestry (LULUCF) activities, consequently, the exchange of CO_2 (carbon cycle) between the terrestrial biosphere system and the atmosphere is altered. LULUCF activities play a crucial role in the mitigation of climate change by increasing the removals of greenhouse gases (GHGs) from the atmosphere or decrease emissions by sources leading to an accumulation of carbon stocks (UNFCCC, 2018).

References

Atkins J. and Atkins B. (2016). *The Business of Bees: An Integrated Approach to Bee Decline and Corporate Responsibility*, Routledge, New York.

Atkins J., Barone E., Maroun W. and Atkins B. (2018). From the Big Five to the Big 4? Exploring Extinction Accounting for the Rhinoceros, *Accounting, Auditing and Accountability Journal*, in press.

Atkins J. and Maroun W. (2018). Integrated Extinction Accounting and Accountability: Building an Ark, *Accounting, Auditing and Accountability Journal*, in press.

CDP (2017). *Learning from the Leaders*, CDP, Berlin.

Eisenhardt K.M. (1989). Building Theories from Case Study Research, *Academy of Management*, vol. 14, issue 4, pp. 532–550.

Elad C. (2014). Forest Certification and Biodiversity Accounting in the Congo Basin Countries, in M.J. Jones (ed.), *Accounting for biodiversity*, Routledge, New York, pp. 189–212.

EU (2018). Land Use and Forestry Regulation for 2021–2030, https://ec.europa.eu/clima/lulucf_en.

FAO (2016). *Forests and Agriculture: Land-Use Challenges and Opportunities*, State of the World's Forests report, FAO, Rome.

FSC (2015). The Ten Rules for Responsible Forest Management, https://ic.fsc.org/en/what-is-fsc-certification/principles-criteria/fscs-10-principles.

Global Canopy (2017a). *Achieving 2020: How Can the Private Sector Meet Global Goals of Eliminating Commodity-Driven Deforestation?*, Global Canopy, Oxford.

Global Canopy (2017b). *Linking Deforestation Risks to Investment Value*, November, Global Canopy, Oxford.

Gray R.H. (1992), Accounting and Environmentalism: An Exploration of the Challenge of Gently Accounting for Accountability, Transparency and Sustainability, *Accounting, Organizations and Society*, vol. 17, issue. 5, pp. 399–425.

IPCC (2014). *Climate Change 2014: Synthesis Report*, Contribution of Working Groups I, II and III to the Fifth Assessment Report of the Intergovernmental Panel on Climate Change, ed. R.K. Pachauri and L.A. Meyer, IPCC, Geneva, www.ipcc.ch/pdf/assessment-report/ar5/syr/AR5_SYR_FINAL_SPM.pdf (accessed 10 March 2018).

Jones M.J. (1996). Accounting for Biodiversity, *British Accounting Review*, vol. 28, pp. 281–303.

Jones M.J. (2010). Accounting for the Environment: Towards a Theoretical Perspective for Environmental Accounting and Reporting, *Accounting Forum*, vol. 34, pp. 123–138.

Jones M.J. and Matthews J. (2000). *Accounting for Biodiversity: A Natural Inventory of the Elan Valley Nature Reserve*, ACCA, London.

Jones M.J. and Solomon J.F. (2013). Problematising Accounting for Biodiversity, *Accounting, Auditing and Accountability Journal*, vol. 26, issue 5, pp. 668–687.

Kimberly-Clark (2009). Fiber Procurement, www.cms.kimberly-clark.com/umbraco images/UmbracoFileMedia/FiberProcurementPolicy_umbracoFile.pdf.

Kimberly-Clark (2011). Update to "Protection of Biosphere" and "Sustainable Use of Natural Resources", adopted on 25 October 1991, Protection of Environment, adopted on 1 November 2011, www.cms.kimberly-clark.com/umbracoimages/UmbracoFileMedia/Protection_of_Environment_umbracoFile.pdf.

Kimberly-Clark (2014). *Leading the World in Essentials for a Better Life*, sustainability report, Kimberly-Clark.

Kuijik M., Putz F.E. and Zagt R. (2009). *Effects of Forest Certification on Biodiversity*, Tropenbos International, Wageningen, the Netherlands.

Maroun W. and Atkins J. (2018). The Emancipatory Potential of Extinction Accounting: Exploring Current Practice in Integrated Reports, *Accounting Forum*, in press.

Ndidi E.C. and Suleiman G.A. (2009). Species Diversity Patterns along the Forest Savanna Boundary in Nigeria, *Management of Environmental Quality: An International Journal*, vol. 20, issue 1, pp.64–72.

PPI (2017). Pulp and Paper Price Index, www.risiinfo.com/service/prices.

Ryan B., Scapens R. and Theobald, M. (2002). *Research Method and Methodology in Finance and Accounting*, Thomson, London.

SCA (2016). *SCA's Vision is "Dedicated to Improving Well-Being through Leading Hygiene and Health Solutions"*, sustainability report, SCA.

Shah, A. (2014). Loss of Biodiversity and Extinctions, *Global Issues*, 19 January, www.globalissues.org/article/171/loss-of-biodiversity-and-extinctions (accessed 10 March 2018).

Sofidel (2013). *Endless Care, Innovative Life*, integrated report, Sofidel.

Swift T.A., Hamprey C. and Gor V. (2000). Great Expectations? The Dubious Financial Legacy of Quality Audits, *British Journal of Management*, vol. 11, issue 1, pp. 31–45.

UNFCCC (2018). Land Use, Land-Use Change and Forestry (LULUCF), http://unfccc.int/land_use_and_climate_change/lulucf/items/1084.php

WWF (2018). Threats: Deforestation: Overview, www.worldwildlife.org/threats/deforestation.

Yin R.K. (2008). *Case Study Research: Design and Methods*, fourth edition, Sage Publishing, New York.

III.3

Extinction accounting in the USA, Mexico and Canada

16 Accounting for captive belugas

A whale of a business

Aris Solomon and Margaret Clappison

Introduction

When the Vancouver Aquarium was first opened there was far less knowledge and understanding of animals in general, and even less of cetaceans such as Beluga whales, than today. Animals have often been considered as having less value than humans and have therefore not always been respected in industrialized counties. Societal norms have, however, altered over time. For example, in a human species context, there are now international human rights to ensure "freedom from fear and want for all, without discrimination" (OHCHR, 2012, p. 11). In the same way, societies' norms around animal species have evolved – this is certainly the case for cetaceans who "are wide-ranging, deep diving, exceptionally active, highly intelligent, extremely social" beings (ibid.) but it seems that often there is not the same consideration given to cetaceans as to the human species. This chapter begins by discussing the lives of belugas and other whales, as well as dolphins in aquariums, compared with their lives in the oceans.

The life of cetaceans in aquariums

The Vancouver Aquarium was founded almost 70 years ago. Cetaceans such as belugas and killer whales were kept for a breeding program (Hrynyshyn and Sorg, 2006). In contrast, MarineLand, which was opened around the same time, was created as a company with the motive of using cetaceans and other animals mainly for people's amusement (Vancouver et al., 2016). By 2006 only a small proportion of cetaceans born in the Vancouver Aquarium had survived with losses as follows: nine orcas, seven narwhals, six belugas, and four Pacific white-sided dolphins (Hrynyshyn and Sorg, 2006). This high mortality rate suggests these beings' life spans may be shorter in captivity (many survived only ten years or less; ibid.). However, MarineLand does not state the number of cetacean deaths, although records state that 18 whales and dolphins died between 1999 and 2006 (Niagara This Week, 2006). It is sad to note that five of those who died were under seven years old (ibid.). In contrast, when these creatures are in their natural environment they have a similar life span to humans.

In Canada whales and /or dolphins are kept in captivity in the Vancouver aquarium located in Vancouver British Columbia and in MarineLand located in Niagara Falls Ontario. Although Canada has banned the capturing and exporting of belugas since 1992, they remain on display in Canada (Hrynyshyn and Sorg, 2006). The Vancouver Aquarium keeps, breeds, and exports cetaceans (belugas, orcas, and dolphins) while MarineLand imports them from Russia (ibid.). "MarineLand Ontario in Canada is still importing live-caught cetaceans, at a time when the practice of keeping cetaceans in captivity there is controversial" (Rose et al., 2009, p. 9). MarineLand imported 10 dolphins and 36 belugas from the wild between 1999 and 2008 and has not given any indication it will stop this practice (ibid.).

Belugas are one of the smallest whales, which makes it manageable to keep them in small swimming-pool-sized tanks (Hrynyshyn and Sorg, 2006). If the whales survive capture and transportation to an aquarium they are put on display and made to perform tricks (ibid.). In 2005, MarineLand had 26 belugas in captivity while the Vancouver Aquarium had four (ibid.). Although this industry claims they are helping to conserve, breed and teach the public to understand these beings, it could be suggested that keeping whales and dolphins in captivity has led to their demise, at the same time generating profits from the whales. "Worst yet, it desensitizes people to captivity's inherent cruelties – for virtually all captive marine mammals, the world is a tiny enclosure, and life is devoid of naturalness" (ibid., 2006, p. IV).

> The claim that conservation is a primary purpose of the public display industry as a whole is highly misleading at best. Fewer than five to 10 percent of zoos, dolphinaria, and aquaria are involved in substantial conservation programs either in natural habitat or in captive settings, and the amount spent on these programs is a mere fraction of the income generated by the facilities.
>
> (Rose et al., 2009, p. 4)

Life of cetaceans in their native habitat

Cetaceans such as the Atlantic right whales, Pacific right whales, beluga whales, as well as narwhals and dolphins (this includes orcas, also called killer whales) swim in Canadian waters. For example, beluga whales live in the northern coastal waters of the Northern hemisphere and are native to Canada, Greenland, Russian Federation, Svalbard and Jan Mayen, and the United States (International Union for Conservation of Nature and Natural Resources, 2017). Their main habitats in Canada are the Eastern Beaufort Sea/Beaufort Sea (Canada and Alaska), Cumberland Sound, Ungava Bay, Hudson Bay, the St Lawrence River, the Eastern High Arctic/Baffin Bay (about 30% migrate to West Greenland to overwinter (ibid.). In contrast, the Atlantic right whale migrates into the northern waters for the summer in the Bay of Fundy in Canada and as far as Greenland (Cupka and Murphy, 2005). In contrast, the Pacific right whales migrate into northern Asia and Canadian waters (Reilly and

B, 2015). Many of these beings are facing potential extinction. For example, in 2008 the *Delphinapterus leucas* (beluga) in the Cook Inlet were determined to be near threatened (International Union for Conservation of Nature and Natural Resources, 2017). In Canada it was discovered that there are seven different distinct Beluga populations where only three of the beluga populations are not yet endangered (Hrynyshyn and Sorg, 2006). Not only are these beings considered threatened, it seems they are not necessarily appreciated and valued for their intrinsic value.

Morality

Unfortunately, in some societies, animals have not always been considered sentient and have been afforded less priority than humans, often leading to their use and abuse. With increased scientific observation and philosophic research, animal welfare (implying humans determine what is acceptable in a particular situation) and animal rights (similar to human rights such as the right to avoid pain and abuse) have gained traction (Carbone, 2004). The concept of morality is subjective and determines how, humans relate to each other in the world as they judge what is right and wrong. Morality has been considered unique to humans such that species tended to be divided on moral principles such that humans were considered to have moral values but animals none (ibid.). An important debate has been the consideration of what constitutes a sentient being. One definition is that a sentient being has intelligence, consciousness, awareness and self-analysis, and is able to feel distress, pain, anxiety, suffering and fear (Bekoff and Goodall, 2000; Carbone, 2004). Furthermore, the concept of morals being intrinsically appropriate to particular species attributes is vital (Carbone, 2004). However, cognitive ethology (the study of animals' minds) takes the previous definition further to encapsulate animal's beliefs and how they think (Bekoff, 2007). Charles Darwin suggested animals experience emotions such as guilt, joy, shame, pride, dejection, grief, love, devotion, determination, astonishment, shyness, and modesty (Darwin, 1871). Therefore, the emotions exhibited by animals to varying degrees, seem to span the total range of human emotions, which also varies depending on the person. There is little fundamental difference between man and "higher" mammals in their mental faculties (ibid., p. 66). Thus the differences between humans and animals, such that, "similarities and contrasts among species are nuance or shades of gray, not stark black-and-white differences" (Bekoff, 2007, p. 33). Thus this results in a continuity in evolution (Bekoff and Goodall, 2000). Furthermore, since animals are sentient, "their own pain and suffering is no less important [than human] . . . pain and suffering" (ibid., p. 62).

The life of cetaceans in the ocean

Once the animals are considered sentient, then humans should, it may be argued, adjust their ways and treat them fairly and with respect. Beluga whales, other whales, and dolphins are mammals – like humans. They have the same brain structures allowing them to process emotions although cetaceans do not tend to hide their emotions (Bekoff, 2010). The females of sperm whales take turns babysitting, so that the young whales are protected while the mother is finding food (ibid.). These beings can navigate over great distances to different locations (Barringer, 2012). This compares to people traveling from their home to a summer cottage on a different continent. Humans are social beings that use the voice to communicate with other. Likewise, belugas and other cetaceans are very social and use acoustic communication (ibid.). Noc, a beluga in captivity, decided to learn English words and then told a diver to get out of the water (Bekoff and Goodall, 2000). Dolphins chuckle when happy and have long-term social relationships. Killer whales allow their curious youngsters to explore their environment whilst monitoring for danger (Bekoff, 2002). In addition, they have strong family ties so if one being in the family unit (pod) is captured it can negatively affect all of them – similar to a situation where a child is kidnapped in an extended family (ibid.). Humans also chuckle, have long-term strong relationships with the extended family, and diligently watch over their young children while allowing them to explore their environment and be curious. This suggests that there are many similarities between these beings and humans. In a documentary on belugas in St Laurence, the researchers found a live baby beluga beached and decided to try and return it to the sea (Suzuki, 2017). The baby beluga was found by a group of males, which stayed for an hour to make sure the baby was safe, then dispersed to find a mother beluga (ibid.). Between the time they left and when a mother came (an hour and a half later), the baby remained calm. It seemed that they recognized the researchers were no threat to the child.

While we may not be surprised that cetaceans help their own kind, helping others including humans shows that they have compassion for those in need of assistance. One instance of this was a beluga who saved a diver when she was unable to return to the surface of the water by gently grasping her leg to propel her to the surface (Bekoff, 2010). In another instance a dolphin helped two pygmy sperm whales, stuck on a New Zealand beach by leading them back into deep water (ibid., p. 86). Stories like these suggest that these creatures have a moral sense that compels them to help. This is similar to a human's good deeds – making a choice to make a difference and another being.

If animals are both sentient then our human language should perhaps change to show respect and compassion for the animals. Are they really "in the wild" or is this a human perception that arose because we do not understand them and assume they are not as advanced as humans are. By labelling these beings as "wild", we are perhaps still considering them as lesser to humans. Instead, we could call them friends from the sea and learn their language to understand them. We do not have to take care of them. We are responsible to clean up the mess we have made of the environment since we have polluted their home environment rendering them uninhabitable. Thus, we have the responsibility to keep the environment clean for future generations of all beings on this world.

Animals (beings from the sea) in aquariums tend to be stressed because they live their lives in an environment that tries to replicate their home but still live unnatural lives – impoverished lives (Bekoff, 2002). In addition, these beings are denied rights and freedoms as they are loaned, bought and sold (ibid.). This is similar to slavery where certain groups of people were clearly considered to have less rights than others, being denied rights and freedoms and families were torn apart as slaves were bought and sold.

In 2012 some park attractions tried to obtain a license to purchase 18 Belugas even though experts stated "there is no way even the best captive situation has even the slightest approximation to their home] environment" (Barringer, 2012, para.6). Thus treating them with respect and consideration is vital. In contrast, other experts insist that capture, confinement and breeding programs are essential to conserve and understand these beings (ibid.). Aquariums have made profits from allowing humans to play with or view these beings (ibid.). This splits up families of cetaceans (pods) and can cause evident grief.

Animals (including humans) interact with others though their actions, reactions, impulses, senses, and perceptions which give meaning to their subjective universe. Human actions, perceptions, and emotions colour, create and shape the human world. In the same way dolphins, belugas, and other cetaceans create and shape their world. This is because they are intelligent, have extensive cognitive abilities, complex language and abstract thinking (Marino, 2013). Like humans, they are self-aware and live in a complex society (ibid.). They too use their actions, reactions, impulses, senses, perceptions, and emotions to give meaning and colour to their world.

Whales and dolphins in human care

Ceta Base estimates that, as of June 2017, there were:

> approximately 623 captive whales and dolphins in human care in the US and Canada. Of this total, 133 (21%) were acquired through capture, 455 (73%) are the result of captive births and 34 (6%) are the result of rescue and were declared unreleasable. There is also 01 animal currently in rehabilitation. They are exhibited in 34 facilities, 32 in the U.S. and 02 in Canada, for the purpose of public display, research and rescue/rehabilitation.
>
> (Ceta Base, 2017)

Canada and the Vancouver Aquarium

Currently there are no belugas at the Vancouver Aquarium. However, the Vancouver Aquarium owns five belugas outside the facility; this number is made up of three transfers and two born outside the facility. In addition the Vancouver Aquarium owns one orca born outside the facility. It is somewhat concerning that eleven Belugas died between 1976 and 2017. Further five of the eleven (45.45%) deaths were young belugas with only one living past four years of age (see Appendix A.2). The Vancouver Aquarium has had a total of sixteen belugas and of these eleven died (68.75% died). When all cetaceans are included there are eight alive and forty have died, making a death rate of 83.33% between 1976 and 2010.

MarineLand: captive belugas

MarineLand bought twenty-eight belugas from Russia between 1998 and 2008 (all except one beluga was captured from the Sea of Okhotsk in Russia (see Appendix A.4). It seems that MarineLand purchased and imported beluga between 2004 and 2008 despite the keeping of wild-caught cetaceans in captivity was controversial (Rose et al., 2009). They also imported 10 wild-caught Black Sea bottlenose dolphins around the same time (ibid.). As with other live captures, the cetaceans are traumatized, put in shallow pools, and forced to eat dead fish (ibid.). MarineLand bought females to start a breeding program even though the taking of so many females from the wild could be a problem for their complex society (ibid.). As a result of the breeding programme, between 2006 and 2013 there were thirty baby belugas born in captivity. There was, however, a poor survival rate for the baby belugas (see Appendix A.4). This raises questions about whether the wellbeing of the cetaceans was subordinated to profit maximization.

United States and Georgia: captive belugas

Currently the Georgia Aquarium has three belugas in the Aquarium (see Appendix B.1). All belugas were born in captivity although this aquarium does not own any of them. The belugas are on lease from MarineLand, SeaWorld San Antonio, and Shedd Aquarium (see Appendix B.1). In June 2012, the aquarium applied to import eighteen belugas from Russia but their application was rejected by the United States National Oceanic and Atmospheric Administration Fisheries in 2013 (Guardian, 2015). The aquarium appealed and a US Federal Judge ruled that they could not import the belugas (McKay, 2015). Although the Georgia Aquarium applied to import the belugas (therefore having ownership), the belugas were intended to be sent to other aquaria such as SeaWorld of Florida, SeaWorld of Texas, SeaWorld of California, and Shedd Aquarium (NMFS, 2015).

Mystic Marinelife Aquarium and SeaWorld Orlando: captive belugas

The aquariums Mystic Marinelife Aquarium and Orlando SeaWorld have only two belugas each (see Appendices B.2 and B.3). Mystic Marinelife has a beluga on lease from MarineLand (see Appendix B.2). SeaWorld Orlando has a beluga born in captivity on lease from another SeaWorld in San Antonio (see Appendix B.3).

SeaWorld San Antonio, SeaWorld San Diego, and John G. Shedd Aquarium: captive belugas

In contrast to the aquariums discussed above, SeaWorld San Antonio, SeaWorld San Diego, and John G. Shedd Aquarium have many belugas. All three have wild belugas caught from Hudson Bay, Canada. SeaWorld San Antonio has the most belugas at four captured wild beluga and five born in captivity at their facility) (see Appendix B.4). The John G. Shedd Aquarium has two wild captured belugas and 4 born in captivity at their facility (see Appendix B.6). However, they own two while the other two are on lease (see Appendix B.6). Lastly, SeaWorld San Diego has the fewest belugas at two wild caught and three born in captivity (see Appendix B.5). Two belugas born in captivity are on lease: one is from SeaWorld San Antonio and the other one from MarineLand (see Appendix B.5). All these Facilities form part of a consortium of aquariums that have a breeding program which they say is needed for research, and education (Morell, 2012). By keeping belugas or breeding them in captivity, the risk from predators and starvation has been removed, yet they tend to die around 30 instead of 50 to 60 when free (Page, 2012). Perhaps it is simply that in captivity they lose purpose and self-determination, which means they lose the will to live.

While the parks and aquariums say they need belugas in captivity for research and education, it is also possible that income is an overriding reason as they can generate $1 million a year (Kestin, 2018, para 1). It is even possible for owners

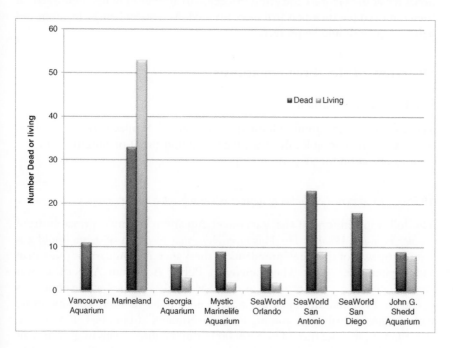

Figure 16.1 Summary of dead and living beluga, Canada and the USA, 1975–2017

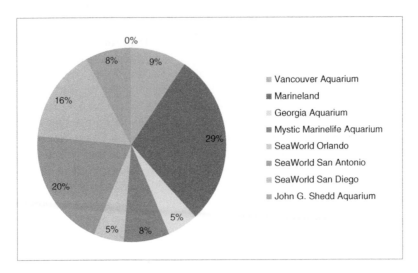

Figure 16.2 Dead beluga by place, Canada and the USA, 1975–2017

of belugas to use them as collateral for loans, as well as being able to cover them with life insurance (ibid.). Customers can swim with a beluga whale for an additional fee at the Georgia aquarium (Morell, 2012). Not only has their freedom been removed but their personal space invaded. As sentient beings, freedom and personal space should be protected.

Overview of the three aquariums

The Vancouver Aquarium

The Vancouver Aquarium[1] is located in Vancouver's Stanley Park, an area held in great esteem among locals. It is a registered non-profit organization and has been in operation for 61 years.

1956–2018: a period of changing consensus towards cetaceans in captivity

The following history of the Vancouver Aquarium is drawn primarily from *People, Fish and Whales, The Vancouver Aquarium Story*, an 88-page booklet is written by two of the three presidents of the Vancouver Aquarium (Newman and Nightingale, 2006). The Vancouver Public Aquarium Association was incorporated by a group of aquarists on 22 March 1951. The "whale pool" was opened in 1971 and the Aquarium was intended to be "entirely self supporting with no operational funds coming from government" (ibid., p. 17). Newman and Nightingale state that "The $300,000 from the three levels of government was entirely used up to create the building and its empty displays" (ibid., p. 18).

Figure 16.3 Entrance to the Vancouver Aquarium, 2017

The tanks were stocked as a result of a fundraising effort involving the Hudson's Bay department store in downtown Vancouver raising $12,000:

> The accountant told us we had to draw 125,000 in our first year or we'd be out of business . . . We got our 125,000 in the first month . . . By the year's end a total of 340,870 had passed through the turnstiles . . . the official city population at the time of was 344,833 . . .
>
> (Newman and Nightingale, 2006, p. 19)

The 2016 Vancouver Aquarium Annual Report discloses "record attendance" (Vancouver Aquarium Annual Report, 2016, p. 2) although no figure is disclosed. However, we do have a number for 2015 of 1,116,075 visitors (Vancouver Aquarium Annual Report, 2015, p. 4). The 2016 Canadian census recorded a population of 631,486 for Vancouver (Statistics Canada, 2016). Today a better comparison would be Greater Vancouver with a population of 2,463,431 (ibid.). The Vancouver Aquarium is also reported to be a major tourist attraction. TripAdvisor rate the aquarium as number 8 out of 360 things to do in Vancouver, while Tourism Vancouver ranks it as number 2 out of 10 (2018 data).

There is a chequered history relating to whales captured or bred and displayed. Newman and Nightingale (2006) give a rendition of the capture and demise of the orca "Moby Doll" whereas Sorg (2013) provides a rather different report of events which involved a killer whale being harpooned but not killed, being instead brought to the aquarium and displayed as an exhibit until it died 87 days later (ibid.).

Vancouver aquarium had 11 orcas between 1967 and 2001. The last one, Bjossa, was transferred to SeaWorld San Diego in April 2001, and died the same year. However, Springer, a then two-year-old orca, was found orphaned in 2002 in Puget Sound, Washington State, emaciated. There was much controversy over whether or not to interfere with nature (Messenger, 2014). Donna Sandstrom of Orca Alliance told Seattle's KING 5 News at the time:

> It's going to be heart-breaking if we see the worst thing happen, which is to see her die . . . But we would rather bear that heartbreak than to know she's enduring it alone in a concrete tank.
>
> (Messenger, 2014)

Following deliberations, the decision was taken to intervene and the Vancouver Aquarium played a major role in her rehabilitation and reuniting her to Pod A4. (Newman and Nightingale, 2006). Springer was spotted in 2013 with a calf off the coast of BC (CBC, 2013).

In 1967 the Vancouver aquarium captured two Belugas located in Bristol Bay, Alaska. They were flown to Vancouver and placed in the "old dolphin pool" (Newman and Nightingale, 2006). They named them Bella, who was an adult female (died 1976), and Lugosi, who was a male calf (died 1980). In 1991 the Vancouver Aquarium decided to establish a beluga breeding program with the completion of "the Arctic Canada Gallery" (Newman and Nightingale, 2006). In 1996 the first beluga was born in a Canadian aquarium, Quila. The last reaming beluga died at the Vancouver Aquarium on November 24 2017 (CBC, 2017a), her daughter Qila died November 16, 2017 (CBC, 2017b). On 15 June 2006 Canada Post issued a 51-cent domestic rate stamp to commemorate the 50th anniversary of the aquarium (Figure 16.4).

Figure 16.4 50th anniversary of the Vancouver Aquarium

Source: © Canada Post Corporation 2006. Reproduced with permission.

It is difficult to convey in such a short piece the civic pride that was at the time seen in the Vancouver Aquarium. The issue of a stamp in commemoration of its 50th anniversary is a reflection of both national and provincial pride in the organization at the time.

2017 saw a change in the laws relating to cetaceans in captivity as follows.

Section 9(e) Cetaceans in Vancouver Parks by-law *prior to* May 15, 2017
 . . . no person shall bring into any park, or otherwise keep or maintain in any park, any cetaceans, including baleen whales, narwhals, dolphins, porpoises, killer whales and beluga whales, which have been captured or taken from their wild habitat except:

I) Captive cetaceans caught from the wild prior to September 16, 1996, and cetaceans born into captivity at any time;
 ii) Cetaceans which are already being kept or maintained in a park as of September 16, 1996;
 iii) A member of an endangered cetacean species, provided that approval for bringing it into a park has first been obtained from the Park Board; and
 iv) An animal that has been injured or is otherwise in distress and in need of assistance to survive or rehabilitation, whether or not the intention is to release it back into its natural wild habitat.
 (Vancouver Board of Parks and Recreation, 2017, p. 1)

On May 15, 2017 the Vancouver Parks Board voted to repeal Section 9(e) above and replace it with:

(e) no person shall bring a cetacean into a park.
 (f) No person shall keep a cetacean in a park, except that this prohibition does not apply to cetaceans already in a park on [*date of enactment*] (*May 15, 2017 added*).
 (g) no person shall produce or present in a park a show, performance, or other form of entertainment, which includes one or more cetaceans.
 (Vancouver Board of Parks and Recreation, 2017, p. 8)

2017 also saw the end to the beluga breeding program by 2029 (Vancouver Sun, 2017).

In 2017 the Vancouver Parks Board the landlord of the Vancouver Aquarium banned any new captured cetaceans on its properties, except for rescues or those deemed not to be releasable (ibid.).

However, Vancouver Aquarium sought reversal of the Vancouver Parks Board decision to ban cetaceans at The Supreme Court of British Columbia and succeeded in overturning Vancouver Parks Board decision on banning of keeping cetaceans (CTV, 2018). This reversal coincided with reports that "Public attendance dropped nine percent between December 1, 2016, and

May 31, 2017, CBC's Jason Proctor reports. During the same period, members attendance declined 17 percent and membership renewals declined 22 percent" (Georgia Straight, 2018).

Toys modelled after whales for sale in the aquarium's gift shop began to collect dust on their shelves. Their sales fell 33.6 per cent during the six-month period discussed (ibid.).

How does the Vancouver Aquarium see itself?

We analysed the reports and accounts from Vancouver Aquarium and found a certain lack of transparency. They have recently launched themselves as "Ocean Wise" and residents in Vancouver see the Ocean Wise logo on restaurant menus where fish is designated as "sustainable". Figure 16.5 summarizes the expenses and revenues from the Aquarium below for the period 2011–2015. Although we gained access to the accounts since 2015 we were unable to obtain permission to reproduce them here. Figure 16.5 shows where its revenue comes from; as we can see, 31% of revenues arise from retail sales.

Figure 16.8 shows expenses as a percentage form 2011 to 2015. We feel it is notable that almost as much money is spent on retail operations as on conservation, research and education and animal care combined.

MarineLand

MarineLand is a themed amusement park and zoo for both marine and land animals, in the city of Niagara Falls, Ontario, Canada. The park has been a

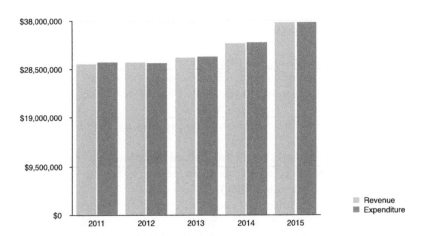

Figure 16.5 Vancouver Aquarium expenses and revenue in Canadian dollars, 2011–2015

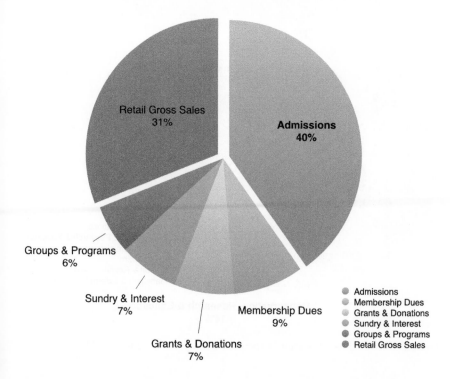

Figure 16.6 Vancouver Aquarium revenue percentage breakdown, 2011–2015

Figure 16.7 Vancouver Aquarium gift shop at Vancouver Airport, March 2018

centre of controversy over its handling of animals at the park. This a one-facility company. The park was founded by John Holer, a Slovenian immigrant who had worked for circuses in Europe before coming to Canada in the late 1950s.

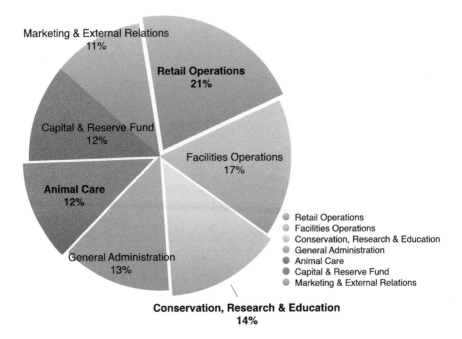

Figure 16.8 Vancouver Aquarium expenses percentage breakdown, 2011–2015

It first opened in 1961 as "Marine Wonderland and Animal Farm". Holer welded two large steel tanks together and brought in three sea lions and charged one quarter for admission and another to feed the animals (Casey, 2011). Although the company has not released details on animal deaths, Zoocheck Canada has suggested that 16 killer whales and 10 belugas have died at the park. MarineLand is a private Canadian company that would be expected to use a paired down, made Canada version of the International Financial Reporting Standards (IFRS) called Accounting Standards Private Enterprise (ASPE). Unlike the IFRS for Small and Medium-sized Entities (SMEs), ASPE does not require an audit nor any financial information disclosure. This makes it impossible compare MarineLand financials to SeaWorld or the Vancouver Aquarium. MarineLand has had the most belugas (53). They have chosen to have no audited disclosure.

SeaWorld

We can gain an idea of how SeaWorld views itself from Form 10-K (SeaWorld, 2016) in Exhibit 16.1.

Exhibit 16.1   SeaWorld Company Overview

PART I.

Item 1. Business

Company Overview

We are a leading theme park and entertainment company providing experiences that matter and inspiring guests to protect animals and the wild wonders of our world. We own or license a portfolio of recognized brands including SeaWorld, Busch Garden and Sea Rescue. Over our more than 50 year history, we have built a diversified portfolio of 12 destination and regional theme parks that are grouped in key markets across the United States, many of which showcase our one-of-a-kind zoological collection. Our theme parks feature a diverse array of rides, shows and other attractions with broad demographic appeal which deliver memorable experiences and a strong value proposition for our guests.

During the year ended December 31, 2016, we hosted approximately 22.0 million guests in our theme parks, including approximately 2.9 million international guests. In the year ended December 31, 2016, we had total revenues of $1.34 billion and generated a net loss of $12.5 million.

We generate revenue primarily from selling admission to our theme parks and from purchases of food, merchandise and other spending. For the year ended December 31, 2016, theme park admissions accounted for approximately 61% of our total revenue, and food, merchandise and other revenue accounted for approximately 39% of our total revenue. Over the same period of time, we reported $37.17 in admission per capita (calculated as admissions revenue divided by total attendance) and $23.93 in-park per capita spending (calculated as food, merchandise and other revenue divided by total attendance).

In November 2015, we communicated our roadmap to stabilize our business to drive sustainable growth. This strategic plan encompasses five key points which include (i) providing experiences that matter; (ii) delivering distinct guest experiences that are fun and meaningful; (iii) pursuing organic and strategic revenue growth; (iv) addressing the challenges we face; and (v) financial discipline. The plan is intended to build on our strong business fundamentals by evolving the guest experience to align with c n m preferences for experiences that matter. Through family entertainment and distinct experiences and attractions, we provide our guests an opportunity to explore and learn more about the natural world

(continued)

(continued)

and the plight of animals in the wild, to be inspired and to act to make a better world. The plan includes a new approach to in-park activities as well as "turning parks inside out" by taking our guests behind the scenes to provide a better understanding of our veterinary care and animal rescue operations. Other elements of the plan include implementing a simplified pricing model, targeted capital investments in new attractions across our parks, and an ongoing focus on cost control as part of a larger commitment to overall financial discipline. Additionally, we announced a new resort strategy that will include evaluating opportunities which could include purchasing or developing resort properties in or near some of our parks. We also recently announced our partnership with Miral Asset Management LLC to develop SeaWorld Abu Dhabi . . .

On March 17, 2016, we announced that we have ended all orca breeding and the orcas currently in our care will be the last generation of orcas at SeaWorld (the "Orca Announcement"). We also announced that we will introduce new, inspiring, natural or a encounters and phase out our current theatrical shows, as part of our ongoing commitment to education, marine science research, and rescue of marine animals. These programs will focus on orca enrichment, exercise, and overall health. This change will start in SeaWorld San Diego Park in 2017, and will be at all three SeaWorld parks by 2019. In conjunction with the Orca Announcement, the orca habitat expansion we previously disclosed (the "Blue World Project"), as originally designed and planned, will not move forward and we will spend significantly less capital than the originally proposed Blue World Project. The "new" SeaWorld will maintain unique value proposition of providing experiences that matter and inspiring guests to protect animals and the wild wonders of o world. We have implemented an integrated marketing plan designed to attract new and repeat guests to the "new" SeaWorld with its unique blend of compelling animal experiences and new rides and attractions for the whole family. . . .

As one of the world's foremost zoological organizations and a global leader in animal welfare, training, husbandry, veterinary care and marine animal rescue, we are committed to helping protect and preserve the environment and the natural world.

Illustrations of accounting for captive belugas, other whales, and dolphins

In this section we consider the disclosures relating to cetaceans by Vancouver Aquarium and SeaWorld as illustrations of cetacean accounting. There are those that see accounting as a science, in that if you have the same set of circumstance you will have the same outcome. However, a more realistic approach is to see accounting as an art in that the same set of circumstances can legitimately lead to a different outcome. For example if you have two identical blank canvases and palettes being used by two artists the outcome would be different possibly radically. If the colour options on the palettes were reduced and the artists asked to paint the same scene it would be similar but not the same even very different! This is one way of interpreting the differences and similarities between the financial statements of the Vancouver Aquarium and SeaWorld. They are both essentially in the same business of caring for cetaceans, the main differences between the two are that Vancouver Aquarium is a nonprofit operating in Canada and SeaWorld a for-profit operating in the United States. Accounting treatment of cetaceans should follow generally accepted accounting principles, which they do.

Generally accepted accounting treatment of cetaceans

Given that the approach taken here is that accounting is an art not a science then it would come as no surprise that there are two legitimate accounting treatments of cetaceans. The first would be to treat them as an asset and depreciate them over their lifetime, this is a typical "commercial approach". To treat them as an asset a market cost would have to be assigned to them, this could include payment for the cetacean (if any) and any costs associated with bring it to its place of exhibition. This approach clearly identifies the cetaceans as being assets of the organization. A second approach would be not to recognize the cetaceans as assets. They would exist as some sort of "off balance sheet asset". The "commercial approach" is straightforward and clearly falls with the remit of generally accepted accounting principles. But how can the "off balance sheet asset approach" be rationalized. Without interviewing the Vancouver Aquarium on this issue we offer some speculative suggestions:

- The cetaceans could be regarded as guests (for want of a better term) who are being cared for and as such are not an asset of the Vancouver Aquarium.
- More and more organizations today are not valued by their physical assets but by their employees, typical examples are advertising and software companies in the, for profit sector and universities and hospitals in the nonprofit sector. However, employees do not appear on the balance sheet, they are in effect "off balance assets" or perhaps some may even be liabilities.

Not putting cetaceans or other animals held at the Vancouver Aquarium on the balance sheet would fit more with its nonprofit status rather than crass commercialization as would be acceptable in the commercial world. Perhaps the Vancouver Aquarium is saying we do not own these cetaceans. This would reinforce the rational that the Vancouver Aquarium exists to help cetaceans and not benefit financially from them being present at the aquarium as guests. However, if you photograph a cetacean within the aquarium you need their permission to publish the photo.

Current accounting treatment of cetaceans

Vancouver Aquarium treatment of cetaceans in annual reports

After some difficulty and the purchase of a membership to the Vancouver Aquarium, making one of the authors a member, we were able to obtain the account for the years 2015 and 2017. However we were unable to obtain permission to reproduce them, and therefore can only provide a non-specific discussion of their contents. The aquarium is built on land owned by the Vancouver Parks Board. Amortization is straight-line. The useful lives of tangible assets are as follows: buildings, 30 years; galleries, 5 to 20 years; building improvements, 30 years; furniture and equipment, 5 to 10 years. Nothing remarkable here. However, were belugas to be treated as assets by Vancouver Aquarium we would expect to find some mention of them or animals in this section. The licensing agreement is from 2010 to 2019, and details of payments are given – again, nothing remarkable here. The presentation of capital assets provides nothing remarkable, with costs, accumulated depreciation and net book value shown over a number of years. The Vancouver Aquarium does not list cetaceans or any animals in its care as assets. As discussed above, this is not unexpected, as it may be in alignment with a non-profit philosophy.

SeaWorld treatment of cetaceans in its annual reports

Exhibit 16.2 consists of extracts from the annual reports for SeaWorld for the years 2015 and 2016 (SeaWorld, 2015, F8; SeaWorld, 2016, F8).

Exhibit 16.2   Extracts from SeaWorld Annual Reports 2015 and 2016

Property and Equipment – Net

SEAWORLD ENTERTAINMENT, INC. AND SUBSIDIARIES
NOTES TO CONSOLIDATED FINANCIAL STATEMENTS
(DOLLARS IN THOUSANDS, EXCEPT PER SHARE AMOUNTS)

2. SUMMARY OF SIGNIFICANT ACCOUNTING POLICIES

Fiscal period ending December 31, 2015

Property and equipment are recorded at cost. The cost of ordinary or routine maintenance, repairs, spare parts and minor renewals is expensed as incurred. Development costs associated with new attractions and products are generally capitalized after necessary feasibility studies have been completed and final concept or contracts have been approved. The cost of assets is depreciated using the straight-line method based on the following estimated useful lives:

Land improvements...10–40 years
Buildings ....5–40 years
Rides, attractions and equipment..........................3–20 years
Animals ....1–50 years

Material costs to purchase animals exhibited in the theme parks are capitalized and amortized over their estimated lives (1–50 years). All costs to maintain animals are expensed as incurred, including in-house animal breeding costs, as they are insignificant to the consolidated financial statements. Construction in process assets consist primarily of new rides, attractions and infrastructure improvements that have not yet been placed in service. These assets are stated at cost and are not depreciated. Once construction of the assets is completed and placed into service, assets are reclassified to the appropriate asset class based on their nature and depreciated in accordance with the useful lives above. Debt interest is capitalized on all active construction projects. Total interest capitalized for the years ended December 31, 2015, 2014 and 2013, was $2,299, $2,629 and $4,347, respectively.

Fiscal Period Ending December 31, 2016

The change between the fiscal periods for this section "Property and Equipment – Net" is: Total interest capitalized for the years ended December 31, 2016, 2015 and 2014, was $2,686, $2,299 and $2,629, respectively.

As can be seen from Exhibit 16.2, SeaWorld does regard its animals as assets and depreciates them over a straight-line basis for 1–50 years. As can be seen in Exhibit 16.3 (SeaWorld, 2015, F-9; SeaWorld, 2016, F-9), SeaWorld also considers any impairment of its long-lived assets (no pun intended).

Exhibit 16.3　Extract from SeaWorld Annual Report 2015 and 2016

Impairment of long-lived assets

SEAWORLD ENTERTAINMENT, INC. AND SUBSIDIARIES
NOTES TO CONSOLIDATED FINANCIAL STATEMENTS
(DOLLARS IN THOUSANDS, EXCEPT PER SHARE AMOUNTS)

Fiscal period ending December 31, 2015

All long-lived assets are reviewed for impairment upon the occurrence of events or changes in circumstances that would indicate that

(continued)

(continued)

the carrying value of the assets may not be recoverable. An impairment loss may be recognized when estimated undiscounted future cash flows expected to result from the use of the asset, including disposition, are less than the carrying value of the asset. The measurement of the impairment loss to be recognized is based upon the difference between the fair value and the carrying amounts of the assets. Fair value is generally determined based upon a discounted cash flow analysis. In order to determine if an asset has been impaired, assets are grouped and tested at the lowest level for which identifiable independent cash flows are available (generally a theme park). No impairment losses were recognized during the years ended December 31, 2015, 2014 and 2013.

Fiscal Period Ending December 31, 2016

The change between the fiscal periods for this section "Impairment of Long-Lived Assets" is: No impairment losses were recognized during the years ended December 31, 2016, 2015 and 2014.

Exhibit 16.4   Extracts from SeaWorld 2015 and 2016 Annual Reports

Property and Equipment Net

SEAWORLD ENTERTAINMENT, INC. AND SUBSIDIARIES
NOTES TO CONSOLIDATED FINANCIAL STATEMENTS
(DOLLARS IN THOUSANDS, EXCEPT PER SHARE AMOUNTS)

8. PROPERTY AND EQUIPMENT, NET

Fiscal period ending December 31, 2015

The components of property and equipment, net as of December 31, 2015 and 2014, consisted of the following:

	2015	2014
Land	$ 286,200	$ 286,200
Land improvements	281,612	289,892
Buildings	618,507	566,112
Rides, attractions and equipment	1,310,645	1,267,832
Animals	158,191	158,362
Construction in process	93,006	43,654
Less accumulated depreciation	(1,029,165)	(867,421)
Total property and equipment, net	$ 1,718,996	$ 1,744,631

Depreciation expense was approximately $174,700, $169,000 and $159,700 for the years ended December 31, 2015, 2014 and 2013, respectively.

In January 2016, the Company made a decision to remove deep-water lifting floors from the killer whale habitats at each of its three SeaWorld theme parks. As a result, in the first half of 2016, the Company expects to record approximately $33,000 of accelerated depreciation related to the disposal of these lifting floors. These lifting floors are included in rides, attractions and equipment in the table above.

Fiscal Period Ending December 31, 2016

Changes between fiscal periods December 31, 2015 and December 31, 2016 for the section "PROPERTY AND EQUIPMENT, NET" are shown in blue below:

The components of property and equipment, net as of December 31, 2016 and 2015, consisted of the following:

	2016	2015
Land	$ 286,200	$ 286,200
Land improvements	316,774	281,612
Buildings	645,013	618,507
Rides, attractions and equipment	1,368,018	1,310,645
Animals	158,199	158,191
Construction in process	54,242	93,006
Less accumulated depreciation	(1,161,631)	(1,029,165)
Total property and equipment, net	$ 1,666,815	$ 1,718,996

Depreciation expense was approximately $191,500, $174,700 and $169,000 for the years ended December 31, 2016, 2015 and 2014, respectively.

In January 2016, the Company made a decision to remove deep-water lifting floors from the orca habitats at each of its three SeaWorld theme parks. As a result, during the first quarter of 2016, the Company recorded approximately $33,700 of accelerated depreciation related to the disposal of these lifting floors. These lifting floors are include in rides, attractions and equipment as of December 31, 2015 in the table above.

Although we are not given a figure for individual species due to the consolidation we do have a figure of $158,199,000 for all animals (SeaWorld, 2015, F-16; SeaWorld, 2016, F17). Further, there has been no impairment loss, given the current (2018) unfavorable "political" climate (SeaWorld, 2016, p. 22) with cetaceans in captivity this is an interesting outlook from SeaWorld.

Overall, it is fair to say there are no surprises here, as SeaWorld treats cetaceans in its care as assets and depreciates them as protocol requires. The Vancouver Aquarium on the other hand chooses not to regard them as assets. This has a consequence of making them absent from their accounting framework.

Risks identified and disclosed by the three aquariums

We shall now look at the risks that SeaWorld and the Vancouver Aquarium face as identified by them. Over the last 30 years how organizations identify and deal with risks has become a very important part of their account-ability to stakeholders. The discharging of accountability is dealt with by adherence to the COSO Framework on Internal Control (COSO, 2013) in North America for listed companies. Non-profits disclosure is set at a much lower standard.

Risk disclosures are provided by Vancouver Aquarium in their 2015 and 2017 annual reports. As stated above we do not have permission to publish them so we are discussing them in a non-specific manner. Our conclusion is that the risk disclosure from the Vancouver Aquarium is at a minimal level and only deals with obvious economic risks, interest rate, credit, liquidity and cur-rency fluctuations.

MarineLand does not disclose any information on risks as it is a private com-pany and is not legally obliged to do so. However, there is no reason to believe that it does not face the same risks as the Vancouver Aquarium and SeaWorld.

SeaWorld, however, provides a very comprehensive list of risks as we can see from Exhibit 16.5 below.

Exhibit 16.5   Extracts from SeaWorld 2015 and 2016 Annual Reports

Risk Factors – animal-related elements

Item 1A. Risk Factors

Risks Related to Our Business and Our Industry
Fiscal period ending December 31, 2015

- We are subject to complex federal and state regulations governing the treatment of animals, which can change, and to claims and lawsuits by activist groups before government regulators and in the courts.
- Various factors beyond our control could adversely affect attendance and guest spending patterns at our theme parks.
- Featuring animals at our theme parks involves risks.

- Animals in our care are important to our theme parks, and they could be exposed to infectious diseases.
- If we lose licenses and permits required to exhibit animals and/or violate laws and regulations, our business will be adversely affected.

In Exhibit 16.5 we have deleted a lot of the information leaving those disclosures relating specifically to animal-related risks, for the sake of brevity. It is clear that substantial efforts have been made to disclose animal-related risks. This leads us to suggest that animal-related risk disclosure from SeaWorld demonstrates a higher level of transparency than that of the Vancouver Aquarium. Disclosure from the Vancouver Aquarium appears to lack both substance and depth. Following the COSO (2013) SeaWorld appears to have produced a realistic and useful risk discussion. This comparison raises an interesting question: why would two organizations which are essentially in the same business irrespective of legal form, provide such different sets of disclosures?

Some reflections

From the discussion we feel that there is a case based on moral reasoning for aquaria being made accountable for captive cetaceans. Accountability can be discharged by transparent disclosure. However, currently disclosure is totally inadequate and the legal form of the organization private, public, non profit is being used to further restrict disclosure. The outcome of this situation is that a reality is being communicated and constructed that deliberately does not allow transparent disclosure (see Hines, 1988, for the back ground discussion) and as such allows these organizations to remain unaccountable for captive cetaceans

The Vancouver Aquarium is run as a not for profit and is very secretive and does not disclose any accountability information about cetaceans, the same for MarineLand which is a private company. SeaWorld as listed for profit provides some consolidated disclosure on its animals falling far short of disclosure required to discharge accountability for cetaceans.

Transparent cetacean accountability disclosure could include any or more of the following:

- no consolidation of belugas;
- demographic type information should be disclosed on each beluga (name, age);
- history of transfers between aquaria;
- statement on their wellbeing;

- how much space each beluga has within the facility;
- births, deaths and captures dates;
- statement of how the belugas spend their time at the aquaria. (education of public, entertainment and/or recuperation); and
- photos of Belugas and facilities.

Organizations are hiding behind their legal form this should desist for cetacean disclosure. There are a multitude of frameworks they can use to do this and some are discussed below.

Concluding remarks and some recommendations for cetacean accounting

We have looked at three legal forms of organizations (profit, not for profit and private) none of which, in our view, has acknowledged accountability to cetaceans and subsequently have not provided adequate transparent disclosure to discharge their accountability. We now consider some possible frameworks for the discharging of accountability to cetaceans.

If the accounting framework is to be used for the discharging of accountability to cetaceans, they must fall into the elements for measuring financial position, these are assets, liability and equity. The International Accounting Standards Board (IASB) conceptual framework defines them as follows:

(a) An asset is a resource controlled by the entity as a result of past events and from which future economic benefits are expected to flow to the entity.

(b) A liability is a present obligation of the entity arising from past events, the settlement of which is expected to result in an outflow from the entity of resources embodying economic benefits"

(c) Equity is the residual interest in the assets of the entity after deducting all its liabilities.

(IASB, 2010, para 4.4)

Anyone who has seen a cetacean performance at aquaria will be able to relate to the definition of an asset. The definition could have been written specifically for this discussion. The trainers have complete control over them and patrons pay to see them. This makes it clear why SeaWorld classifies them as assets.

It is relatively easy to draw a comparison between an aquarium displaying performing animals and recording them as assets and a football company providing entertainment from its players, who are recorded as an asset. The only real difference is the footballers have a choice – and receive an income. The classification of cetaceans as assets is not to confuse them as livestock as defined in an animal-farming situation. Manchester United football club (soccer in the US) has football players on their balance sheet as "players registrations" and amortizes them, see Exhibit 16.6 below

Exhibit 16.6 Manchester United: consolidated balance sheet

| | Note | As of 30 June | |
		2014	2013
		£'000	£'000
ASSETS			
Non-current assets			
Property, plant and equipment	12	254,859	252,808
Investment property	13	13,671	14,080
Goodwill	14	421,453	421,453
Players' registrations	15	204,572	119,947
Trade and other receivables	18	41	1,583
Deferred tax asset	25	129,631	145,128
		1,024,227	954,999
Current assets			
Derivative financial instruments	17	–	260
Trade and other receivables	18	125,119	68,619
Cash and cash equivalents	19	66,365	94,433
		191,484	163,312
Total assets		1,215,711	1,118,311

Source: Manchester United (2014, 122: F-5)

In a similar way, captive cetaceans can be classified as assets, such as tangible, long-term, fixed, plant property and equipment, as can be seen in the SeaWorld financial statements (Exhibit 16.7).

Exhibit 16.7 Manchester United: operating results

The following table shows selected audited consolidated income statement data for the year ended 30 June 2014, 2013 and 2012

| | Year End 30 June | | |
	2014	2013	2012
	£'000		
Income Statement Data			
Revenue	433,164	363,189	320,320

(continued)

(continued)

	Year End 30 June		
	2014	*2013*	*2012*
	£'000		
Analyzed as:			
Commercial revenue	189,315	152,441	117,611
Broadcasting revenue	135,746	101,625	103,991
Matchday revenue	108,103	109,123	98,718
Operating expenses – before exceptional items	(367,056)	(304,120)	(274,411)
Analyzed as:			
Employee benefit expenses	(214,803)	(180,523)	(161,688)
Other operating expenses	(88,298)	(74,114)	(66,983)
Depreciation	(8,665)	(7,769)	(7,478)
Amortization of players' registrations	(55,290)	(41,714)	(38,262)
Operating expenses – exceptional items	(5,184)	(6,217)	(10,728)
Total operating expenses	(372,240)	(310,337)	(285,139)
Operating profit before profit on disposal of players' registrations	60,924	52,852	35,181
Profit on disposal of players' registrations	6,991	9,162	9,691
Operating profit	67,915	62,014	44,872
Finance costs	(27,668)	(72,082)	(50,315)
Finance income	256	1,275	779
Net finance costs	(27,412)	(70,807)	(49,536)
Profit/(loss) on ordinary activities before tax	40,503	(8,793)	(4,664)
Tax (expense)/credit	(16,668)	155,212	27,977
Profit for year	23,835	146,419	23,313
Attributable to:			
Owners of the parent	23,835	146,250	22,986
Non-controlling interest	–	169	327

Source: Manchester United (2014, p. 60)

As in Exhibit 16.7, cetaceans can also be amortized and expensed, again as with the SeaWorld's approach. We may well ask: would a cetacean be an asset or a liability? This might depend on where it is in its life. Would an older animal be destroyed or put out to pasture. Should a fund be set up to deal with retirement? However distasteful in some respects (and perhaps why the Vancouver Aquarium takes a different approach), cetaceans can be accounted for, but this is not the same as discharging transparent accountability.

Using cetaceans as an example an international accounting standard and accompanying US GAAP standard could be developed which overrides legal form. This approach could be applied to other areas were disclosure is desired, such as equal opportunities. This could even lead to a new set of accounting standards. Again, this leads us to ask what could an overriding legal form accounting standard look like? It would be based on cetaceans as either assets or liabilities depending on their life cycle and include some or all of the items indicated in form of disclosure. One of the issues with this approach is the amount of time it would take to develop a standard.

Perhaps cetaceans are above being placed on a balance sheet and should be disclosed as legitimate off-balance items. Special Purpose Entities could be set up. Organizations can include cetaceans as assets or liabilities using an off balance sheet approach. They can do this immediately. This approach, as opposed to the accounting approach used by SeaWorld, could psychologically show them as an asset of the organization but as somehow different, that they are perhaps not commercialized but living beings in their care. That they should not be classified as tangible, or long-term, or fixed assets or plant property and equipment? This is a small distinction yet one we feel worth mentioning.

Perhaps the overriding vehicle for cetacean accountability disclose is in the area of corporate governance. The corporate governance framework (for example FRC, 2016) allows the most flexibility for legal entities of any form to discharge their accountability as soon as possible. Typically the Board appoints four committees: audit, corporate governance, human resources and risk. Further, committees are appointed as necessary for example corporate social responsibility or information technology are not uncommon. In our case a committee that overseas cetaceans could be appointed with Board members and outside advisers such as veterinarians to provide transparent disclosure that discharges cetacean accountability. Employing the corporate governance framework there is no need to classify cetaceans as assets, as in reality it does not matter as we are just dealing with artificial construct (see Hines, 1988), it is the discharging of accountability that is the issue. There are two broad areas the corporate governance framework can be used to discharge cetacean accountability, internal control and corporate social responsibility, which we will look at below.

Another possibility is to look at risk and internal control mechanisms. Most listed companies in North America use the Committee of Organizations of the Treadway Commission (COSO) Internal Control – Integrated framework (COSO, 2013) framework to discharge their legal requirements in financial reporting. However, COSO has a more advanced framework Enterprise Risk Management Integrating with Strategy and Performance Framework (COSO, 2017). This could be applied relatively easily to discharge cetacean accountability. As can be seen below this formal process allows organizations to systematically embed enterprise risk management within the whole enterprise.

Incorporating cetaceans into this framework would bring out the attitudes and subsequently the responsibilities of the organization and how they align with society's requirement for cetacean accountability. For example in Governance and Cultured principle 3 is to define desired culture and principle 4 is to demonstrate commitment to core values. With these in place and following through the framework transparent cetacean accountability can be disclosed, as the ERM framework is auditable. Again it is not a requirement to include cetacean as assets.

Over the last 40 years, corporate social reporting (CSR) has developed largely as a voluntary means by which organizations discharge their accountability to society. CSR can also facilitate the discharging of accountability to society for cetaceans. There is no framework such as the accounting framework that is applicable to CSR, companies are free to do what they want generally and when they want. However, with the increased pressure on companies to be socially responsible many report annually and use a recognized framework such as the Global Reporting Initiative G4 Sustainability Reporting Guidelines.

The GRI framework is designed to be used across legal form and be audited. One of the defining aspects of the GRI is that stakeholders are identified and their requirements taken into account when producing a sustainability report and it is at this point that cetacean accountability can be incorporated. Again this can be implemented at any time and cetaceans do not need to be categorized as assets.

All of the above possibilities provide alternative ways in which transparent cetacean accountability could happen.

The writing of this chapter has been an enlightening experience for both of the authors. We both have a discomfort concerning the way animals are treated by humans. We found the commercialization of belugas and the apparent lack of accountability somewhat incomprehensible, yet to some extent understandable given the way that most organizations choose to operate. Belugas (as are other cetaceans and animals) are captured from the wild, separated from their pods (families), placed in tanks, artificially inseminated, transported across continents, traded, leased, forced to entertain the masses. This all seems worthy of a Stephen King novel. Owners of these animals, whatever their legal form, appear to have little disregard for belugas, cetaceans or animals generally and certainly discharge a low level of accountability. Segments of society are however moving towards equality for men, women, the environment and the animal world. As we go to press Joel Manby has resigned as CEO of SeaWorld after mounting losses, suggesting that society's love affair with captive cetaceans is ending (Whale Sanctuary Project, 2018). Society has a long way to go. By making owners of belugas accountable for their ownership of them above legal form a new standard for humanity is set. The owners have at their disposal a myriad of mechanisms to discharge their accountability, which they declined to use in a voluntary capacity. The reason is clear that any accountability disclosure will not be favourable towards them. In a perfectly accountable and utopian world there should be no room for accountants to use accounting techniques in this way. In a perfect world the Whale Sanctuary Project, which is "building a model sanctuary where captive whales and dolphins can be reha- bilitated and live permanently in their natural environment" (ibid.), would be unnecessary. Further, the Ceta Base (2018) should not need to exist to keep track of cetaceans in captivity. As accountants we have the ability and tech- niques to bring reliable and relevant information to the table, but we currently have our hands tied. There needs to be a new category of disclosure above legal form, not only for belugas, cetaceans and animals, but also in areas of corporate governance, corporate social responsibility and the environment.

> I think that in 50 years, we'll look back and go "My God, what a barbaric time".

> (Blackfish, 2013)

Note

1 Officially the Vancouver Aquarium Marine Science Centre, 845 Avison Way, Vancouver, British Columbia V6G 3E2, Canada, main website http://www.vanaqua. org/about

References

Barringer, F. (2012). Opposition as Aquarium Seeks Import of Whaled. *New York Times Magazine*, 9 October.
Bekoff, M. (2002). *Minding Animals: Awarness, Emotions, and Heart*. New York: Oxford University Press.
Bekoff, M. (2007). *The Emotional Lives of Animals*. Novato, CA: New World Library.
Bekoff, M. (2010). *The Animal Manifesto*. Novato, CA: New World Library.
Bekoff, M. and Goodall, J. (2000). *Animals Matter*. Boston, MA: Shambhala Publications.
Blackfish (2013). *Blackfish*. Documentary film. See www.blackfishmovie.com.
Carbone, L. (2004). *What Animals Want*. New York: Oxford University Press.
Casey, L. (2011). The Man behind MarineLand: 50 Years of Controversy. *Toronto Star*, 3 October.
CBC (2013). Springer the Killer Whale Spotted with 1st Calf Off B.C. *Coast*. 8 July. Retrieved from www.cbc.ca/news/canada/british-columbia/springer-the-killer-whale-spotted-with-1st-calf-off-b-c-coast-1.1316859
CBC (2017a). 2nd Beluga Whale Dies at Vancouver Aquarium in Less than Two Weeks. Retrieved from www.cbc.ca/news/canada/british-columbia/aurora-beluga-van couver-aquarium-dies-1.38692412017a).
CBC (2017b). Quila the Beluga Dies at Vancouver Aquarium, Retrieved from www. cbc.ca/news/canada/british-columbia/qila-the-beluga-dies-at-vancouver-aquar ium-1.3853742.
Ceta-Base (2018). Living Population of Whales, Dolphins & Porpoises in North America. Retrieved from www.cetabase.org/captive/cetacean/us-canada
Ceta Base (2017). Living Population of Whales, Dolphins & Porpoises in North America. Retrieved from www.cetabase.org/captive/cetacean/us-canada
COSO (2013). Internal Control – Integrated Framework. Retrieved from www.coso. org/Documents/990025P-Executive-Summary-final-may20.pdf.

COSO (2017). Enterprise Risk Management Integrating with Strategy and Performance. Retrieved from www.coso.org/Documents/2017-COSO-ERM-Integrating-with-Strategy-and-Performance-Executive-Summary.pdf.

CTV (2018). BC Supreme Court Overturns Cetacean Ban at Vancouver Aquarium. Retrieved from https://bc.ctvnews.ca/b-c-supreme-court-overturns-cetacean-ban-at-vancouver-aquarium-1.3797227.

Cupka, C. D., and Murphy, M. (2005). North Atlantic Right Whale *Eubalaena Glacialis*. South Carolina State Documents Depository, 8235.

Darwin, C. (1871). *The Descent of Man and Selection in Relation to Sex*. New York: D. Appleton and Co.

FRC (2016). The UK Corporate Governance Code. Retrieved from www.frc.org.uk/getattachment/ca7e94c4-b9a9-49e2-a824-ad76a322873c/UK-Corporate-Governance-Code-April-2016.pdf.

Georgia Straight (2018). Vancouver Aquarium Revenues Fell Ahead of Decision to Cease Keeping Whales and Dolphins in Captivity. *The Georgia Straight*. Retrieved from www.straight.com/news/1022186/vancouver-aquarium-profits-fell-ahead-decision-cease-keeping-whales-and-dolphins

Guardian (2015). Georgia Aquarium's Plan to Import 18 Beluga Whales Meets Broad Opposition. *Guardian*, 24 March. Retrieved from www.theguardian.com/us-news/2015/mar/24/georgia-aquarium-import-beluga-whales-opposition.

Hines, R. D. (1988). Financial Accounting: In Communicating Reality We Construct Reality. *Accounting, Organizations and Society*, 13(3): 251–261.

Hrynyshyn, J., and Sorg, A. (2006). *Canada's Beluga Whales: Hunted, Poisoned, Unprotected*. Arctic series. Canadian Marine Environment Protection Society.

IASB (2010). The Conceptual Framework for Financial Reporting, Retrieved from www.ifrs.org/issued-standards/list-of-standards/conceptual-framework

International Union for Conservation of Nature and Natural Resources. (2017). The IUCN Red List of Threatened Species. Retrieved from www.iucnredlist.org.

Kestin, S. (2018). Captive Mammals Can Net Big Profits for Exhibitors. *South Florida Sun Sentinel*, 16 March. Retrieved from www.sun-sentinel.com/sfl-dolphins-moneydec31-story.html

Manchester United (2014). Manchester United PLC, Form 20-F. Retrieved from http://ir.manutd.com/~/media/Files/M/Manutd-IR/Annual%20Reports/manchester-united-plc-20f-20141027.pdf.

Marino, L. (2013). Humans, Dolphins, and Moral Inclusivity. In A. Corcsy and R. Lanjouw (eds), *The Politics of Species: Reshaping our Relationships with Other Animals*. Cambridge: Cambridge University Press.

McKay, R. (2015). US Judge Stops Georgia Aquarium from Importing Belugas from Russia. Retrieved from www.reuters.com/article/us-usa-georgia-whales/u-s-judge-stops-georgia-aquarium-from-importing-belugas-from-russia-idUSKCN0RS2G620150928.

Messenger S. (2014). Why One Wild Orca and Her Baby Are Making SeaWorld Look REALLY Bad. 14 July. Retrieved from www.thedodo.com/why-one-orcas-stunning-return--637166847.html.

Morell, V. (2012). Changing Planet: Should We Import Belugas for Display? Retrieved from https://blog.nationalgeographic.org/2012/10/22/should-we-import-belugas-for-display.

Newman, M. A. and Nightingale, J. (2006). *People, Fish and Whales: The Vancouver Aquarium Story*. Harbour Publishing.

Niagara This Week. (2006). Kandu Dies; MarineLand Killer Whale Entertained for Decades. *Niagara This Week*, January 11.

NMFS. (2015). Georgia Aquarium Application to Import 18 Beluga Whales (File No. 17324). Retrieved on 8 March 2018 from www.nmfs.noaa.gov/pr/permits/geor gia_aquarium_belugas.htm.

OHCHR. (2012). *Towards Freedom from Fear and Want: Human Rights in the Post-2015 Agenda*. Thematic Think Piece, May. Retrieved from www.un.org/millenni umgoals/pdf/Think%20Pieces/9_human_rights.pdf

Page, T. (2012). US Marine Parks Trying to Import Wild Beluga Whales into Life-Long Captivity. Retrieved from https://greenerideal.com/news/environment/1009-us-marine-parks-import-beluga-whales-into-captivity.

Reilly, A. and B., S. (2015). *Eubalaena Japonica*, North Pacific Right Whale. South Carolina State Documents Depository, 8235.

Rose, N., Parsons, E. C. M. and Farinato, R. (2009). The Case against Marine Mammals in Captivity. Retrieved from www.humanesociety.org/assets/pdfs/marine_mam mals/case_against_marine_captivity.pdf

SeaWorld (2015). SeaWorld Entertainment 2015 Annual Report, p:18–30. Retrieved from http://s1.q4cdn.com/392447382/files/doc_financials/Annual%20 Reports/2015-SEAS-Annual-Report.pdf

SeaWorld (2016). SeaWorld Entertainment 2016 Annual Report, p:24–33. Retrieved from http://s1.q4cdn.com/392447382/files/doc_financials/Annual%20Reports/ Annual/359096_012_web_bmk11.pdf

Sorg A. (2013). Puncturing Vancouver's Moby Doll Myth. *Huffington Post*, 8 August. Retrieved from www.huffingtonpost.ca/annelise-sorg/vancouver-moby-doll_b_3704819.htmlC

Statistics Canada (2016). 2016 Census. Retrieved from www12.statcan.gc.ca/census-recensement/2016/dp-pd/prof/details/download-telecharger/comp/page_dl-tc. cfm?Lang=E.

Suzuki, D. (2017). *The Nature of Things: Call of the Baby Beluga*. Canada: CBC. Retrieved from www.cbc.ca/natureofthings/episodes/call-of-the-baby-beluga

Vancouver, B., Society, H. and November, Z. (2016). A Crumbling Case for Cetacean Captivity? A Review of Several Key Education and Conservation Research Factors. Retrieved from www.vancouverhumanesociety.bc.ca/wp-content/uploads/2016/ 12/MM-Education-and-Conservation-Report-Dec-9-2016-v1.pdf

Vancouver Aquarium (2015). Annual Report. Retrieved from www.vanaqua.org/annu alreport2015/assets/dist/pdfs/annualreport2015.pdf.

Vancouver Aquarium (2016). Annual Report. Retrieved from www.vanaqua.org/annu alreport2016/assets/dist/pdfs/annualreport2016.pdf.

Vancouver Board of Parks and Recreation (2017). Cetaceans in Vancouver Parks By-law Amendment. 9 May. Retrieved from http://parkboardmeetings.vancou ver.ca/2017/20170515/REPORT-CetaceansInVancouver ParksBy-lawAmend ment-20170515.pdf

Vancouver Sun (2017). Five Things about Proposed Bylaw to Ban Cetaceans at Vancouver Aquarium. 15 May. Retrieved from http://vancouversun.com/news/ local-news/five-things-about-proposed-bylaw-to-ban-cetaceans-at-vancouver-aquarium

Whale Sanctuary Project (2018). Our Work, The Whale Sanctuary Project. Retrieved from https://whalesanctuaryproject.org

Appendix: captive belugas in Canada and the United States

Canada

Data for this section are compiled from the CETA Captive Cetacean Database.

A.1 Vancouver Aquarium: cetaceans: historical data

No.	Cetacean	Living	Dead	Transfers	Born at another facility
1	Beluga Whale	0	11	3	2
2	Harbor Porpoise	0	2	0	0
3	Narwhal Whale	0	6	0	0
4	Orca (Killer Whale)	0	10	0	1
5	Pseudorca Dolphin	1	0	0	0
6	White-sided Pacific Dolphin	1	11	0	0

A.2 Vancouver Aquarium: beluga deaths

No.	Name	Sex	Origin	Origin date	Captured/born	Died
1	Bela	F	Capture	1967	Bristol Bay, Alaska	1976
2	Lugosi	M	Capture	1967	Bristol Bay, Alaska	1980
3	Sanaq	M	Capture	1976	Hudson Bay, Canada	1985
4	Kavna	F	Capture	1976	Hudson Bay, Canada	2012
5	Tuaq	M	Born	1977	Vancouver Aquarium	1977
6	Churchill	M	Capture	1985	Hudson Bay, Canada	1990
7	Aurora	F	Capture	1990	Hudson Bay, Canada	2016
8	Qila	F	Born	1995	Vancouver Aquarium	2016
9	Tuvaq	M	Born	2002	Vancouver Aquarium	2005
10	Tiqa	F	Born	2008	Vancouver Aquarium	2011
11	Nala	F	Born	2009	Vancouver Aquarium	2010

A.3 Vancouver Aquarium: living beluga transfers

No.	Name	Sex	Origin	Origin date	Captured/born	Transfer location
1	Allua	F	Capture	1985	Hudson Bay, Canada	SeaWorld San Diego
2	Imaq	M	Capture	1990	Hudson Bay, Canada	SeaWorld San Antonio
3	Nanuq	M	Capture	1990	Hudson Bay, Canada	SeaWorld Orlando

A.4 Vancouver Aquarium: Belugas born and kept at another facility

No.	Name	Sex	Origin	Origin date	Captured/born	Last location
1	Grayson	M	Born	Jun, 2007	SeaWorld San Antonio	Shedd Aquarium
2	Qinu	F	Born	Jul, 2008	SeaWorld San Antonio	Georgia Aquarium

A.5 MarineLand: captive belugas

No.	Name	Sex	Origin	Origin date	Captured/born
1	Andre	M	Capture	1998	Barents Sea, Russia
2	Charmin	F	Capture	1999	Sea of Okhotsk, Russia
3	Gemini	F	Capture	1999	Sea of Okhotsk, Russia
4	Xena	F	Capture	1999	Sea of Okhotsk, Russia
5	Isis	F	Capture	2000	Sea of Okhotsk, Russia
6	Caspian	F	Capture	2003	Sea of Okhotsk, Russia
7	Cleopatra	F	Capture	2003	Sea of Okhotsk, Russia
8	Jubilee	F	Capture	2003	Sea of Okhotsk, Russia
9	Osiris	F	Capture	2003	Sea of Okhotsk, Russia
10	Sierra	F	Capture	2003	Sea of Okhotsk, Russia
11	Kelowna	F	Capture	2004	Sea of Okhotsk, Russia
12	Peekachu	F	Capture	2004	Sea of Okhotsk, Russia
13	Skyla	F	Capture	2004	Sea of Okhotsk, Russia
14	Kodiak	M	Capture	2004	Sea of Okhotsk, Russia
15	Orion	M	Capture	2004	Sea of Okhotsk, Russia
16	Tofino	M	Capture	2004	Sea of Okhotsk, Russia
17	Tuktoyaktuk	M	Capture	2004	Sea of Okhotsk, Russia
18	Acadia	F	Capture	2008	Sea of Okhotsk, Russia
19	Aurora	F	Capture	2008	Sea of Okhotsk, Russia
20	Lillooet	F	Capture	2008	Sea of Okhotsk, Russia
21	Meeka	F	Capture	2008	Sea of Okhotsk, Russia
22	Rain	F	Capture	2008	Sea of Okhotsk, Russia
23	Secord	F	Capture	2008	Sea of Okhotsk, Russia
24	Horus	M	Born	2006	MarineLand
25	Burnaby	M	Born	2006	MarineLand
26	Jelly Bean	F	Born	2007	MarineLand
27	Eve	F	Born	2008	MarineLand
28	Mira	F	Born	2009	MarineLand
29	Neva	F	Born	2009	MarineLand
30	Qila	F	Born	2010	MarineLand
31	Tank	M	Born	2011	MarineLand
32	Frankie	M	Born	2012	MarineLand
33	Xavier II	M	Born	2012	MarineLand
34	Gia	F	Born	2012	MarineLand
35	Ruby	F	Born	2013	MarineLand
36	Penny-Wink	F	Born	2013	MarineLand
37	Yara	F	Born	2013	MarineLand
38	Titan	M	Born	2014	MarineLand
39	Jetta	F	Born	2014	MarineLand
40	Kharabali	F	Born	2014	MarineLand
41	Ivy	F	Born	2014	MarineLand
42	Sahara	F	Born	2014	MarineLand
43	Nahanni	F	Born	2015	MarineLand

(continued)

(continued)

No.	Name	Sex	Origin	Origin date	Captured/born
44	Skara	F	Born	2015	MarineLand
45	Havok	M	Born	2015	MarineLand
46	Artemis	F	Born	2016	MarineLand
47	Bubba	M	Born	2016	MarineLand
48	Bull	M	Born	2016	MarineLand
49	Jasper	M	Born	2016	MarineLand
50	Valor	M	Born	2016	MarineLand
51	Aslan	M	Born	2016	MarineLand
52	Cyprus	M	Born	2016	MarineLand
53	Eve's Calf	F	Born	2017	MarineLand

United States

Data for this section are compiled from the CETA Captive Cetacean Database (2018)

B.1 Georgia Aquarium: captive belugas

No.	Name	Sex	Origin	Origin date	Captured/born
1	Maple	F	Born	2005	MarineLand
2	Qinu	F	Born	2008	SeaWorld San Antonio
3	Nunavik	M	Born	2009	Shedd Aquarium

B.2 Mystic Marinelife Aquarium: captive belugas

No.	Name	Sex	Origin	Origin date	Captured/born
1	Kela	F	Capture	1985	Hudson Bay, Canada
2	Juno	M	Born	2002	MarineLand

B.3 SeaWorld Orlando: captive belugas

No.	Name	Sex	Origin	Origin date	Captured/born
1	Naluark	M	Capture	1992	Hudson Bay, Canada
2	Whisper	F	Born	1999	SeaWorld San Antonio

B.4 SeaWorld San Antonio: captive belugas

No.	Name	Sex	Origin	Origin date	Captured/born
1	Natasha	F	Capture	1984	Hudson Bay, Canada
2	Crissy	F	Capture	1988	Hudson Bay, Canada
3	Martha	F	Capture	1988	Hudson Bay, Canada
4	Imaq	M	Capture	1990	Hudson Bay, Canada

5	Luna	F	Born	2000	SeaWorld San Antonio
6	Oliver	M	Born	2007	SeaWorld San Antonio
7	Samson	M	Born	2013	SeaWorld San Antonio
8	Kenai	M	Born	2016	SeaWorld San Antonio
9	Crissy's Calf	M	Born	2017	SeaWorld San Antonio

B.5 SeaWorld San Diego: captive belugas

No.	Name	Sex	Origin	Origin date	Captured/born
1	Ferdinand	M	Capture	1975	Hudson Bay, Canada
2	Allua	F	Capture	1985	Hudson Bay, Canada
3	Klondike	M	Born	2002	MarineLand
4	Atla	F	Born	2010	SeaWorld San Antonio
5	Pearl	F	Born	2010	SeaWorld San Diego

B.6 John G. Shedd Aquarium: captive belugas

No.	Name	Sex	Origin	Origin date	Captured/born
1	Mauyak	F	Capture	1984	Hudson Bay, Canada
2	Beethoven	M	Born	1992	SeaWorld San Antonio
3	Naya	F	Capture	1992	Hudson Bay, Canada
4	Kayavak	F	Born	1999	Shedd Aquarium
5	Aurek	M	Born	2003	MarineLand
6	Bella	F	Born	2006	Shedd Aquarium
7	Grayson	M	Born	2007	SeaWorld San Antonio
8	Kimalu	F	Born	2012	Shedd Aquarium

B.7 Summary of dead and living belugas, Canada and the USA, period 1975–2017

Facility	Dead	Living
Vancouver Aquarium	11	0
MarineLand	33	53
Georgia Aquarium	6	3
Mystic Marinelife Aquarium	9	2
SeaWorld Orlando	6	2
SeaWorld San Antonio	23	9
SeaWorld San Diego	18	5
John G. Shedd Aquarium	9	8
Total	**115**	**89**

17 An ecological auto-ethnography of a monarch butterfly

Sanjay V. Lanka

Introduction

As I sit in the beautiful sunshine here on the central coast of California, I look around and see that there are far fewer of my family than there used to be. I begin to wonder how much longer my kin will be able to continue our existence. I am a monarch butterfly, or *Danaus plexippus* for those who are more focused on scientific nomenclature, and one among a rapidly dwindling species of butterflies in North America. I am taking this opportunity to provide you with the background on how we got to be a threatened species and what are the factors that have caused and continue to cause our decline. I will also provide some context on what used to be the life of our species including details of our annual migration and the changes to our habitat here in North America. In doing so, I will discuss the impact of the regulatory environment on the continuation of our way of life.

Our habitat and annual migration

We are unique among butterfly species on Earth due to the multi-generational migration that we undertake over the North American continent spanning Canada, the United States and Mexico. The process of migration from Canada and the northern states of the United States begins in late summer to either the mountains of central Mexico or the California coast where we will spend the winter months. Those of us that survive the winter will then return to the Southern region of the United States that was traditionally the region where milkweed plants which are our main food source, used to be found. The females of our species lay their eggs only on milkweed plants and then these eggs hatch into caterpillars, which feed on the milkweeds, leading to their metamorphosis into butterflies. Until the start of the 1990s this used to be a rather routine process for us since there was plenty of milkweed to be found among the landscapes of the Midwest region of the United States. Things started to change for us at this time with the introduction of what is referred to as genetically modified crops. I will elaborate on the havoc that this caused in our lives a little later.

Figure 17.1 Monarch butterfly

Our eggs are laid singly, on the underside of a young leaf or on a flower bud and take three to eight days to develop and hatch into larvae (caterpillars). Larval monarchs take nine to 14 days to go through five instar stages before pupating. Our larvae in the final stages of development stop feeding to search for a location to form a pupa, or chrysalis, the last stage of development before their emergence as adults. At the end of metamorphosis, our adults emerge from the chrysalis, expand their wings and fly away. The body mass of our fifth stage caterpillars increases about 2000-fold from first stage instars. Our larvae must eat constantly to ingest enough milkweed to increase in mass so dramatically within a few weeks. We then continue our northern journey in search of newly emerging milkweeds. This migration continues on throughout the year during which time the process of laying eggs, these eggs turning in caterpillars and then into butterflies is completed several times until what you would call our "great-great-grandchildren", in relation to those of us who would have left our winter home each year in the spring, return to the overwintering sites the following autumn.

An area of 56,259 hectares (ha) is protected as the Monarch Butterfly Biosphere Reserve in Mexico and its core area of about 13,551 ha includes our wintering forest habitat where we migrate each fall from Canada and the United States to the states of Michoacán and Estado de Mexico (WWF, 2016). Our population in the Rosario and Sierra Chincua colonies make up our entire breeding stock for the eastern United States and Canada. After wintering in Mexico, we then begin our mass migration north from Mexico each spring, flying north, until we stop to lay eggs in the south of the United States. Those of us who survive this stage are born and continue the journey, and by summer we reach as far north as Canada.

Severe weather conditions over the mountains of the state of Michoacán, west of Mexico City which are home to two-thirds of our population in our Mexican sanctuaries, in the year 2002 was the most catastrophic event in recent memory with the death of around 220 to 270 million monarch butterflies (Yoon, 2002). This was a devastating blow to our extended family from which we have never recovered since it left us vulnerable to the changes in weather caused by climate change which has been further compounded by increasing deforestation in and around our winter habitat in Mexico (WWF, 2015, 2016).

Since forest trees can act as an umbrella against the rain and a blanket that can retain heat, scientists and conservationists have been warning for years that the thinning of the forests in the relatively small area we have chosen for our habitats could threaten our existence by increasing our exposure to these elements (Yoon, 2002). The severity of the weather, with a combination of rain followed by freezing temperatures, had a major role to play in the extent of loss of life among our colonies in Mexico in 2002 (ibid.). It goes without saying that deforestation has also played a significant role since trees in the forest have tended to provide us with protection by acting as a blanket that can store the heat that we generate by our action of being clumped together in close knit communities (Stevenson, 2015). Thus, the loss of our population in 2002 could be attributed not only to climate change (Zipkin et al., 2012; Lemoine, 2015), but also to the loss of about 50% of the pristine forest cover in the mountains of central Mexico over the past 50 years (Brower et al., 2002).

There is hope for improvement since the conception of the WWF–Telcel Alliance in 2003, in partnership with local communities. Also the Mexican federal and state governments, have supported both the conservation and management of our habitat through the reforestation of 24,273 acres with more than 10.73 million trees (WWF, 2015). However, we live a precarious existence since even a small area of deforestation has a large impact on our population. Despite progress elsewhere the loss of about 19 hectares of habitat in the rural hamlet of San Felipe de los Alzati in the state of Michoacán due to logging has been compounded by the impact of drought and pests (Stevenson, 2015). However, our problems are not limited to the issues that we face in our wintering habitat in Mexico. A larger issue that needs to be understood is the loss of our breeding habitat in the United States due to the expansion over the last twenty years of the cultivation of crops which are resistant to genetically modified (GM) herbicides (Brower et al., 2012).

The impact of the growth of industrial agriculture

While considering the factors impacting the continued existence of my species, it is pertinent to begin by looking at the system of agriculture in North America that consists of the use of chemical inputs such as fertilizers and pesticides. The problem is that the monetary cost, which is often the only consideration for you humans, does not as yet include the impact of these farming practices in terms of environmental degradation, which is one among the principal causes of the reduction in the numbers of my species. The system of agriculture that has been introduced in the past one hundred years is the basis for an industrial form of food production which replaces local markets and local cultures that have traditionally been places of crop diversity, promoted through the ingenuity of indigenous farmers that enabled the survival and growth of my species through the conservation of seeds and plant varieties (Shiva, 2000).

Farmland biodiversity is an important characteristic in assessing sustainability of agricultural practices which have promoted the numbers of my species, but has seen a drastic fall due to the adoption of herbicide resistant crops almost twenty years ago (Tappeser, Reichenbecher and Teichmann, 2014). Glyphosate and its related herbicides are the most widely used in the world and apart from being toxic to plants, have adverse effects on mammals, some invertebrates, aquatic species and the soil micro flora and are particularly toxic to amphibians (ibid.). An estimated amount of 239 million kg of additional herbicides were applied due to the rising dependence on glyphosate in the whole period of 1996–2011, with herbicide resistant soybean accounting for two thirds of the total increase (ibid.). Despite this, the industrial method of farming is actively promoted by the large transnational corporations (TNCs), governments and civil society organizations alike accompanied with the rhetoric of a responsible approach to business (Craig and Amernic, 2004). There is however clear evidence that intensive high input farming is one of the main drivers of ongoing biodiversity losses in agricultural landscapes that has made it increasingly challenging for the continuation of my species (Tappeser, Reichenbecher and Teichmann, 2014).

Another important constraint to ensuring our continued survival has been the loss of soil fertility which is a prerequisite for the abundance of the milkweed that is our main source of sustenance. So in order to ensure that we have sufficient food, there is a need to prioritize the maintenance and regeneration of soil fertility which is linked to promoting the soil organic carbon (SOC) (Bationo et al., 2007). Since the increasing intensification of agriculture along with increase in the usage of pesticides is causing a loss in biodiversity including the loss in the numbers of my species, a way to mitigate this would be to get more humans to learn about sustainable agricultural practices (Pretty and Bharucha, 2014, 2015; Tappeser, Reichenbecher and Teichmann, 2014).

Industrial agriculture is harmful to the survival of my species since it involves the clearing of forests and tree-covered land for the purpose of cultivation, along with promotion of inappropriate fertilizer use among other unsustainable practices which will increase the emission of GHG and worsen the process and extent of climate change (Bationo et al., 2007). As noted earlier, climate change was the cause for the most extensive loss of the population of my species during the severe weather conditions in Mexico in 2002. Industrial agriculture makes extensive use of fertilizers and pesticides which in turn require the use of larger amounts of water, along with an associated decrease in the organic inputs to soil (Sanderman and Baldock, 2010; Meersmans et al., 2011). Further, this industrial system of agriculture involves insufficient crop rotations in a seasonal fashion with damage caused to the soil structure through rampant intensive soil tillage leading to soil compaction which causes a depletion of SOC and soil biodiversity (Brady et al., 2015; Meersmans et al., 2011). Unfortunately, all of these have had an adverse impact on the existence of milkweed which is the only source of food for us.

In the context of the development of modern industrial agriculture in the USA, its impact consisting of an extensive use of fertilizers and pesticides and the resulting loss in soil fertility is that it requires extended fallow periods for the soil to regenerate itself (Follett, 2001). This is part of the planning process of the United States Department of Agriculture (USDA) and the US Department of the Interior's Bureau of Land Management, where there is land left fallow that is called "set-aside land" (McGranahan, Brown, Schulte and Tyndall, 2015). What this means for the survival of my species is that each year larger and larger areas of the United States Midwest are becoming fallow indicating that the milkweed that used to grow in these areas does not grow anymore.

This has made it increasingly difficult for us to find food as we make our annual migration across North America. Thus, with these types of practices, industrial agriculture with its monopoly power within the agriculture industry which in turn is further strengthened by patents over seeds and industrial chemicals is destroying biodiversity and hence is the greatest threat to the continued survival of my species among others. The industrial method of farming currently incentivizes monocultures and cash crops and is one of the main drivers of ongoing biodiversity losses in agricultural landscapes (Altieri, 1983; Shiva, 1997) which has contributed to the overshooting of the biodiversity planetary boundaries (Rockström et al., 2009). Monocultures by their very nature of representing uniformity without diversity are vulnerable to ecological catastrophes while compromising the survival of nature's diversity by promoting large scale species extinction (Shiva, 1997).

As a result of the growth of industrial agriculture across the United States, the habitat of my species has been significantly reduced and degraded especially due to the significant increase in the use of genetically modified crops that are meant to be resistant to the use of pesticides. There has been a reduction in the availability of our main food source, the milkweed, which is the only plant on which we lay our eggs and this has not been modified to withstand the use of such crops. The primary threat that we face is the loss of our food source, the milkweed. This is caused by the widespread planting of genetically engineered, herbicide-resistant corn and soybeans in the Corn Belt region of the United States along with the planting of genetically engineered cotton in California.

In the Midwest region of the United States, where the majority of my species originates, the adoption of genetically modified crops involves the increasing use of glyphosate, the pesticide developed by Monsanto, which has led to the severe loss of milkweed (Hoppe, 2010). In the Midwest region of the United States, genetically modified corn and soybeans were introduced in the 1990s by the Monsanto Corporation under the brand names "Roundup Ready soybeans" introduced in 1996 and "Roundup Ready corn" introduced in 1998. These varieties of both soybean and corn are genetically modified to survive when glyphosate (Roundup) is applied and now comprise 94% of soybeans and 89% of all corn grown in the United States (Benbrook, 2012).

Glyphosate is being applied both more intensively than before as well as to larger and larger areas of the area in the Midwest of the United States that we consider home. Since 1995 when Roundup Ready soybeans were introduced, there has been a significant increase in the total glyphosate use on corn and soybeans besides the additional use of neonicotinoids since the year 2002 which has meant an all-out attack on milkweed and hence on our habitat (Douglas and Tooker, 2015). Additional loss of our habitat is being caused by the rapid conversion of grasslands and other milkweed-containing land types to corn and soybean fields to produce biofuels under US biofuels policy despite an attempt by the US government to create Conservation Reserve Program (CRP) lands in the Midwest of the United States. The conflict between one US government policy and another has led to my species losing a large percentage of milkweed from our habitats due to the shrinkage of CRP acreage by 11.2 million acres (30%) since 2007, with more than half of the decline taking place in the US Midwest, which has lost 6.2 million CRP acres (Hoppe, 2010).

In the period 1999 to 2012, it is estimated that there was a 64% decline in overall milkweed in the US Midwest, due to changes in the use of croplands (Pleasants, 2015). Milkweed that used to grow among crops used to be four times as much as the milkweed available in other settings. The loss of milkweed due to the fundamental changes made to both the way corn and soybean are cultivated, in terms of the increased density of these plants within the genetically modified fields, has had a disproportionate impact on the numbers of my species so that as of 2012, it is estimated that our numbers in the US Midwest have decreased by 88% compared with 1999 (ibid.). What I have just presented to you is a rather scary picture of the situation that our species is facing in North America since we are under attack by the forces of industrial agriculture. In this situation we are rather helpless and this is despite the creation of institutions such as the Environmental Protection Agency (EPA). It might make you wonder, what role if any does the EPA play in the protection of the habitat of species such as my own? To answer this question, it would be important to consider the regulatory environment in the United States which has allowed the creation of GM crops which are the basis of the chemical attack on my species.

Impact of the regulatory environment on our way of life

In this final section of my auto-ethnography, I would like to bring to your attention the debate surrounding the approval of genetically modified organisms (GMOs) within the international food system. As you have seen from the situation in the Midwest of the United States where genetically modified soy and corn have decimated the food supply for my species and put under risk our continued survival, I would like to make the case for changes to the regulatory system in the United States since, in my opinion, that is the most important change that, if made, would promote the survival of my species.

I will engage specifically with the accountability of the United States food and drug administration (FDA) and the environmental protection agency (EPA) which have approved genetically modified foods for human consumption based on the concept of "substantial equivalence". Before I can explain what "substantial equivalence" is, I would like to first explain to you what is meant by GMOs, or "herbicide-tolerant crops". Farmers often use broad-spectrum herbicides, which kill nearly all kinds of plants to control weeds. Scientists have applied biotechnology to create crops that are resistant to certain herbicides. Herbicide tolerant crops contain new genes that allow the plant to tolerate these herbicides. The most common herbicide-tolerant crops (cotton, corn, soybeans, and canola) are those that are resistant to glyphosate, an effective herbicide used on many species of grasses, broadleaf weeds, and sedges.

The EPA does not regulate these crops. Rather, the USDA regulates the crops and the EPA regulates the herbicide. The EPA regulates pesticides, including genetically engineered pesticides, using two laws. The first of them is called the Federal Insecticide, Fungicide, and Rodenticide Act (FIFRA). This act provides the legal requirements for EPA's registration process for all pesticides. With regard to biotechnology, EPA's jurisdiction under FIFRA covers regulation of the new substance and DNA in the plant when it is pesticidal in nature. The second law is called the Federal Food, Drug, and Cosmetics Act (FFDCA), as amended by the Food Quality Protection Act (FQPA). The FFDCA requires the EPA to set tolerances, or exemptions from tolerances, for the allowable residues of pesticides that are applied to food and animal feed.

Before a pesticide can be marketed and used in the United States, FIFRA requires that the EPA evaluate the proposed pesticide thoroughly to ensure that the pesticide will not pose unreasonable risks of harm to human health or the environment. In the case of genetically modified plants, the EPA considers many factors by conducting studies that assess the risks to human health as well as studies that assess risks to non-target organisms and the environment. Pesticides that pass the EPA's evaluation under FIFRA are granted a license or "registration" that permits their sale and use according to the requirements set by EPA to protect human health and the environment.

In making regulatory decisions, the EPA evaluates the risks of pesticide use and balances these risks with the benefits derived from pesticide use. It is important to understand that the regulatory system that has compromised the survival of my species is a combination of a regulatory partnership between the EPA, USDA and the FDA. In this regulatory system, the USDA's Animal and Plant Health Inspection Service (APHIS) is responsible for protecting American agriculture against pests and diseases.

The APHIS regulates the field testing of genetically engineered plants that may be the products of biotechnology. The USDA's regulatory jurisdiction includes the regulation of herbicide-tolerant crops, which do not fall under EPA's jurisdiction because these crops do not produce pesticides. The FDA which is a part of the Department of Health and Human Services assesses food safety and nutritional aspects of new plant varieties. The FDA bases its biotechnology policy on existing food law and requires that genetically engineered foods meet the same rigorous safety standards required of all other foods.

The FDA also sets labelling standards for foods and enforces the tolerances of allowable pesticide residues that EPA establishes. This is the scary part for my species and should be scary for humans as well, because instead of mandating that dangerous chemicals that harm my species and yours should not exist, this partnership between the EPA and the FDA creates a "legal loophole", as you humans like to call it. This legal loop hole means that since the regulatory agencies have allowed for and set the tolerances for certain dangerous chemicals such as the pesticides that can be used in the context of GM foods, the presence of these dangerous chemicals under the tolerances provides a legal protection to the companies that produce them. The only aspect that the companies need to ensure is that the existence of these dangerous chemicals is kept below the tolerance defined by the FDA and the EPA.

As long as the companies are able to follow this requirement, their liability for damage to humans and death to species like my own will go unquestioned and they can continue as they have since the introduction of GMOs making profits at the expense of our lives. Keeping this information in mind, we can now begin to understand how food safety is defined using the concept of substantial equivalence. Substantial equivalence holds that the safety of a new food, particularly one that has been genetically modified (GM), may be assessed by comparing it with a similar traditional food that has proven safe in normal use over time.

As part of a food safety testing process, substantial equivalence is the initial step, establishing toxicological and nutritional differences in the new food compared with a conventional counterpart – differences are analysed and evaluated, and further testing may be conducted, leading to a final safety assessment. Substantial equivalence is the underlying principle in GM food safety assessment for a number of national and international agencies, including the Canadian Food Inspection Agency (CFIA), Japan's Ministry of Health, the US Food and Drug Administration (FDA), and the United Nations' Food and Agriculture Organization (FAO) and the World Health Organization.

The US Food and Drug Administration says that consuming GMOs is safe. There have been no human studies on the long-term health impact of consuming GMOs, only animals' studies, as is typical in determining the safety of food. Anti-GMO groups like Green America and Center for Food Safety point to published studies that say there are signs of toxic effects in animals that ate genetically modified crops and say more research needs to be done. GMO critics also raise concerns about the health effects of the toxin inserted into corn DNA to make it insect-resistant, and about glyphosate, the main herbicide used on GMO crops. GMO proponents contest those studies, and say other research shows that the products are safe. They say that GMOs are simply a technological extension of the plant breeding people have done for centuries. Unfortunately, while this debate rages and the court case brought against the Monsanto Corporation by the state of California goes through a slow legal process, the time for species such as my own is running out. I know that you humans will not act until your own lives and those of your families are threatened. I hope that you will pay greater attention to the regulation of these dangerous chemicals in time to save my species from extinction.

References

Altieri, M. A. 1983. The Question of Small Farm Development: Who Teaches Whom? *Agriculture, Ecosystems and Environment*, 9, pp. 401–405.

Bationo, A., Kihara, J., Vanlauwe, B., Waswa, B. and Kimetu, J. 2007. Soil Organic Carbon Dynamics, Functions and Management in West African Agro-ecosystems. *Agricultural Systems*, 94(1), pp. 13–25.

Benbrook, C. M. (2012). Impacts of Genetically Engineered Crops on Pesticide Use in the US: The First Sixteen Years. *Environmental Sciences Europe*, 24(1), 24.

Brady, M. V., Hedlund, K., Cong, R. G., Hemerik, L., Hotes, S., Machado, S., Mattsson, L., Schulz, E. and Thomsen, I. K. (2015). Valuing Supporting Soil Ecosystem Services in Agriculture: A Natural Capital Approach. *Agronomy Journal*, 107(5), 1809–1821.

Brower, L. P., Castilleja, G., Peralta, A., Lopez-Garcia, J., Bojorquez-Tapia, L., Díaz, S. . . . and Missrie, M. (2002). Quantitative Changes in Forest Quality in a Principal Overwintering Area of the Monarch Butterfly in Mexico, 1971–1999. *Conservation Biology*, 16(2), pp. 346–359.

Brower, L. P., Taylor, O. R., Williams, E. H., Slayback, D. A., Zubieta, R. R. and Ramirez, M. I. (2012). Decline of Monarch Butterflies Overwintering in Mexico: Is the Migratory Phenomenon at Risk? *Insect Conservation and Diversity*, 5(2), pp. 95–100.

Craig, R. J. and Amernic, J. H. 2004. Enron Discourse: The Rhetoric of a Resilient Capitalism. *Critical Perspectives on Accounting*, 15, pp. 813–852.

Douglas, M. R. and Tooker, J. F. (2015). Large-Scale Deployment of Seed Treatments has Driven Rapid Increase in Use of Neonicotinoid Insecticides and Preemptive Pest Management in US Field Crops. *Environmental Science and Technology*, 49(8), pp. 5088–5097.

Follett, R.F. 2001. Soil Management Concepts and Carbon Sequestration in Cropland Soils. *Soil and Tillage Research*, 61(1), pp. 77–92.

Hoppe, R. A. (2010). *Small Farms in the United States: Persistence under Pressure*. Collingdale, PA: Diane Publishing.

Lemoine, N. P. (2015). Climate Change May Alter Breeding Ground Distributions of Eastern Migratory Monarchs (*Danaus plexippus*) via Range Expansion of Asclepias Host Plants. *PLoS ONE*, 10(2), e0118614.

McGranahan, D. A., Brown, P. W., Schulte, L. A. and Tyndall, J. C. 2015. Associating Conservation/Production Patterns in US Farm Policy with Agricultural Land-Use in Three Iowa, USA Townships, 1933–2002. *Land Use Policy*, 45, pp. 76–85.

Meersmans, J., van Wesemael, B., Goidts, E., Van Molle, M., De Baets, S. and De Ridder, F. 2011. Spatial Analysis of Soil Organic Carbon Evolution in Belgian Croplands and Grasslands, 1960–2006. *Global Change Biology*, 17(1), pp. 466–479.

Pleasants, J. M. 2015. Monarch Butterflies and Agriculture. In K. S. Oberhauser, K. R. Nail and S. Altizer (eds), *Monarchs in a Changing World: Biology and Conservation of an Iconic Butterfly*, pp. 169–178. Ithaca, NY: Comstock Publishing Associates

Pretty, J. and Bharucha, Z. P. 2014. Sustainable Intensification in Agricultural Systems. *Annals of Botany*, 114(8), pp. 1571–1596.

Pretty, J. and Bharucha, Z. P. 2015. Integrated Pest Management for Sustainable Intensification of Agriculture in Asia and Africa. *Insects*, 6(1), pp. 152–182.

Rockström, J., Steffen, W., Noone, K., Persson, Å., Chapin, F.S., Lambin, E. F., Lenton, T. M., Scheffer, M., Folke, C., and Schellnhuber, H. J. 2009. A Safe Operating Space for Humanity. *Nature*, 461, pp. 472–475.

Sanderman, J. and Baldock, J. A. 2010. Accounting for Soil Carbon Sequestration in National Inventories: A Soil Scientist's Perspective. *Environmental Research Letters*, 5(3), p. 034003.

Shiva, V. 1997. *Biopiracy: The Plunder of Nature and Knowledge*. Cambridge, MA: South End Press.

Shiva, V. 2000. *Stolen Harvest: The Hijacking of the Global Food Supply*. New Delhi: India Research Press.

Stevenson, M. 2015. Deforestation in Mexico Butterfly Reserve More Than Triples. 25 August. Available at: https://phys.org/news/2015-08-deforestation-mexico-butterfly-reserve-triples.html [Accessed on December 15, 2017]

Tappeser, B., Reichenbecher, W. and Teichmann, H. 2014. Agronomic and Environmental Aspects of the Cultivation of Genetically Modified Herbicide-Resistant Plants. Available at: www.bfn.de/fileadmin/MDB/documents/service/skript362.pdf [Accessed 6 July 2017].

WWF. 2015. 96% of all Deforestation within Mexico's Monarch Butterfly Sanctuaries Occur in a Single Community. WWF-Telmex-Telcel Foundation Alliance, the National Commission of Natural Protected Areas, and the Institute of Biology of the National Autonomous University of Mexico, 25 August. Available at: www.wwf.org.mx/noticias/noticias_mariposa_monarca.cfm?uNewsID=251391 [Accessed 17 December 2017].

WWF. 2016. Forest Degradation in the Core Zone of the Monarch Butterfly Biosphere Reserve 2015–2016. WWF-Telmex-Telcel Foundation Alliance, the National Commission of Natural Protected Areas, and the Institute of Biology of the National Autonomous University of Mexico, 23 August. Available at: https://c402277.ssl.cf1.rackcdn.com/publications/932/files/original/Forest_Degradation_Monarch_Biosphere_Final_Report.pdf?1471881367 [Accessed 17 December 2017].

Yoon, C. K. 2002. Storm in Mexico Devastates Monarch Butterfly Colonies. *The New York Times*, 12 February. Available at: www.nytimes.com/2002/02/12/world/storm-in-mexico-devastates-monarch-butterfly-colonies.html [Accessed 16 December 2017].

Zipkin, E. F., Ries, L., Reeves, R., Regetz, J., and Oberhauser, K. S. 2012. Tracking Climate Impacts on the Migratory Monarch Butterfly. *Global Change Biology*, 18(10), 3039–3049.

III.4

Extinction accounting in polar regions

18 Accounting for survival of polar bears

An arctic icon on thin ice

Kristina Jonäll and Svetlana Sabelfeld

Are oil companies taking the polar bear extinction problem seriously?

One of the effects of global warming is that the Arctic's ice is dramatically shrinking, opening up access to huge oil resources in the area. The number of oil companies involved in drilling activities in the Arctic has increased in recent years. We wonder, however, how these companies are taking their stakeholders' concerns into account in that region, whether local inhabitants or polar bears. This chapter discusses the ways Russian and Norwegian oil companies, which have joint collaboration in the Arctic, are reporting on how polar bears are affected by their activities and on actions taken to reduce the threat of extinction for this iconic species.

The polar bear, once the apex predator of the Arctic, now finds itself threatened by an adversary far deadlier and more powerful than any it has ever faced. Can the polar bear survive? The polar bear is on the list of threatened species and has become a symbol of our impact on the planet. We are all familiar with the polar bear story. Polar bears depend on ice as it is their lifeline, their highway, essential for hunting and travelling. Over a 30-year period the ice has rapidly vanished. Satellite data show that since 1978 the extent of Arctic sea ice has decreased by about 12 per cent per decade.[1] Sea ice is often classified by age; there is new ice and multi-year ice. New ice is thin and shallow, while multi-year ice is stable and thick, often between 6 and 12 feet. Multi-year ice lasts during melting seasons and is important to polar bears for their survival. November 2016 showed the lowest amount of Arctic sea ice since satellite measuring began, 28 per cent less than the average for 1980–2010.[2] However, ice is also thinning, 22 per cent of the ice cover was multi-year ice in November 2016 compared to 45 per cent of ice cover in 1985.

Increased water and air temperatures due to human-induced global warming are one of the reasons for the melting and ice loss in the Arctic sea. Without the sea ice the polar bears are not able to reach their food in the natural way. Many manage to survive without the ability to hunt on the ice for food – but others don't. For those who plunge into the warming sea in search for food, many are drowned. The dramatic shrinkage of Arctic ice is opening up access to huge oil resources in the area. In recent years, the world's major oil companies have realized that the access to the region's enormous oil resources would open a range of business opportunities and gains in the future. Large oil companies have started oil exploration and drilling activities in the area. For example, in May 2012, Russian and Norwegian large oil companies, Rosneft and Statoil, signed a Cooperation Agreement in May 2012 to explore jointly areas of the Russian shelf and for Rosneft to join in the exploration of the Norwegian shelf, aiming to implement strategic cooperation on joint exploration in the Norwegian Barents Sea and Joint Technical evaluation covering two Russian onshore assets.

While oil companies are increasing their business activities in the Arctic region to maximize their future gains, there is a risk that these activities will have, and are having, a negative impact on Arctic marine biodiversity, which will also be exacerbated by climate change. What is especially worrying is the lack of a shared agenda for protecting marine and coastal biodiversity, agreed between all businesses operating in the Arctic region. Even if there are soft law instruments such as *The Convention on Biological Diversity* (1993), there is room for interpretation of such frameworks, and thereby a variety of ways of measuring the corporate impact on biodiversity. There is simply neither shared strategy nor set of measurements related to the protection of marine biodiversity in the Arctic region. Moreover, as the region's local population is extremely sparse, the oil companies are not exposed to local stakeholder pressure as they normally are in more populated areas.

This chapter studies how large oil companies account for their impact on polar bears in the Arctic in annual and sustainability reports and how sustainability accounting can serve companies and society as a tool for organizational change towards more sustainable businesses. Sustainability accounting can serve organizations in their communication with different stakeholders, but it can also serve as an organizing tool inside organizations, helping them to relate current performance to future goals, which enables a development towards improved performance. Incorporating the protection of marine biodiversity in Arctic areas into part of corporate strategy, where different companies in Arctic are in agreement, can elicit change.

Businesses are driven by the logic of profit maximization. In areas such as the Arctic, where there are few people, there are consequently few voices to promote their cause. For companies, their interest is primarily to be first to be able to benefit from newly found resources. In areas where there are legally and national blurred boundaries companies have a better chance of exploiting gaps in systems and laws. Since it is difficult to see where the limits are, and who is responsible for what, companies have a chance to exploit their potential of profit maximization often with little concern for negative impacts on society and the environment.

Business, as a direct cause of habitat loss and an indirect cause of climate change, has a responsibility to slow and, ultimately, prevent the ongoing extinction crisis. The GRI reporting principle GRI-EN14 calls for companies to report information on red listed species whose habitat is affected by their operations. By identifying threats and being led to disclose the information, companies can initiate actions and thereby start to do something to avoid extinction.

In this chapter, we aim to explore the ways large oil companies' measure and communicate their impact in the Arctic region and to analyse the question how this can lead to a change inside companies, which contributes to a movement towards more sustainable business behaviour and hopefully a more sustainable world.

Polar bears in the Arctic region

The polar bear was first documented in 1774 by Constantin John Phipps. Phipps led an expedition to sail as close as possible to the North Pole. The ship reached Spitzbergen, but was prevented from travelling further north by an ice barrier. In Spitzbergen the expedition found a great number of white bears. Phipps described them as "an animal much larger than the black bear"[3] and gave it its scientific name *Ursus maritimus*, which is Latin for "maritime bear".

Polar bears are found in Alaska, Canada, Greenland, Norwegian Arctic, Russia and areas that surround the North Pole. Measuring the exact number of Polar Bears is impossible since the animals often occur at low densities, in distant habitats, far from civilization. The Polar Bear Specialist Group (PBSG) has, since 1993, provided a global population estimate for polar bears. Estimations are expensive and difficult, depending on the factors being measured. Although estimates have improved in recent decades, information remains poor or outdated for some subpopulations.[4] There are 19 subpopulations of polar bears in the arctic regions spread across different areas. Today the total population of polar bears is estimated to be between 20,000 and 25,000 individuals.[5] The total numbers of estimated polar bears have been quite stable since the measuring started but some areas are more affected than others. The Polar Bear has been on the IUCN's red list of threatened species since 1982 and is currently categorized as vulnerable.[6] In addition to estimating number of bears, the PBSG also estimates the trend, i.e. the change in population size, over a 12-year period, centred on the time of assessment. The current trend according to estimates in 2015 suggests that one subpopulation has increased, six were stable, three were considered to have declined and for the remaining nine there were insufficient data to provide an assessment of current trend[7]. Table 18.1 below shows the population trends of the polar bears subpopulations in 2015.

Polar bear ecology

The polar bear's reproductive rate is among the lowest of all mammals.[8] Females mature when they are between four and five years old and successfully mate for the first time between the ages of six and eight.[9] Whether or not there will be cubs depends of the condition of the female. Mating takes place in spring,

Table 18.1 Trends in polar bear subpopulations

Area	No. of bears	Population trend (2015)
Arctic Basin	Unknown	Data deficient
Chukchi Sea	Unknown	Data deficient
Southern Beaufort Sea	500–1000	Declining
Northern Beaufort Sea	500–1000	Stable
Viscount Meville Sound	< 500	Data deficient
Norwegian bay	< 500	Data deficient
Kane Basin	< 500	Declining
Lancaster Sound	2000–3000	Data deficient
Baffin Bay	1000–2000	Declining
M'Clintock Channel	< 500	Increasing
Gulf of Boothia	1000–2000	Stable
Foxe Basin	2000–3000	Stable
Western Hudson Bay	1000–2000	Stable
Southern Hudson Bay	500–1000	Stable
Davis Strait	2000–3000	Stable
East Greenland	Unknown	Data deficient
Barents Sea	2000–3000	Data deficient
Kara Sea	Unknown	Data deficient
Laptev Sea	Unknown	Data deficient

Source: Polar Bear Specialists Group (January 2015)

pregnant females enter dens in snow drifts or slopes on land, close to the sea, or on sea ice in autumn. She gives birth inside the den, usually in late December to early January to, commonly, twin cubs (one or three cub litters are less frequent). Cubs are small at birth but grow rapidly. They are fed on milk from their mother and they leave the den in spring. At this time the female may not have eaten for a period of up to eight months. Mortality is high in the first year of a polar bear's life. Cubs that have a mother with large fat stores in the fall are more likely to survive. The cubs stay with their mother for about two and a half years. This means that females on average do not enter a new reproductive cycle more often than every third year, such that a female only has about five litters in her lifespan.

Polar bears rely on the sea ice to find and catch their prey. They get their food mostly from seals but even larger species such as walrus and beluga are on the menu. Birds, fish, vegetation and kelp are eaten during the ice free-season when the bears are trapped on land. In summer this food is adequate but polar bears would not gain enough nutrition to survive primarily on a terrestrial diet.[10]

Threats

There are a range of threats that might impact the future population of the polar bears. The first and most serious threat to future polar bear survival is climate change.[11] The sea ice is retreating because of global warming, leading to decreased habitat both in quality and area. Polar bears depend on sea ice as a platform for hunting. The ice also facilitates seasonal movements and mating. The melting of the ice makes it increasingly difficult for the polar bears to travel, hunt and raise their young. An ongoing and continued climate warming will increase future uncertainty and pose severe risks to the welfare of polar bear populations.[12] The polar bear is an apex predator which means that it is at the top of the food web. Polar bears, therefore, like a canary in a cage taken down a coal mine, can give an early signal that there are problems in the Arctic marine ecosystem. The bears are likely to be among the most affected species as the Arctic warms and sea-ice melts. Studies based on sea-ice data show that an excessive part of the Arctic will be ice-free for more than 5-month by the middle of the 21st century.[13] If sea ice diminishes, hunting areas will be lost and it is not known how climate change will change denning locations and habitats. One can expect that declining sea ice availability likewise can impair the ability of pregnant females to reach their ordinary denning areas, or indeed injure all denning for polar bears.[14]

Oil and gas development also pose a major risk to polar bears. With global warming leading to sea ice decline, previously inaccessible areas are, as mentioned eearlier, exposed to development. Oil development in the Arctic poses a wide of range of threats to polar bears ranging from oil spills to increased human-bear interactions. It is probable that an oil spill in sea ice habitat would result in oil being concentrated in leads and between ice floes, resulting in both polar bears and their main prey, such as seals, being directly exposed to oil.

Not only the threat of oil spills from oil and gas development but also other forms of activities, such as trans-Arctic shipping from vessels and tourism, affect the life of polar bears. Some studies suggest that polar bears are sensitive to disturbance at maternity den sites. Polar bears are often attracted by the smells and sounds associated with human activity. Oil and gas drilling, transportation and tourism may contribute to such disturbances[15]. Stress resulting from a more crowded Arctic, may play a destructive role in the future.

Polar bear hunting management is also something that needs to be taken into consideration. In Norway and Russia hunting is prohibited, whereas the US, Canada, and Greenland allow and manage a subsistence "harvest" of polar bears. The annual legal harvest of polar bears is between 700 and 800 or 3–4 per cent of the estimated size of the total population. The principle use of polar bears is in meat consumption; use of their hides for clothing; and small scale handicrafts. Whole hides may be used for subsistence needs, kept as trophies, or sold on open markets. The recorded legal trade between the years 1992–2006 were 31,000 body parts include skins, claws teeth and skulls.

Reporting for sustainability

Sustainability reporting is used by companies to communicate with different stakeholders. Such reporting can also be used as a tool within companies to help relate current results to future goals, enabling development towards improved result and performance. When companies report sustainability, it is more than just a description of the company's business, often disclosure beyond what laws, rules, codes or best practices determine.[16] Environmental and sustainability issues have become increasingly important for both society and companies over the last years. Reports from, among others, WWF[17] and the IPCC[18] about human impact on climate and accelerated climate change have reflected each other. Sustainability reporting can play a significant role in how a company is perceived by the outside world, as non-governmental organizations like Greenpeace, Amnesty International and others can contribute to a public disaster if certain aspects of the business are perceived to be darkened or hidden in the accounts.[19] Accounting has become more than a response to social pressure on sustainability issues or a way to deal with threats to an organization's credibility.[20] A focus on sustainability helps companies manage their environmental impact and improve operating efficiency and natural resource stewardship. It also remains a vital component of shareholder and stakeholder relations.

Studies show that companies, through their written and oral communication about nature and the environment, try to appear as responsible companies.[21] Companies also tend to adopt particular linguistic strategies in their communications related to climate change.[22] Over the years, research has also shown that companies are tending to disclose more information about threatened species and how to protect them.[23] GRI and the new G4 help companies that follow the guidelines to identify and report activities that could endanger vulnerable plants and animals. By identifying threats and being effectively forced to disclose the information companies can initiate actions and thereby start to do something to avoid extinction. However, it is not certain that companies reporting according to GRI's guidelines are committed to sustainability issues or are taking responsibility for maintaining diversity and protection for endangered species. Similarly, it is hard to say whether the increased sustainability reporting, shows greater transparency, increased awareness of the importance of sustainability issues or increased accountability.[24] Instead, there is a risk that increased reporting on sustainability issues can strengthen "business-as-usual" and thus contribute to greater unsustainability.[25]

The purpose of GRI is to create uniformity in sustainability reporting and to make it easier to assess and compare companies from social, environmental and economic perspectives. Research shows that the GRI guidelines, to some extent, have influenced how sustainability work is organized in companies. Results from prior research indicates that sustainability issues have become more integrated in companies in the sense that more employees are involved in taking responsibility for sustainability work and finding new ways to get the sustainability issues spread in the organization.[26]

When companies provide sustainability information, it not only contributes to inform and solve social and environmental issues, research has shown that it also gives economic benefits to businesses.[27] Depending on how companies express themselves in the reporting, they can also enhance the image that they are really doing something about sustainability.[28] Companies need to disclose that they are willing to change if it should be of help to prevent threats against endangered species. The general information that companies often leave, which follows codes and best practices, needs to be complemented by reporting specific strategies, plans and measures that are implemented to prevent extinction[29] as outlined in chapters one and two.

Research method

We performed a content analysis of annual reports and sustainability reports produced by Statoil and Rosneft from 2012, when the Arctic collaboration project started, to 2015. The analysis was conducted in two stages. A content overview was done by screening all information related to polar bears and the aspects that directly or indirectly can harm polar bears or the environment needed for their survival, based on existing knowledge on polar bears. At this stage, we captured a map of the information items that the two companies accounted for – or did not account for. In a second stage, we carried out an interpretive analysis of the accounts given (or not given) on the issue of polar bears, aiming to identify linguistic strategies[30] that companies use in their reports. Table 18.2 presents a list of information categories screened during Step 1.

Table 18.2 Content categories screened in annual reports and sustainability reports 2012–2015

Content categories
1 Total amount of oil spill (tons)
2 Oil spill in the Arctic
3 Employee training for prevention of oil spill
4 Number of trainees
5 Number of hours of training
6 Prevention of risks
7 Pollution in general
8 Pollution in Arctics
9 Account on cleaning activities in the Arctic
10 Seismic testing/seismic survey, general info
11 Impact from seismic testing
12 Noise from aircraft and other vehicle in the Arctic
13 Research on polar bears
14 Arctic research activities
15 Agenda related to polar bears protection
16 Goals related to polar bears protection
17 Follow up of the goals related to polar bears protection
18 Accounts related to protective measures
19 Follow up of the protective measures
20 Total spending on environmental protection

Categories 1–17 are based on previous knowledge on polar bears and how industrial activities, such as oil spills, pollution, cleaning activities, seismic testing, noise from vehicles and aircraft in the Arctic region and aircraft in Arctic region, absence of agenda and research related to polar bear protection can negatively affect them. Items 18–19 are not directly related to the threat of polar bear extinction, but rather are summative categories related to protective measures that are articulated in the Polar code, an international code for ships operating in polar waters, to prevent environmental damage of business operations in the area.[31]

The coding was performed according using a binary approach, where 1 indicated that information was found, and 0 indicated that no information was found, for each category. Despite its limitations,[32] binary coding gives an overview of the type and amount of content presented in the reports,[33] which is an objective of the first stage of this study.

After having received an overview of the content in the annual and sustainability reports, which is related to the polar bear extinction problem (stage one), we proceeded with a closer analysis of the accounts at the level of sentences, in order to identify strategic tactics that companies use in their communication.[34] At this stage, the whole text of the report was first read by the authors, and then the meaning the polar bear-related sentences was scrutinized and interpreted in a context of what is being communicated, how it is communicated[35] and what is not said, or where there are silences[36] concerning the impact of corporate activities on polar bears.

Findings from the content analysis: accounting for polar bears

Investigation of the annual reports and sustainability reports of Rosneft and Statoil, both involved in the oil drilling project in the Arctic, enabled us to see how oil companies account for the impact of their business in the Arctic to stakeholders and how they address the problem of decreasing populations of Polar bears. In general, most of the information relating to environment and biodiversity is disclosed in sustainability reports. Both Statoil and Rosneft write about their activities in the Arctic as a "business opportunity". The focus is on what they do in the Arctic in order to be able to conduct oil exploration in the region. Companies report on their research in the Arctic, they do seismic testing, they buy "modern and environment-friendly" equipment, and this is presented as a good investment in their new business. The companies also show their awareness of the consequences of climate change in the Arctic region, such as ice melting and the risk of local fauna decrease. A short overview of the amount of information from 2012–2015 is presented in Figures 18.1 (annual reports) and 18.2 (sustainability reports).

How do companies talk about collaboration in the Arctic?

The extract below shows that companies refer to their initiative to develop a Declaration, with ministries and governmental agencies, that would help

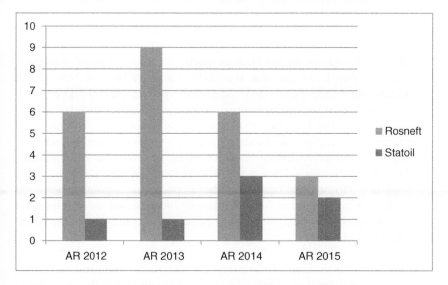

Figure 18.1 Amount of information presented in annual reports 2012–2015

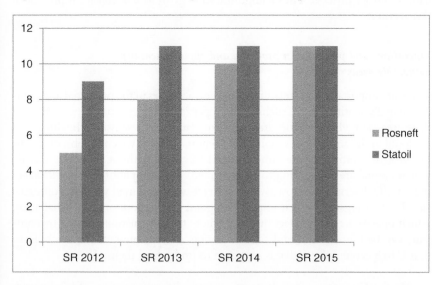

Figure 18.2 Amount of information presented in sustainability reports 2012–2015

companies involved in business activities in the Arctic region to achieve a uni-fied environmental strategy for business in the region. However, the problems or critical questions to be addressed when developing such a strategy are not articulated (there is a silence in the reports). In other words, details of how such a strategy will be put into progress, and what problems/risks the compa-nies need to consider together and think about, are totally missing from the discourse visible in the annual report.

Recognizing that the Arctic environment comprises fragile ecosystems with unique natural features and resources, the Company initiated the development of the Declaration on the Protection of the Environment and Conservation of Biodiversity during the Exploration and Development of Mineral Resources on the Russian Arctic Continental Shelf. Alongside Rosneft, the document was signed by ExxonMobil and Statoil; Eni declared its willingness to sign it. At present, the Company works together with ministries and governmental agencies to ensure effective implementation of the Declaration provisions, e.g. regarding the creation of effective cooperation mechanisms for the prevention of and coordinated response to emergencies, conservation of the environment and the biota. The document provides for the development of uniform approaches towards environmental safety of offshore operations, ongoing monitoring of changes in the state of Arctic landscapes and seas, and the development of international cooperation with the environmental strategy for the Arctic taken into account.[37]

As stated in the beginning of the paragraph above, the company recognizes the Arctic environment as a fragile ecosystem, presenting it as the outcome of natural history process. Thus a linguistic strategy of *naturalization*[38] is present in this account.

Operations and priorities in protected and environmentally vulnerable areas

There are important issues relating to business activities in the protected and environmentally sensitive areas, such as which particular operations are performed in these areas and what priorities are made. In relation to these issues, the discussion disclosed in the annual and sustainability reports, as far as we could observe, indicate that the companies use rather abstract language, without specifying exactly which natural areas are going to be protected. An example of a *standardization*[39] used in the description below, where abstract words are used without contextualized details regarding what impacts are going to be monitored, in what areas, which operations might affect the area, where the information collated by company can be found. Such undetailed accounts are thus presented as symbols, or signals to a certain group that is supposed to understand them.

As the Company expands its operations, the conservation of biodiversity and ecosystems becomes increasingly important. The top priority in this regard is environmental safety of operations in protected areas and their buffer zones. The Company has created and maintains a registry of protected natural areas potentially affected by operations of its subsidiaries. The registry is intended to support the monitoring and management of impacts of the Company's operations on protected environmental features. The registry contains information about the Company's relevant facilities (or license areas); specific operations carried out in protected areas and associated impact mitigation measures; engagement of the respective subsidiary with local authorities; and results of environmental inspections by regulators. The Company collects information on its industrial and infrastructure facilities adjacent to protected natural areas.[40]

The above account is followed by an account relating tor another priority, namely "the implementation of a system of measures for the conservation of biodiversity and prevention of adverse environmental impacts in the context of offshore projects",[41] where a list of general activities as summarized below is stated without further elaboration on which legislation, which experts, which measures, and so on:

- environmental impact assessment prior to the commencement of work, which includes public consultations, identification of biodiversity conservation measures and other actions to prevent or mitigate environmental impacts, and calculation of compensation for environmental damage;
- obtaining licenses and permits required by the legislation, including a positive conclusion of the state environmental expert review;
- engagement with international and regional environmental NGOs, relevant authorities, and the expert community;
- a broad range of environmental assessment and protection works, including an assessment of the background state of the natural environment and the biota, integrated environmental monitoring, self-monitoring, studies of marine ecology, and special measures to protect marine mammals;
- planning and development of specific internal regulations and standards addressing the specifics of offshore operations and taking into account risk assessment results for both exploration and production phases.

So, as illustrated above, when communicating to their stakeholders about prevention of biodiversity decrease, the company is not communicating a particular agenda for prevention, but rather mentioning general institutional words such as "legislations", "consultations", "regulations", "calculations" without filling these words with a specific context.[42]

Both companies mention their ongoing research projects in the Arctic region. In the accounts describing the research projects, the companies, however, do not account for the key results of their research. An example of how Rosneft describes one of their research projects is illustrated below.

In 2014, the research centre plans to implement large-scale research projects in the Arctic Seas in such fields as: regional environmental studies; development of new techniques for the removal of oil spills in the Arctic; remote monitoring and studies of marine mammal populations; ensuring safety of operations; conceptual design of drilling platforms for exploratory drilling; ice and hydrometeorological studies (with two exploratory expeditions planned for 2014); and the study of sea bottom conditions. These projects will help study the conditions and the state of the environment on the continental shelf, thus supporting the designing of effective measures to minimize environmental impacts of the company's subsequent operations.[43]

"Displaced" accounts on threatened spaces and polar bear protection

While Statoil is silent about the topic of polar bears in their annual and sustainability reports, Rosneft is yearly addressing this theme via both text and images. Examples of such accounts are illustrated in the accounts below:

> In June 2013, Rosneft and WWF Russia signed a Protocol of Intent concerning the establishment of a constructive dialogue on environmental protection, including conservation of polar bears and other Arctic animals. The signatories agreed to develop a roadmap that would include their joint actions.[44]

> As part of its program to support the conservation of threatened animal species, the Company sponsors polar bears kept in the Moscow Zoo. In 2013, it spent RUB 8 mln on this program.[45]

> Rosneft has a program for the preservation of endangered animal species, including polar bears. The world's polar bear population currently stands at 20,000–25,000 and may fall to a third of that by 2050 due to human interference. In 2015 Rosneft supported Russian zoos that have polar bears in Omsk Region, the Udmurt Republic, Krasnoyarsk Territory, Sverdlovsk Region, Perm Territory, Chelyabinsk Region and the Sakha Republic (Yakutia). The species preservation program includes improving the living conditions and care of the animals, enlarging and maintaining cages, monitoring the animals with modern equipment, improving security, etc.[46]

As the company states, the conservation program means, for example, a sponsorship of polar bears in Russian zoos, something which is positive, but not really about how polar bears are protected in their homeland, the Arctic region. Here we can witness a linguistic strategy of *displacement*,[47] the use of a term/object from a completely different context. The reader still gets a positive impression about polar bears being "protected" and "taken care of".

Further, a number of protection agreements and meetings (not the actual protective actions) are mentioned in order to rationalize (legitimize)[48] the operations in the Arctic region, as mirrored in the following excerpt from a sustainability report.

Following up on the Protocol of Intentions between Rosneft and the World Wildlife Fund (WWF Russia) on Organizing Interaction for a Constructive Dialogue in Environment Protection Including Protection of Polar Bears and other Representatives of Arctic Wildlife, the following events were held:

- joint working meetings and consultations on actions aimed at studying Red Book animals, conservation of Arctic biodiversity and ecosystems, and protection and rescue of animals and birds while responding to emergency oil spills at Company sites;
- a number of joint meetings on sharing practical experience (participation in environment impact assessment of the Company's planned activities, including on the Arctic shelf, and in searching for new environment protection technologies);
- International Conference Holarctic Sea Mammals organized by the World Wildlife Fund with the Company's support;
- working meetings on walrus conservation when operating in the Company's Arctic offshore license areas as part of the Expert Consultative Group on Atlantic Walrus Species Preservation.[49]

Silence on companies' impact on polar bears

We found one account of the impact on polar bears provided by Rosneft over the studied years:

> In 2015, the Company also conducted studies on polar bears (ship, air, and land-based monitoring) and implemented an environmental monitoring program on the population of Atlantic walrus subspecies and other mammal species inhabiting the Nenetsky State Nature Reserve. No impact on marine mammals was identified from geophysical studies during the entire period of observations.[50]

When it comes to the Statoil accounts on the issues of polar bear extinction, no mention was found in the texts of annual or sustainability reports. The company, however, mentions the collaboration with Rosneft in the initial phase in 2012.

In November 2012, Rosneft and Statoil signed a "Declaration on Protection of the Environment and Biodiversity for Oil and Gas Exploration and Development on the Russian Arctic Continental Shelf". The pact reaffirms our commitment to sustainable development, including minimising the impact of oil and gas activities on indigenous populations and climate change.[51]

Companies do seem to avoid talking about any impact of their activities in the Arctic region on polar bears. Rosneft mentions research results showing that no impact is identified. However, the companies do not provide any account on methodology on how research was performed and what exactly was in focus of their research of the impact. Silence can be seen as a communication strategy that companies use in their communication with stakeholders.[52] Our study reveals that oil companies are generally silent in their accounts on the material impact that their operations have on the polar bears and other species in the Arctic region.

Discussion

Are oil companies taking polar bear extinction problem seriously? Are they discharging accountability on this issue? If we look at the amount of environmental disclosure related to Arctic region provided in annual and sustainability reports, we find that companies account for their operations in the Arctic, as well as they show awareness about polar bear distinction problem. However, a deeper question of HOW they account for the issue reveals that companies are using various linguistic strategies when they talk about the polar bears and the impact in Arctic region in general. Polar bears are vulnerable when the companies perform harmful oil exploration activities, and in this way they are therefore stakeholders, insofar as they are affected by the companies' operations. However, they are obviously unable to put any pressure on the oil companies. In Russia there have been a number of protests addressed to the Rosneft plans to start drilling in the Arctic[53]. The polar bear was a symbol used in the protests, which may explain why Rosneft (in contrast to Statoil) mentions polar bears in annual and sustainability reports (even if displaced into the context of the protection in Russian zoos).

Displacement, silence, standardization and usage of abstract words are the linguistic strategies used in the accounts related to the polar bears protection and environmental impact of oil industry. Thus, even though both oil companies follow GRI guidelines on CSR disclosure, the outcome seems to be an

Figure 18.3 Polar bear

increase in the amount of disclosure, rather than an increase in accountability on the important issue of polar bear extinction. Allowing companies to be opportunistic in their accounting for sustainability involves a risk that reporting only strengthens the legitimacy of "business-as-usual" mode of oil business. Such a risk means enormous losses for society and ecology in the future. The implication of this study would thus be for regulators to consider a possibility to develop more contextualized guidelines for the oil industry, including disclosures related to the environmentally sensitive Arctic region. As mentioned in the introduction, the region has a specific setting where the legal and national boundaries can be blurred. The study suggests that GRI-EN14 call to report on red listed species needs a further development for various industries operating in certain regions where particular red species need protection. Additionally, it is also important to increase society's awareness of the negative impact of oil industry in Arctic region. A more aware society would be able to represent voices of stakeholders (e.g. polar bears) in Arctic region and this would create more pressure on the oil companies. It would potentially turn the accounts from being linguistically strategic to more engaging accounts that would enable transparent communication with various stakeholders as well as enable organizational change towards more sustainable businesses.

Finally, the results of the study reveal that oil companies having a joint project in the Arctic do not report a joint agenda and goals related to polar bear protection. This leads us to recommend that managers of oil companies in the Arctic region seek to develop a shared strategy and goals regarding polar bear impact and protection. Attaching a set of quantitative and qualitative measures to those shared goals will enable a managerial dialogue on these issues and also a follow up over time. This in turn could be disclosed in a form of extinction accounting to stakeholders and such disclosure could result in a virtuous circle of action and reporting.

Notes

1 F. Fetterer et al. *Sea Ice Index Version 2.* (Boulder, Colorado USA. NSIDC, National Snow and Ice Data Center, 2016).
2 J. Richter-Menge, J. E. Overland and J. T. Mathis, "Arctic Report Card 2016", www.arctic.noaa.gov/Report-Card.
3 John Phipps Mulgrave, *A Voyage Towards the North Pole* (London: Bowyer & Nichols, 1773), page 185.
4 M. E. Obbard et al., *Polar Bears,* in *Proceedings of the 15th Working Meeting of the IUCN/SSC Polar Bear Specialist Group,* Gland, Switzerland and Cambridge, UK.
5 PBSG, "Global Polar Bear Population Estimates". Accessed July 14, 2017. http://pbsg.npolar.no/en/status/pb-global-estimate.html
6 Ø. Wiig, S. Amstrup, T. Atwood, K. Laidre, N. Lunn, M. Obbard, E. Regehr & G. Thiemann. "Ursus Maritimus" The IUCN Red List of Threatened Species 2015: e.T22823A14871490. http://dx.doi.org/10.2305/IUCN.UK.2015-4.RLTS.T228 23A14871490.en.
7 PBSG. 2017. "Summary of Polar Bear Population Status per 2017". Accessed: 16 July 2017 pbsg.npolar.no/en/status/status–table.html

8 Ø. Wiig. "Survival and Reproductive Rates for Polar Bears at Svalbard." Ursus 10 (1998): 25–32.

9 Amstrup, Steven C. "Polar Bear – Ursus Maritimus. Biology, Management, and Conservation." In George A. Feldhamer, Bruce C. Thomson and Joseph A. Chapman (eds), *Wild Mammals of North America: Biology, Management, and Conservation* (Baltimore, MD, USA.: John Hopkins University Press, 2003): 587–610.

10 Karyn Rode, Charles Robbins, Lynne Nelson, and Steven Amstrup. "Can Polar Bears Use Terrestrial Foods to Offset Lost Ice-Based Hunting Opportunities?" *Frontiers in Ecology and the Environment* 13, no. 3 (2015): 138–145.

11 Wiig et al., "Ursus Maritimus."

12 A. E. Derocher, J. Aars, S.C. Amstrup, A. Cutting, N. J. Lunn, P. K. Molnár, and M. E. Obbard. "Rapid Ecosystem Change and Polar Bear Conservation." *Conservation Letters* 6, no. 5 (2013): 368–375.

13 T. C. Atwood, B. G. Marcot, D. C. Douglas, S.C. Amstrup, K. D. Rode, G. M. Durner, and J. F. Bromaghin. 2015. "Evaluating and Ranking Threats to the Long-Term Persistence of Polar Bears". U.S. Geological Survey Open-File Report 2014–1254.

14 S. G. Cherry, Derocher, A. E. Thiemann, G. W. and Lunn, N. J. "Migration Phenology and Seasonal Fidelity of an Arctic Marine Predator in Relation to Sea Ice Dynamics." *Journal of Animal Ecology* 82, no. 4 (2013): 912–921.

15 N. J. Lunn, I. Stirling, D. Andriashek, and E. Richardson. "Selection of Maternity Dens by Female Polar Bears in Western Hudson Bay, Canada and the Effects of Human Disturbance." *Polar Biology* 27 (2004): 350–356.

16 Markus J. Milne, Helen Tregidga, Sara Walton, "Words Not Actions! The Ideological Role of Sustainable Development Reporting", *Accounting, Auditing & Accountability Journal* 22, no. 8 (2009): 1211–1257; Michael. J. Jones, Jill. F. Solomon, "Problematising around Biodiversity" *Accounting, Auditing & Accountability Journal* 26 no. 5 (2013): 668–687; C. H. Cho, M. Laine, R. W. Roberts and M. Rodrigue, "Organized Hypocrisy, Organizational Façades, and Sustainability Reporting", *Accounting, Organizations and Society* 40, no. 0 (2015): 78–94.

17 M. Grooten, R. Almond, R. McLellan, *Living Planet Report 2012: Biodiversity, Biocapacity and Better Choices*, WWF, Zoological Society of London, Global Footprint Network, European Space Agency (2012)

18 IPCC, *Climate Change 2013: The Physical Science Basis* (Cambridge: Cambridge University Press, 2013)

19 J. D., Mahadeo, V., Oogarah-Hanuman and T., Soobaroyen. "Changes in Social and Environmental Reporting Practices in an Emerging Economy (2004–2007): Exploring the Relevance of Stakeholder and Legitimacy Theories". *Accounting Forum* 35, no. 3 (2011): 158–175.

20 Milne et al., "Words Not Actions!"; M. J. Jones, J. F. Solomon, "Problematising around biodiversity" *Accounting, Auditing & Accountability Journal* 26, no. 5 (2013): 668–687; C. H. Cho, M. Laine, R. W. Roberts and M. Rodrigue, "Organized Hypocrisy, Organizational Façades, and Sustainability Reporting", *Accounting, Organizations and Society* 40, no. 0 (2015): 78–94.

21 Milne et al., "Words Not Actions!"

22 J. Ferguson, T. R. Sales de Agiuar and A. Fearful, "Corporate Response to Climate Change: Power and Symbolic Construction" *Accounting Auditing and Accountiability Journal* 29, no 2 (2016).

23 J. F. Atkins, W. Maroun, B. Atkins and E. Barone "From the Big Five to the Big Four? Exploring Extinction Accounting for the Rhinoceros." *Accounting Auditing and Accountability Journal* 31, no. 2 (2017): 674–702.

24 Milne et al., "Words Not Actions!"

25 Ibid.

26 T. Borglund, M. Frostensson and K. Windell, "Effekterna av hållbarhetsredovisning: En studie av konsekvenserna av de nya riktlinjerna om hållbarhetsinformation i statligt ägda företag", Regeringskanslit (2010).

27 M. Laine, "Towards Sustaining the Status Quo: Business Talk of Sustainability in Finnish Corporate Disclosures 1987–2005" *European Accounting Review* 19, no. (2010): 247–274.

28 Milne et al., "Words Not Actions!"

29 C. H. Cho, M. Laine, R. W. Roberts and M. Rodrigue, "Organized Hypocrisy, Organizational Façades, and Sustainability Reporting", *Accounting, Organizations and Society* 40, no. 0 (2015): 78–94; J. F. Atkins, E. Barone, W. Maroun and B. Atkins, "Bee Accounting and Accountability in the UK" in J.F. Atkins and B. Atkins (eds.) "The Business of Bees: An Integrated Approach to Bee Decline and Corporate responsibility" Sheffield (2016).

30 Ferguson et al., "Corporate Response to Climate Change."

31 International Maritime Organization. "Shipping in Polar Waters" (2017) www.imo.org/en/MediaCentre/HotTopics/polar/Pages/default.aspx

32 V. Beattie and S. Thomson. "Lifting the Lid on the Use of Content Analysis to Investigate Intellectual Capital Disclosures in Corporate Annual Reports" *Accounting Forum* 31, no. 2 (2007):

33 K. Krippendorf. *Content Analysis: an Introduction to its Methodology* (Thousand Oaks, CA: Sage, 2004).

34 Ferguson et al., "Corporate Response to Climate Change."

35 Ibid.

36 D. Merkl-Davies and N. Brennan. "A Theoretical Framework of External Accounting Communication: Research Perspectives, Traditions, and Theories", *Accounting, Auditing & Accountability Journal* 30, no. 2 (2017):

37 Rosneft. *Sustainability Report 2012*, Page 36

38 Ferguson et al., "Corporate Response to Climate Change."

39 Ibid.

40 Rosneft. *Sustainability Report 2012*, p. 36.

41 Ibid., p. 37.

42 Ibid., p. 37

43 Rosneft. *Sustainability Report 2013*, pp. 47–48.

44 Ibid., p. 54

45 Ibid., p. 100

46 Rosneft. *Sustainability Report 2015*, p. 110.

47 Ferguson et al., "Corporate Response to Climate Change."

48 Ibid.

49 Rosneft. *Sustainability Report 2014*, p. 63.

50 Rosneft. *Sustainability Report 2015*, p. 72.

51 Statoil. *Sustainability Report 2012*, p. 43.

52 Merkl-Davies and Brennan, "A Theoretical Framework of External Accounting Communication."

53 For example, see www.greenpeace.org/russia/ru/news/2013/10-04-2013_Medvedi_na_platforme_Statoil.

References

Amstrup, Steven C. "Polar Bear – Ursus Maritimus. Biology, Management, and Conservation." Chap. 27 In *Wild Mammals of North America: Biology, Management, and Conservation*, edited by Feldhamer George A., Thomson Bruce C. and Chapman Joseph A., 587–610. Baltimore, MD, USA.: John Hopkins University Press, 2003.

Atkins, J., F., E. Barone, W. Maroun, and B. Atkins, eds. *Bee Accounting and Accountability in the Uk.* Edited by J. Atkins, F. and B. Atkins, The Business of Bees: An Integrated Approach to Bee Decline and Corporate Responsibility. Sheffield: Greenleaf Publishers, 2016.

Atkins, J., F., W. Maroun, B. Atkins, and E. Barone. "From the Big Five to the Big Four? Exploring Extinction Accounting for the Rhinoceros." *Accounting, Auditing & Accountability Journal* 31, no. 2 (2017): 674–702.

Atwood, T.C., B.G. Marcot, D.C. Douglas, S.C. Amstrup, K.D. Rode, G.M. Durner, and , and J.F. Bromaghin. "Evaluating and Ranking Threats to the Longterm Persistence of Polar Bears." In *U.S. Geological Survey Open*, 2015.

Beattie, Vivien, and Sarah Thomson. "Lifting the Lid on the Use of Content Analysis to Investigate Intellectual Capital Disclosures in Corporate Annual Reports." *Accounting Forum* 31, no. 2 (2007): 129–163.

Borglund, Tommy, Magnus Frostensson, and Karolina Windell. "Effekterna Av Hållbarhetsredovisning: En Studie Av Konsekvenserna Av De Nya Riktlinjerna Om Hållbarhetsinformation I Statligt Ägda Företag." *Regeringskanslit*, 2010.

Cherry, S.G., A.E. Derocher, G.W. Thiemann, and N.J. Lunn. "Migration Phenology and Seasonal Fidelity of an Arctic Marine Predator in Relation to Sea Ice Dynamics.". *Journal of Animal Ecology* 82, no. 4 (2013): 912–921.

Cho, Charles H., Matias Laine, Robin W. Roberts, and Michelle Rodrigue. "Organized Hypocrisy, Organizational Façades, and Sustainability Reporting." *Accounting, Organizations and Society* 40 (2015/01/01/ 2015): 78–94.

Derocher, A.E., J. Aars, S.C. Amstrup, A. Cutting, N.J. Lunn, P.K. Molnár, M.E. Obbard, *et al.* "Rapid Ecosystem Change and Polar Bear Conservation. ." *Conservation Letters 6*, no. 5 (2013): 368–375.

Ferguson, John, Thereza Raquel Sales de Aguiar, and Anne Fearfull. "Corporate Response to Climate Change: Language, Power and Symbolic Construction." *Accounting, Auditing & Accountability Journal* 29, no. 2 (2016): 278–304.

Fetterer, F., Kenneth Knowles, Walt Meier, and Matthew Savoie. "Sea Ice Index, Version 2." Boulder, Colorado USA. NSIDC, National Snow and Ice Data Center, http://nsidc.org/data/G02135.

Grooten, Monique, Rosamunde Almond, and Richard McLellan. "Living Planet Report 2012: Biodiversity, Biocapacity and Better Choices." WWF, Zoological Society of London, Global Footprint Network and European Space Agency, 2012.

IMO. "Shipping in Polar Waters." International Maritime Organization (IMO), www.imo.org/en/MediaCentre/HotTopics/polar/Pages/default.aspx.

IPCC. "Climate Change 2013: The Physical Science Basis." Cambridge: Intergovernmental Panel on Climate Change, 2013.

Jones, Michael John, and Jill Frances Solomon. "Problematising Accounting for Biodiversity." *Accounting, Auditing & Accountability Journal* 26, no. 5 (2013): 668–687.

Krippendorff, Klaus. *Content Analysis: An Introduction to Its Methodology.* 2. ed. Thousand Oaks, Calif.: Sage, 2004.

Laine, Matias. "Towards Sustaining the Status Quo: Business Talk of Sustainability in Finnish Corporate Disclosures 1987–2005." *European Accounting Review* 19, no. 2 (2010/06/01 2010): 247–274.

Lunn, N.J., I. Stirling, D. Andriashek, and E. Richardson. "Selection of Maternity Dens by Female Polar Bears in Western Hudson Bay, Canada and the Effects of Human Disturbance. ." *Polar Biology* 27 (2004): 350–356.

Mahadeo, Jyoti Devi, Vanisha Oogarah-Hanuman, and Teerooven Soobaroyen. "Changes in Social and Environmental Reporting Practices in an Emerging Economy (2004–2007): Exploring the Relevance of Stakeholder and Legitimacy Theories." *Accounting Forum* 35, no. 3 (2011/09/01/ 2011): 158–175.

Merkl-Davies, Doris, M., and Niamh Brennan, M. "A Theoretical Framework of External Accounting Communication: Research Perspectives, Traditions, and Theories." *Accounting, Auditing & Accountability Journal 30*, no. 2 (2017): 433–469.

Milne, Markus J., Helen Tregidga, and Sara Walton. "Words Not Actions! The Ideological Role of Sustainable Development Reporting." *Accounting, Auditing & Accountability Journal* 22, no. 8 (2009): 1211–1257.

Obbard, M.E. , G.W. Thiemann, E. Peacock, and T.D DeBruyn. "Polar Bears." Paper presented at the 15th Working Meeting of the IUCN/SSC Polar Bear Specialist Group, Copenhagen, Denmark, 29 June–3 July 2009, 2010.

PBSG. "Global Polar Bear Population Estimates." Polar Bear specialist group, http://pbsg.npolar.no/en/status/pb-global-estimate.html.

PBSG. "Summary of Polar Bear Population Status Per 2017." http://pbsg.npolar.no/en/status/status-table.html.

Phipps Mulgrave, Constantine John. *A Voyage Towards the North Pole*. London: Bowyer & Nichols, 1773.

Richter-Menge, J, J.E. Overland, and J.T. Mathis. "Arctic Report Card 2016." 2016.

Rode, Karyn .D., Charles T. Robbins, Lynne Nelson, and Steven C. Amstrup. "Can Polar Bears Use Terrestrial Foods to Offset Lost Ice-Based Hunting Opportunities?." *Frontiers in Ecology and the Environmen* 13, no. 3 (2015): 138–145.

Rosneft. *Sustainability Report 2012*. Moscow: Rosneft.

Rosneft. *Sustainability Report 2013*. Moscow: Rosneft.

Rosneft. *Sustainability Report 2014*. Moscow: Rosneft.

Rosneft. *Sustainability Report 2015*. Moscow: Rosneft.

Statoil. *Sustainability Report 2012*. Stavanger: Statoil.

Wiig, Øystein. "Survival and Reproductive Rates for Polar Bears at Svalbard." *Ursus* 10 (1998): 25–32.

Wiig, Ø., S. Amstrup, T. Atwood, K. Laidre, N.J. Lunn, M. Obbard, E. Regehr, and G. Thiemann. "Ursus Maritimus, Polar Bear." In *The IUCN Red List of Threatened Species*. http://dx.doi.org/10.2305/IUCN.UK.2015-4.RLTS.T22823A14871490.en.

III.5

Extinction accounting in East Asia

19 Panda accounting and accountability

Preventing giant panda extinction in China
熊猫

Longxiang Zhao and Jill Atkins

The loss of biodiversity globally and the continuing trend of species extinctions represent the most significant threats to the continuance of life on planet earth – human and non-human. Species are disappearing by the hour, some before they have even been discovered and the sad truth is that we do not really know how many species inhabit our planet let alone how many are disappearing. Unfortunately, it is now indisputable that this sixth period of mass extinction on earth are being caused directly and indirectly by human activity, especially business activity. Climate change, global warming, habitat degradation, pollution, invasion by alien species, agriculture, over-fishing, excessive consumption of natural resources, pesticide and herbicide use, are all contributing to species extinction. The role of corporations and other forms of organisation is vital if current extinction trends are to be altered. Businesses have not only a responsibility but also a duty to act as better stewards of our ecosystems and biodiversity. The need to encourage businesses worldwide to embrace this responsibility and to be proactive in slowing biodiversity loss is becoming more and more acknowledged and accepted.

The Convention on Biological Diversity (CBD) came into force in 1993, and has three main objectives: biodiversity conservation; sustainable use of biodiversity; and fairly share the benefits from biodiversity (CBD, 1993). Since the concept of 'corporate (private sector) participation in biodiversity' was first proposed in the third meeting of the Conference of the Parties (COP-3) to CBD in 1996 (CBD, 1996), 'Business and Biodiversity' has gradually developed as an important issue in CBD negotiation. Moreover, in the ISO 26000 guidance on social responsibility, biodiversity has been listed in the environment core subject as 'Protection of the environment, biodiversity and restoration of natural habitats' (ISO, 2010, p. 12). Furthermore, the G3.1 of GRI's Sustainability Reporting Guidelines has two core indicators (EN11 and EN12) and four additional indicators (EN13, EN14, EN15 and EN25) specifically deal with biodiversity disclosure, including reporting information on species and habitats which affected by corporate operations; the impact of corporate operations, products and services on biodiversity; and how corporations managing these impacts (GRI, 2011).

In 2010, the COP-10 approved the 'Strategic Plan for Biodiversity 2011–2020', and identified the 2020 global biodiversity targets, which is also named as Aichi Biodiversity Targets (CBD, 2010a). In Aichi Biodiversity Targets, corporate position and function in biodiversity conservation have been greatly valued in Strategic Goal A, which is: 'address the underlying causes of biodiversity loss by mainstreaming biodiversity across government and society' (CBD, 2010b, p. 2). Corporations are involved in all the detailed targets. The second target suggests biodiversity values to be integrated into national accounting and reporting systems, and the fourth target points out the requirement for business participation (CBD, 2013). Biodiversity is an unavoidable issue for modern corporations, no matter from their corporate social responsibility perspective or their survival and development perspective (Zhang et al., 2014).

There has been a recent growth in academic research which explores the role of accounting in helping to conserve and enhance biodiversity as well as to prevent extinctions of species. Recent work has provided a range of frameworks which may be implemented to prevent extinction. Further, a number of studies have explored the practice of extinction accounting around the world focusing on high profile species such as rhinoceros, bees, polar bears, and butterflies. However, these studies have all centred around the West and developing economies. There has been no research to date which has focused on how accounting may contribute to extinction prevent in countries in the Far East. This paper seeks to address this gap in the existing literature by exploring the extent to which Chinese companies are accounting for biodiversity and whether or not they are seeking to prevent extinction through their initiatives and practice as well as whether they are accounting for extinction in their reports and disclosures. Further, we have chosen to focus on the extent to which one particular species is being protected: the giant panda. Panda are one of the most charismatic species on the planet, they are so beloved the world over that they have been chosen for the WWF symbol. As we shall see in this paper, there have been grave concerns about the survival of panda for many years, with their habitat disappearing and their natural environment being destroyed. We seek to discover the extent to which Chinese companies and other organisations are working together (or separately) to enhance panda populations and ensure the survival of this wonderful species.

In this chapter, we seek to provide a tentative panda accounting framework, developed from the extinction accounting framework of Atkins and Maroun (2018) and that found in chapter one, for companies and other organisations to use as a basis for accounting for their efforts to protect and enhance panda populations, as well as to demonstrate the extent to which these efforts are working. This framework is intended to act as an emancipatory accounting tool which will assist in saving the panda from extinction. We also present a panda-centric accounting and accountability framework which incorporates the various mechanisms which are currently in place and which are seeking to save the panda.

As discussed at length in chapter two, there has been a recent surge of interest in accounting for biodiversity and extinction accounting among the academic accounting community. Research into accounting for biodiversity has ranged from studies of corporate disclosures of biodiversity-related information, to more theoretical discussions around the role of corporations in destroying as well as in seeking to preserve and enhance biodiversity. Early attempts to formulate a means of accounting for (or really auditing) biodiversity were explored by Jones (see Jones 1996, 2003; Jones and Matthews, 2000). A special issue of *Accounting, Auditing and Accountability Journal*, published in 2013, included a series of papers which considered biodiversity accounting practice by companies in different countries as well as frameworks and techniques for addressing biodiversity loss. Indeed, a framework for problematising biodiversity identified theoretical motivations underlying accounting for biodiversity and explored the role of humans in the ongoing loss of biodiversity (Jones and Solomon, 2013). Further, a book entitled *Accounting for Biodiversity* was published in 2014 (Jones, 2014). A study of biodiversity accounting practice by UK and German companies found that there were a wide range of disclosures but that they were concentrated in certain industries (Atkins et al., 2014). This study concluded that contemporary biodiversity accounting practice was anthropocentric, with the focus being on preserving and enhancing biodiversity where this was useful to humans and from the perspective of managing and reducing financial risk to the companies from biodiversity loss.

More recently, research has focused on the need for, nature of, and practice of, a new form of accounting, namely extinction accounting, which is the subject of this whole book. We do not feel it necessary to summarise this literature again in this chapter and refer our readers to chapter two for a full discussion. This chapter aims to build on existing research and the framework in chapter two by considering their applicability to saving panda.

Biodiversity loss and extinction threats in a Chinese context

China is one of twelve countries with the richest biodiversity on the planet, with a share of 13.7% of global vertebrates, and it is one of four centres of genetic resources origin in the world (Li, 2015). Moreover, China accounts for 20% of the worldwide human population, but only has 7% of global arable land and fresh water resources. Under such conditions, China is the most important place to purchase, process and consume global key commodities, the current production mode of these commodities is placing great pressure on biodiversity and sustainable utilisation of renewable resources, which have higher conservation value (WWF China, 2015a). Currently, China is also one of the countries highly threatened by biodiversity loss, mainly caused by over exploitation of resources, loss and degradation of living environment, environmental pollution and climate change (Zang et al., 2016).

Based on the Living Planet Report (LPR) produced by WWF (2014), the number of species globally has reduced by 52% since 1970, and humanity now requires 1.5 planets' worth of resources to satisfy their needs for future, and this pressure is multiplied due to the double effect of growing population and higher ecological footprint per capita. According to the Stockholm Resilience Centre (2015), humans have already overstepped 3 of the 9 planetary boundaries (the safe space defined for life on earth). The loss of biodiversity represents one of the planetary boundaries and we are now in a sixth period of mass extinction on planet earth. At the 10th Conference of the Parties of the Convention on Biological Diversity (CBD), scientists pointed out that the current rate of species extinction is estimated at around one species per hour, which is the fastest rate of extinction since the extinction of the dinosaurs. Due to the impact of human activities, the current extinction rate is more than 1,000 times the natural extinction rate. At this rate, over one million terrestrial species will disappear from earth within 50 years (Jiang et al., 2015).

The Chinese government states that it highly values biodiversity conservation and significant progress has been made throughout years. In 2010, the State Council approved and released the China Biodiversity Conservation Strategy and Action Plan (2011–2030), which promoted biodiversity conservation as a national strategy. In 2011, the State Council approved the establishment of the China biodiversity conservation national commission (Li, 2015). The Biodiversity Conservation Major Projects Implementation Plan (2015–2020) was approved by the commission in 2014. One of the basic tasks within this plan was to carry out national biodiversity surveys and evaluations, in order to build national biodiversity database and information platform based on the unit as county territory (Wu et al., 2016). Moreover, in 2015, the draft leading group for 'regulations for bio-genetic resources obtain and benefit sharing' was established. The Central Committee of the Communist Party of China and State Council released 'comments on speeding up the development of ecological civilisation', which identified 'getting basic control of the biodiversity loss rate, strengthening national ecosystem stability' as main targets. It also confirmed the main tasks of implementing biodiversity conservation key projects, through actively participating in international convention negotiations of biodiversity, and strengthening natural reserve construction and management (Zang et al., 2016).

By the end of 2014, China had established 2,729 natural reserves, covering 1.47 million square kilometres land, constituting 14.84% of China's land area. 85% of national key protected wild fauna and flora species are now protected through legislation. Moreover, ecosystem protection and restoration have made effective achievements; the forestry area has grown by 20% over the last decade. Furthermore, the publicity and education of biodiversity has also had significant success, after the State Council approved to implement 'the United Nations biodiversity ten years China operation', media publicity has affected hundreds of millions of people, such that social awareness of, and enthusiasm about, biodiversity conservation have risen significantly (Li, 2015).

However, the overall trend of biodiversity degradation has not been fundamentally reduced; the issues of species habitat loss and fragmentation, and invasion of alien species continue to present challenges to biodiversity conservation (Wei, 2015). At present, 90% of the nation's grasslands are degenerating and suffering desertification at various levels, 40% of the key wetlands are facing the threat of degeneration, and 10.9% of the higher plants and 21.2% of the vertebrates are under threat. Some rare endangered species have not been protected, and the phenomenon of genetic resources loss still exists (Li, 2015).

Zang et al. (2016) point out that biodiversity conservation work in China is still inadequate and that there is a lack of comprehensive understanding regarding the threatened status of wild flora and fauna, which renders the conservation efforts as less than systemic, scientific and concentrated approaches. Therefore, it is essential to establish China's biodiversity 'red list' to support further conservation works.

The 'China Biodiversity Red List 2015' was released by the China Environmental Protection Department and Chinese Academy of Sciences. The list completes the threatened status assessment for 34,450 advanced plant species and 4,357 kinds of vertebrate species (except marine fishes) in China. The results of the assessment show that the current trend of biodiversity loss in China has not been contained effectively (Jiang et al., 2015). The list also provides a reassessment of advanced plant species and vertebrate species which have been assessed in 'China Biodiversity Red List 2004'. Within 11 years, over half of assessed advanced plant species' threatened status are improved or been removed from the list; and there are less threatened vertebrate species. However, in consideration of the threatened status of listed vertebrate species, the number of species getting worse is more than the number of improved (Zang et al., 2016). One positive sign is that the threatened mammals in China have reduced from 223 to 178, which suggests initial success of protection for threatened mammals. For example, the combination of on-site and off-site conservation has strengthened conservation for giant pandas (Jiang et al., 2015).

The 'China Biodiversity Red List 2015' identifies the threatened status of known advanced plants and vertebrates, as well as their distributional differences and threatened factors. It provides important scientific evidence for local government and related departments to formulate related policies and plans, and promote the reasonable utilisation of resources. Moreover, it provides reference for environmental impact evaluation of construction projects. Furthermore, it could be used as essential material for biodiversity education and public awareness raising (Zang et al., 2016).

Biodiversity conservation is a complex issue that cuts across different regions, disciplines and departments. Firstly, biodiversity conservation is multidisciplinary including biology, ecology, meteorology, geography, sociology. These different disciplines all provide theories and technical support for conservation activities, and their theoretical bases are essential for conservation awareness raising and education. Secondly, biodiversity conservation is a challenge referring to multi fields including legislations, policies, environment, forestry, customs, culture, international communication and etc. Effective conservation requires the integration of knowledge and strengths of these fields. These two features of biodiversity protection mean it needs to be a coordinated process among many departments. It needs government departments to provide legislation, policy, strategic and macro planning support; local communities' direct involvement; research institutions to responsible for technical development, theory exploration, education promotion and awareness raising; NGOs to introduce and promote international advanced concepts, experiences and methods; and corporations to provide funding support and implement conservation in their development. Therefore, effective biodiversity conservation requires participation from a wide range of stakeholders; it has been recognised as one effective approach internationally (Zhang and Liu, 2015).

However, the current biodiversity conservation process in China is characterised by a lack of participation from multi stakeholders. Therefore it is necessary to establish a stakeholder participation mechanism that complies with Chinese characteristics, considers China's actual conditions, problems and demands exist in China's biodiversity conservation. In China, the main obstacles to such a mechanism are: conflicts of interests and responsibilities among different departments; lack of coordination and cooperative mechanisms; lack of legislation; lack of policy and technical support; and lack of corporate participation (Zhang and Liu, 2015).

According to Hou (2014), biodiversity protection is one of the important contents of social responsibility, but it has not been valued as well as other components like public welfare by corporations. In China, corporations are the main bodies that utilise the biodiversity, but they did not realise the seriousness of the issue. According to the GoldenBee CSR Index Report (2007–2013), published by China WTO Tribune and GoldenBee (Beijing) Management Consulting in 2013, 15% of Chinese companies believe China does not need to worry about biodiversity, only 13% of companies develop technical research about biodiversity, and there are only 7% of companies use professional reports to spread and report biodiversity. This indicates that the majority of companies lack relevant knowledge, technical research, publicity and guidance concerning biodiversity protection.

The Chinese government was invited to attend the forum of Global Partnership for Business and Biodiversity (GPBB), and on the GPBB-4, China firstly announced that it has prepared to join GPBB. Correspondingly, the Ministry of Environmental Protection of China has already organised some activities like business and biodiversity case study collection, corporations' awareness for biodiversity conservation survey, and biodiversity and green development international forum. It also organises business representatives in different industries to sign the 'initial written proposal for corporate participation in biodiversity conservation', initially establish the communication and cooperation platform between government and corporations (Wang et al., 2015).

Some corporations in China are beginning to take action, actively participating in biodiversity related forums and etc. However, China does not have experience in organising and guiding corporations to participate in biodiversity conservation, sustainable utilisation and benefit sharing. In order to meet the requirements for further biodiversity conservation work, several recommendations for Chinese government have been proposed: firstly, actively participate in the GPBB. Secondly, strengthen technical research to formulate related standards and guidelines for business and biodiversity. Thirdly, deepen the platform construction, set up a business and biodiversity partnership in China. Finally, establish a coordination mechanism that across departments to guide the specific work of corporations' participation in biodiversity (Wang et al., 2015).

Giant panda in China: threats, challenges and conservation efforts

The giant panda is one of 13 flagship species which has been given global conservation priority. Conservation of giant pandas and their habitats also benefits all species living in the same area, including other rare species such as the golden monkey, the lesser panda, the blood pheasant, the crested ibis as well as the ecosystems like forest and wet land (WWF China, undated a). The giant panda has been established as an 'indicator species', such that the performance of giant panda conservation is taken to represent the performance of nature reserves in the region (Green Homeland, 2003). Giant pandas play an important role in their habitats as they spreading seeds in their droppings all over the forest, thus to keep the forest thrive (WWF UK, 2015). Where the giant panda lives has been called the green heart of China, which is the Upper Reaches of the Yangtze River (WWF, 2009). The Yangtze River is the 'mother river' of China, it provides water to one-third of the Chinese population, and over 500 million people live around it (WWF, 2010). Moreover, the forest that giant panda lives in is also crucial for the livelihoods of local people, who depend it on food, medicine, income and fuel (WWF, 2015). Furthermore, giant pandas are culturally and economically valuable to China, they can generate income through tourism. They are the national symbol of China and are recognised as the 'national treasure' (WWF, 2015). They have been rented to overseas as the Goodwill Ambassadors of China, promote and maintain friendship between China and other countries (China Conservation and Research Centre for the Giant Panda, undated).

China has conducted a systemic survey of giant panda since 1974, and updates the survey every ten years. The geologic record shows that the current giant panda (*Ailuropoda melanoleuca*) is the descendant of *Ailuropoda melanoleuca baconi*, it was widely distributed in southern and eastern China, northern Burma and northern Vietnam. In the middle of the twentieth century, giant pandas' habitats have shrunk to just 6 isolated mountain ranges, approximately 23 isolated habitats in Szechwan, Gansu and Shaanxi Provinces. 13 out of these isolated habitats have higher risk of extinction due to smaller giant panda population. Climate change might contribute to the long term trend of habitat reduction, but the main reason is the human activity in modern times. Chinese population explode from 0.47 billion in 1949 to 1.3 billion in 2000, with the rapid development of industry and agriculture, human activities and expansion significantly affect giant pandas' habitats (Conservation International and Shanshui Conservation Centre, 2009).

According to the WWF's research, various factors contribute to the degeneration, fragmentation and loss of giant panda's habitats. Traditional threats such as grazing, collection of medicinal herbs, and poaching have not been eliminated completely, and new threats are emerging: large-scale road construction, tourism, mining, and the dam construction. These factors intensify the isolation of giant panda groups and the extinction risk of isolated small group of giant pandas. Isolation among small groups of giant pandas is fatal for their long term survival. Reduction of effective breeding individuals leads to inbreeding and failure of breeding, thus drop the population's abilities to adapt environment and resist diseases. Ultimately, small groups' survivability is reduced, even leading to extinction (WWF China, 2016a).

Research by Wu et al. (2014) shows that the most suitable habitats for giant panda are gradually reducing, and some of these habitats have not been covered in current giant pandas' conservation network. The suitable habitats for giant pandas have lower tolerance of environment change due to their specialities; the future climate change could lead to the degradation of these habitats. Moreover, various researches (Wu and Lv, 2009; Liu, 2012; Wu et al., 2016) point out that giant pandas' habitats will shrink, and some new suitable habitats will expand to west and higher altitude, with the trend of fragmentation. The future works of conservation and recovery of giant pandas' habitats are facing great challenge. It is urgent to identify and complement the conservation gaps of the most suitable habitats (current and potential) for giant pandas, and take actions to prevent the reduction of these habitats. The following monitoring and evaluation works are also required.

Bamboo is the main source of food for giant pandas and the distribution range of bamboo is one of the main factors that determine the distribution of giant pandas (Wu et al., 2016). Bamboo naturally dies off every 40–120 years, giant pandas normally move from die-offs bamboo area to healthy bamboo area (WWF, 2015). However, bamboo has flowering periods and it is a one-time reproductive plant which withers intensely when flowering. Currently the inner mechanism of this phenomenon remains unknown, and the periodic bloom of bamboo is a main threat to giant pandas (Wu et al., 2016). Interference from human activities creates more threats. Due to human expansion and over harvesting of bamboo, 65% of giant panda's habitats declined between 1974 and 2001. Accordingly, the population of wild giant panda experienced a sharp decrease from 2,459 to only 1,596 during the same period (Conservation International and Shanshui Conservation Centre, 2009).

Panda protection in China

Government and NGOs such as the WWF and other organisations have been working hard to save the panda. In response to problems associated with bamboo loss, as identified above, the Chinese government has banned logging activities in giant panda's habitats since 1998, and focused on the establishment and expansion of natural reserves and green corridors. The green corridors are composed of bamboo and forest, and act as a bridge to connect habitats to expand giant pandas' range of activities, thus to help them find more foods and companions to breed (WWF Global, undated). By 2008, there were 63 giant panda reserves in China, covering 32,077.59 square kilometres. Sixteen of these are national level nature reserves, which is higher than the national average. Currently, establishing nature reserve is the main approach to conserve giant pandas and their habitats. However, lots of habitats, potential habitats and habitat corridors are still have not covered by nature reserves. A number of local residents are living in these areas. Therefore, it is important to encourage local community conservation (Conservation International and Shanshui Conservation Centre, 2009).

Government efforts to save the panda

The investment that central government provides for wild giant panda conservation is severely low and fundamental change is required (Conservation International and Shanshui Conservation Centre, 2009). One of the main reasons for this low level of investment according to Wu et al. (2010) is a lack of legislation. Without legal protection, the national investment in giant panda conservation cannot satisfy the actual needs. Similarly, the current wildlife conservation legislations and major conservation project have lots of contradictions and inconsistencies with local economic development. For example, some local economic projects like highway and railway construction could segment giant pandas' habit result in isolation of population. The concomitant pollution like sound pollution and light pollution also could impact giant pandas and their habitats. The current legislations and standards are not enough to limit or solve these issues. Furthermore, some current conservation legislation is unclear about implementation parties or approaches, or have issues on enforcement. China also lacks specific legislation about international governments' and organisations' participation in China's wildlife conservation and giant panda conservation. This not only affects the motivation of these parties, but also creates difficulties to manage and coordinate them. All these legislation issues are not favourable for the construction and management of giant panda nature reserves and conservation works.

Giant panda conservation receives the most significant investment from the Chinese government, compared with their other species' conservation projects (Wu et al., 2016). The 'Wildlife Conservation Law' was issued in 1988; over 50 legal documents related to giant panda conservation were released in the following two decades. They provide positive legal basis for giant panda conservation. Furthermore, in order to fundamentally save giant panda from endangered status, Chinese government put great effort in the conservation of giant pandas' habitats. After the implementation of 'China Giant Panda and Related Habitat Conservation Project (1992)', numerous giant panda nature reserves have been established, effectively contain the trend of habitat degradation. However, as discussed earlier, there are still some gaps and blanks in the current legislations for giant panda conservation (Wu et al., 2010) In respond, the State Forestry Administration of China has put the formulation of 'giant panda conservation regulation' on the agenda; this will be the first proposed legal regulation in China for a single species. Zhiyong Fan, who is the executive director of WWF China policy research centre, believes that the potential threats of giant panda conservation not only have not being eliminated, but also more serious than ever before. Moreover, the current wildlife conservation law cannot satisfy the needs for national key conservation species. Fan believes that after this special legislation has been implemented, the trend of fragmentation of giant panda's habitats can be restrained, and this legislation will be a good example for other species (Paper, 2016).

The WWF and Shanshui's efforts to save the panda

The WWF (World Wide Fund for Nature) was the first international organisation invited by the Chinese government in 1980, to help protect giant pandas. WWF was carrying out the first giant panda protection research program, cooperate with State Forestry Administration (SFA) to implement the national giant panda survey and formulate the 'giant panda and habitats conservation project'. In the last 30 years, WWF's giant panda strategy has developed from pure species protection expand to the ecosystem protection that focus on giant panda's habitats. The main contributions of WWF are: promote the effective management of giant panda habitats; reduce the negative impact of infrastructure construction; promote sustainable development of community; demonstrate sustainable tourism; exploring response and adaptation strategy of climate change (WWF China, undated a).

In 2013, China has completed the fourth national giant panda survey, which shows there are 1,864 giant pandas alive in the wild, increased by 17% (268) compare to the survey in 2003. Moreover, there are 375 giant pandas in captivity in China and 42 giant pandas in overseas in 12 countries. Furthermore, the habitat of giant panda also increased by 11.8% to 2.58 million hectares over the decade (Guardian, 2015). This is evidence that the population of giant panda has stabilised and is starting to increase, as well as the available habitats, the IUCN Red List decided to downlist the giant panda from Endangered to Vulnerable on 4 September 2016 suggesting the success of conservation efforts by the Chinese government in recent decades (IUCN, 2016).

However, the State Forestry Administration of China (2016) responds that although giant panda has been downlisted from endangered, it is still an endangered species and requires stronger protection and support. As the direct management department of giant panda protection, the State Forestry Administration explains that IUCN's report is just based on related data and technical index. If consider the actual performance and protection situation, it is too early to downlist the giant panda from endangered. Habitat fragmentation is still the main threat of local population of giant pandas, it obstructs the gene exchange between local populations, affects the genetic diversity of giant pandas. Gong et al. (2016) emphasise that the fragmentation pattern of habitats has not changed at all, as well as the human interference. Accelerated local infrastructure construction and resources development in giant pandas' distribution area further the fragmentation degree of local habitats. This result in various fragmentation type, increase the uncertainty of integral fragmented habitats. Moreover, as IUCN (2016) points out, the wild giant pandas are still facing severe survival risk; more than 35% of panda's bamboo habitat is predicted to be eliminated in the next 80 years due to climate change. Furthermore, WWF China (2016a) mentions that much of panda's habitat is threatened by poorly planned infrastructure projects.

Based on these factors, the endangered situation of giant panda has not improved; decades of conservation work just maintain the existing status. More effort is needed to realise the long term survival of giant panda. The key for future conservation work is to try not to lose any inch of giant pandas' habitats, and to expand and connect potential habitats. Meanwhile, the impacts of climate change also need to be considered. Moreover, the transformation and upgrade of conservation approaches are also needed to cope with new conservation requirements (Gong et al., 2016).

The State Forestry Administration concerns that this downlist might cause relaxed protection work, thus lead to irreversible damage and loss (State Forestry Administration of China, 2016). Only the broader conservation policy and measures could ensure the survival of wild giant panda and their unique habitats in future. The public should have more extensive understanding about the importance of conservation of wild species and their habitats for human life. Lambertini, the general secretary of WWF global is appealing to establish and deepen the integrated cooperative relationships among government, local communities, NGOs, corporations and individuals to facing the greater conservation challenge (WWF China, 2016b).

The Shanshui Conservation Center (Shanshui) is a non-governmental biodiversity protection organisation which supported by and cooperates with Conservation International (CI). Its programmes are mainly based on the western China, carry out field protection to demonstrate the harmony between human and nature, thus to promote the mainstreaming of nature conservation in the nation, local policy and public awareness (Shanshui, 2014b). Shanshui was founded by an academic team which has proficient experiences in nature conservation researches and practices; its academic background helps it to create wide cooperative relationships with communities, research institutions, government, corporations, media and other organisations. Shanshui's strategy is formed by 'practice station', 'research institute' and 'value chain' (Shanshui, 2014a).

'Practice station' is focus on implementing field protection works by training protectors and innovating new protection approaches (Shanshui, 2014a). Community protection is one of these new approaches, different with traditional approach, Shanshui is providing fund and technology to support the

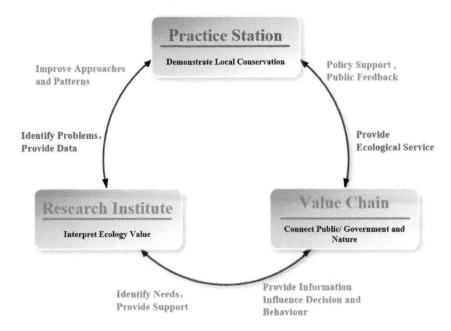

Figure 19.1 Three modules that inform Shanshui's work

community residents to perform protection works rather than conservation organisations. The residents who lived around giant panda nature reserves always been rely on nature resources to make a living, which threaten wildlife habitats and create intense human–animal conflicts. Shanshui believes that only the local residents can solve this issue as they create this threat to environment at the first place. It is important for Shanshui to maintain good cooperation relationships with funders and local resource manager as the community protection usually takes long time to see the effects. Thus, the projects are threatened by various factors, for example, any regional economy development could destroy a five year project in just one month (Shanshui, 2015).

Only society's acknowledgement of ecological value could open channels to fund nature. Therefore, 'Value chain' aims to connect public, government and nature together by delivering the concept of ecological value and ecological justice products to society (Shanshui, 2014a). One of the products, named China nature watch report, is an independent assessment of China's ecological status that jointly issued by NGOs and university research institutions every year. Based on accumulated data from these organisations, the report attempts to explain the changes of China's natural ecology in the last decade, provide information for public and decision makers. Research points out that in China, threatened species have not been protected and data new species data is urgently needed. A large number of blanks in species' population and distribution data are being filled by nature watchers from public. Indeed, the general public are becoming a major and reliable force for basic information collection of species. Funded by HSBC and CEPF, a database website named Nature Watch Map (www.hinature.cn) has been introduced. The website has a public interaction function that allows people to upload information about species' population and distribution, uncovered key habitats and etc. that they discovered to fill the scientific information gaps. A matched application is also being developed to be used by mobile phones (Shanshui, 2014b). China nature watch is continually searching for more partners and trying to cooperate with more conservation NGOs, nature reserves and citizen scientist groups to create a real-time update database for threatened species in China (Shanshui, 2015).

The 'Bee Panda' honey is an ecological justice product initiated by Shanshui Partner, a social enterprise established through the support of Shanshui Conservation Center, which aims to explore commercial approaches to support ecological protection, focusing on producing pure forest honey (Shanshui Partner, 2016a). 'Bee Panda' is only produced in giant panda habitats, and has to satisfy certain requirements for the bees. The bee keepers are local villagers, who also act as watchmen of the forest, giant pandas and pure water (Shanshui, 2013). The villagers used to rely on natural resources to make a living, mainly gathering medical herbs, in so doing threatening giant panda habitats. Therefore, the 'Bee Panda' program provides an alternative livelihood for these local villagers (Shanshui Partner, 2016b). The honey is produced by traditional methods, with only one harvest a year to ensure the highest quality (Shanshui, 2013). The product design and market research including pricing were conducted by Shanshui's academic research team (Zhang and Lv, 2014). All profits from the sales of 'Bee Panda' honey is returned to Shanshui for local communities' ecological conservation activities. Currently, the 'Bee Panda' program supports five conservation areas and 1,194 watchmen in the local community. The programme has benefited 4,175 species of plant, 248 bird species, and 92 species of animals (Shanshui, 2014b).

Jie Feng, who is the programme director of Shanshui points out that 40% of wild giant pandas are living in local communities instead of nature reserves. The protection of these giant pandas is dependent on community residents who need to prevent illegal activities like illegal hunting and deforestation. The 'Bee Panda' programme directly protects the ecological environment of giant pandas' habitats by providing local people with a livelihood and encouraging them to protect the pandas and their habitat. By linking city dwellers with villagers through honey consumption, 'Bee Panda' can be a medium through which the public recognise the value of nature resources and the need for environmental protection (CCTV News, 2014). Further, 'Bee Panda' provides an innovative means for NGOs to cooperate with social enterprises, and connect urban public with conservation programs.

Research method and data collection

We sought to extract any examples of emergent extinction accounting for panda from the sustainability reports and annual reports of Chinese listed companies as well as from websites. Initially, we analysed the annual reports, CSR reports and corporate websites for Chinese listed extractive companies but found nothing relating to panda. Second, we analysed the websites and annual reports of the NGOs involved in panda conservation and protection in China, namely WWF China and Shanshui to find evidence of these NGOs partnering with business and listed companies in order to protect panda and their habitat. This analysis provided rich illustrations from the NGO sector of panda accounting and accountability. As we can see from Chapter 11, public sector extinction accounting is as important, necessary and urgent to species preservation as reporting and accounting for species by listed companies. It is not the sole responsibility of listed companies to practise extinction accounting but is just as necessary for the public sector, charities, NGOs, governmental bodies and voluntary organisations. Only by collaborating across organisational groups can species stand a chance of being preserved. As discussed in Atkins et al. (2018) in relation to rhinoceros conservation and protection, one of the leading ways in which companies are actively attempting to preserve species is through their partnerships with NGOs, such as the WWF.

As well as information about how companies in China are engaging with NGOs to help save the panda, gathered from articles and the media, we also analysed corporate reports and websites to find illustrations of panda accounting. We found panda reporting by three Chinese companies (HIK Vision, Shangri-La, Panda Green Energy Group), as well as by six international companies (L'Oreal, Mercedes-Benz, Seagate, HSBC, Carrefour, Canon) that are either based in China or are joint ventures with Chinese companies. We also carried out an extensive internet search for news and media articles and reports relating to corporate participation in panda conservation. In China this involves using the Baidu function which is the Chinese equivalent of Google.

Panda accounting on partnerships between companies and NGOs in China

WWF partnering with Carrefour

Carrefour has participated in WWF's Sichuan pepper project since 2002; the project aims to protect giant pandas by providing alternative livelihood for villagers living around giant panda nature reserves. The sale of pepper used to be villagers' main income source, but the majority of profits were taken by middlemen. Thus, villagers have to collect medical herbs and firewood from the wild to make a living (Carrefour China, 2011). WWF helps villagers form a cooperative to grow sustainable Sichuan pepper and introduce to Carrefour. By making direct purchase from cooperative, Carrefour can provide fresh, traceable products to its customers. Villagers' incomes are improved and secured by this long term project ensuring the long term protection of giant panda's habitat. This holistic approach provides a sustainable solution and benefits all the involved stakeholders (WWF, 2012).

WWF and Canon China's efforts to save the panda

Canon Company was established in 1937 and entered China in 1997; 'mutualism' is its corporate philosophy. Since Canon China participated in China's wildlife photo training camp in 2004, it has become involved in wildlife conservation work. In 2008, the Wenchuan earthquake caused significant damage to wild giant pandas' habitats. There is a need for research into giant pandas' habitat and giant pandas' post-earthquake ecological habit, as well as the following conservation work (FECO, 2013) and Canon China disclosed the following in its 2014 CSR report:

> Canon donates 16 sets of office equipment and image documentation equipment for wild giant panda protection stations in Szechwan Minshan and Shaanxi Qinling to recover their daily conservation work and post-earthquake behaviour researches for wild giant pandas.
>
> (Canon China, 2014, p. 76)

Further, Canon China is seeking to help reduce the difficulties and improve efficiency of nature reserves' conservation work by providing the high-end field surveillance cameras to monitor wild giant pandas' habitat and moving direction (FECO, 2013). As Canon China disclosed in its 2013 CSR report:

> In 2012, Canon China launch the 'Image·Tracker' program in wild life reserves. It establishes giant panda conservation fund in Wolong Nature Reserve to support the researches about breeding and wild training of giant panda. Moreover, the program also provides a complete set of high-definition video field monitoring system to Fengtongzhai Natural Reserve to support the conservation and salvation of wild giant pandas and other wild animals.
>
> (Canon China, 2013, p. 52)

The most advanced video monitor technology contributes the first-hand video data for long term researches of giant pandas' environment, habitat, breeding and etc. (FECO, 2013). Canon China continually tracking the development and real effect of wild giant panda conservation programs, keep updating and debugging the monitoring equipment (Canon China, 2014). Currently Canon China also work with WWF on other programs to record image data of China's biodiversity and raise public awareness by providing the high-end imaging technology. Meanwhile, it also considers expanding the program for conservation of other endangered wild species (FECO, 2013).

Shanshui and L'Oreal China's efforts to save the panda

One of 'Bee Panda's marketing approach involves cooperating with companies on CSR. For example, the skin care brand, Kiehl, collaborates with celebrities to design and promote a limited edition product incorporating the 'Bee Panda concept' with the aim of donating some of the profits from sales to Shanshui to support panda conservation programs (L'Oreal China, 2015, p. 11). Moreover, L'Oreal China is also working with Shanshui to expand sale channels for Bee Panda and has purchased Bee Panda honey as raw material for its own products since 2016, donating 10% of its income to the community for local ecological conservation (Sina Public Welfare, 2017).

CI, Shanshui and HSBC's efforts to save the panda

HSBC China disclosed its Giant Panda National Park Demonstration project in its 2015 CSR report (p. 27). The company believes that the main problem for giant panda conservation is lack of a unified management mechanism and decided to support Conservation International (CI) which participates in nature reserve management as an NGO in Sichuan. CI has worked with local government departments to creates a pilot national park at Sichuan Anzihe Giant Panda Nature Reserve, to develop a more scientific, systematic and open management. This should allow more institutions, groups and individuals to participate in conservation activities (HSBC China, 2015).

Shanshui is funded by and cooperates with CI on the China Nature Watch project, as disclosed in Shanshui's Annual Report (2014, p. 42; 2015, p. 10) and the project is also partly funded by HSBC. HSBC China states that it aims to 'fully mobilise public resources to obtain information about endangered species and promote the public's participation in biodiversity conservation' (HSBC China, 2015, p. 26).

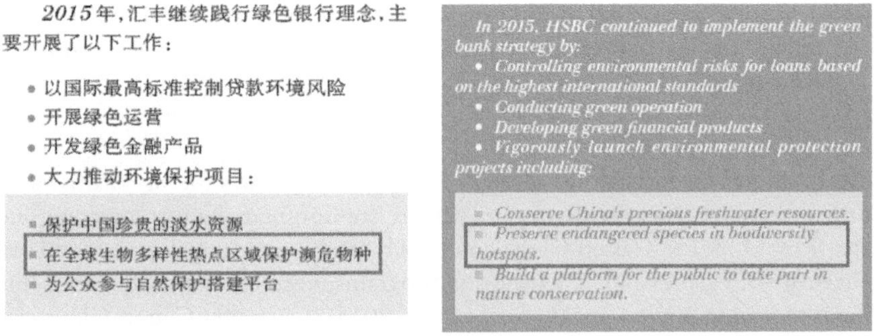
2015年，汇丰继续践行绿色银行理念，主要开展了以下工作：

- 以国际最高标准控制贷款环境风险
- 开展绿色运营
- 开发绿色金融产品
- 大力推动环境保护项目：

- 保护中国珍贵的淡水资源
- 在全球生物多样性热点区域保护濒危物种
- 为公众参与自然保护搭建平台

In 2015, HSBC continued to implement the green bank strategy by:

- *Controlling environmental risks for loans based on the highest international standards*
- *Conducting green operation*
- *Developing green financial products*
- *Vigorously launch environmental protection projects including:*

- *Conserve China's precious freshwater resources.*
- *Preserve endangered species in biodiversity hotspots.*
- *Build a platform for the public to take part in nature conservation.*

Figure 19.2 Protecting environment and building green bank

Source: HSBC China (2015, p. 23)

Panda accounting by Mercedes–Benz

We also found that one of the world's most significant car makers, Mercedes–Benz, is involved in panda conservation. There is information in the media which describes the efforts of Mercedes Benz to assist in panda protection. For example, the company has funded a panda kindergarten for rearing baby panda (Han, 2009; Campaign China, 2012). The launch of the Mercedes–Benz Panda Kindergarten was in response to the 2008 Sichuan Earthquake, which seriously damage giant pandas' habitat, the automaker is reinforcing its commitment to panda conservation with the release of five PANDA tips to help preserve the species which include sharing information about panda on facebook and other social media in order to raise public awareness of their plight (Campaign China, 2012). This project forms part of Mercedes–Benz's Green Legacy Program with United Nations Educational, Scientific and Cultural Organization (UNESCO) in support of World Heritage Sites in China (Han, 2009). Until 2012, the Mercedes–Benz Kindergarten has housed almost 20 pandas, contributed to the research for pandas' eventual survival in the wild and to raised public awareness (Campaign China, 2012).

Panda accounting by Shangri–La

The hotel chain Shangri–La disclosed substantial panda related information in its report; for example the extract shown in Figure 19.3 (Shangri–La, 2012b, p. 31). The sections outlined in the figure translate into English as follows:

Shangri–La's Care for Nature Project

In Shaanxi Province (a panda hometown), two hotels participate and support the projects of Zhouzhi Nature Reserve. Zhouzhi Nature Reserve is the home of golden monkeys and panda. Xian Shangri–La Hotel and Xian Jinhua Hotel renew the patrol equipment for Reserve's patrols, which improve patrols' equipment and capacities. Moreover, they also support the alternative livelihood project, such as bee keeping and Chinese herbal planting projects thus replacing traditional field herbal collection. We hope our support on these projects can reduce the pressures of human activity on the Reserve.

Shangri–La's Care for Panda Project

As part of Shangri–La's Care for Panda Project, we provide support to the planting of 1.6 hectares of bamboo forest in Sichuan Provence (a panda hometown) . . . This bamboo forest is planted within the Dujiangyan Center for Panda Care and Disease Control, located at the foot of Qingcheng Mountain. Shangri_La will plant 9,000 Phyllostachys violascens (a species of bamboo) and 90 trees. This bamboo forest will provide food for the giant pandas in the Dujiangyan Center. The Dujiangyan

Giant Panda Center is currently under construction, and is estimated to open to the public in 2013. The Center will receive and cure ill or aged giant pandas, and carry out research for disease control.

(Shangri-La, 2012b, p. 31)

In Shangri-La (2016, p. 15) the company states that they are continuing their efforts to protect habitat and biodiversity:

From reef care, turtle care, panda care to wetland protection and showcasing flora and fauna, our Sanctuary projects combine conservation with raising public awareness, guest engagement, staff engagement and education programs to address bio-diversity challenges from various angles.

The tourist industry has been noted for its greater incidence of biodiversity reporting, when compared with other industries. This may be motivated by a desire to reduce biodiversity related risks which could affect their hotel trade as well as by an incentive to increase profitability arising from eco-tourism (Atkins et al., 2014).

The company also highlights its partnership initiatives as follows:

Hotels with Sanctuary projects also form partnerships with relevant external parties including accredited non-government organizations, academic bodies, and community groups to ensure local endorsement and professional input.

(Shangri-La, 2016, p. 15)

Figure 19.3 Shangri-La's Care for Panda project

Further the company explains that they carry out audits of biodiversity in order to inform further strategy, which does resemble an emancipatory element in this emergent extinction accounting: 'Biodiversity data is collected on a regular basis to measure results and inform decision makers on the next steps required for each project' (Shangri-La, 2016, p. 15). The company provides details of the hotel involved in panda conservation, as the Shangri-La Hotel, Chengdu, stating that:

> in 2014, Shangri-La Hotel, Chengdu further developed its Care for Panda project. . . . through the development of bamboo plantations and panda feeding facilities. The Group set up a panda kitchen to produce food for the endangered bears, as well as a system to allow guests to share their views on the centre. As of the end of 2014, a total of 1.6 hectares of bamboo had been planted.
>
> (Shangri-La, 2015, p. 15)

This excerpt from their report provides some quantitative information as well as qualitative narrative. It also suggests evidence of stakeholder engagement.

The company discusses its Sanctuary project and states:

> The Qinling region in one of the areas with the richest biodiversity in China, and is home to the most well-known species of the giant panda and the golden monkey. The hotels have invested in the much-needed upgrading of the patrolling facilities to enable the nature reserve staff to better monitor species count and security.
>
> (Shangri-La, 2014, p. 11)

These initiatives are reminiscent of the attempts to protect rhinoceros from poaching in South Africa, as disclosed by South African listed companies (Atkins et al., 2018). However, the text was almost identical to that disclosed in Shangri-La (2013), which is indicative of a rather boiler-plate approach to the panda accounting rather than a more dynamic, emancipatory form of reporting.

Panda accounting by Panda Green Energy Group

Panda Green Energy Group provided information about their new mascot, a Giant Panda called Qiyi, adopted by the company in 2017. The article explains that the CEO of Panda Green Energy went to the Chengdu Research Base at the Giant Panda Breeding Centre and selected a panda for adoption. The articles stated that Qiyi would serve as the active mascot for the United Nations Development Program's (UNDP), 'Youth Leadership Summer Camp for Climate Action and Panda Green Energy's World's First 'Panda Power Plant' and will participate in the opening ceremony held in the United Nations headquarters in Beijing on 10 August (Panda Green Energy Group, 2017). As disclosed in Panda Green Energy Group's 2016 Environmental, Social and

Governance Report (pp. 12–13), the Group plans to establish more Panda Solar Plant and Summer Camps along 'One Belt, One Road' to provide global youth a deep understanding of climate change and green energy, thus to encourage next generation to get involved in future innovate development (Panda Green Energy Group, 2016, p. 13).

Panda accounting by HIK and Seagate

HIK Vision disclosed information (HIK Vision, 2017, p. 26) about how the company and Seagate were cooperating with WWF to support the WWF giant panda conservation project (Figure 19.4). The content in the figure translates into English as follows:

> HIK Vision and Seagate work together to support WWF's giant panda conservation work in Sichuan province Yele Nature Reserve. Based on the environmental features of Yele Nature Reserve, HIK VISION provides design and implementation services for the development of hardware equipment for the cooperative project. The company needs to overcome the limitations of complicated terrain and atrocious weather, work

二、自然

牵手国际 NGO 助力 WWF 大熊猫保护项目

WWF 大熊猫保护项目是由海康威视与希捷助力 WWF 共同打造的针对四川省冶勒自然保护区保护大熊猫的公益项目。依据冶勒自然保护区的环境特征，海康威视提供合作项目硬件设备的开发和实施方案的设计与落地，克服复杂地形与恶劣气候的限制，与合作伙伴希捷共同助力自然保护区完善技术防范体系，提供高稳定性、全天候的安全防护，旨在减少人为活动对保护区生态环境的干扰，提升保护区监控能力与管理效率，为大熊猫珍稀种群逐步恢复提供保障。未来，公司会更加关注生态环境的保护，为更多的野生动植物保护做出努力。

Figure 19.4 Cooperate with international NGO to support WWF giant panda conservation project

Source: HIK Vision (2017, p. 26)

with partner Seagate to support technical defence system of the Nature Reserve, to provide high stability and 24/7 safety protection. It aims to reduce the human activities' interference for the ecological environment of Nature Reserve, improve the Nature Reserves' monitoring capability and management efficiency, thus to guarantee the gradual recovery of rare population of giant pandas. In the future, the company will pay more attention on ecological conservation, strive for the conservation of more wild flora and fauna.

(HIK Vision, 2017, p. 26)

Seagate have also disclosed information relating to panda preservation on their corporate website:

In partnership with the World Wildlife Fund, Seagate donated surveillance and storage equipment to a giant panda habitat in Western China. The equipment is being used to monitor the pandas and their environment as part of conservation and preservation efforts.

(Seagate, undated)

There has been media attention on the company for their wildlife protection efforts. Xi Zhinong is a famous wildlife photographer in China capturing pictures of panda and other threatened species. He states that he depends on Seagate storage products in his work to document China's endangered species. Indeed, Xi explains that photography can be a 'potent weapon' in educating people about the plight of these animals and in motivating them to take an active role in caring for the environment (see Zhang, 2018). This resonates with claims in the accounting literature that a botanical drawing, an etching or other form of pictorial 'account' is an important and emancipatory means of conveying the urgency of extinction prevention and the need to protect biodiversity. These elements are included in the extinction accounting framework presented in Atkins and Maroun (2018) as well as in chapter two of this book.

A panda-centric accounting and accountability framework

An outcome from this research was to develop a panda-centric depiction of the accountability and accounting mechanisms currently in operation within China which aim to save the panda. Figure 19.5 brings together all of the actors involved in saving the panda.

The diagram brings together the current mechanisms for giant panda conservation in China based on this study. With the giant panda in the centre, different stakeholders are placed in two different rings represent their relationship with and influence on giant panda conservation. Government, NGOs, local communities, academic community, international companies and other internal stakeholders are placed in the inner ring as they directly involved in or contribute for giant panda programs or activities. In the outer ring, IUCN,

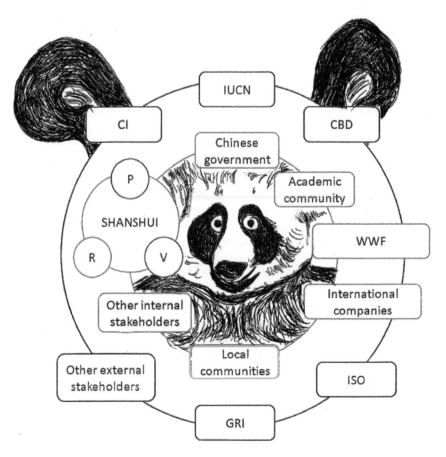

Figure 19.5 Accountability for giant panda conservation

CBD, CI, GRI, ISO, WWF, international companies and other external stakeholders representing as external parties to support or put pressures for stakeholders which within the ring in relation to giant panda conservation. It needs to be noticed that WWF and international companies are in both rings as they creating connections between internal and external stakeholders; and Shanshui is specialised due to it has own research institution and social enterprise. The closer the collaboration between these parties, the more likely panda conservation will be to succeed.

Another outcome from this research has been to develop a panda–centric extinction accounting framework, which builds on the extinction accounting framework presented in Atkins et al. (2018) but adapts it for saving panda, incorporating the various agencies and bodies we have found to be involved in panda conservation (see Table 19.1).

Table 19.1 A panda–centric extinction accounting framework

Element	Purpose	Elements
1 Panda extinction accounting context	Describe the level of panda extinction risk in the context of the organisation's business and the diverse reasons for wanting to address this risk	Record numbers of panda in habitats affected by the company's activities Report where (if relevant), geographically, the company's activities pose a threat to panda Report potential risks/impacts on panda arising from the company's operations Incorporate images (such as photographs, etchings, botanical drawings example) of panda affected by the company's operations and which the company has a duty of care to protect Report full details (narrative as well as financial figures) relating to any fines or ongoing claims relating to breaches in panda conservation legislation Report corporate expressions of moral, ethical, emotional, financial and reputational motivations for preserving panda
2 Action-focused reporting	Explain the actions the company takes and plans to take to reduce panda extinction risk	Report actions/initiatives taken by the company to avoid harm to, and to prevent extinction of, panda including efforts to protect habitats and local ecosystems
3 Partnership reporting	Complement action-focused reporting by explaining broader partnerships/initiatives formed to combat/reverse extinction trends	Report partnerships between NGOs such as WWF China and Shanshui and the company which aim to address corporate impacts on panda as well as to develop reserves and other panda conservation initiatives and report the outcome of such partnerships on panda populations, their habitats and ecosystems
4 Analysis and reflection	Evaluation of panda extinction prevention initiatives against aims/targets to inform changes to actions and partnerships	Report assessment and reflection on outcomes of partnerships and decisions taken about necessary changes to policy/initiatives going forward

(continued)

Table 19.1 (continued)

Element	Purpose	Elements
5 Assessment	Audit of panda populations and habitat	Report regular assessments (audit) of panda populations in areas affected by corporate operations as well as assessments of habitat degradation or improvement
6 Reporting	Provide an account of the progress made to date on preventing panda extinction, planned future actions and risk exposure	Report assessment of whether or not corporate initiatives/actions are assisting in prevention of species extinction and habitat protection Report strategy for the future development and improvement of panda conservation initiatives: an iterative process Ensure that the whole process of 'panda extinction accounting' is integrated into corporate strategy and is incorporated into the company's integrated report, the company's business plan, corporate strategy and risk management/internal control system not resigned to separate sustainability reports or websites. Report potential liabilities relating to future possible legal fines/claims relating to panda impacts. Discuss ways in which the company is working to prevent future liabilities related to harming panda Provide pictorial representations of success in panda conservation – and of failure

Our research shows that currently in China, most corporate participants in biodiversity conservation are international companies, with only a few Chinese companies involved in initiatives and usually their involvement is limited to a form of donation. This might be due to low levels of public awareness. As a number of international and national NGOs and the Chinese government are making efforts to raise awareness and encourage corporations to start or take further participation in biodiversity conservation practices, Chinese corporations are starting to take action.

The giant panda is the most famous species in China and it has become endangered as a result of human activity. The giant panda may be considered one of the most well protected species in the world, with the recent IUCN's downlisting of giant panda's threatened status suggesting effective conservation efforts. However, a number of challenges still exist, and continuous conservation is required. There are still some spaces for improvement. As we saw in chapter five, the downlisting of a species is not necessarily a positive sign for the species and can send an inappropriate signal. By downlisting panda, could this give the impression the species is safe, when this is clearly not the case. Numbers may be increasing but habitat is being destroyed and threats to their survival continue to mount.

One recommendation is that it is necessary to speed up the establishment of specific 'giant panda conservation regulation' to fill gaps in legislation protecting giant panda and their habitat. It is essential to ensure future investment in nature reserves and other conservation programs, and solve the conflicts with local economic development which have arisen from previous legislative loopholes. Secondly, a standard and set of guidelines for business and biodiversity are required as those currently in place are provided by international organisations. China needs to formulate a specific set of standard and guideline that fits the current Chinese context.

Our research has shown that although partnerships exist between NGOs and companies, and that Shanshui and the WWF are all involved in various initiatives, there seems to be little collaboration among these parties. Working more closely together and collaborating with each other would have a synergistic effect, increasing the impact of the initiatives. In relation to multi-stakeholder engagement, the Chinese government could improve mechanisms by which corporations can contact other stakeholders in order to participate in direct conservation practices, and integrate these practices into corporate operations or products, thus releasing the weighty potential conservation from the private sectors. Moreover, government could further introduce local communities, NGOs and other stakeholders into these mechanisms to multiply conservation dynamics. Furthermore, NGOs could create partnerships with each other, share information and integrate resources to achieve mutual goals. They could form a stronger force to create greater impacts on programme implementation, awareness raising, policy formulation, and supervision.

In order to support the formulation of proposed mechanisms, an equal dialogue platform is required to solve the obstacles among stakeholders. The key is to let each stakeholder share equal right to express their opinions and concerns, thus to create a fair context to combine interests, mediate conflicts, identify goals and assign responsibilities. Successful implementation of this dialog could integrate different stakeholders as a whole, speed up conservation progress, and create more conservation approaches and opportunities. Secondly, it is also important to create dialog platform with international conservation organisations, expand cooperative networks and exchange experiences to make further improvements. Meanwhile, there is also a great demand for academics' research and investigation on effectiveness of corporate practice on giant panda conservation. Finally, further strengthen the involvement of stakeholders like media and public could help the society form a supervisory environment, thus to force private sector pay more attention and take actions. These recommendations are not limited to the giant panda but for all other endangered species as well.

References

Atkins, J. and Maroun, W. 2018. Integrated Extinction Accounting and Accountability: Building an Ark. *Accounting, Auditing and Accountability Journal*, 31, 750–786.

Atkins, J., Gräbsch, C. and Jones, M. 2014. Biodiversity Reporting: Exploring its Anthropocentric Nature. *Accounting for Biodiversity*, 215–245.

Atkins, J., Maroun, W., Atkins, B. C. and Barone, E. 2018. From the Big Five to the Big Four? Exploring Extinction Accounting for the Rhinoceros. *Accounting, Auditing and Accountability Journal*, 31, 674–702.

Campaign China, 2012. Mercedes Benz reinforces commitment to panda conservation. Retrieved from www.campaignasia.com/article/mercedes-benz-reinforces-com mitment-to-panda-conservation/294190 [Accessed 5 Jan 2018].

Canon China, 2013. *Canon China CSR Report*. s.l.: Canon China.

Canon China, 2014. *Canon China CSR Report*. s.l.: Canon China.

Carrefour China, 2011. Multiple initiatives to ensure food security. [Retrieved from www.carrefour.com.cn/News/CarrefourNewsDetail.aspx?NewsID=147 [Accessed 12 Feb 2017].

CBD, 1993. About the Convention. Retrieved from www.cbd.int/intro/default.shtml [Accessed 12 Feb 2017].

CBD, 1996. COP 3 Decision III/6: Additional financial resources. Retrieved from www.cbd.int/decision/cop/default.shtml?id=7102 [Accessed 12 Feb 2017].

CBD, 2010a. COP 10 Decision X/21: Business engagement. Retrieved from www. cbd.int/decision/cop/default.shtml?id=12287 [Accessed 12 Feb 2017].

CBD, 2010b. Strategic Plan for Biodiversity 2011–2020 and the Aichi Targets: 'Living in Harmony with Nature'. s.l.: CBD.

CBD, 2013. Quick Guides to the Aichi Biodiversity Targets. s.l.: CBD.

CCTV News, 2014. Taking and giving: panda honey shows ecological justice. Retrieved from http://news.cntv.cn/2014/09/11/ARTI1410411157349994.shtml [Accessed 12 Feb 2017].

China Conservation and Research Centre for the Giant Panda, undated. Cooperation and communication. Retrieved from www.chinapanda.org.cn/cooperation.php [Accessed 12 Feb 2017].

China WTO Tribune and GoldenBee (Beijing) Management Consulting, 2013. *GoldenBee CSR Index Report (2007–2013)*, Beijing: China WTO Tribune and GoldenBee (Beijing) Management Consulting.

Conservation International and Shanshui Conservation Centre, 2009. *China Wild Giant Panda Survival and Security Evaluation*. s.l.: Conservation International and Shanshui Conservation Centre.

FECO, 2013. Chinese Corporations' Participation in Biodiversity: Case Study Collection. s.l.: FECO.

Gong, M., Cui, L., Fan, Z., Zhu, Y., Liu, G., Guo, J. and Li, H., 2016. *Habitat Fragmentation's Impact on Giant Panda's Long Term Suvival*. s.l.: WWF China.

Green Homeland, 2003. Giant panda specialist: Lv Zhi: 'My protection target is Not just giant panda'. Retrieved from www.people.com.cn/GB/huanbao/8220/30473/31759/32140/2351100.html [Accessed 12 Feb 2017].

GRI, 2011. *Sustainability Reporting Guidelines*. s.l.: GRI.

Guardian, 2015. Giant panda numbers up 17%, China reports. Retrieved from www.theguardian.com/environment/2015/mar/02/giant-panda-numbers-up-17-china-reports [Accessed 12 Feb 2017].

Han, T., 2009. Mercedes-Benz sponsors giant panda kindergarten. Retrieved from www.chinadaily.com.cn/bw/2009-09/07/content_8660786.htm [Accessed 05 Jan 2018].

HIK Vision, 2017. *HIK Vision 2016 CSR Report*. s.l.: HIK Vision.

Hou, M., 2014. Three dimensions of biodiversity protection. Retrieved from www.cneo.com.cn/info/2014-11-25/news_17052.html [Accessed 12 Feb 2017].

HSBC China, 2015. *HSBC China Corporate Sustainability Report*. s.l.: HSBC China.

ISO, 2010. *ISO 26000: Guidance on Social Responsibility*. s.l.: ISO.

IUCN, 2016. The IUCN Red List of Threatened Species: *Ailuropoda melanoleuca*. Retrieved from www.iucnredlist.org/details/712/0 [Accessed 12 Feb 2017].

Jiang,Z., Qin,H., Liu,Y., Ji,L. and Ma,K., 2015. Protecting biodiversity and promoting sustainable development: in memory of the releasing of Catalogue of Life China 2015 and China Biodiversity Red List on the International Day for Biological Diversity 2015. *Biodiversity Science*, 23(3), 433–434.

Jones, M. 1996. Accounting for biodiversity: a pilot study. *The British Accounting Review*, 28(4), 281–303.

Jones, M. 2003. Accounting for biodiversity: operationalising environmental accounting. *Accounting, Auditing and Accountability Journal*, 16(5), 762–789.

Jones, M. 2010. Accounting for the environment: Towards a theoretical perspective for environmental accounting and reporting. *Accounting Forum*, 34(2), 123–138.

Jones, M. 2014. *Accounting for Biodiversity*. Abingdon: Routledge.

Jones, M. J. and Solomon, J. F. 2013. Problematising accounting for biodiversity. *Accounting, Auditing and Accountability Journal*, 26 (5), 668–687.

Jones, M. J. and Matthews, J. 2000. *Accounting for Biodiversity: A Natural Inventory of the ElanValley Nature Reserve*. London: Association of Chartered Certified Accountants (ACCA).

Li, G., 2015. How to perform well the biodiveristy protection work in China under the new situation. Retrieved from http://epaper.gmw.cn/gmrb/html/2015-04/23/nw.D110000gmrb_20150423_1-07.htm?div=-1 [Accessed 12 Feb 2017].

Liu, Y., 2012. *Impact of Climate Change to Minshan's Giant Panda and Habitat*. Beijing: Beijing Forestry University.

L'Oreal China, 2015. *L'Oreal China Sustainable Development Result Summary*. s.l.: L'Oreal China.

Panda Green Energy Group, 2016. *Panda Green Energy Group Limited 2016 Environmental Social and Governance Report: Committed to Providing Affordable Clean Energy*. s.l.: Panda Green Energy Group.

Panda Green Energy Group, 2017. Panda Green Energy welcomes new member to the family. Giant panda Qiyi adopted as the company mascot. Retrieved from http://unitedpvgroup.com/en/news-events/press-releases//article/panda-green-energy-welcomes-new-member-to-the-family-giant-panda-qiyi-adopted-as-the-company-mascot [Accessed 4 Jan 2018].

Paper, 2015. Chian going to formulate specialized protection legislation for giant panda, how about cowfish and Chinese sturgeon?. Retrieved from www.thepaper.cn/newsDetail_forward_1319306 [Accessed 12 Feb 2017].

Seagate, undated. Community snapshots. Retrieved from www.seagate.com/gb/en/global-citizenship/community-snapshots [Accessed 5 Jan 2018].

Seagate, 2015. Seagate And WWF To Start Seagate Giant Panda Habitat Monitoring And Restoration Demonstration Program In China's Western Mountainous Areas Retrieved from www.seagate.com/about-seagate/news/seagate-wwf-to-start-seagate-giant-panda-habitat-monitoring-restoration-demonstration-program-in-china-pr/ [Accessed 5 Jan 2018].

Shangri-La, 2012a. Shangri-La hotels and resorts' Care for Panda project takes root in Sichuan Provence, China. Retrieved from www.shangri-la.com/corporate/press-room/press-releases/shangri-la-hotels-and-resorts-care-for-panda-project-takes-root-in-sichuan-prov/ [Accessed 4 Jan 2018]

Shangri-La, 2012b. *Sustainability Report*. s.l.: Shangri-La.

Shangri-La, 2013. *Shangri-La Hotels and Resorts 2012 UN Global Compact Communication on Progress*. s.l.: Shangri-La.

Shangri-La, 2014. *Shangri-La Hotels and Resorts 2013 UN Global Compact Communication on Progress*. s.l.: Shangri-La.

Shangri-La, 2015. *Shangri-La Hotels and Resorts 2014 UN Global Compact Communication on Progress*. s.l.: Shangri-La.

Shangri-La, 2016. *Shangri-La Hotels and Resorts 2015 UN Global Compact Communication on Progress*. s.l.: Shangri-La.

Shanshui, 2013. Public benefit honey: not just honey. Retrieved from www.beepanda.com/gyfm.html [Accessed 12 Feb 2017].

Shanshui, 2014a. About Shanshui Conservation Center. Retrieved from www.shanshui.org/ArticleShow.aspx?id=69 [Accessed 12 Feb 2017].

Shanshui, 2014b. *Shanshui Conservation Center 2014 Annual Report*. s.l.: Shanshui.

Shanshui, 2015. *Shanshui Conservation Center 2015 Annual Report*. s.l.: Shanshui.

Shanshui Partner, 2016a. Shanshui Partner: ecological justice product enterprise. Retrieved from https://wap.koudaitong.com/v2/showcase/feature?alias=1irkd1oc8 [Accessed 12 Feb 2017].

Shanshui Partner, 2016b. The meaning of panda honey towards Baishui River Jinxingou Retrieved from https://wap.koudaitong.com/v2/showcase/feature?alias=d4w6eh30 [Accessed 12 Feb 2017].

Sina Public Welfare, 2017. L'Oreal purchase the 'Bee Panda Honey' and propose for green consumption. Retrieved from http://gongyi.sina.com.cn/actype/qy/2017-06-06/doc-ifyfuzny3452017.shtml [Accessed 11 Feb 2018].

State Forestry Administration of China, 2016. Giant panda is still a endangered species, still needs stronger conservation. Retrieved from www.forestry.gov.cn/main/195/content-903457.html [Accessed 12 Feb 2017].

Stockholm Resilience Centre, 2015. The nine planetary boundaries. Retrieved from www.stockholmresilience.org/research/planetary-boundaries/planetary-boundaries/about-the-research/the-nine-planetary-boundaries.html [Accessed 12 Feb 2017].

Wang, A., Wu, J, and Liu, J, 2015. Business and biodiversity: a review of the negotiation progress of a new issue under the Convention on Biological Diversity. *Biodiversity Science*, 23(5), pp. 689–694.

Wei, B., 2015. Biodiveristy is the strategic resources to promote the green transformation. Retrieved from www.china.com.cn/guoqing/2015-06/29/content_35936305.htm [Accessed 12 Feb 2017].

Wu, J. and Lv. J, 2009. Climate change's potential impact on giant panda's distribution. *Environmental Science and Technology*, 12, pp. 168–177.

Wu, J., Liu, Z. and Teng, L., 2010. *Research and Evaluation of China Giant Panda Conservation Policy.* s.l.: WWF China.

Wu, X., Fan, Z., Gao, J., Zhao, Z., Tian, Y., Li, J., Li, G., Hu, L. and Chang, Y., 2014. *Research about Climate Change's Potential Impact on Giant Panda's Habitats and Population, and Future Conservation Strategy.* s.l.: WWF China.

Wu, X., Fan, Z., Zhao, Z., Li, J., Gao, J., Tian, Y., Li, G., Chang, Y. and Li, Y, 2016. *Climate Change's Potential Impact of Giant Panda's Habitat and Population in Qinling and Minshan Area, and Research for Future Conservation Strategy.* s.l.: WWF China.

WWF, 2009. *Newsletter.* s.l.: WWF.

WWF, 2010. *WWF China Programme Annual Report 2010.* s.l.: WWF.

WWF, 2012. Peppers help pandas in China's Sichuan Province. Retrieved from www.worldwildlife.org/stories/peppers-help-pandas-in-china-s-sichuan-province [Accessed 12 Feb 2017].

WWF, 2014. *Living Planet Report.* s.l.: WWF.

WWF China, 2015a. Market transformation proposal. Retrieved from www.wwf china.org/programmedetail.php?id=7 [Accessed 12 Feb 2017].

WWF China, 2015b. The fourth national giant panda survey. Retrieved from www. wwfchina.org/specialdetail.php?pid=205andpage=1 [Accessed 12 Feb 2017].

WWF China, 2016a. WWF giant panda conservation research report. s.l.: WWF.

WWF China, 2016b. Giant panda is not lised as endangered, but still facing serious survival risk. Retrieved from www.wwfchina.org/pressdetail.php?id=1711 [Accessed 12 Feb 2017].

WWF China, undated a. Giant pandas. Retrieved from www.wwfchina.org/program medetail.php?id=8 [Accessed 12 Feb 2017].

WWF China, undated b. WWF China corporate partners. Retrieved from www.wwf china.org/sponsor.php [Accessed 12 Feb 2017].

WWF Global, 2016. Giant panda no longer endangered, but iconic species still at risk. Retrieved from http://wwfcn.panda.org/?5441/Giant-panda-no-longer-endangered-but-iconic-species-still-at-risk [Accessed 12 Feb 2017].

WWF Global, undated. Giant panda. Retrieved from http://wwf.panda.org/what_we_do/endangered_species/giant_panda [Accessed 12 Feb 2017].

WWF UK, 2015. Giant pandas: living proof that conservation works. Retrieved from www.wwf.org.uk/wildlife/giant-pandas [Accessed 12 Feb 2017].

Zang, C., Cai, L., Li, J., Wu, X. and Li, J., 2016. Preparation of China Biodiversity Red List and its significance for biodi-versity conservation of China. *Biodiversity Science*, 24(5), pp. 1–5.

Zhang, K. 2018. Storage is a potent weapon for protecting endangered species. Retrieved from www.seagate.com/gb/en/do-more/storage-is-potent-weapon-protecting-endangered-species-master-dm [Accessed 5 Jan 2018]

Zhang, F., Fang, J. and Yin, G., 2014. Problem, current status and approach of corpo rations' participation in biodiversity. *China WTO Tridune*, 11, pp. 71–5.

Zhang, F. and Liu, W., 2015. Current status of stakeholder's participation in bio diversity conservation and research about mechanism construction. *Environmental Protection*, 43(5).

Zhang, X. and Lv, Z., 2014. *The Ecological Impact and Value of Chinese Honey Bee in Giant Panda Habitat, and its Contribution to Giant Panda Conservation.* Peking: Peking University.

20 Some reflections on extinction accounting, engagement and species

Jill Atkins and Barry Atkins

This book has taken a new look at the current mass extinction crisis enveloping our world. We have sought to bring accounting, extinction, investor and NGO engagement, and deep ecology perspectives under one roof. Rather than seeing business and global capitalism as the perpetrator that must be removed in order to retain the balance of nature, we have tried to show that as perpetrator, the business world also has the responsibility to address extinction of species urgently. Although an emancipatory extinction accounting cannot solve the crisis, it can be one mechanism among many which can assist in addressing species extinctions. Similarly, engagement of business by responsible investment institutions and NGOs such as the WWF and RSPB represents a powerful mechanism within the global capitalist system which can address, and as we can see from chapters in this book, is addressing species loss and extinctions.

This final chapter seeks to reflect on the content of this book. We take a brief look at some themes and commonalities that span chapters and then draw some tentative conclusions on how to take the framework for extinction accounting and engagement forward to enable it to act as an effective emancipatory mechanism.

We can see from the various chapters of this book the vast range of different mechanisms, institutions and organisations which are collaborating to address extinction, from those addressing imminent bird extinctions, as discussed from an RSPB perspective, to efforts by the responsible investment community, to save marine species and habitat. The crucial role of zoos, aquaria and national parks in saving species and providing safe habitat is emphasised by contributors with illustrations from eastern and southern Africa, across Europe, in North America and the Far East. At times their role can be somewhat controversial and their effectiveness in helping species debatable, as seen especially from Solomon and Clappison in Chapter 16. Corporate efforts, often in partnership with NGOs such as the WWF, and as evidenced from analysis of corporate disclosures, are discussed with evidence from companies in China, Russia, Italy and South Africa inter alia.

Figure 20.1 brings together in a comprehensive (although perhaps not exhaustive) manner the many initiatives, NGOs, mechanisms and efforts mentioned throughout the contributors' chapters to show their diversity.

UK
RSPB
UK Wildlife Trusts
LEAF
Countryside Stewardship Scheme
DEFRA
Sustainable Agricultural Network
Local Nature Partnerships
Natural Improvement Areas
Countryside Management Scheme
Game & Wildlife Conservation Trust
Moorland Association
National Gamekeepers Organisation
National Parks
Natural England
Wildlife Trusts and Butterfly Conservation
BOCC

Far East
WWF China
China Biodiversity Red List
Golden Bee
Ministry of Environmental Protection of China
SHANSHUI
Wildlife Conservation Law'
State Forestry Administration of China
Bee Panda
Fengtongzhai Natural
Sichuan Anzihe Giant Panda Nature Reserve
Zhouzhi Nature Reserve
Dujiangyan Center for Panda Care and Disease Control
Yele Nature Reserve

European Union (EU)
EU Zoos Directive Good Practice
EAZA
EU Birds Directive
EU Habitats Directive
Norden's Ark
Zoocheck
Stockholm Resilience Centre

USA/Canada/South America
NOAA
ESA
SASB
FSB Taskforce on Climate Related Financial Disclosure
US ESA
Monarch Butterfly Biosphere Reserve
WWF-Telcel Alliance
Conservation Reserve Program CRP
Federal Insecticide, Fungicide, and Rodenticide Act (FIFRA)
Federal Food, Drug, and Cosmetics Act (FFDCA)
Animal and Plant Health Inspection Service (APHIS)

Extinction Accounting
Extinction Engagement

Africa
SANBI
WWFSA
IRCSA
SANParks
KNP
GKEPF
AMPAA
GRU
MLC
MTPA

International
UNEP CBD
WWF
GRI
IIRC
SDGs
NCP
NCC
IUCN
CITES
Greenpeace
MIKE
ETIS
PIKE
NIAPs
Nagoya Protocol
LRC
WAZA
BLI
Albatross Task Force
FSC
PEFC
ODP
FIP
SFP
CETA
GPBB

Polar Regions
Polar Bear Specialist Group PBSG
Polar Code

Figure 20.1 Protection mechanisms included in extinction accounting and engagement

Extinction accounting, as well as providing a basis for enhancing integrated thinking within organisations on the urgent need to act on extinction prevention also represents a platform, a basis for demonstrating collaboration between various organisations, partnerships, governments. Through extinction accounting, all the various engagements, initiatives and other extinction prevention mechanisms can be collated. Such collation assists in ensuring genuine collaborative, interdisciplinary and international efforts which together can save species.

It is also interesting to see the ways in which contributors to this book have employed such a broad variety of communication strategies and techniques. Chapters proffered by practitioners such as King (Chapter 6) and Herron (Chapter 7) are hard-hitting and effective in driving home the need for mechanisms of extinction accounting and engagement. They are necessarily focused on accounting and investment practice as a critically important tool for extinction prevention. Some chapters are more academic in style, arising from research by members of the international academic accounting community. Novel approaches, such as the autoethnographic writing by Lanka (Chapter 17), who writes from a butterfly's perspective, are especially effective and also inkeeping with the idea of placing nature at the centre. By 'being a butterfly' this chapter attempts to move away from an anthropocentric approach and imagine what it really feels like to be a threatened species of butterfly – albeit a very highly educated one who maybe attended Harvard.

Similarly, the use of dialogue – a conversation between several people in a pub – by Christian (Chapter 3) represents another innovative means of communicating extinction threats and clashing philosophies and ideas of morality and ethics to the reader. The way in which the hiker (clearly Christian himself) explores deeply held beliefs in his conversations with others in the pub but also his ponderings when alone, brings home the personal nature of the extinction problem – the way in which mass extinction threatens all of us at a deep psychological level and poses problems of such immensity it is often hard to come to terms with them.

As is evident from the title of the book, the aim was to explore extinction, extinction accounting and engagement around the world and our contributors have provided illustrations of species as well as examples of engagement and accounting on extinction prevention from just about every corner of the globe including the Far East, North America, Latin America, Europe, Scandinavia and Africa. We are hugely indebted to the contributors for the immense effort and diligent research that they have committed to bringing this book to fruition and ensuring that it really does provide a global portrait of the current state of affairs for species and their relationship with business and the capitalist system, as well as the huge international efforts of NGOs, the general public, governments and local communities in trying to save species, habitats and ecosystems.

The chapters of this book have not only covered species across all areas of the planet but also across different groups of flora and fauna. Birds were the focus of Punkari in Chapter 14, which adopts an accounting perspective and focuses on two species: the red kite and the sparrow, whereas we get a broad perspective of UK bird species from Amaral Rogers (Chapter 13), who looks at the work of the RSPB in preventing bird extinctions. Flora – in terms of forests and trees – are the subject of Martini, Doni and Corvino's Chapter 15, which not only considers the substantial impact of industrial tissue production on forest but also seeks to apply the extinction accounting framework in that context, demonstrating how the use of this framework could potentially prevent extinction of tree species. Highly charismatic mammals are the subject of Zhao and Atkins in Chapter 19, concerning protection and conservation of the giant panda, as well as Jonäll and Sabelfeld in Chapter 18, on polar bears and the extent to which extractive companies are attempting (or not) to save the species from extinction. The potential extinction of the mighty rhinoceros in eastern Africa is the focus of discussion by Sibanda and Mulama (Chapter 10). Insects are also critically important to the survival of our ecosystem, as discussed in Chapter 1, and the monarch butterfly's plight is addressed by Lanka (Chapter 17), highlighting the urgency of preventing this spectacular creature's imminent extinction. Creatures of the sea, especially whales such as the beluga, orca and grey whale, are the focus of Solomon and Clappison (Chapter 16) and Nicolov (Chapter 5).

We are also delighted to have so many disciplines integrated into this book, as the need to escape from academic silos and cross disciplinary boundaries was highlighted in the early chapters as crucial to the effectiveness of extinction prevention initiatives. We are immensely fortunate to be able to include contributions from a legal perspective (Chapter 8), the investment industry (Chapter 7), wildlife NGOs (the WWF in Chapter 10 and the RSPB in Chapter 13), professional practice in law, governance and accounting (Chapters 6 and 14), as well as from a large number of international accounting scholars whose research focus is in the domain of social and environmental, ecological and biodiversity accounting. Their views and perspectives range from those embedded in deep ecology (Chapters 3 and 4) to accounting academics who may be seen as more oriented towards a 'within system' approach to social and environmental accounting (Chapters 11 and 18).

It is beyond the scope of this chapter to summarise and discuss all of the interesting, urgent and compelling issues which arise throughout the varied chapters and indeed not the intention, as the chapters stand to be read individually. However, a couple of issues are worthy of reflection here. For example, issues relating to categorising species according to extinction risk are also a theme common to many chapters of the book. Nicolov (Chapter 5) questions the recategorisation of the grey whale, providing an eloquent discussion of the real meaning underlying classifications, especially in relation to historical species populations. Similarly, the uncomfortable approach towards red kite and sparrows in terms of the species' classification and reclassification is raised by Punkari in Chapter 14. The recent recategorisation of panda, whose status has been downgraded given population increase is also called into question by Zhao and Atkins (Chapter 19). Is this really a 'good' thing or can it send the wrong message and shift attention away from preservation for that particular species?

There is also an issue in relation to protection of a species and the need to protect their habitat. Both in the case of companies reporting on polar bears, in Chapter 18, and Chinese companies disclosing information about panda protection, they discuss initiatives whereby they sponsor the species in zoos or nature parks. Similarly, the immense efforts of European zoos, as described by Rimmel (Chapter 12), and the work of the SANParks in South Africa (Chapter 11) while critically important to species preservation cannot replace the urgent need to protect and enhance natural habitat. As Jonäll and Sabelfeld point out in Chapter 18, a focus on species related initiatives within oil company accounts seems to make up for a lack of information on how the companies are seeking to protect the species' natural habitat in areas where their activities may affect these. This suggests that illustrations of extinction accounting in practice for some businesses may be more akin to philanthropic accounting, involving charitable giving and donations, rather than strategies which aim to transform and change their impact on species through habitat loss or environmental degradation. Such forms of extinction accounting are not emancipatory and these findings indicate far more needs to be done to ensure real change in approach and strategy.

Another interesting issue is the perceived difference in scope and nature between corporate social and environmental accounting and accounts produced by NGOs. Chapter 14 by Punkari emphasises and highlights the need to develop a more ecological form of accounting for organisations and corporations by comparing the reporting practice of wildlife NGOs with current corporate environmental and sustainability reporting. The fact that they are so deficient, based on such differing objectives implies that corporate environmental reporting does not incorporate issues of species extinction in a way which engenders change.

This does, of course, bring us to the elephant in the room. How can an extractive business find a way of ensuring oil extraction will not have a negative impact on polar bear populations? The paradox evident in Chapter 18 is that the more oil they extract, the greater will be global warming due to the use of the extracted fossil fuels, which again releases more Arctic areas for exploitation leading to a vicious circle of effect. Maybe the only solution to this is to encourage oil companies away from oil and into other forms of energy production. Recent moves such as insurance companies considering refusing to sell insurance to businesses for their oil or gas pipelines could help to change the focus of such companies. Probably the only way to prevent polar bear extinction is to stop companies extracting oil. This is where the real problems begin – and end. How can we reformulate the corporate and financial worlds to do things completely differently, to change their modes and foci of production and business activities for good? Perhaps extinction accounting, by forcing them to disclose actual impacts and what they are doing to prevent these, could encourage such moves and engender real change. Or maybe it is simply too late?

Corporate silence, or absence in reporting on their impacts on threatened species, as highlighted in Chapter 18, could not occur were a dynamic and perhaps even mandatory form of extinction accounting imposed on organisations. Is this impossible? Are we dreaming to think this could happen in reality? Maybe not. As the evidence mounts and points to our own imminent extinction if we do not prevent mass extinctions of non-human species perhaps governments and supranational organisations may actually implement legally binding mechanisms to ensure species protection, such as making emancipatory extinction accounting and emancipatory extinction engagement by investors and NGOs compulsory? We cannot answer these questions but we can pose them. One motivation for writing this book was to engender genuine change – both in societal attitudes and in practice – and to pose difficult questions which require an urgent response.

Another issue to reflect on is where we go from here. In considering new paths for research into extinction accounting, one avenue we are exploring in ongoing work is to see how theories, techniques and practice in counselling and therapeutic engagement can be applied to engagement of businesses by responsible investors and NGOs in order to enhance the effectiveness and render it more emancipatory as a tool to prevent extinction. Concepts such as externalisation, used in narrative therapies and counselling, seem potentially useful for investors or wildlife organisations in seeking to communicate the severity and reality of extinction threats to species. Externalisation can involve making something visible, and less abstract, whether through imagination, art or music. In bringing etchings of endangered species into this book we were attempting to externalise the richness and beauty of species as well as to communicate through a different media from the written word the need to preserve them for aesthetic and moral reasons as well as through the business case built in the text. It is only by bringing all these different dimensions together, as well as a wide range of disciplines, that the urgency of extinction can be truly communicated to people.

All of the chapters in the book point towards an urgent need to develop, implement and promote an extinction accounting and engagement among businesses and other organisations in order to stem the tide of species extinctions. Punkari's Chapter 14 concludes by highlighting the need to develop a framework for sustainability and environmental reporting which bridges the gaps he outlined between such reporting by wildlife NGOs and corporate sustainability reporting. He mentions the need for reporting on habitat, temperature and the impact of changes in these on species. In fact, his conclusion presents a strong rationale for developing and implementing a form of extinction accounting, similar to that presented in Chapter 2, for companies, wildlife NGOs and other organisations. Indeed, the extinction accounting framework presented in Chapter 2 allows for the inclusion of these types of information and seeks a reporting outcome which incorporates deep green perspectives, trends in species as well as action to prevent extinctions into the heart of corporate reporting and disclosures by all organisations at all levels. Martini, Doni and Corvino (Chapter 15) demonstrate the need for an emancipatory extinction accounting framework, which they refer to as an EFEAA and show how emergent forms of such accounting already exist among companies in the tissue sector and show how this could work. Similarly, Chapters 9, 11, 18 and 19 all provide a rationale for, and a need for, an extinction accounting framework within their specific contexts.

Reading Chapter 4, by Gray and Milne, it may seem logical to conclude that accounting cannot provide an answer to the extinction crisis. However, considering their arguments a little more deeply leads us to a different conclusion. From their three points, the first, that 'accounts of species extinction make no sense unless grounded in the context of causes – these being humanity's manifest failures', is consistent with our own viewpoint as evidenced in Chapter 1, that the extinction crisis has one root cause: ourselves. The case of pollinator decline clearly demonstrates how extinction of a species could lead to our own demise, never mind mass extinction. Point two, that 'the systematic extinction of species leads to the very real possibility of humanity's extinction (and, as an ethical aside, the potential desirability of such extinction)' again does not differ from our own arguments in Chapter 1, based on the interdependence of all species within the ecosystem and our reliance on that interdependence and ecosystem. We beg to differ however regarding desirability as we believe people generally do not want to go extinct. Point three, 'the bewildering inability, it seems, of mainstream argument – whether in politics or academe, business or the media – to follow through the arguments of causes and effects and thus address the potential need for deep, fundamental, root and branch change in our organs of modernity (most notably, such shibboleths as accounting, financial markets, multinational corporations and growth) again leads naturally, in our view, to the need for a shaking up of accounting and finance, as described throughout this book, to render it emancipatory in the sense of assisting in extinction prevention. Similarly, with the investment function: responsible investment can be emancipatory and can also prevent extinctions. Evidence from Herron (Chapter 7) suggests this is already happening. The crucial role of wildlife NGOs, especially the WWF, in liaising and engaging with accounting, finance and financial markets cannot be underestimated. Business as usual and cosmetic accounts of biodiversity and environmental/ecological impacts will get us nowhere. If accounting is to become emancipatory and save species it has to alter radically and perhaps such a transformation in motivation, intent and outcome is not possible.

In our view, a radical and progressive emancipatory form of accounting with the flawed system which will undo the evil caused is the only solution in the current crisis.

Extinction has now become one of the most significant threats to the very survival and continuance of global capitalism and as such the capitalist system has to eradicate it. There are other threats: global warming, terrorism, asteroid strikes and also, according to the late Stephen Hawking, artificial intelligence. But extinction is the most substantial, human-caused, threat to the survival of the capitalist system we have created and ultimately to the human race. Extinction, at its current rate, will ensure that financial markets and businesses will collapse, which will happen shortly before extinction of the human race if no urgent action is taken.

Our objectification and externalisation of the concept of extinction demonstrates that it is a real and present danger to capitalism, to businesses and to financial markets. By seeing capitalism as an evil which must be done away with if we are to survive fails to address how we can use it as a potential solution. We have shown how preventing species extinctions is actually crucial to the future continuance of capitalism and its many mechanisms. Capitalism is good at dealing with and eliminating anything which gets in its way, or slows down its progress. Tropical rainforests are a notorious example.

If extinction of species (rather than the existence of 'irritating' species which prevent 'progress' such as the orang-utan for organisations wanting to create more palm oil plantations) is suddenly recognised as an obstacle, a threat to capitalism, then 'it' will be destroyed. Extinction will suddenly become the focus of extermination. The iron cage of capitalism suddenly becomes extinction. Indeed, it is obvious from the discussions throughout this book that capitalism can only continue if extinctions are prevented. Capitalism can only continue to protect itself from extinction if it learns to accommodate species protection, at its core.

Perhaps another poignant case of arbsurdity is that capitalism may soon become more committed to deep ecology and saving species than the deep ecologists themselves? Perhaps the capitalist system must embrace the theory of Gaia if it is to survive? What we are offering in this book, as suggested in Chapter 2, is a new form of capitalism which places species protection and protection of habitats and ecosystems at the very heart of business, financial markets and investment. We are suggesting a form of ecological, Gaian capitalism. A capitalism which embraces Gaia would be one where capitalism, as a system *per se*, becomes part of Gaia rather than operating in opposition to the natural system of our planet.

Extinction engagement within responsible investment and extinction accounting give a voice to all of those working within companies and investment houses around the world who are themselves passionate about nature but have, until now, had to separate their day job from their beliefs and feelings. These ecological extinction prevention mechanisms within capitalism allow people to bring people and planet into the heart of their work, merging their personal and working life for the good of all species. It is only by embracing nature that we can save the planet – and ourselves.

We found Gray and Milne's reference in Chapter 4 to the absurd (especially with reference to Albert Camus) an enticing avenue for further reflection. As they conclude: 'An increasingly well-developed sense of our absurdity might not go amiss either.' This could be the focus of further research in the academic sphere but also one which enlightens society into the contradictions inherent in our global thinking and decision making.

Clearly, the majority of this book focuses on large organisations, companies and even supranational organisations and governments and many readers may feel that it is not within their power in everyday life to implement the solutions proposed. So what can we do in our personal lives? If we follow Christian's hiker (Chapter 3) in getting closer to nature, this may help us to become more aware of issues and how we can contribute to saving species at a more local level. We can join local wildlife groups and assist in community data collection exercises with volunteers, such as counting butterflies or birds in gardens and local areas. If we are part of an occupational pension scheme, or a client of any investment institution (life insurance, unit trusts) which are invested in company shares, we can ask whether our pension, or the financial institution, is taking account of extinction in their investment. We can seek to ensure our own garden or land is free from chemicals that may kill insects, 'weeds', small mammals and otherwise pollute the environment and natural habitat. We can avoid putting dangerous and harmful chemicals on pets and livestock. For some a vegan lifestyle may be an option (although the authors have to be honest and admit that at present they have not embraced veganism). We can consider what we are eating and look at labelling to check supply chains and protection of species, for example are food products compliant with the MSC, the FSC and other eco-labelling. We can seek to educate children in the importance of preserving species. We can also try to integrate extinction issues into our own spheres of influence at work, through family and other communities in which we may be involved. We can participate in online petitions and activism through social media, for example initiatives from wildlife organisations. We can donate to ecological and wildlife charities and hold fundraising events for local habitat protection, for example.

Everyone the world over is busy in their lives looking after families, bringing up children, working, earning money to be able to live and often the plight of other species cannot be a priority, especially in countries where survival is paramount, where water supplies are dwindling, where there is political upheaval. However much we care and are passionate about the environment and the other creatures we share the planet with, it is hard to find the time and resources to do anything and it is often easy to feel overwhelmed. As a final reflection we feel that despite all the constraints and difficulties faced by people, day to day, in all corners of the planet, there is still space for hope: hope in human nature and in the power and potential of interdisciplinary, international collaborative efforts to reverse ecological damage and stop mass extinction dead in its tracks.

Almost a Requiem

Silence is not golden:
it has many sounds,
the most chilling one of which is
. . . nothingness.
Isolation is an extreme form of absence.
Absence is nothingness.

For the Renaissance man and woman,
cosmology mirrored the Chain of Being,
as it had done in Medieval times.
God
King
peasant,
reflecting all Creation in links
ascending to the Creator,
and descending to the heat of Hell.

This hierarchy equated order, a pattern,
even in the face of war, disease and death.

Centuries have slipped away:
the Chain no longer exists;
the links are broken.

There is little awareness of the old values:
these have been replaced by the first-person doctrine,
'I, me, myself, my, mine'
and by the maxim,
'Profit at all costs.'

In Africa we have the Big Five,
unique but facing extinction.
The question is,
'Can we still protect the Small Five?'

A new Chain of Being needs to reflect the balance:
the earth = our existence.

How many humans live in space?

A world of silence is already dead:
no sound of bees dispersing gold;
no mornings greeted by birds;
no eggs in nests;
no frogs creating a roar at night;
no beetles and worms busy under damp earth.
Extinction is worse than Mad Max's apocalypse:
it has no sound at all.

                                    Lelys Maddock

Index

and vulnerable areas 346–8; research method 343–4; silence in 349, 394; *see also* corporate disclosure; corporate sustainability reporting
corporate social accounting 393
corporate social responsibility (CSR) 199, 249, 256, 317, 350, 359, 360, 393
corporate sustainability reporting 254, 341–3; audits 259; standards for 257–9; *see also* sustainability reporting
Countryside Stewardship scheme 95
Creationism 39
crested ibis 365
critical accounting theory 66
critical habitat 162; *see also* habitat
critical theory 185
crocodile lizards 42
CSEAR *see* Centre for Social and Environmental Accounting Research (CSEAR)
cultural heritage 101
cultured landscapes 264–5
Cupido minimus 244
Cuvier, George 7
cybergenetics 41
Cyprian grey bush cricket 30

Darwin, Charles 291
DDT pesticides 15; *see also* pesticides
deadzones 149
decomposition of waste 41
deep ecology 53, 55, 68, 69, 74, 77, 93, 96, 106, 209; and biodiversity 178; capitalism and 396; in South Africa 177–8; *see also* ecology
Deepwater Horizon 57
deer farming 102
deforestation 24, 165; in Asia 278; and forest certifications 273–6; and the tissue industry 278–9; tropical 17
democracy: agonistic 92; in South Africa 202
dengue fever 28
desert rat kangaroo 10
desertification 120
dinosaurs 33
displacement 348
dodo bird 10
dolphins 289, 290; acts of compassion by 292; bottlenose 294; in captivity 289, 290, 294; in MarineLand 294; *see also* cetaceans
Downes, Azzedine 158–9
drought mitigation 41

Dujiangyan Center for Panda Care and Disease Control 375–6
dune reserve 103
dwarf bear-poppy 18
Dwarf naupaka 18

East African black rhino 192–200; *see also* black rhinoceros
eastern North Pacific (ENP) grey whale *see* grey whales
Eaton, Mark 253
eco capitalism 55
eco-tourism 177, 194, 195, 196
Eco, Umberto 119
ecological accounts 202
ecological civilisation 362
ecological justice products 371
ecology 38, 41, 56, 60, 66, 105, 351, 363; in China 370; destruction of 124; marine 347; planetary 125; polar bear 339–40; restoration 44; *see also* deep ecology
economic growth 128n9
economics, neo-classical 166–7
Economics of Ecosystems and Biodiversity (TEEB) 81n81
ecosophy 93, 105
ecosystem services 41, 69, 177
ecosystems: 46n6, 56, 101, 153; appropriation of 122; Arctic marine 341; corporate impact on 59; destruction of 69; interdependence of 395; management of 204; unpredictability of 40; *see also* habitat
Ehrlich, Paul 120
El Niño-Southern Oscillation (ENSO) cycle 135
El Niño/La Niña weather event 135, 138
eland 194
Elephant Trade Information System (ETIS) 159
elephants 8, 19, 166, 176, 178, 194; African 158–9; impact interventions 210; in SANParks 206
Ellen MacArthur Foundation 150
elongate bitterling 33
emancipatory accounting 64–7, 68, 70, 179; by SANParks 203–14
emancipatory extinction engagement 75–7
emancipatory framework for extinction accounting and accountability (EFEAA) 276–7, 282–3
emissions 59
Encyclopedia of Life (online) 9, 33